Important Instruction

Students, Parents, and Teachers can use the URL or QR code provided below to access two full-length Lumos OST practice tests. Please note that these assessments are provided in the Online format only.

URL	QR Code
Visit the URL below and place the book access code **http://www.lumoslearning.com/a/tedbooks** **Access Code: G7EOST-92584-P**	

Lumos Learning
Developed by Expert Teachers

Ohio State Test Prep: Grade 7 English Language Arts Literacy (ELA) Practice Workbook and Full-length Online Assessments: OST Study Guide

Contributing Editor   - Stacy Zeiger
Contributing Editor   - Mechelle Craig
Contributing Editor   - George Smith
Executive Producer   - Mukunda Krishnaswamy
Designer and Illustrator - Harini N.

First Edition - 2020

NGA Center/CCSSO are the sole owners and developers of the Common Core State Standards, which does not sponsor or endorse this product. © Copyright 2010. National Governors Association Center for Best Practices and Council of Chief State School Officers.

Ohio Department of Education is not affiliated to Lumos Learning. Ohio department of education, was not involved in the production of, and does not endorse these products or this site.

ISBN-10:1-945730-46-3

ISBN-13:978-1-945730-46-7

Printed in the United States of America

For permissions and additional information contact us

Lumos Information Services, LLC
PO Box 1575, Piscataway, NJ 08855-1575
http://www.LumosLearning.com

Email: support@lumoslearning.com
Tel: (732) 384-0146
Fax: (866) 283-6471

lumos learning
Developed by Expert Teachers

INTRODUCTION

This book is specifically designed to improve student achievement on the Ohio State Test (OST). With over a decade of expertise in developing practice resources for standardized tests, Lumos Learning has designed the most efficient methodology to help students succeed on the state assessments (See Figure 1).

Lumos Smart Test Prep Methodology provides students OST assessment rehearsal along with an efficient pathway to overcome any standards proficiency gaps. Students perform at their best on standardized tests when they feel comfortable with the test content as well as the test format. Lumos online practice tests are meticulously designed to mirror the OST assessment. It adheres to the guidelines provided by the OST for the number of questions, standards, difficulty level, sessions, question types, and duration.

The process starts with students taking the online diagnostic assessment. This online diagnostic test will help assess students' proficiency levels in various standards.

After completion of the diagnostic assessment, students can take note of standards where they are not proficient. This step will help parents and educators in developing a targeted remedial study plan based on a student's proficiency gaps.

Once the targeted remedial study plan is in place, students can start practicing the lessons in this workbook that are focused on specific standards.

After the student completes the targeted remedial practice, the student should attempt the second online OST practice test. Record the proficiency levels in the second practice test to measure the student progress and identify any additional learning gaps. Further targeted practice can be planned to help students gain comprehensive skills mastery needed to ensure success on the state assessment.

Lumos Smart Test Prep Methodology

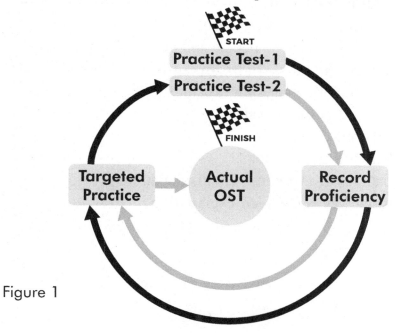

Figure 1

Table of Contents

Sign Up Online

OST

Grade 7 ELA Practice

Unlock Digital Access

2 OST Practice Tests

3 ELA Strands

Sign Up Now

Url: https://LumosLearning/a/tedbooks

Access Code: G7EOST-92584-P

Access OST Test Practice Resources On Your Mobile Device

Online Access

for

OST Practice

+

Printed Workbook

for

Skills Practice

Download Lumos StepUp App
from Google Play Store or Apple App Store

After installing the StepUp App, scan this **QR Code** via **tedBook** section of the mobile app

Chapter 1

Lumos Smart Test Prep Methodology

Step 1: Access Online OST Practice Test

The online OST practice tests mirror the actual Ohio State Test(OST) in the number of questions, item types, test duration, test tools, and more.

After completing the test, your student will receive immediate feedback with detailed reports on standards mastery and a personalized study plan to overcome any learning gaps. With this study plan, use the next section of the workbook to practice.

Use the URL and access code provided below or scan the QR code to access the first OST practice test to get started.

URL	QR Code
Visit the URL below and place the book access code **http://www.lumoslearning.com/a/tedbooks** **Access Code: G7EOST-92584-P**	

Step 2: Review the Personalized Study Plan Online

After students complete the online Practice Test 1, they can access their individualized study plan from the table of contents (Figure 2) Parents and Teachers can also review the study plan through their Lumos account (parent or teacher) portal.

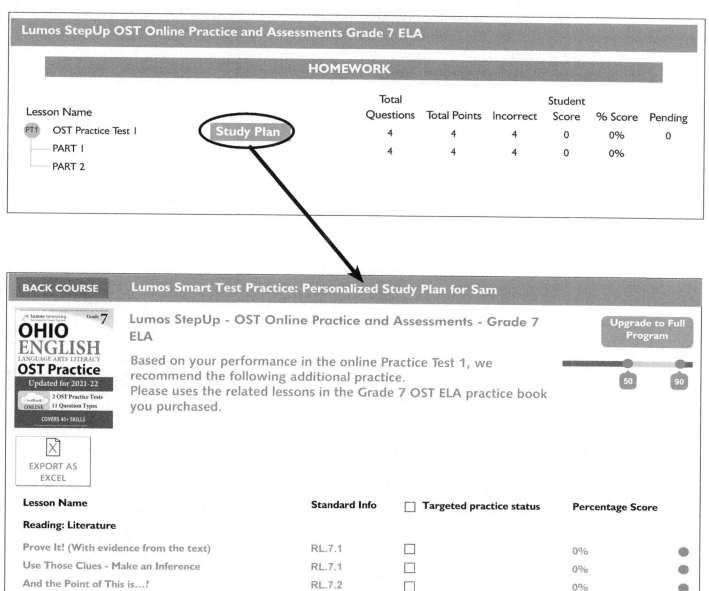

Step 3: Complete Targeted Practice

Using the information provided in the study plan report, complete the targeted practice using the appropriate lessons to overcome proficiency gaps. With lesson names included in the study plan, find the appropriate topics in this workbook and answer the questions provided. Students can refer to the answer key and detailed answers provided for each lesson to gain further understanding of the learning objective. Marking the completed lessons in the study plan after each practice session is recommended.(See Figure 3)

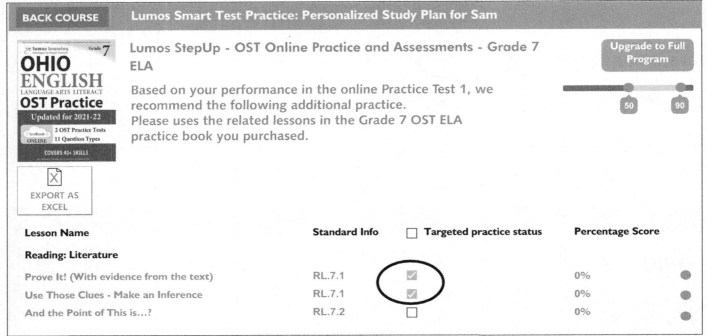

Figure 3

Step 4: Access the Practice Test 2 Online

After completing the targeted practice in this workbook, students should attempt the second OST practice test online. Using the student login name and password, login to the Lumos website to complete the second practice test.

Step 5: Repeat Targeted Practice

Repeat the targeted practice as per Step 3 using the second study plan report for Practice test 2 after completion of the second OST rehearsal.

Visit http://www.lumoslearning.com/a/lstp for more information on Lumos Smart Test Prep Methodology or Scan the QR Code

Test Taking Tips

1) **The day before the test,** make sure you get a good night's sleep.

2) **On the day of the test,** be sure to eat a good hearty breakfast! Also, be sure to arrive at school on time.

3) **During the test:**

- **Read every question carefully.**

    - Do not spend too much time on any one question. Work steadily through all questions in the section.
    - Attempt all of the questions even if you are not sure of some answers.
    - If you run into a difficult question, eliminate as many choices as you can and then pick the best one from the remaining choices. Intelligent guessing will help you increase your score.
    - Also, mark the question so that if you have extra time, you can return to it after you reach the end of the section.
    - Some questions may refer to a graph, chart, or other kind of picture. Carefully review the infographics before answering the question.
    - Be sure to include explanations for your written responses and show all work.

- **While Answering EBSR questions.**

    - EBSR questions come in 2 parts - PART A and B.
    - Both PART A and B could be multiple choice or Part A could be multiple choice while Part B could be some other type.
    - Generally, Part A and B will be related, sometimes it may just be from the same lesson but not related questions.
    - If it is a Multiple choice question, Select the bubble corresponding to your answer choice.
    - Read all of the answer choices, even if think you have found the correct answer.
    - In case the questions in EBSR are not multiple choice questions, follow the instruction for other question types while answering such questions.

- **While Answering TECR questions.**

    - Read the directions of each question. Some might ask you to drag something, others to select, and still others to highlight. Follow all instructions of the question (or questions if it is in multiple parts)

Chapter 2 - Reading: Literature

The objective of the Reading Literature standards is to ensure that the student is able to read and comprehend literature (which includes stories, drama and poetry) related to Grade 7.

To help students master the necessary skills, information to help the student understand the concepts related to the standard is given. Along with this, we encourage the student to go through the resources available online on EdSearch to gain an in depth understanding of these concepts. The EdSearch page for each lesson can be accessed with the help of the url or the QR code provided.

A small map is provided after each passage or text in which the student can enter the details as understood from the literary text. Doing this will help the student to refer to key points that help in answering the questions with ease.

Chapter 2

Lesson 1: Prove It! (With evidence from the text)

Let us understand the concept with an example.

Inferences from a text: After reading a text, an inference is an idea or conclusion that the reader has made or reached that was not in the text but is based on information that was in the text.

Managing the North American Lobster Population

Lobsters are an expensive delicacy today, but they were not always so highly valued or regarded. Hundreds of years ago, lobsters were so plentiful and easy to catch in shallow water near the shore-line that Native Americans used them to fertilize their fields and to bait their hooks for fishing. In colonial times, lobsters were considered "poverty food" and harvested by hand along the shoreline to be served to prisoners and indentured servants, and widows and children dependent on charitable donations.

Until about 1840, the lobster industry was fairly localized to the areas where the lobsters were caught, because lobster meat would spoil easily if not refrigerated, and there were no refrigerated trucks or air freight capabilities or dry ice sufficient to protect them in shipment. But then a new food manufacturing process changed all that.

What manufacturing process are we referring to? It is believed that the single most important factor which resulted in the exploitation of the lobster resource was the sudden success of the canning industry. The spreading fame of Maine lobsters and the lack of adequate facilities for the distribution of fresh product were the factors that stimulated the beginning of the canning industry in 1840. According to United States government data, the number of canneries grew and the volume of canned lobster meat produced increased also. The canneries were very efficient at processing.

Why, then, did the lobster meat canning industry collapse 40 years later? Because they were so efficient and canned so many pounds of the larger lobsters, there reached a time when the only lobsters being caught were smaller lobsters. Only twenty years later, the canneries were stuffing meat from half-pound lobsters into the tins for processing, a sign that the fishery had been overfished by then. The success of the canning industry made obvious the need for preservation and law enforcement if the fishery was to survive. Following the collapse of the canning industry, the fresh lobster industry took over the commercialization of the fishery. This meant the building of lobster pounds. Using the circulating salt water facilities at the pounds for storing lobsters live, dealers could wait for the price of lobster to increase or allow a newly-molted lobster time to harden its shell. These live-storage facilities became the backbone of the modern lobster industry. State government licensing data indicates that the number of lobster pounds established grew steadily from the 1880's until the 1990's. Laws to protect the lobster population from overfishing were introduced, including minimum size limits, specific periods during the year when lobstering is not allowed, requiring lobstermen to throw back female lobsters carrying eggs and the requirement that lobstermen be licensed.

Your assignment: Summarize the main ideas of this article and text that supports these ideas, and explain any inferences you make from the text.

This is what you might write.

Lobsters were plentiful and not highly valued as food up until the 1840's. One reason they were plentiful was that they were only consumed locally; canning and refrigeration equipment had not yet been invented, so lobsters could not be shipped very far. But the reputation of lobsters as desirable food was growing, so there was increasing demand.

The need to send lobsters long distances to meet a growing demand resulted in the development of equipment that could seal lobster meat in cans, eliminating the need for refrigeration and allowing shipment over long distances. And so the canning industry was born and grew in size, according to U.S. government data. But some 40 years later, the canning industry for lobster meat collapsed. The canning process was so efficient it depleted the lobster population so that only younger, smaller lobsters were left to be caught. The lobster population had been overfished. The success of the canning industry made obvious the need for preservation and law enforcement if the fishery was to survive.
The fresh lobster industry emerged to replace the canning industry. Keeping lobsters alive meant building lobster pounds, which used circulating salt water for storing lobsters live. These live-storage facilities became the backbone of the modern lobster industry and are helping it survive today. Also helping the industry and the lobster population survive are legal protections, such as minimum size limits, specific periods during the year when lobstering is not allowed, requiring lobstermen to throw back female lobsters carrying eggs and the requirement that lobstermen be licensed.

What I infer from this article is that government agencies and conservationists must be alert and focused on the protection of all animal and plant species, and must take actions to prevent these species from extinction. Otherwise, situations like overfishing of the lobster population or polluting the environment can be a threat to these species.

You can scan the QR code given below or use the url to access additional EdSearch resources including videos and mobile apps related to *Prove it! (With evidence from the text).*

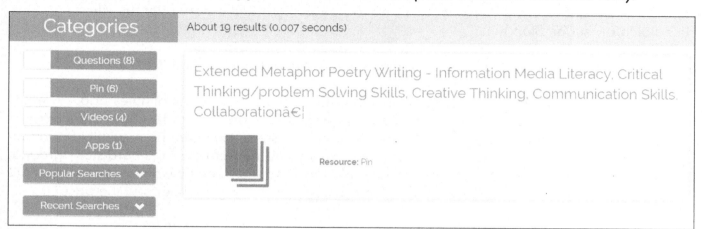

Categories	About 19 results (0.007 seconds)
Questions (8)	Extended Metaphor Poetry Writing - Information Media Literacy, Critical Thinking/problem Solving Skills, Creative Thinking, Communication Skills, Collaborationâ€¦
Pin (6)	
Videos (4)	
Apps (1)	Resource: Pin
Popular Searches ⌄	
Recent Searches ⌄	

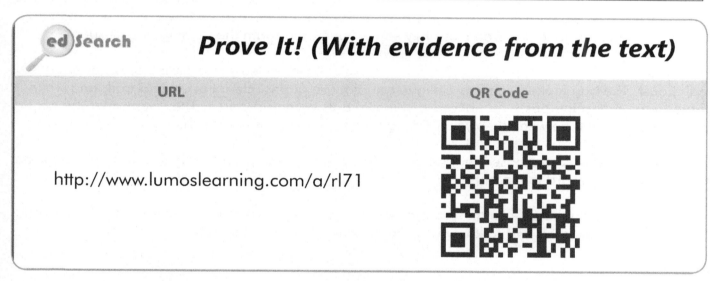

ed Search

Prove It! (With evidence from the text)

URL	QR Code
http://www.lumoslearning.com/a/rl71	

From *Scouting for Boys*

"Hi! Stop Thief!" shouted old Blenkinsopp as he rushed out of his little store near the village. "He's stolen my sugar. Stop him."

Stop whom? There was nobody in sight running away, "Who stole it?" asked the policeman.

"I don't know, but a whole bag of sugar is missing. It was there only a few minutes ago." The policeman tried to track the thief, but it looked a pretty impossible job for him to single out the tracks of the thief from among dozens of other footprints about the store. However, he presently started off hopefully, at a jog-trot, away out into the bush. In some places, he went over the hard stony ground, but he never checked his pace, although no footmarks could be seen. People wondered how he could possibly find the trail. Still, he trotted on. Old Blenkinsopp was feeling the heat and the pace

At length, he suddenly stopped and cast around, having evidently lost the trail. Then a grin came on his face as he pointed with his thumb over his shoulder up the tree near which he was standing. There, concealed among the branches, they saw a young man with the missing bag of sugar.

How had the policeman spotted him? His sharp eyes had detected some grains of sugar sparkling in the dust. The bag leaked, leaving a slight trail of these grains. He followed that trail, and when it came to an end in the bush, he noticed a string of ants going up a tree. They were after the sugar, and so was he, and between them, they brought about the capture of the thief.

Old Blenkinsopp was so pleased that he promptly opened the bag and spilled a lot of the sugar on the ground as a reward to the ants.

He also appreciated the policeman for his cleverness in using his eyes to see the grains of sugar and the ants, and in using his wits to know why the ants were climbing the tree.

After reading the story, enter the details in the map below. This will help you to answer the question with ease.

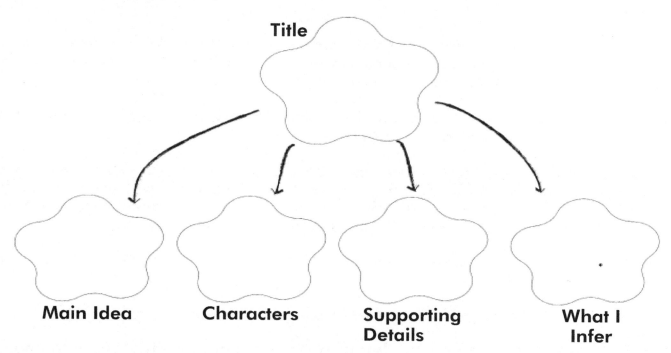

1. Why could the policeman not find the footprints from among the others in the shop?

Ⓐ   because they were clearly marked
Ⓑ   there were dozens of footprints
Ⓒ   there were no footprints to be found
Ⓓ   the footprints had been cleaned

Tryouts

For years, Sam had dreamed of being the best tennis player in the world. He went to tennis practice every single morning and night. He spent every summer at tennis camp, and he gave up long week-ends at the beach to work on his game. Now, it seemed his hard work was finally paying off. He was invited to try out for the state tennis team!

Still, there was something that was bothering Sam. The tryouts for the tennis team were on the same day as his mom's birthday, and he knew his family was planning a huge surprise party for her. He didn't want to hurt his mom's feelings by missing the party, but he also didn't want to miss his one shot at being a champion tennis player. He was in a quandary; he didn't know what to do.

For days, Sam went to bed, worrying about the decision. If he went to the tryout, he worried he would seem selfish. If he stayed home, he would miss his one big shot at making the state team. In fact, despite the honor of being invited to try out, he hadn't even told his family about the opportunity. He was so stressed about deciding whether to go or not that he couldn't even think about sharing the news.

Weeks went by, and Sam was making no progress. Every day his coach asked him if he was ready for the tryout, and Sam couldn't even respond. Finally, Sam couldn't bear the stress any longer. He decided to talk to his grandfather about his predicament.

"You know, your mom wants you to be happy," he told Sam. "It would be a great birthday present for her to know you are making your dream come true."

Sam had never thought of it that way before, and after talking to his grandfather, he knew what he had to do. He immediately went home and sat down with his parents to let them know about the opportunity to try out for the state team. When Sam apologetically told his parents what day the tryouts were, they were so busy shrieking with excitement that he thought maybe they hadn't heard.

"But Mom, that means I'm going to miss your birthday," Sam said. "I am happy you are so nice about it, but I still feel really bad."

"Are you kidding?" his mom asked. "This is the best present I could ask for!"

After reading the story, enter the details in the map below. This will help you to answer the questions with ease.

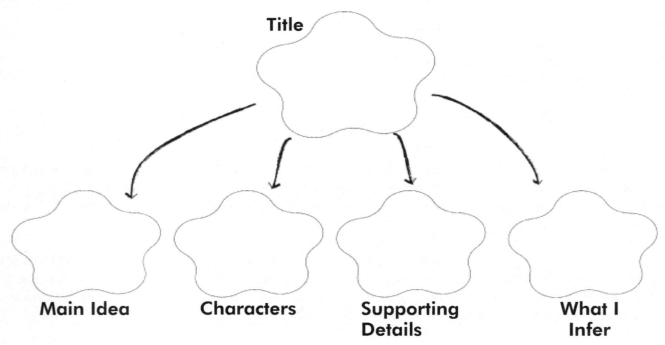

2. In this passage, who helps Sam make his choice?

Ⓐ His dog
Ⓑ His neighbor
Ⓒ His grandfather
Ⓓ His mom

3. Which of the following is NOT a sign that Sam's parents raised him well?

Ⓐ He understood that family and tennis were both priorities he needed to balance in his life.
Ⓑ He sought guidance from his grandfather instead of running from the problem.
Ⓒ He knew that to become a great tennis player he had to put in a lot of hard work.
Ⓓ Sam didn't care about missing the party.

Fairy Tales by A Brothers' Grimm

A certain king once fell ill, and the doctor declared that only a sudden fright would restore him to health, but the king was not a man for anyone to play tricks on, except his fool. One day, when the fool was with him in his boat, he cleverly pushed the king into the water. Help had already been arranged, and the king was drawn ashore and put to bed. The fright, the bath, and the rest in bed cured the diseased king.

The king wanted to frighten the fool for his act, so he told him that he would be put to death. He directed the executioner privately not to use the ax but to let fall a single drop of water on the fool's neck. Amidst shouts and laughter, the fool was asked to rise and thank the king for his kindness. But the fool never moved; he was dead; killed by the master's joke.

4. What trick did the fool plan to cure the king?

Ⓐ a lot of medicines
Ⓑ injections
Ⓒ the sudden push into the water
Ⓓ the ride in the boat

From "The Owl and the Pussy-Cat" by Edward Lear

The Owl and the Pussy-Cat went to sea
 In a beautiful pea-green boat,
They took some honey, and plenty of money
 Wrapped up in a five-pound note.
The Owl looked up to the stars above,
 And sang to a small guitar,

"O lovely Pussy! O Pussy, my love,
 What a beautiful Pussy you are,
    You are,
    You are!
What a beautiful Pussy you are!"
Pussy said to the Owl, "You elegant fowl!
 How charmingly sweet you sing!
O let us be married! too long we have tarried:
 But what shall we do for a ring?"
They sailed away for a year and a day,
 To the land where the Bong-tree grows,
And there in a wood a Piggy-wig stood,
 With a ring at the end of his nose,
    His nose,
    His nose,
 With a ring at the end of his nose.

5. Who provides the wedding ring for the wedding?

Ⓐ The Owl
Ⓑ The Pussy-Cat
Ⓒ The Pig
Ⓓ The Bong-tree

"The Boys and the Frogs"
From <u>Aesop's Fables</u>, adapted by Marmaduke Park

Some boys, beside a pond or lake,
Were playing once at duck and drake;
When, doubtless to their heart's content,
Volleys of stones were quickly sent.
But there were some (there will be such)
Who did not seem amused so much;
These were the frogs, to whom the game,
In point of sport was not the same.

For scarce a stone arrived, 'tis said,
But gave some frog a broken head;
And scores in less than half an hour,
Perished beneath the dreadful shower.
At last, said one, "You silly folks, I say,
Do fling your stones another way;
Though sport to you, to throw them thus,
Remember, pray, 'tis death to us!"

6. Part A

Why does the frog scold the boys?

Ⓐ The boys hit the frog in the head with a rock.
Ⓑ The boys are polluting the pond that the frog lives in.
Ⓒ The boys refuse to let the frog play with them.
Ⓓ The boys are trying to catch the frog to keep as a pet.

Part B

According to this poem what are the boys doing at the pond?

Ⓐ Trying to catch fish
Ⓑ Trying to catch frogs
Ⓒ Killing frogs
Ⓓ Throwing stones into the pond

From "The Dog and the Wolf" by Marmaduke Park

A wolf there was, whose scanty fare
Had made his person lean and spare;
A dog there was, so amply fed,
His sides were plump and sleek; 'tis said
The wolf once met this prosp'rous cur,
And thus began: "Your servant, sir;
I'm pleased to see you look so well,
Though how it is I cannot tell;
I have not broke my fast to-day;
Nor have I, I'm concern'd to say,
One bone in store or expectation,
And that I call a great vexation."

7. Who is speaking in the dialogue of this selection?

Ⓐ The wolf
Ⓑ The dog
Ⓒ The dog's owner
Ⓓ The narrator

The Use of Transitions

(1)The wind was blowing with the gale force of over 55 miles an hour. (2) The windows of the house began to shake as we silently waited for the worst of all possible storms. (3) Kitchen plates crashed to the floor, and we trembled with fear.

(4)My trusty dog was by my side, and my little brother huddled under the table. (5) Our parents had gone to a neighbor's house for a community meeting. (6) This storm was not predicted by the weatherman earlier on TV. (7) We knew nothing of the impending danger.

(8)Within moments, the tornado warning sounded from the fire station downtown. (9) I grabbed my brother, Danny, and headed straight for the hallway. (10) On the way, I remembered to pull the mattress off of his bed. (11) We fell to the floor, pulled the mattress on top of us, and the faint sound of a train whistle began. (12) Suddenly it was as loud as if we were crossing the tracks. (13) Yes, my greatest fear was realized. (14) We were on the path of a pop-up tornado!

(15)Then as quickly as it began, silence. (16) No more wind, I thought to myself. (17) Boy, was I wrong! (18) Extremely loud crashing and banging of pane glass windows surrounded us. (19)The tornado was on top of us!

(20)Moments later, a gentle breeze came down the hall. (21) The calm after the storm, yes, that phrase fit. (22) I quickly checked Danny, who was underneath me. (23) He was as white as a sheet but grunted that he was ok. (24)Sapphire was fine, as well. (25) Not so for our living room, kitchen, and bedrooms. (26) The wind force had blown out all windows and lifted our roof to the street

(27)We just sat there in the hallway after checking the house and began to cry.

(28)Within moments the fire trucks were coming down our street. (29) Their megaphone was on and announcing an all clear. (30)They wanted everyone who could come outside.

(31)My brother and I went out slowly and carefully to avoid the glass fragments. (32) Our dog followed yelping all the way. (33) Our parents were running down the street, fearing for what had happened. (34) Ours was the only house touched by the tornado! (35) Debris was everywhere. (36) Praises to the man up above, we were safe.

(37)Family and life are more important than personal belongings. (38) That I can say.

8. Given the information in the selection, a substantiated critique of this selection would best read as follows. Circle the correct answer choice.

Ⓐ The author notes that tornados are frightening and can cause damage.
Ⓑ The author makes valid statements to back up his/her account of a damaging tornado that destroyed property but not lives.
Ⓒ The author fabricates the information and does not give supportive evidence to back up the selection.
Ⓓ The author gave limited information in regards to the tornado damage and its impact on his/her family's survival.

Lines Written In A Young Lady's Album
By George W. Sands

'Tis not in youth, when life is new, when but to live is sweet,
When Pleasure strews her starlike flow'rs beneath our careless feet,
When Hope, that has not been deferred, first waves its golden wings,
And crowds the distant future with a thousand lovely things; -

When if a transient grief o'ershades the spirit for a while,
The momentary tear that falls is followed by a smile;
Or if a pensive mood, at times, across the bosom steals,
It scarcely sighs, so gentle is the pensiveness it feels

It is not then the, restless soul will seek for one with whom
To share whatever lot it bears, its gladness or its gloom, -
Some trusting, tried, and gentle heart, some true and faithful breast,
Whereon its pinions it may fold, and claim a place of rest.

But oh! when comes the icy chill that freezes o'er the heart,
When, one by one, the joys we shared, the hopes we held, depart;
When friends, like autumn's withered leaves, have fallen by our side,
And life, so pleasant once, becomes a desert wild and wide; -

As for her olive branch the dove swept o'er the sullen wave,
That rolled above the olden world - its death-robe and its grave! -
So will the spirit search the earth for some kind, gentle one,
With it to share her destiny, and make it all her own!

9. What do you think the poet is writing about in this poem? Write your answer in the box below.

Chapter 2

Lesson 2: Use Those Clues - Make an Inference

Inferences from a text: After reading a text, an inference is an idea or conclusion that the reader has made or reached that was not in the text but is based on information that was in the text.

You can scan the QR code given below or use the url to access additional EdSearch resources including videos and mobile apps related to *Use Those Clues - Make an Inference*.

 **Search**   ***Use Those Clues - Make an Inference***

URL	QR Code
http://www.lumoslearning.com/a/rl71	

"The Lament"
by SRAVANI

It is twilight. Thick wet snow is slowly twirling around the newly lighted street lamps and lying in soft thin layers on roofs, on horses' backs, on people's shoulders and hats. The cab driver, Iona Potapov, is quite white and looks like a phantom: he is bent double as far as a human body can bend double; he is seated on his box; he never makes a move. If a whole snowdrift fell on him, it seems as if he would not find it necessary to shake it off. His little horse is also quite white, and remains motionless; its immobility, its angularity, and its straight wooden-looking legs, even close by, give it the appearance of a gingerbread horse worth a kopek. It is, no doubt, plunged in deep thought. If you were snatched from the plough, from your usual gray surroundings, and were thrown into this slough full of monstrous lights, unceasing noise and hurrying people, you too would find it difficult not to think.

Iona and his little horse have not moved from their place for a long while. They left their yard before dinner and, up to now, not a fare. The evening mist is descending over the town, the white lights of the lamps are replacing brighter rays, and the hubbub of the street is getting louder.

'Cabby for Viborg Way!' suddenly hears Iona. 'Cabby!'
Iona jumps and, through his snow-covered eyelashes, sees an officer in a greatcoat, with his hood over his head.

'Viborg way!' the officer repeats. 'Are you asleep, eh? Viborg way!'
With a nod of assent, Iona picks up the reins, in consequence of which layers of snow slip off the horse's back and neck. The officer seats himself in the sleigh, the cab driver smacks his lips to encourage his horse, stretches out his neck like a swan, sits up and, more from habit than necessity, brandishes his whip. The little horse also stretches its neck, bends its wooden-looking legs, and makes a move undecidedly.

'What are you doing, werewolf!' is the exclamation Iona hears from the dark mass moving to and fro, as soon as they have started.
'Where the devil are you going? To the r-r-right!'
'You do not know how to drive. Keep to the right!' calls the officer angrily. A coachman from a private carriage swears at him; a passerby, who has run across the road and rubbed his shoulder against the horse's nose, looks at him furiously as he sweeps the snow from his sleeve. Iona shifts about on his seat as if he was on needles, moves his elbows as if he were trying to keep his equilibrium, and gasps about like someone suffocating, who does not understand why and wherefore he is there.
'What scoundrels they all are!' jokes the officer; 'one would think they had all entered into an agreement to jostle you or fall under your horse.'
Iona looks around at the officer and moves his lips. He evidently wants to say something but the only sound that issues is a snuffle.
'What?' asks the officer.
Iona twists his mouth into a smile and, with an effort, says hoarsely:
'My son, Barin, died this week.'
'Hm! What did he die of?'

Iona turns with his whole body towards his fare and says: 'And who knows! They say high fever. He was three days in the hospital and then died… God's will be done.'
"Turn round! The devil!' sounds from the darkness. 'Have you popped off, old doggie, eh? Use your eyes!'

'Go on, go on,' says the officer, 'otherwise we shall not get there by tomorrow. Hurry up a bit!'
"If you were snatched from the plough, from your usual gray surroundings, and were thrown into this slough full of monstrous lights, unceasing noise and hurrying people, you too would find it difficult not to think."

After reading the story, enter the details in the map below. This will help you to answer the question with ease

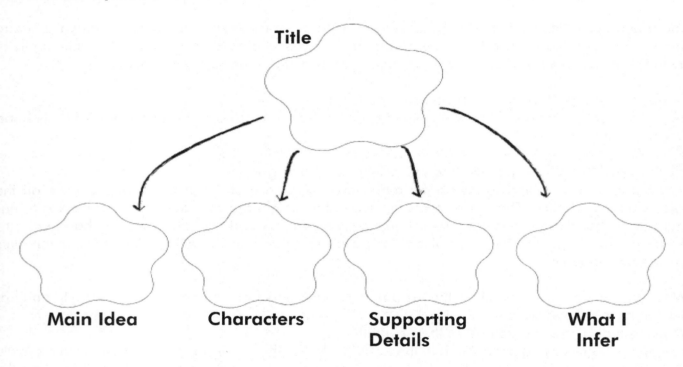

Title

Main Idea   **Characters**   **Supporting Details**   **What I Infer**

1. What can be inferred from the first two paragraphs of the passage?

Ⓐ that the cab driver was very sad
Ⓑ that the cabby was from a village or a very small town
Ⓒ that the cab driver did not want to think
Ⓓ that the cab driver was not thinking

"Bruno the Bear"
Excerpt from *The Bond of Love*

I will begin with Bruno, my wife's pet sloth bear. I got him for her by accident. Two years ago, we were passing through the cornfields near a small town in Iowa. People were driving away the wild pigs from the fields by shooting at them. Some were shot, and some escaped. We thought that everything was over when suddenly a black sloth bear came out panting in the hot sun.

Now I will not shoot a sloth bear wantedly, but unfortunately for the poor beast, one of my companions did not feel the same way about it and promptly shot the bear on the spot.

As we watched the fallen animal, we were surprised to see that the black fur on its back moved and left the prostrate body. Then we saw it was a baby bear that had been riding on its mother's back when the sudden shot had killed her. The little creature ran around its prostrate parent, making a pitiful noise. I ran up to it to attempt a capture. It scooted into the sugarcane field. Following it with my companions, I was at last able to grab it by the scruff of its neck while it snapped and tried to scratch me with its long, hooked claws.

We put it in one of the large jute-bags we had brought, and when I got back home, I duly presented it to my wife. She was delighted! She at once put a blue colored ribbon around its neck, and after discovering the cub was a 'boy,' she christened it Bruno.

Bruno soon took to drinking milk from a bottle. It was but a step further, and within a very few days, he started eating and drinking everything else. And everything is the right word, for he ate porridge made from any ingredients, vegetables, fruit, nuts, meat (especially pork), curry and rice regardless of condiments and chilies, bread, eggs, chocolates, sweets, pudding, ice-cream, etc. As for drink: milk, tea, coffee, lime juice, aerated water, buttermilk, beer, alcoholic liquor, and, in fact, anything liquid. It all went down with relish.

The bear became very attached to our two dogs and all the children living in and around our farm. He was left quite free in his younger days and spent his time playing, running into the kitchen, and going to sleep in our beds.

One day an accident befell him. I put down poison (barium carbonate) to kill the rats and mice that had got into my library. Bruno entered the library as he often did and ate some of the poison. Paralysis set into the extent that he could not stand on his feet. But he dragged himself on his stumps to my wife, who called me. I guessed what had happened.

Off I rushed him in the car to the vet's residence. A case of poisoning! Tame Bear—barium carbonate—what to do? Out came his medical books, and a feverish reference to index began: "What poison did you say, sir?" he asked, "Barium carbonate," I said.

"Ah yes—B—Ba—Barium Salts—Ah! Barium carbonate! Symptoms— paralysis—treatment—injections of . .. Just a minute, sir. I'll bring my syringe and the medicine." Said the doc. I dashed back to the car. Bruno was still floundering about on his stumps, but clearly, he was weakening rapidly; there was some vomiting, he was breathing heavily, with heaving flanks and gaping mouth. I was really scared and did not know what to do. I was feeling very guilty and was running in and out of the vet's house doing everything the doc asked me.

"Hold him, everybody!" In goes the hypodermic—Bruno squeals — 10 c.c. of the antidote enters his system without a drop being wasted. Ten minutes later: condition unchanged! Another 10 c.c. Injected! Ten minutes later: breathing less torturous— Bruno can move his arms and legs a little although he cannot stand yet. Thirty minutes later: Bruno gets up and has a great feed! He looks at us disdainfully, as much as to say, 'What's barium carbonate to a big black bear like me?' Bruno was still eating. I was really happy to see him recover.

The months rolled on, and Bruno had grown many times the size he was when he came. He had equaled the big dogs in height and had even outgrown them. But was just as sweet, just as mischievous, just as playful. And he was very fond of us all. Above all, he loved my wife, and she loved him too! And he could do a few tricks, too. At the command, 'Bruno, wrestle,' or 'Bruno, box,' he vigorously tackled anyone who came forward for a rough and tumble. Give him a stick and say 'Bruno, hold the gun,' and he pointed the stick at you. Ask him, 'Bruno, where's baby?' and he immediately produced and cradled affectionately a stump of wood which he had carefully concealed in his straw bed. But because of the neighborhoods' and our renters' children, poor Bruno, had to be kept chained most of the time.

Then my son and I advised my wife and friends advised her, too, to give Bruno to the zoo. He was getting too big to keep at home. After some weeks of such advice, she at last consented. Hastily, and before she could change her mind, a letter was written to the curator of the zoo. Did he want a tame bear for his collection? He replied, "Yes." The zoo sent a cage in a truck, a distance of hundred – eighty – seven miles, and Bruno was packed off. We all missed him greatly, but in a sense, we were relieved. My wife was inconsolable. She wept and fretted. For the first few days, she would not eat a thing. Then she wrote a number of letters to the curator. How was Bruno? Back came the replies, "Well, but fretting; he refuses food too."

After that, friends visiting the zoo were begged to make a point of seeing how Bruno was getting along. They reported that he was well but looked very thin and sad. All the keepers at the zoo said he was fretting. For three months, I managed to restrain my wife from visiting the zoo. Then she said one day, "I must see Bruno. Either you take me by car, or I will go myself by bus or train myself." So I took her by car. Friends had conjectured that the bear would not recognize her. I had thought so too. But while she was yet some yards from his cage, Bruno saw her and recognized her. He howled with happiness. She ran up to him, petted him through the bars, and he stood on his head in delight.

For the next three hours, she would not leave that cage. She gave him tea, lemonade, cakes, ice cream, and whatnot. Then 'closing time' came and we had to leave. My wife cried bitterly; Bruno cried bitterly; even the hardened curator and the keepers felt depressed. As for me, I had reconciled myself to what I knew was going to happen next.

"Oh please, sir," she asked the curator, "may I have my Bruno back"? Hesitantly, he answered, "Madam, he belongs to the zoo and is Government property now. I cannot give away Government property. But if my boss, the superintendent, agrees, certainly, you may have him back."

There followed the return journey home and a visit to the superintendent's office. A tearful pleading: "Bruno and I are both fretting for each other. Will you please give him back to me?" He was a kind-hearted man and consented. Not only that, but he wrote to the curator, telling him to lend us a cage for transporting the bear back home.

Back we went to the zoo again, armed with the superintendent's letter. Bruno was driven into a small cage and hoisted on top of the car; the cage was tied securely, and a slow and careful return journey back home was accomplished.

Once home, a squad of workers were engaged for special work around our yard. An island was made for Bruno. It was twenty feet long and fifteen feet wide and was surrounded by a dry moat, six feet wide and seven feet deep. A wooden box that once housed fowls was brought and put on the island for Bruno to sleep in at night. Straw was placed inside to keep him warm, and his 'baby,' the gnarled stump, along with his 'gun,' the piece of bamboo, both of which had been sentimentally preserved since he had been sent away to the zoo, were put back for him to play with. In a few days, the workers hoisted the cage on to the island, and Bruno was released. He was delighted; standing on his hind legs, he pointed his 'gun' and cradled his 'baby.' My wife spent hours sitting on a chair there while he sat on her lap. He was fifteen months old and pretty heavy too!

The way my wife reaches the island and leaves it is interesting. I have tied a rope to the overhanging branch of a maple tree with a loop at its end. Putting one foot in the loop, she kicks off with the other, to bridge the six-foot gap that constitutes the width of the surrounding moat. The return journey back is made the same way.

But who can say now that a sloth bear has no sense of affection, no memory, and no individual characteristics?

After reading the story, enter the details in the map below. This will help you to answer the question with ease

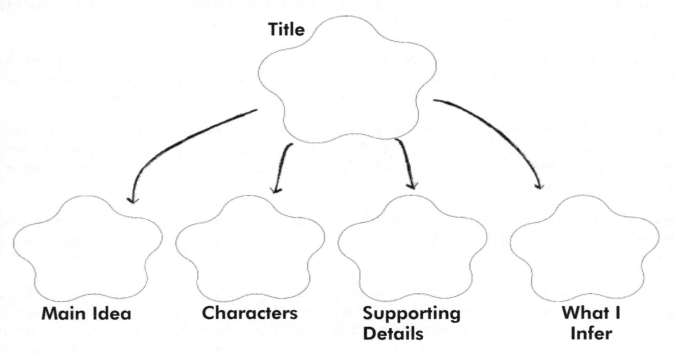

2. How can the reader infer the bear was depressed?

- Ⓐ because both the bear and the author's wife cried bitterly while departing
- Ⓑ because the bear did not recognize its mistress
- Ⓒ because the author's wife was lean and depressed
- Ⓓ because Bruno would not eat anything.

Best Friend

Ever since they were kids, Julie and Max had been best friends. They went to kindergarten together. They went to summer camp together. They hung out together every weekend. But suddenly, things between the two had started to change.

Max had started playing on the football team and didn't have much time for Julie anymore. He was always busy, and he never seemed to make it to study hall, where the two used to swap stories about their favorite (or least favorite) teachers. In class, Julie noticed that Max never seemed to have his homework done on time anymore. She even noticed that he got a 'D' on his last paper. She knew something was going on with him – but what?

At first, Julie decided to play it cool and see how things went. She tried waiting in the hall for Max after class to see if she could ask if he was OK. But days went by, and he never had time to stop.

He'd rush right past her in the hall, only to leave her feeling even worse about what was happening between them.

Even though she wasn't sure she could handle the situation herself, Julie didn't want to talk to her parents because she was afraid they would tell her not to hang out with Max anymore. She barely saw him as it was, so she knew it would just make things worse if her parents didn't approve of him. She didn't want to tell Max's parents either because she didn't want him to get in trouble. Still, it seemed like something needed to change. Julie decided to go to one of her school counselors and let her know she was concerned.

When she walked into Mrs. Smith's room, she was surprised to see that Max was already sitting there.
"I'm sorry, I'll come back," Julie said.
"No, stay," said Max. "Maybe you can help."
Julie was surprised to find that Max had visited the counselor's office for the same reason she had: He was starting to feel overwhelmed with all of the things he was supposed to be doing as a student, an athlete, and a friend. He needed some guidance on how to determine what truly mattered and how to divide his time between all of the things that were important to him. When she realized that Max was still the same old Max (just a little more stressed), Julie was relieved. She was also happy to know that he had come to a conclusion on his own, without her having to talk to someone else about it. She decided it was a sign they were both growing up.

After reading the story, enter the details in the map below. This will help you to answer the question with ease.

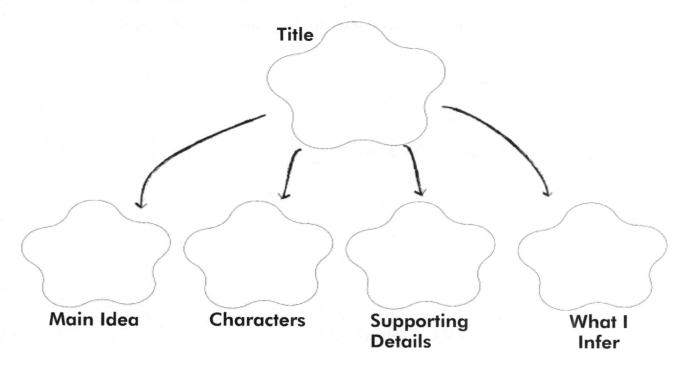

3. What can you infer about relationship between Julie and Max?

Ⓐ They were best of friends who cared about each other.
Ⓑ They really hated each other, so they went to the counselor alone.
Ⓒ They were just acquaintances who only occasionally talked.
Ⓓ They were neighbors.

From "The Dog and the Wolf" by Marmaduke Park

A wolf there was, whose scanty fare
Had made his person lean and spare;
A dog there was, so amply fed,
His sides were plump and sleek; 'tis said
The wolf once met this prosp'rous cur,
And thus began: "Your servant, sir;
I'm pleased to see you look so well,
Though how it is I cannot tell;
I have not broke my fast to-day;
Nor have I, I'm concern'd to say,
One bone in store or expectation,
And that I call a great vexation."

4. Which of the following can be inferred about the dog based on this poem?

Ⓐ That the dog was a golden retriever
Ⓑ That the dog had a caring master
Ⓒ That the dog was tall
Ⓓ That the dog belonged to the king

5. What does the wolf represent in this poem?

Ⓐ the basic idea of dieting
Ⓑ how to fast (not eat)
Ⓒ the basic needs of living
Ⓓ being a wild animal

6. What does the dog represent in this poem?

Ⓐ being a tamed animal
Ⓑ the comforts of having everything needed in life
Ⓒ being greedy
Ⓓ sharing with others

"The Boys and the Frogs" by Marmaduke Park

Some boys, beside a pond or lake,
Were playing once at *duck and drake*;
When, doubtless to their heart's content,
Volleys of stones were quickly sent.
But there were some (there will be such)
Who did not seem amused so much;
These were the frogs, to whom the game,
In point of sport was not the same.
For scarce a stone arrived, 'tis said,
But gave some frog a broken head;
And scores in less than half an hour,
Perished beneath the dreadful shower.
At last, said one, "You silly folks, I say,
Do fling your stones another way;
Though *sport* to *you*, to throw them thus,
Remember, pray, 'tis *death* to us!"

7. What is most likely true about the boys in this poem? Circle the correct answer choice.

Ⓐ They dislike frogs and want to hurt them.
Ⓑ They did not realize that the rocks would harm the frogs.
Ⓒ They want to catch the frogs to keep as pets.
Ⓓ They like rocks more than they like frogs.

From <u>The Children of France</u> by Ruth Royce

Before the "Squire's" son went away to war, the neighborhood children knew him only by sight and by hearing their parents speak of him as the son of "the richest man in Titusville," who never had done a day's work in his life.

Perhaps the parents were not quite right in this, for, even if Robert Favor had not gone out in the fields to labor, he had graduated from high school and college with high honors. He never spoke to the village children nor noticed them, and was not, as a result, very popular with the young people of his home town. The neighbors said this was all on account of his bringing up.

It was therefore a surprise to them when, at the beginning of the great war, after Germany swept over Belgium, Robert Favor hurried to Europe. It was later learned that he had joined what is known as the "Foreign Legion" of the French Army. Titusville next heard that he had been made a lieutenant for heroic conduct under fire. But Titusville did not believe it; it said no Favor ever did anything but run away in such circumstances. But they believed it when, later on, they read in the newspapers how

Lieutenant Favor had sprung out of the trenches and ran to the rescue of a wounded private soldier who had lain in a shell hole in No Man's Land since the night before.

The village swelled with pride and the eyes of the children grew wide with wonder as they listened to the story of the heroism of the Squire's son. But this was as nothing to what occurred later. "Bob" Favor was brought home one day to the house on the hill, pale and weak from wounds received in battle.

Spring was at hand, and as soon as he was able, Captain Favor—you see he had again been promoted—was taken out on the lawn where, in his wheel chair he rested in the warm sunshine. The bright red top of his gray-blue cap, and the flash of the medal on his breast excited the wonder of the children, who pressed their faces against the high iron fence and gazed in awe. It was the first real hero any of them ever had seen.

Finally, chancing to look their way, the Captain smiled and waved a friendly hand. A little girl clapped her hands, others started to cheer and a little man of ten dragged an American flag from his pocket and waved it. The Captain beckoned to the children.

"Come in, folks," he called. "I wish someone to talk to me and make me laugh. Are you coming?" They were. The children started, at first hesitatingly, then with more confidence, led by the boy with the American flag, which he was waving bravely now.

"What's your name?" demanded the Captain.
"Joe Funk, sir."

The Captain laughed. "No boy so patriotic as you are should have a name like that," he said. "We all are going to be great friends, I am sure, and when I get this leg, that a German shell nearly blew off, in working order again, we shall have some real sport and I'll teach you all how to be soldiers. Just now I cannot do much of anything."

"Yes, you can," interrupted Joe. "You can tell us how you rescued the soldier when the Germans were shooting at you and—"
"Master Joseph," answered the Captain gravely, "a real soldier never brags about himself; but what you say does give me an idea. How would you like to have me tell you about the brave little children of France?"
"Well, I'd rather hear about how you killed the Germans, lots of 'em; I want to hear about battles and dead men and—"

"We shall speak of the children first, and I will begin right now. Let me see. Ah! I have it. Sit down on the grass, all of you, and be comfortable. Be quiet until I finish the story, then ask what questions you wish. Now listen!"

After reading the story, enter the details in the map below. This will help you to answer the question with ease.

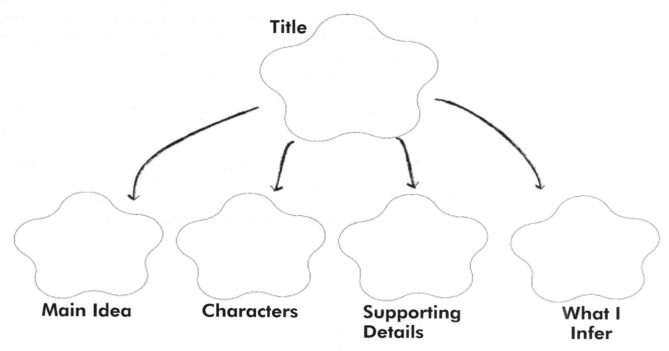

Title

Main Idea   **Characters**   **Supporting Details**   **What I Infer**

8. **Based on the details in this story, what do you think brought the Captain back to Titusville? Circle the correct answer choice.**

Ⓐ He was injured during the war and could no longer fight.
Ⓑ He wanted to tell the people of Titusville his heroic stories.
Ⓒ He wanted to make the people of Titusville proud of him.
Ⓓ He wanted to work on his father's farm again.

"Hi! Stop Thief!" shouted old Blenkinsopp as he rushed out of his little store near the village. "He's stolen my sugar. Stop him."

Stop whom? There was nobody in sight running away, "Who stole it?" asked the policeman.

"I don't know, but a whole bag of sugar is missing. It was there only a few minutes ago." The policeman tried to track the thief but it looked a pretty impossible job for him to single out the tracks of the thief from among dozens of other footprints about the store. However, he presently started off hopefully, at a jog-trot, away out into the bush. In some places he went over hard stony ground but he never checked his pace, although no footmarks could be seen. People wondered how he could possibly find the trail. Still he trotted on. Old Blenkinsopp was feeling the heat and the pace

At length the tracker suddenly stopped and cast around having evidently lost the trail. Then a grin came on his face as he pointed with his thumb over his shoulder up the tree near which he was standing. There, concealed among the branches, they saw a young man with the missing bag of sugar.

How had the policeman spotted him? His sharp eyes had detected some grains of sugar sparkling in the dust. The bag leaked, leaving a slight trail of these grains. He followed that trail and when it came to an end in the bush he noticed a string of ants going up a tree. They were after the sugar, and so was he, and between them they brought about the capture of the thief.

Old Blenkinsopp was so pleased that he promptly opened the bag and spilled a lot of the sugar on the ground as a reward to the ants.

He also appreciated the policeman for his cleverness in using his eyes to see the grains of sugar and the ants, and in using his wits to see why the ants were climbing the tree.

9. The details of this story show that no one is present at the scene. Who is likely the narrator of this selection?

Ⓐ the shopkeeper
Ⓑ the narrator
Ⓒ the people
Ⓓ the thief

Tryouts

For years, Sam had dreamed of being the best tennis player in the world. He went to tennis practice every single morning and night. He spent every summer at tennis camp, and he gave up long weekends at the beach to work on his game. Now, it seemed his hard work was finally paying off. He was invited to try out for the state tennis team!

Still, there was something that was bothering Sam. The tryouts for the tennis team were on the same day as his mom's birthday, and he knew his family was planning a huge surprise party for her. He didn't want to hurt his mom's feelings by missing the party, but he also didn't want to miss his one shot at being a champion tennis player just because the tryouts were on his mom's birthday. He was in a quandary; he didn't know what to do.

For days, Sam went to bed, worrying about the decision. If he went to the tryout, he worried he would seem selfish. If he stayed home, he would miss his one big shot at making the state team. In fact, despite the honor of being invited to try out, he hadn't even told his family about the opportunity. He was so stressed about making the decision of whether to go that he couldn't even think about sharing the news.

Weeks went by, and Sam was making no progress. Every day his coach asked him if he was ready for the tryout, and Sam couldn't even respond. Finally, Sam couldn't bear the stress any longer. He decided to talk to his grandfather about his predicament.

"You know, your mom wants you to be happy," he told Sam. "It would be a great birthday present for her to know you are making your dream come true."

Sam had never thought of it that way before, and after talking to his grandfather, he knew what he had to do. He immediately went home and sat down with his parents to let them know about the opportunity to try out for the state team. His parents were so excited that when he told them, apologetically, what day the tryouts were, and they were so busy shrieking with excitement that he thought maybe they hadn't heard.

"But Mom, that means I'm going to miss your birthday," Sam said. "I am happy you are so nice about it, but I still feel really bad."

"Are you kidding?" his mom asked. "This is the best present I could ask for!"

10. Which of the following is a sign that Sam's parents raised him well?

Ⓐ He understood that family and tennis were both priorities he needed to balance in his life
Ⓑ He sought guidance from his grandfather instead of running from the problem
Ⓒ He knew that to become a great tennis player he had to put in a lot of hard work
Ⓓ All of the above

Chapter 2

Lesson 3: And the Point of This is...

Before answering questions related to this standard, it is important to understand the term "Inference"

Inferences from a text: After reading a text, an inference is an idea or conclusion that the reader has made or reached that was not in the text but is based on information that was in the text.

You can scan the QR code given below or use the url to access additional EdSearch resources including videos and mobile apps related to *And the Point of This is...*

And the Point of This is...

URL	QR Code
http://www.lumoslearning.com/a/rl72	

"Bruno the Bear"
Excerpt from *The Bond of Love*

I will begin with Bruno, my wife's pet sloth bear. I got him for her by accident. Two years ago, we were passing through the cornfields near a small town in Iowa. People were driving away the wild pigs from the fields by shooting at them. Some were shot, and some escaped. We thought that everything was over when suddenly a black sloth bear came out panting in the hot sun.

Now I will not shoot a sloth bear wantedly, but unfortunately for the poor beast, one of my companions did not feel the same way about it and promptly shot the bear on the spot.

As we watched the fallen animal, we were surprised to see that the black fur on its back moved and left the prostrate body. Then we saw it was a baby bear that had been riding on its mother's back when the sudden shot had killed her. The little creature ran around its prostrate parent, making a pitiful noise. I ran up to it to attempt a capture. It scooted into the sugarcane field. Following it with my companions, I was at last able to grab it by the scruff of its neck while it snapped and tried to scratch me with its long, hooked claws.

We put it in one of the large jute-bags we had brought, and when I got back home, I duly presented it to my wife. She was delighted! She at once put a blue colored ribbon around its neck, and after discovering the cub was a 'boy,' she christened it Bruno.

Bruno soon took to drinking milk from a bottle. It was but a step further, and within a very few days, he started eating and drinking everything else. And everything is the right word, for he ate porridge made from any ingredients, vegetables, fruit, nuts, meat (especially pork), curry and rice regardless of condiments and chilies, bread, eggs, chocolates, sweets, pudding, ice-cream, etc. As for drink: milk, tea, coffee, lime juice, aerated water, buttermilk, beer, alcoholic liquor, and, in fact, anything liquid. It all went down with relish.

The bear became very attached to our two dogs and all the children living in and around our farm. He was left quite free in his younger days and spent his time playing, running into the kitchen, and going to sleep in our beds.

One day an accident befell him. I put down poison (barium carbonate) to kill the rats and mice that had got into my library. Bruno entered the library as he often did and ate some of the poison. Paralysis set into the extent that he could not stand on his feet. But he dragged himself on his stumps to my wife, who called me. I guessed what had happened.

Off I rushed him in the car to the vet's residence. A case of poisoning! Tame Bear—barium carbonate—what to do? Out came his medical books, and a feverish reference to index began: "What poison did you say, sir?" he asked, "Barium carbonate," I said.

"Ah yes—B—Ba—Barium Salts—Ah! Barium carbonate! Symptoms— paralysis—treatment—injections of . .. Just a minute, sir. I'll bring my syringe and the medicine." Said the doc. I dashed back to the car. Bruno was still floundering about on his stumps, but clearly, he was weakening rapidly; there was some vomiting, he was breathing heavily, with heaving flanks and gaping mouth. I was really scared and did not know what to do. I was feeling very guilty and was running in and out of the vet's house doing everything the doc asked me.

"Hold him, everybody!" In goes the hypodermic—Bruno squeals — 10 c.c. of the antidote enters his system without a drop being wasted. Ten minutes later: condition unchanged! Another 10 c.c. Injected! Ten minutes later: breathing less torturous— Bruno can move his arms and legs a little although he cannot stand yet. Thirty minutes later: Bruno gets up and has a great feed! He looks at us disdainfully, as much as to say, 'What's barium carbonate to a big black bear like me?' Bruno was still eating. I was really happy to see him recover.

The months rolled on, and Bruno had grown many times the size he was when he came. He had equaled the big dogs in height and had even outgrown them. But was just as sweet, just as mischievous, just as playful. And he was very fond of us all. Above all, he loved my wife, and she loved him too! And he could do a few tricks, too. At the command, 'Bruno, wrestle,' or 'Bruno, box,' he vigorously tackled anyone who came forward for a rough and tumble. Give him a stick and say 'Bruno, hold the gun,' and he pointed the stick at you. Ask him, 'Bruno, where's baby?' and he immediately produced and cradled affectionately a stump of wood which he had carefully concealed in his straw bed. But because of the neighborhoods' and our renters' children, poor Bruno, had to be kept chained most of the time.

Then my son and I advised my wife and friends advised her, too, to give Bruno to the zoo. He was getting too big to keep at home. After some weeks of such advice, she at last consented. Hastily, and before she could change her mind, a letter was written to the curator of the zoo. Did he want a tame bear for his collection? He replied, "Yes." The zoo sent a cage in a truck, a distance of hundred – eighty – seven miles, and Bruno was packed off. We all missed him greatly, but in a sense, we were relieved. My wife was inconsolable. She wept and fretted. For the first few days, she would not eat a thing. Then she wrote a number of letters to the curator. How was Bruno? Back came the replies, "Well, but fretting; he refuses food too."

After that, friends visiting the zoo were begged to make a point of seeing how Bruno was getting along. They reported that he was well but looked very thin and sad. All the keepers at the zoo said he was fretting. For three months, I managed to restrain my wife from visiting the zoo. Then she said one day, "I must see Bruno. Either you take me by car, or I will go myself by bus or train myself." So I took her by car. Friends had conjectured that the bear would not recognize her. I had thought so too. But while she was yet some yards from his cage, Bruno saw her and recognized her. He howled with happiness. She ran up to him, petted him through the bars, and he stood on his head in delight.

For the next three hours, she would not leave that cage. She gave him tea, lemonade, cakes, ice cream, and whatnot. Then 'closing time' came and we had to leave. My wife cried bitterly; Bruno cried bitterly; even the hardened curator and the keepers felt depressed. As for me, I had reconciled myself to what I knew was going to happen next.

"Oh please, sir," she asked the curator, "may I have my Bruno back"? Hesitantly, he answered, "Madam, he belongs to the zoo and is Government property now. I cannot give away Government property. But if my boss, the superintendent, agrees, certainly, you may have him back."

There followed the return journey home and a visit to the superintendent's office. A tearful pleading: "Bruno and I are both fretting for each other. Will you please give him back to me?" He was a kind-hearted man and consented. Not only that, but he wrote to the curator, telling him to lend us a cage for transporting the bear back home.

Back we went to the zoo again, armed with the superintendent's letter. Bruno was driven into a small cage and hoisted on top of the car; the cage was tied securely, and a slow and careful return journey back home was accomplished.

Once home, a squad of workers were engaged for special work around our yard. An island was made for Bruno. It was twenty feet long and fifteen feet wide and was surrounded by a dry moat, six feet wide and seven feet deep. A wooden box that once housed fowls was brought and put on the island for Bruno to sleep in at night. Straw was placed inside to keep him warm, and his 'baby,' the gnarled stump, along with his 'gun,' the piece of bamboo, both of which had been sentimentally preserved since he had been sent away to the zoo, were put back for him to play with. In a few days, the workers hoisted the cage on to the island, and Bruno was released. He was delighted; standing on his hind legs, he pointed his 'gun' and cradled his 'baby.' My wife spent hours sitting on a chair there while he sat on her lap. He was fifteen months old and pretty heavy too!

The way my wife reaches the island and leaves it is interesting. I have tied a rope to the overhanging branch of a maple tree with a loop at its end. Putting one foot in the loop, she kicks off with the other, to bridge the six-foot gap that constitutes the width of the surrounding moat. The return journey back is made the same way.

But who can say now that a sloth bear has no sense of affection, no memory, and no individual characteristics?

After reading the story, enter the details in the map below. This will help you to answer the questions with ease.

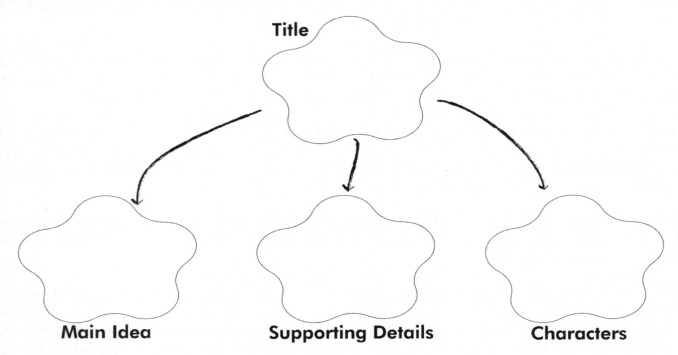

1. Which of the following would make the best alternate title for this selection?

   Ⓐ The Pet
   Ⓑ Hungry for Love
   Ⓒ The Author's Wife
   Ⓓ The Animal in the Zoo

2. What is this story mostly about?

   Ⓐ about having a bear as a pet and how to care for it
   Ⓑ about the bond that the bear and the author's wife shared
   Ⓒ about rescuing a bear
   Ⓓ about animals

3. What is the central idea of this portion of the selection? Circle the correct answer choice.

   Ⓐ Bruno eats rat poison, but doesn't die.
   Ⓑ An accident almost causes the narrator's family to lose its pet.
   Ⓒ A vet treats a pet bear.
   Ⓓ The narrator feels guilty about accidentally poisoning his pet bear.

THE OLD MAN AND THE DEVILS - A Gaelic Folk Tale
(Ed. Kate Douglas Wiggin)

A long time ago there was an old man who had a big lump on the right side of his face. One day he went into the mountain to cut wood when the rain began to pour and the wind to blow so very hard that, finding it impossible to return home, and filled with fear, he took refuge in the hollow of an old tree. While sitting there doubled up and unable to sleep, he heard the confused sound of many voices in the distance gradually approaching to where he was. He said to himself: "How strange! I thought I was all alone in the mountain, but I hear the voices of many people." So, taking courage, he peeped out and saw a great crowd of strange-looking beings. Some were red, and dressed in green clothes; others were black, and dressed in red clothes; some had only one eye; others had no mouth; indeed, it is quite impossible to describe their varied and strange looks. They kindled a fire so that it became as light as day. They sat down in two cross-rows, and began to drink wine and make merry just like human beings. They passed the wine cup around so often that many of them soon drank too much. One of the young devils got up and began to sing a merry song and to dance; so also many others; some danced well, others badly. One said: "We have had uncommon fun tonight, but I would like to see something new."

Then the old man, losing all fear, thought he would like to dance, and saying, "Let come what will, if I die for it, I will have a dance, too," crept out of the hollow tree and, with his cap slipped over his nose and his ax sticking in his belt, began to dance. The devils in great surprise jumped up, saying, "Who is this?" but the old man advancing and receding, swaying to and fro, and posturing this way and that way, the whole crowd laughed and enjoyed the fun, saying: "How well the old man dances! You must always come and join us in our sport; but, for fear you might not come, you must give us a pledge that you will. " So the devils consulted together, and, agreeing that the lump on his face, which was a token of wealth, was what he valued most highly, demanded that it should be taken. The old man replied: "I have had this lump many years, and would not without good reason part with it; but you may have it, or an eye, or my nose either if you wish." So the devils laid hold of it, twisting and pulling, and took it off without giving him any pain, and put it away as a pledge that he would come back. Just then the day began to dawn, and the birds to sing, so the devils hurried away.

The old man felt his face and found it quite smooth, and not a trace of the lump left. He forgot all about cutting wood, and hastened home. His wife, seeing him, exclaimed in great surprise, "What has happened to you?" So he told her all that had befallen him.

Now, among the neighbors there was another old man who had a big lump on the left side of his face. Hearing all about how the first old man had got rid of his misfortune, he determined that he would also try the same plan. So he went and crept into the hollow tree, and waited for the devils to come. Sure enough, they came just as he was told, and they sat down, drank wine, and made merry just as they did before. The second old man, afraid and trembling, crept out of the hollow tree. The devils welcomed him, saying: "The old man has come; now let us see him dance." This old fellow was awkward, and did not dance as well as the other, so the devils cried out: "You dance badly, and are getting worse and worse; we will give you back the lump which we took from you as a pledge." Upon this, one of the devils brought the lump, and stuck it on the other side of his face; so the poor old fellow returned home with a lump on each side.

After reading the story, enter the details in the map below. This will help you to answer the question with ease.

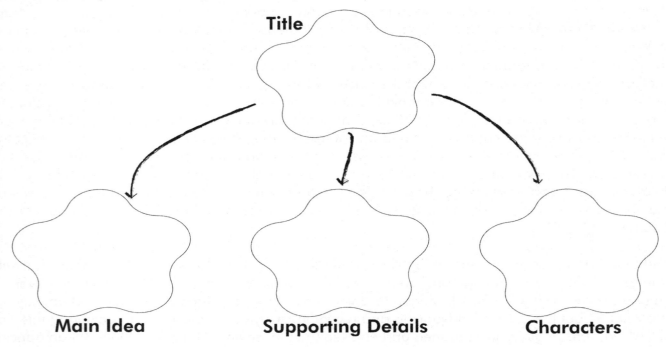

4. Which is the best summary of the second paragraph of the story?

Ⓐ   Two men who have deformities are "cured" in different ways by a group of devils.
Ⓑ   An old man with a lump on his face dances freely with a group of devils.
Ⓒ   An old man dances freely and is rewarded for his talent by a group of devils who cure him of a deformity that never really bothered him.
Ⓓ   The old man returns to his home free of the lump on his face. His wife is shocked by his trans formation.

Tryouts

For years, Sam had dreamed of being the best tennis player in the world. He went to tennis practice every single morning and night. He spent every summer at tennis camp, and he gave up long week-ends at the beach to work on his game. Now, it seemed his hard work was finally paying off. He was invited to try out for the state tennis team!

Still, there was something that was bothering Sam. The tryouts for the tennis team were on the same day as his mom's birthday, and he knew his family was planning a huge surprise party for her. He didn't want to hurt his mom's feelings by missing the party, but he also didn't want to miss his one shot at being a champion tennis player. He was in a quandary; he didn't know what to do.

For days, Sam went to bed, worrying about the decision. If he went to the tryout, he worried he would seem selfish. If he stayed home, he would miss his one big shot at making the state team. In fact, despite the honor of being invited to try out, he hadn't even told his family about the opportunity. He was so stressed about deciding whether to go or not that he couldn't even think about sharing the news.

Weeks went by, and Sam was making no progress. Every day his coach asked him if he was ready for the tryout, and Sam couldn't even respond. Finally, Sam couldn't bear the stress any longer. He decided to talk to his grandfather about his predicament.

"You know, your mom wants you to be happy," he told Sam. "It would be a great birthday present for her to know you are making your dream come true."

Sam had never thought of it that way before, and after talking to his grandfather, he knew what he had to do. He immediately went home and sat down with his parents to let them know about the opportunity to try out for the state team. When Sam apologetically told his parents what day the tryouts were, they were so busy shrieking with excitement that he thought maybe they hadn't heard.

"But Mom, that means I'm going to miss your birthday," Sam said. "I am happy you are so nice about it, but I still feel really bad."
"Are you kidding?" his mom asked. "This is the best present I could ask for!"

After reading the story, enter the details in the map below. This will help you to answer the question with ease.

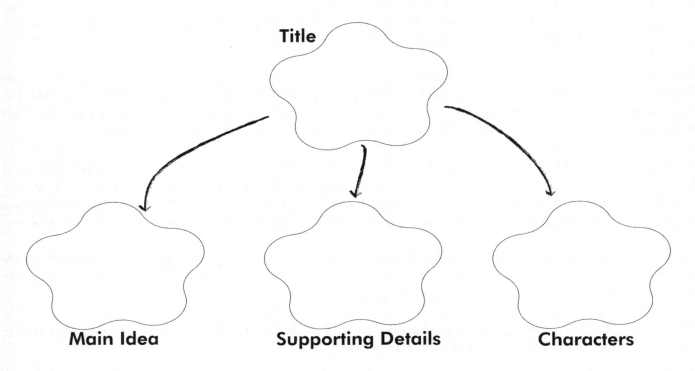

Title

Main Idea   **Supporting Details**   **Characters**

5. What would be an appropriate alternate title for this story?

Ⓐ   The Birthday Present
Ⓑ   Tennis Trouble
Ⓒ   Sam and His Mother
Ⓓ   How Sam Ruined His Mother's Birthday

MY SHADOW by Robert Louis Stevenson

I have a little shadow that goes in and out with me,
And what can be the use of him is more than I can see.

He is very, very like me, from the heels up to the head;
And I see him jump before me, when I jump into my bed.

The funniest thing about him is the way he likes to grow—
Not at all like proper children, which is always very slow;

For he sometimes shoots up taller, like an India-rubber ball,
And he sometimes gets so little that there's none of him at all.

6. What is the summary of the above two stanza of the poem, My Shadow?

Ⓐ A little boy who does not understand shadows delights in playing with his shadow.
Ⓑ A little boy plays with a friend.
Ⓒ A little boy is confused by the shadow that is following him around as he plays.
Ⓓ A little boy tries to control his shadow as he plays.

THE WONDERFUL HAIR by A. H. Wraitslaw

There was a man who was very poor, but so well supplied with children that he was utterly unable to maintain them, and one morning more than once prepared to kill them, in order not to see their misery in dying of hunger, but his wife prevented him. One night a child came to him in his sleep, and said to him: "Man! I see that you are making up your mind to destroy and to kill your poor little children, and I know that you are distressed thereat; but in the morning you will find under your pillow a mirror, a red kerchief, and an embroidered pocket-handkerchief; take all three secretly and tell nobody; then go to such a hill; by it, you will find a stream; go along it till you come to its fountain-head; there you will find a damsel as bright as the sun, with her hair hanging down over her back. Be on your guard, that the ferocious she-dragon do not coil around you; do not converse with her if she speaks; for if you converse with her, she will poison you, and turn you into a fish or something else, and will then devour you but if she bids you examine her head, examine it, and as you turn over her hair, look, and you will find one hair as red as blood; pull it out and run back again; then, if she suspects and begins to run after you, throw her first the embroidered pocket-handkerchief, then the kerchief, and, lastly, the mirror; then she will find occupation for herself. And sell that hair to some rich man, but don't let them cheat you, for that hair is worth countless wealth; and you will thus enrich yourself and maintain your children."

When the poor man awoke, he found everything under his pillow, just as the child had told him in his sleep; and then he went to the hill. When there, he found the stream, went on and on alongside of it, till he came to the fountain-head. Having looked about him to see where the damsel was, he espied her above a piece of water, like sunbeams threaded on a needle, and she was embroidering at a frame on stuff, the threads of which were young men's hair. As soon as he saw her, he made a reverence to her, and she stood on her feet and questioned him: "Whence are you, unknown young man?" But he held his tongue. She questioned him again: "Who are you? Why have you come?" and much else of all sorts, but he was as mute as a stone, making signs with his hands as if he were deaf and wanted help. Then she told him to sit down on her skirt. He did not wait for any more orders but sat down, and she bent down her head to him, that he might examine it. Turning over the hair of her head, as if to examine it, he was not long in finding that red hair, and separated it from the other hair, pulled it out, jumped off her skirt, and ran away back as he best could. She noticed it and ran at his heels full speed after him. He looked around, and seeing that she was about to overtake him, threw, as he was told, the embroidered pocket-handkerchief on the way, and when she saw the pocket-handkerchief, she stooped and began to overhaul it in every direction, admiring the embroidery, till he had got a good way off. Then the damsel placed the pocket-handkerchief in her bosom and ran after him again.

When he saw that she was about to overtake him, he threw the red kerchief, and she again occupied herself, admiring and gazing, till the poor man had again got a good way off. Then the damsel became exasperated, and threw both the pocket-handkerchief and the kerchief on the way, and ran after him in pursuit. Again, when he saw that she was about to overtake him, he threw the mirror. When the damsel came to the mirror, the like of which she had never seen before, she lifted it up, and when she saw herself in it, not knowing that it was herself, but thinking that it was somebody else, she, as it were, fell in love with herself in the mirror, and the man got so far off that she was no longer able to overtake him. When she saw that she could not catch him, she turned back, and the man reached his home safe and sound. After arriving at his home, he showed his wife the hair and told her all that had happened to him, but she began to jeer and laugh at him. But he paid no attention to her and went to a town to sell the hair. A crowd of all sorts of people and merchants collected round him; one offered a sequin, another two, and so on, higher and higher, till they came to a hundred gold sequins. Just then, the emperor heard of the hair, summoned the man into his presence, and said to him that he would give him a thousand sequins for it, and he sold it to him. What was the hair? The emperor split it in two from top to bottom and found registered in it in writing many remarkable things, which happened in the olden time since the beginning of the world. Thus the man became rich and lived on with his wife and children. And that child, that came to him in his sleep was an angel sent by the Lord God, whose will it was to aid the poor man and to reveal secrets which had not been revealed till then.

After reading the story, enter the details in the map below. This will help you to answer the question with ease.

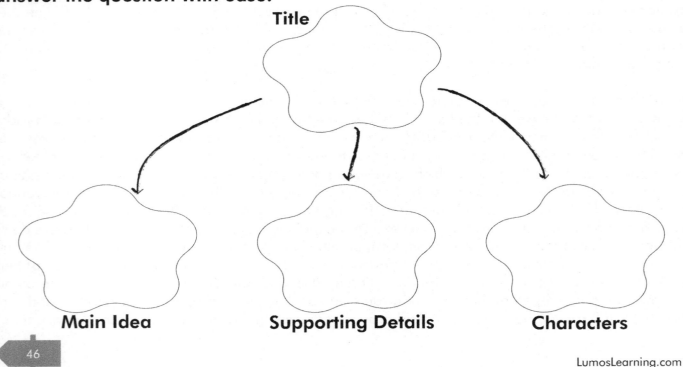

7. Which best summarizes the directions the child gives the poor man while he is sleeping?

Ⓐ Go to the stream and find a damsel who will give you a great deal of money.
Ⓑ You should not kill your children because there is a damsel at the stream who will help you by giving you a lock of her hair.
Ⓒ You will find a hair masked as blood that will cause you great trouble.
Ⓓ At the stream, there is a damsel who can help you make money for your family. You must not speak to her and may need to trick her to get a piece of her hair that you can sell for a great deal of money.

"The Smith and the Fairies": A Gaelic Folk Tale (Ed. Kate Douglas Wiggin)

Years ago, there lived in Crossbrig, a smith of the name of MacEachern. This man had an only child, a boy of about thirteen or fourteen years of age, cheerful, strong, and healthy. All of a sudden, he fell ill, took to his bed, and moped whole days away. No one could tell what was the matter with him, and the boy himself could not, or would not, tell how he felt. He was wasting away fast; getting thin, old, and yellow; and his father and all his friends were afraid that he would die.

At last one day, after the boy had been lying in this condition for a long time, getting neither better nor worse, always confined to bed, but with an extraordinary appetite—one day, while sadly revolving these things, and standing idly at his forge, with no heart to work, the smith was agreeably surprised to see an old man, well known for his sagacity and knowledge of out-of-the-way things, walk into his workshop. Forthwith he told him the occurrence which had clouded his life.

The old man looked grave as he listened, and after sitting a long time pondering over all he had heard, gave his opinion thus: "It is not your son you have got. The boy has been carried away by the 'Daione Sith,' and they have left a Sibhreach in his place." "Alas! and what then am I to do?" said the smith. "How am I ever to see my own son again?" "I will tell you how," answered the old man. "But, first, to make sure that it is not your own son you have got, take as many empty egg-shells as you can get, go into his room, spread them out carefully before his sight, then proceed to draw water with them, carrying them two and two in your hands as if they were a great weight, and arrange them when full, with every sort of earnestness around the fire." The smith accordingly gathered as many broken egg-shells as he could get, went into the room, and proceeded to carry out all his instructions.

He had not been long at work before there arose from the bed a shout of laughter, and the voice of the seeming sick boy exclaimed, "I am eight hundred years of age, and I have never seen the like of that before."

The smith returned and told the old man. "Well, now," said the sage to him, "did I not tell you that it was not your son you had: your son is in Borracheill in a digh there (that is, a round green hill frequented by fairies). Get rid as soon as possible of this intruder, and I think I may promise you your son.

You must light a very large and bright fire before the bed on which this stranger is lying. He will ask you, 'What is the use of such a fire as that?' Answer him at once, 'You will see that presently!' and then seize him and throw him into the middle of it. If it is your own son you have got, he will call out to you to save him; but if not, the thing will fly through the roof."

The smith again followed the old man's advice: kindled a large fire, answered the question put to him as he had been directed to do, and seizing the child flung him in without hesitation. The Sibhreach gave an awful yell and sprang through the roof, where a hole had been left to let the smoke out.

On a certain night, the old man told him the green round hill, where the fairies kept the boy, would be open, and on that date the smith, having provided himself with a Bible, a dirk, and a crowing cock, was to proceed to the hill. He would hear singing and dancing, and much merriment going on, he had been told, but he was to advance boldly; the Bible he carried would be a certain safeguard to him against any danger from the fairies. On entering the hill he was to stick the dirk in the threshold, to prevent the hill from closing upon him; "and then," continued the old man, "on entering you will see a spacious apartment before you, beautifully clean, and there, standing far within, working at a forge, you will also see your own son. When you are questioned, say you come to seek him, and will not go without him."

Not long after this, the time came round, and the smith sallied forth, prepared as instructed. Sure enough, as he approached the hill, there was a light where the light was seldom seen before. Soon after, a sound of piping, dancing, and joyous merriment reached the anxious father on the night wind.

Overcoming every impulse to fear, the smith approached the threshold steadily, stuck the dirk into it as directed, and entered. Protected by the Bible he carried on his breast, the fairies could not touch him; but they asked him, with a good deal of displeasure, what he wanted there. He answered, "I want my son, whom I see down there, and I will not go without him."

Upon hearing this, the whole company before him gave a loud laugh, which wakened up the cock he carried dozing in his arms, who at once leaped upon his shoulders, clapped his wings lustily, and crowed loud and long.

The fairies, incensed, seized the smith and his son and throwing them out of the hill, flung the dirk after them, and in an instant, all was dark.

For a year and a day the boy never did a turn of work, and hardly ever spoke a word; but at last one day, sitting by his father and watching him finishing a sword he was making for some chief, and which he was very particular about, he suddenly exclaimed, "That is not the way to do it;" and taking the tools from his father's hands he set to work himself in his place, and soon fashioned a sword, the like of which was never seen in the country before.

From that day the young man wrought constantly with his father and became the inventor of a peculiarly fine and well-tempered weapon, the making of which kept the two Smiths, father and son, in constant employment, spread their fame far and wide, and gave them the means in abundance, as they before had the disposition, to live content with all the world and very happy with each other.

After reading the story, enter the details in the map below. This will help you to answer the question with ease.

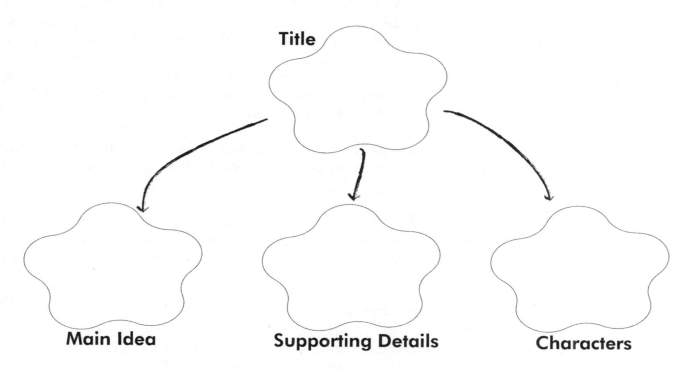

Title

Main Idea   Supporting Details   Characters

8. Which sentence best summarizes from the second to last paragraph in this story?

Ⓐ   The smith's son returns to his father and does not speak for a year and a day.
Ⓑ   The smith's son criticizes his father's work.
Ⓒ   When the smith's son finally speaks after a year and one day of silence, he offers valuable advice to his father on how to make a sword.
Ⓓ   The smith's son has nothing to say until he sees his father not doing his best work.

HOW WISDOM BECAME THE PROPERTY OF THE HUMAN RACE
(West African Folktale)

THERE once lived, in Fanti-land, a man named Father Anansi. He possessed all the wisdom in the world. People came to him daily for advice and help.

One day the men of the country were unfortunate enough to offend Father Anansi, who immediately resolved to punish them. After much thought, he decided that the severest penalty he could inflict would be to hide all his wisdom from them. He set to work at once to gather again all that he had already given. When he had succeeded, as he thought, in collecting it, he placed all in one great pot.

This he carefully sealed and determined to put it in a spot where no human being could reach it.

Now, Father Anansi had a son, whose name was Kweku Tsin. This boy began to suspect his father of some secret design, so he made up his mind to watch carefully. The next day he saw his father quietly slip out of the house, with his precious pot hung around his neck. Kweku Tsin followed. Father Anansi went through the forest until he had left the village far behind. Then, selecting the highest and most inaccessible-looking tree, he began to climb. The heavy pot, hanging in front of him, made his ascent almost impossible. Again and again, he tried to reach the top of the tree, where he intended to hang the pot. There, he thought, Wisdom would indeed be beyond the reach of everyone but himself. He was unable, however, to carry out his desire. At each trial, the pot swung in his way.

For some time, Kweku Tsin watched his father's vain attempts. At last, unable to contain himself any longer, he cried out: "Father, why do you not hang the pot on your back? Then you could easily climb the tree."

Father Anansi turned and said: "I thought I had all the world's wisdom in this pot. But I find you possess more than I do. All my wisdom was insufficient to show me what to do, yet you have been able to tell me." In his anger he threw the pot down. It struck on a great rock and broke. The wisdom contained in it escaped and spread throughout the world.

9. Which sentence best summarizes the first paragraph?

Ⓐ   Father Anansi wanted to teach the men a lesson.
Ⓑ   The men wanted Father Anansi to provide them with wisdom and he refused.
Ⓒ   To punish the men for offending him, Father Anansi hid all of his wisdom where they could not find it.
Ⓓ   Father Anansi hid away all of his wisdom until the men apologized.

10. Which sentence best summarizes what Kweku Tsin saw when he followed his father?

Ⓐ   Kweku Tsin saw his father climb the tallest tree in the forest.
Ⓑ   Kweku Tsin watched as father tried and failed to reach the top of the tallest tree.
Ⓒ   Kewku Tsin watched his father hide the pot of wisdom
Ⓓ   Kweku Tisin taught his father his lesson.

Jane Eyre (Excerpt)
by Charlotte Bronte

The red-room was a square chamber, very seldom slept in, I might say never, indeed, unless when a chance influx of visitors at Gateshead Hall rendered it necessary to turn to account all the accommodation it contained: yet it was one of the largest and stateliest chambers in the mansion. A bed supported on massive pillars of mahogany, hung with curtains of deep red damask, stood out like a tabernacle in the centre; the two large windows, with their blinds always drawn down, were half shrouded in festoons and falls of similar drapery; the carpet was red; the table at the foot of the bed was covered with a crimson cloth; the walls were a soft fawn color with a blush of pink in it; the wardrobe, the toilet-table, the chairs were of darkly polished old mahogany. Out of these deep surrounding shades rose high, and glared white, the piled-up mattresses and pillows of the bed, spread with a snowy Marseilles counterpane. Scarcely less prominent was an ample cushioned easy-chair near the head of the bed, also white, with a footstool before it; and looking, as I thought, like a pale throne.

This room was chill because it seldom had a fire; it was silent, because remote from the nursery and kitchen; solemn because it was known to be so seldom entered. The house-maid alone came here on Saturdays, to wipe from the mirrors and the furniture a week's quiet dust: and Mrs. Reed herself, at far intervals, visited it to review the contents of a certain secret drawer in the wardrobe, where were stored divers parchments, her jewel-casket, and a miniature of her deceased husband; and in those last words lies the secret of the red-room--the spell which kept it so lonely in spite of its grandeur.

After reading the story, enter the details in the map below. This will help you to answer the questions with ease.

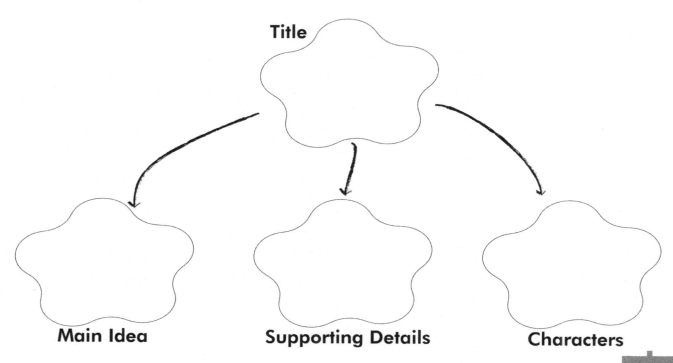

Title

Main Idea   **Supporting Details**   **Characters**

11. Which sentence best summarizes the description of this room?

Ⓐ It was a cold, quiet room.

Ⓑ The cold, dusty bedroom had pinkish walls, a fireplace, a large bed, several chairs, and a wardrobe.

Ⓒ The room was dusty and abandoned.

Ⓓ The room was quiet, lonely and cold and was dominated by a large bed and several red chairs.

12. Why did the author make a point to say "in spite of its grandeur"? Circle the correct answer choice.

Ⓐ Mrs. Reed's husband asked her to leave the room like it was when he lived.

Ⓑ Mrs. Reed does not want to dirty the room after the maid has cleaned.

Ⓒ The room is too pretty to use, so Mrs. Reed only goes there occasionally

Ⓓ The author is saying that the room was so pretty that people would normally want to spend time there, not Mrs. Reed.

Name: _____ Date: _____

Chapter 2

Lesson 4: What is it All About?

Before answering questions related to this standard, it is important to understand the term "Inference"

Inference: This is a conclusion reached by a reader after reading the information in a passage. The reader uses the information in the passage to reach this conclusion on his/her own; it has not been stated by the author. For example, the author may write about large population growth in the world and the negative effects of climate change on the production of food. The reader could draw the inference that there will not be enough food to feed the population.

You can scan the QR code given below or use the url to access additional EdSearch resources including videos and mobile apps related to What is it All About?

What is it All About?

URL	QR Code
http://www.lumoslearning.com/a/rl72	

Tryouts

For years, Sam had dreamed of being the best tennis player in the world. He went to tennis practice every single morning and night. He spent every summer at tennis camp, and he gave up long weekends at the beach to work on his game. Now, it seemed his hard work was finally paying off. He was invited to try out for the state tennis team!

Still, there was something that was bothering Sam. The tryouts for the tennis team were on the same day as his mom's birthday, and he knew his family was planning a huge surprise party for her. He didn't want to hurt his mom's feelings by missing the party, but he also didn't want to miss his one shot at being a champion tennis player. He was in a quandary; he didn't know what to do.

For days, Sam went to bed, worrying about the decision. If he went to the tryout, he worried he would seem selfish. If he stayed home, he would miss his one big shot at making the state team. In fact, despite the honor of being invited to try out, he hadn't even told his family about the opportunity. He was so stressed about deciding whether to go or not that he couldn't even think about sharing the news.

Weeks went by, and Sam was making no progress. Every day his coach asked him if he was ready for the tryout, and Sam couldn't even respond. Finally, Sam couldn't bear the stress any longer. He decided to talk to his grandfather about his predicament.

"You know, your mom wants you to be happy," he told Sam. "It would be a great birthday present for her to know you are making your dream come true."

Sam had never thought of it that way before, and after talking to his grandfather, he knew what he had to do. He immediately went home and sat down with his parents to let them know about the opportunity to try out for the state team. When Sam apologetically told his parents what day the tryouts were, they were so busy shrieking with excitement that he thought maybe they hadn't heard.

"But Mom, that means I'm going to miss your birthday," Sam said. "I am happy you are so nice about it, but I still feel really bad."

"Are you kidding?" his mom asked. "This is the best present I could ask for!"

After reading the story, enter the details in the map below. This will help you to answer the questions with ease.

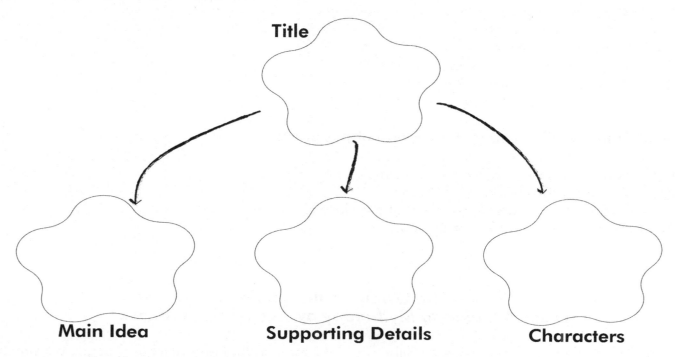

1. **What is the theme of the above story?**

   Ⓐ family values and priorities.
   Ⓑ pleasing everybody in your family
   Ⓒ doing what is very important to you no matter how others feel
   Ⓓ sports above all else

2. **What message about relationship is this story trying to pass on to readers?**

   Ⓐ Friends can come and go out of each others' lives, but mother's love is permanent
   Ⓑ You should always ask friends to help you with your life choices.
   Ⓒ Open communication helps resolve seemingly difficult problems.
   Ⓓ Thinking over a problem in a quiet place is the best way to resolve a conflict.

Moral of "The Dog and the Wolf" by Marmaduke Park

Our neighbors sometimes seem to be
A vast deal better off than we;
Yet seldom 'tis they really are,
Since they have troubles too to bear,
Which, if the truth were really known,
Are quite as grievous as our own.

3. What is the best summary of the moral of this poem?

Ⓐ   It's best to ignore those who complain.
Ⓑ   Dogs and wolves will never get along.
Ⓒ   Everyone else has problems too, that are likely to be grievous as yours.
Ⓓ   Avoid those who look down on you.

"The Origin of the Robin"
From *A Guide to Mythology* by Cornelius Mathews

An old man had an only son, named Iadilla, who had come to that age which is thought to be most proper to make the long and final fast which is to secure through life a guardian genius or spirit. The father was ambitious that his son should surpass all others in whatever was deemed wisest and greatest among his people. To accomplish his wish, he thought it is necessary that the young Iadilla should fast a much longer time than any of those renowned for their power or wisdom, whose fame he coveted.

He, therefore, directed his son to prepare with great ceremony for the important event. After he had been several times in the sweating-lodge and bath, which were to prepare and purify him for communion with his good spirit, he ordered him to lie down upon a clean mat in a little lodge expressly provided for him. He enjoined upon him at the same time to endure his fast like a man, and promised that at the expiration of twelve days he should receive food and the blessing of his father.

The lad carefully observed the command, and lay with his face covered, calmly awaiting the approach of the spirit which was to decide his good or evil fortune for all the days of his life.

Every morning his father came to the door of the little lodge and encouraged him to persevere, dwelling at length on the vast honor and renown that must ever attend him, should he accomplish the full term of trial allotted to him.

To these glowing words of promise and glory the boy never replied, but he lay without the least sign of discontent or murmuring until the ninth day, when he addressed his father as follows:

"My father, my dreams forbode evil. May I break my fast now, and at a more favorable time make a new fast?"

The father answered:
"My son, you know not what you ask. If you get up now, all your glory will depart. Wait patiently a little longer. You have but three days more, and your term will be completed. You know it is for your own good, and I encourage you to persevere. Shall not your aged father live to see you a star among the chieftains and the beloved of battle?"

The son assented; and covering himself more closely, that he might shut out the light which prompted him to complain, he lay till the eleventh day, when he repeated his request.

The father addressed Iadilla as he had the day before, and promised that he would himself prepare his first meal, and bring it to him by the dawn of the morning.

The son moaned, and the father added:
"Will you bring shame upon your father when his sun is falling in the West?"
"I will not shame you, my father," replied Iadilla; and he lay so still and motionless that you could only know that he was living by the gentle heaving of his breast.

At the spring of day, the next morning, the father, delighted at having gained his end, prepared a repast for his son, and hastened to set it before him. On coming to the door of the little lodge, he was surprised to hear his son talking to himself. He stooped his ear to listen, and, looking through a small opening, he was yet more astonished when he beheld his son painted with vermilion over all his breast, and in the act of finishing his work by laying on the paint as far back on his shoulders as he could reach with his hands, saying at the same time, to himself:

"My father has destroyed my fortune as a man. He would not listen to my requests. He has urged me beyond my tender strength. He will be the loser. I shall be forever happy in my new state, for I have been obedient to my parent. He alone will be the sufferer, for my guardian spirit is a just one. Though not propitious to me in the manner I desired, he has shown me pity in another way—he has given me another shape; and now I must go."
At this moment the old man broke in, exclaiming:
"My son! my son! I pray you leave me not!"

But the young man, with the quickness of a bird, had flown to the top of the lodge and perched himself on the highest pole, having been changed into a beautiful robin red-breast. He looked down upon his father with pity beaming in his eyes, and addressed him as follows:

"Regret not, my father, the change you behold. I shall be happier in my present state than I could have been as a man. I shall always be the friend of men, and keep near their dwellings. I shall ever be happy and contented; and although I could not gratify your wishes as a warrior, it will be my daily aim to make you amends for it as a harbinger of peace and joy. I will cheer you by my songs, and strive to inspire in others the joy and lightsomeness of heart I feel in my present state. This will be some compensation to you for the loss of glory you expected. I am now free from the cares and pains of human life. My food is spontaneously furnished by the mountains and fields, and my pathway of life is in the bright air."

Then stretching himself on his toes, as if delighted with the gift of wings, Iadilla caroled one of his sweetest songs, and flew away into a neighboring wood.

After reading the story, enter the details in the map below. This will help you to answer the questions with ease.

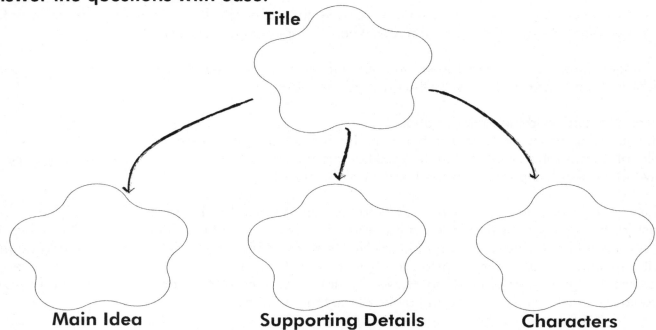

4. What is the theme of this story?

    Ⓐ Disobedient children will be punished.
    Ⓑ Children lead their parents to Heaven.
    Ⓒ Being obedient does not always have the intended result.
    Ⓓ Dying is honorable.

5. What message about parents is the author trying to send through this story?

    Ⓐ Parents should listen to their children.
    Ⓑ Effective parents are strict with their children.
    Ⓒ Parents always know best.
    Ⓓ Children take their parents for granted.

Aesop in Rhyme "The Philosopher and the Acorn" by Marmaduke Park

A philosopher, proud of his wit and his reason,
Sat him under an oak in a hot summer season.
On the oak grew an acorn or two, it is said:
On the ground grew a pumpkin as big as his head.
Thought the sage, "What's the reason this oak is so strong
A few acorns to bear that are scarce an inch long;
While this poor feeble plant has a weight to sustain,
Which had much better hang on the tree, it is plain?"
But just at the time the philosopher spoke
An acorn dropp'd down on his head from the oak;
Then, said he, who just now thought his plan was so clever,
"I am glad that this was not a pumpkin, however."

6. What is the theme of this poem?

Ⓐ   Watch out for falling objects.
Ⓑ   Just because something is small doesn't mean it isn't mighty.
Ⓒ   Don't question the way Mother Nature works.
Ⓓ   Every seed becomes a beautiful plant.

"The Old Man and the Devils"- A Gaelic Folk Tale (Ed. Kate Douglas Wiggin)

A long time ago there was an old man who had a big lump on the right side of his face. One day he went into the mountain to cut wood when the rain began to pour and the wind to blow so very hard that, finding it impossible to return home, and filled with fear, he took refuge in the hollow of an old tree. While sitting there doubled up and unable to sleep, he heard the confused sound of many voices in the distance gradually approaching to where he was. He said to himself: "How strange! I thought I was all alone in the mountain, but I hear the voices of many people." So, taking courage, he peeped out and saw a great crowd of strange-looking beings. Some were red, and dressed in green clothes; others were black, and dressed in red clothes; some had only one eye; others had no mouth; indeed, it is quite impossible to describe their varied and strange looks. They kindled a fire so that it became as light as day. They sat down in two cross-rows, and began to drink wine and make merry just like human beings. They passed the wine cup around so often that many of them soon drank too much. One of the young devils got up and began to sing a merry song and to dance; so also many others; some danced well, others badly. One said: "We have had uncommon fun tonight, but I would like to see something new."

Then the old man, losing all fear, thought he would like to dance, and saying, "Let come what will, if I die for it, I will have a dance, too," crept out of the hollow tree and, with his cap slipped over his nose and his ax sticking in his belt, began to dance. The devils in great surprise jumped up, saying, "Who is this?" but the old man advancing and receding, swaying to and fro, and posturing this way and that way, the whole crowd laughed and enjoyed the fun, saying: "How well the old man dances! You must always come and join us in our sport; but, for fear you might not come, you must give us a pledge that you will." So the devils consulted together, and, agreeing that the lump on his face, which was a token of wealth, was what he valued most highly, demanded that it should be taken. The old man replied: "I have had this lump many years, and would not without good reason part with it; but you may have it, or an eye, or my nose either if you wish." So the devils laid hold of it, twisting and pulling, and took it off without giving him any pain, and put it away as a pledge that he would come back. Just then the day began to dawn, and the birds to sing, so the devils hurried away.

The old man felt his face and found it quite smooth, and not a trace of the lump left. He forgot all about cutting wood, and hastened home. His wife, seeing him, exclaimed in great surprise, "What has happened to you?" So he told her all that had befallen him.

Now, among the neighbors there was another old man who had a big lump on the left side of his face. Hearing all about how the first old man had got rid of his misfortune, he determined that he would also try the same plan. So he went and crept into the hollow tree, and waited for the devils to come. Sure enough, they came just as he was told, and they sat down, drank wine, and made merry just as they did before. The second old man, afraid and trembling, crept out of the hollow tree. The devils welcomed him, saying: "The old man has come; now let us see him dance." This old fellow was awkward, and did not dance as well as the other, so the devils cried out: "You dance badly, and are getting worse and worse; we will give you back the lump which we took from you as a pledge." Upon this, one of the devils brought the lump, and stuck it on the other side of his face; so the poor old fellow returned home with a lump on each side.

After reading the story, enter the details in the map below. This will help you to answer the question with ease.

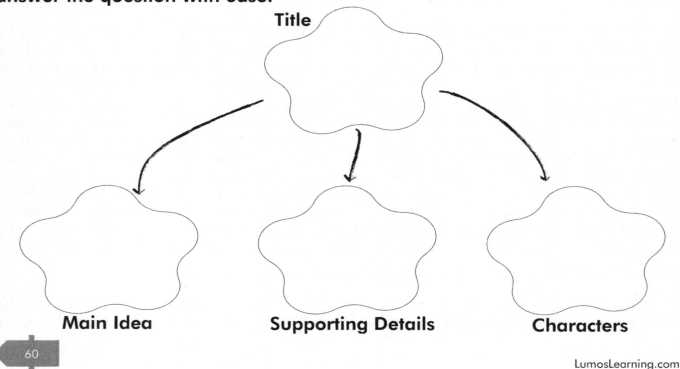

Title

Main Idea   Supporting Details   Characters

7. What is the theme of this selection?

Ⓐ Dance as if no one is watching.
Ⓑ To be healed, you have to make a deal with the Devil.
Ⓒ Blessings come to people who don't expect them.
Ⓓ Changing your appearance will only bring you misery.

"The Land of Nod"
by Robert Louis Stevenson

From breakfast on through all the day
At home among my friends I stay,
But every night I go abroad
Afar into the Land of Nod.

All by myself I have to go,
With none to tell me what to do—
All alone beside the streams
And up the mountain-sides of dreams.

The strangest things are there for me,
Both things to eat and things to see,
And many frightening sights abroad
Till morning in the Land of Nod.

Try as I like to find the way,
I never can get back by day,
Nor can remember plain and clear
The curious music that I hear.

8. What is the theme of this selection?

Ⓐ When we nod our heads, we get to see new places.
Ⓑ Dreams let you travel to new and magical places.
Ⓒ Traveling to the Land of Nod is exciting.
Ⓓ People can travel anywhere they want to go.

"The Lad and the Diel"
by Sir George Webbe Dasent

Once upon a time, there was a lad who was walking along a road cracking nuts, so he found one that was worm-eaten, and just at that very moment, he met the Deil (Devil).

"Is it true, now," said the lad, "what they say, that the Deil can make himself as small as he chooses, and thrust himself on through a pinhole?"

"Yes, it is," said the Deil. "Oh! it is, is it? then let me see you do it, and just creep into this nut," said the lad.

So the Deil did it. Now, when he had crept well into it through the worm's hole, the lad stopped it up with a pin.

"Now, I've got you safe," he said, and put the nut into his pocket.

So when he had walked on a bit, he came to a smith, and he turned in and asked the smith if he'd be good enough to crack that nut for him.

"Ay, that'll be an easy job," said the smith, and took his smallest hammer, laid the nut on the anvil, and gave it a blow, but it wouldn't break.

So he took another hammer a little bigger, but that wasn't heavy enough either. Then he took one bigger still, but it was still the same story, and so the smith got wroth and grasped his great sledge-hammer.

"Now, I'll crack you to bits," he said, and let drive at the nut with all his might and main.

And so the nut flew to pieces with a bang that blew off half the roof of the smithy, and the whole house creaked and groaned as though it were ready to fall. "Why! if I don't think the Deil must have been in that nut," said the smith.

"So he was; you're quite right," said the lad, as he went away laughing.

After reading the story, enter the details in the map below. This will help you to answer the question with ease.

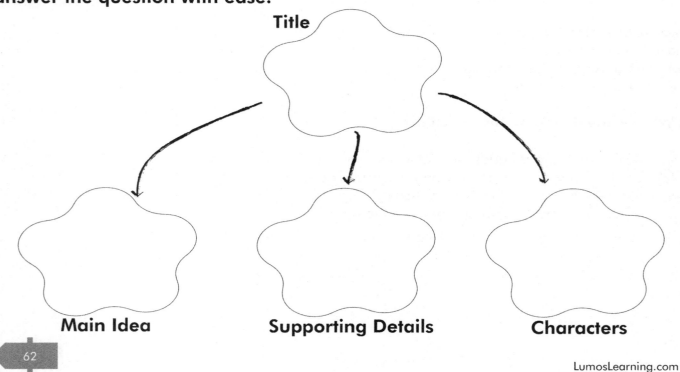

9. What is the theme of this selection?

Ⓐ Violence causes the Devil to come out.
Ⓑ It's not kind to play tricks on unsuspecting people.
Ⓒ Sometimes the Devil is in the smallest, least expected places.
Ⓓ It is important to ask for help.

"The Wonderful Hair"
by A. H. Wraitslaw

There was a man who was very poor, but so well supplied with children that he was utterly unable to maintain them, and one morning more than once prepared to kill them, in order not to see their misery in dying of hunger, but his wife prevented him. One night a child came to him in his sleep, and said to him: "Man! I see that you are making up your mind to destroy and to kill your poor little children, and I know that you are distressed thereat; but in the morning you will find under your pillow a mirror, a red kerchief, and an embroidered pocket-handkerchief; take all three secretly and tell no-body; then go to such a hill; by it, you will find a stream; go along it till you come to its fountain-head; there you will find a damsel as bright as the sun, with her hair hanging down over her back. Be on your guard, that the ferocious she-dragon do not coil around you; do not converse with her if she speaks; for if you converse with her, she will poison you, and turn you into a fish or something else, and will then devour you but if she bids you examine her head, examine it, and as you turn over her hair, look, and you will find one hair as red as blood; pull it out and run back again; then, if she suspects and begins to run after you, throw her first the embroidered pocket-handkerchief, then the kerchief, and, lastly, the mirror; then she will find occupation for herself. And sell that hair to some rich man, but don't let them cheat you, for that hair is worth countless wealth; and you will thus enrich yourself and maintain your children."

When the poor man awoke, he found everything under his pillow, just as the child had told him in his sleep; and then he went to the hill. When there, he found the stream, went on and on alongside of it, till he came to the fountain-head. Having looked about him to see where the damsel was, he espied her above a piece of water, like sunbeams threaded on a needle, and she was embroidering at a frame on stuff, the threads of which were young men's hair. As soon as he saw her, he made a reverence to her, and she stood on her feet and questioned him: "Whence are you, unknown young man?" But he held his tongue. She questioned him again: "Who are you? Why have you come?" and much else of all sorts, but he was as mute as a stone, making signs with his hands as if he were deaf and wanted help. Then she told him to sit down on her skirt. He did not wait for any more orders but sat down, and she bent down her head to him, that he might examine it. Turning over the hair of her head, as if to examine it, he was not long in finding that red hair, and separated it from the other hair, pulled it out, jumped off her skirt, and ran away back as he best could. She noticed it and ran at his heels full speed after him. He looked around, and seeing that she was about to overtake him, threw, as he was told, the embroidered pocket-handkerchief on the way, and when she saw the pock et-handkerchief, she stooped and began to overhaul it in every direction, admiring the embroidery, till he had got a good way off. Then the damsel placed the pocket-handkerchief in her bosom and ran after him again.

When he saw that she was about to overtake him, he threw the red kerchief, and she again occupied herself, admiring and gazing, till the poor man had again got a good way off. Then the damsel became exasperated, and threw both the pocket-handkerchief and the kerchief on the way, and ran after him in pursuit. Again, when he saw that she was about to overtake him, he threw the mirror. When the damsel came to the mirror, the like of which she had never seen before, she lifted it up, and when she saw herself in it, not knowing that it was herself, but thinking that it was somebody else, she, as it were, fell in love with herself in the mirror, and the man got so far off that she was no longer able to overtake him. When she saw that she could not catch him, she turned back, and the man reached his home safe and sound. After arriving at his home, he showed his wife the hair and told her all that had happened to him, but she began to jeer and laugh at him. But he paid no attention to her and went to a town to sell the hair. A crowd of all sorts of people and merchants collected round him; one offered a sequin, another two, and so on, higher and higher, till they came to a hundred gold sequins. Just then, the emperor heard of the hair, summoned the man into his presence, and said to him that he would give him a thousand sequins for it, and he sold it to him. What was the hair? The emperor split it in two from top to bottom and found registered in it in writing many remarkable things, which happened in the olden time since the beginning of the world. Thus the man became rich and lived on with his wife and children. And that child, that came to him in his sleep was an angel sent by the Lord God, whose will it was to aid the poor man and to reveal secrets which had not been revealed till then.

After reading the story, enter the details in the map below. This will help you to answer the question with ease.

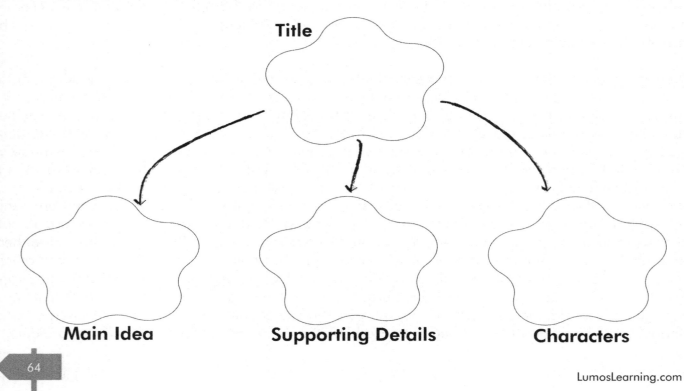

10. What is the theme of this story?

Ⓐ It is wrong for a parent to want to hurt his children.
Ⓑ The things we do for family can bring about great wealth for many.
Ⓒ God rewards those who protect their children.
Ⓓ His character does not have any influence on the plot.

"Gone with the Wind"
by Margaret Mitchell

"'All wars are sacred,' he said. 'To those who have to fight them. If the people who started wars didn't make them sacred, who would be foolish enough to fight? But, no matter what rallying cries the orators give to the idiots who fight, no matter what noble purposes they assign to wars, there is never but one reason for war. And that is money. All wars are, in reality, money squabbles. But so few people ever realize it. Their ears are too full of bugles and drums and fine words from stay-at-home orators. Sometimes the rallying cry is 'Save the Tomb of Christ from the Heathen!' Sometimes it's 'Down with Popery!' and sometimes 'Liberty!' and sometimes 'Cotton, Slavery and States' Rights!'"

11. What is the theme of this excerpt?

"From "The Dog and the Wolf"
by Marmaduke Park

A wolf there was, whose scanty fare
Had made his person lean and spare;
A dog there was, so amply fed,
His sides were plump and sleek; 'tis said
The wolf once met this prosp'rous cur,
And thus began: "Your servant, sir;
I'm pleased to see you look so well,
Though how it is I cannot tell;
I have not broke my fast to-day;
Nor have I, I'm concern'd to say,
One bone in store or expectation,
And that I call a great vexation."

12. Part A
What does the wolf represent in this poem?

Ⓐ the basic idea of dieting
Ⓑ how to fast (not eat)
Ⓒ the basic needs of living
Ⓓ being a wild animal

Part B
What does the dog represent in this poem?

Ⓐ being a tamed animal
Ⓑ the comforts of having everything needed in life
Ⓒ being greedy
Ⓓ sharing with others

Chapter 2

Lesson 5: One Thing Leads to Another

Let us understand the concept with an example.

A Servant's Freedom
By Vivek Krishnaswamy
Revised by George Smith

Late at night when there are people walking around the streets of Spain, I lay in my bed hoping that one day I would be able to be like them, free from being a servant, free to leave this house, and able to get a job that paid more.

It was 12 o'clock in the afternoon and I was washing the dishes when the mistress walked into the kitchen, "Marcos! What is this? What is this? My clothes have been washed but they have not been IRONED!!!! Do it now or you will be punished!" she yelled. So I washed and dried my hands then walked to her room with her dress in my hand, ironed it quickly then got back to my work. This was typical of my relationship with the family members. If I disobeyed any order from the master or the mistress I was beaten by the gardener; that is why my policy was to try and do exactly what they wanted to me to do in the exact manner they asked.

I served this family for five long and dreadful years. Then one evening while doing the dishes in the kitchen, I looked at the back door, and an idea occurred to me. Why couldn't I escape from the house through the back door when the family was gone, look for a job, and come back before the family returned? They always went out every morning. Once I found a job I could ask for permission to leave, telling them I would give back all of the possessions they had given me, owing them nothing. For several weeks I left the house in the mornings and searched for a job that would meet my needs. I finally found a grocery store with an owner who was very kind, would hire me to work in the store, had a small room that was fit for me, would give me free time off from work, and pay a higher salary. The next day, after dinner, I went to my master's office. I knelt on me knee and asked him very politely, "Master?" "What is it?" he replied. "Master I wish to leave this house and find a new job for myself sir." "WHAT? Why would you want to do that now? Have we mistreated you, have we not provided everything that is necessary for your survival?" he asked. "Yes master, but I would like to change my occupation as it has been five years of my service, if it is alright with you then I will take my leave sir." I said. "I may agree however your mistress will be reluctant. If you can find a boy or girl who is as efficient as you then you will be allowed to leave your service." "Sir but I am not allowed to leave the house." I said. "He looked at the ceiling and then spoke, "I will give you two hours in the morning each day to look for someone to replace you, but once your two hours is up you will return to this house and finish your chores. Do you understand?" he said in a very serious tone of voice. "Yes sir, as you say." I left the room with a very happy mood.

The store owner was closing the store for a vacation, and did not need me until he reopened a few days. For the next few days I looked for a replacement and found a girl willing to take my place. I felt sorry for her and honestly described the difficulties that she would have to face when she was at the house, but she still accepted the offer because she was desperate for money. She started work at the house a few days later, and that day I left the house and reported to the grocery store. I felt my life was a paradise. I was free from servitude, I would earn enough money to spend on things I wanted, I had all the food I wanted when I wanted it, for free. This was the life that I had worked for those long five years. I just hope the girl who took my place will eventually find a way to escape to a better life too.

Your assignment is to write about how the plot, characters and setting interact in this story.

This is what you might write.

The plot (main idea) of this story is about the need for the servant to escape his present lifestyle, and to tell how he does this. There are five important characters in this story who play important roles that influence the plot. The master and mistress create living conditions for their servant Marcos that are oppressive (they are disrespectful to him) and restrictive (he cannot leave the house). This treatment is what makes him want to escape which is the source of the plot. The grocery owner and the girl who replaces Marcos are facilitators (those who make something easier to do) for the plot in that they provide what Marcos (and the master and mistress) need to allow him to escape from his servant's role. The settings are the house, which provides a location where he, the master and mistress can live and interact, and the grocery store to which he escapes, both locations are essential to carrying out the plot.

You can scan the QR code given below or use the url to access additional EdSearch resources including videos and mobile apps related to *One Thing Leads to Another.*

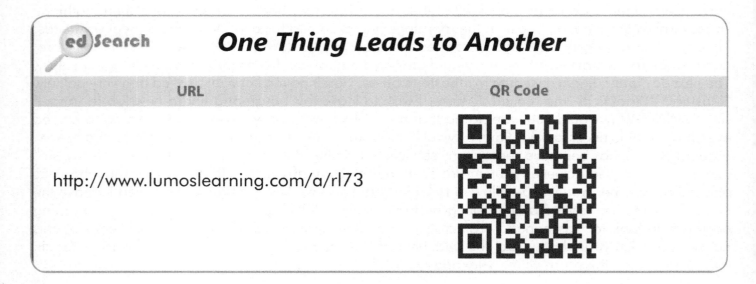

ed Search   **One Thing Leads to Another**

URL	QR Code
http://www.lumoslearning.com/a/rl73	

"The Lament"
by SRAVANI

It is twilight. Thick wet snow is slowly twirling around the newly lighted street lamps and lying in soft thin layers on roofs, on horses' backs, on people's shoulders and hats. The cab driver, Iona Potapov, is quite white and looks like a phantom: he is bent double as far as a human body can bend double; he is seated on his box; he never makes a move. If a whole snowdrift fell on him, it seems as if he would not find it necessary to shake it off. His little horse is also quite white, and remains motionless; its immobility, its angularity, and its straight wooden-looking legs, even close by, give it the appearance of a gingerbread horse worth a kopek. It is, no doubt, plunged in deep thought. If you were snatched from the plough, from your usual gray surroundings, and were thrown into this slough full of monstrous lights, unceasing noise and hurrying people, you too would find it difficult not to think.

Iona and his little horse have not moved from their place for a long while. They left their yard before dinner and, up to now, not a fare. The evening mist is descending over the town, the white lights of the lamps are replacing brighter rays, and the hubbub of the street is getting louder.
'Cabby for Viborg Way!' suddenly hears Iona. 'Cabby!'

Iona jumps and, through his snow-covered eyelashes, sees an officer in a greatcoat, with his hood over his head.
'Viborg way!' the officer repeats. 'Are you asleep, eh? Viborg way!'
With a nod of assent, Iona picks up the reins, in consequence of which layers of snow slip off the horse's back and neck. The officer seats himself in the sleigh, the cab driver smacks his lips to encourage his horse, stretches out his neck like a swan, sits up and, more from habit than necessity, brandishes his whip. The little horse also stretches its neck, bends its wooden-looking legs, and makes a move undecidedly.
'What are you doing, werewolf!' is the exclamation Iona hears from the dark mass moving to and fro, as soon as they have started.

'Where the devil are you going? To the r-r-right!'
'You do not know how to drive. Keep to the right!' calls the officer angrily. A coachman from a private carriage swears at him; a passerby, who has run across the road and rubbed his shoulder against the horse's nose, looks at him furiously as he sweeps the snow from his sleeve. Iona shifts about on his seat as if he was on needles, moves his elbows as if he were trying to keep his equilibrium, and gasps about like someone suffocating, who does not understand why and wherefore he is there.

'What scoundrels they all are!' jokes the officer; 'one would think they had all entered into an agreement to jostle you or fall under your horse.'
Iona looks around at the officer and moves his lips. He evidently wants to say something but the only sound that issues is a snuffle.
'What?' asks the officer. Iona twists his mouth into a smile and, with an effort, says hoarsely: 'My son, Barin, died this week.' 'Hm! What did he die of?'
Iona turns with his whole body towards his fare and says: 'And who knows! They say high fever. He was three days in the hospital and then died... God's will be done.'

"Turn round! The devil!' sounds from the darkness. 'Have you popped off, old doggie, eh? Use your eyes!'

'Go on, go on,' says the officer, 'otherwise we shall not get there by tomorrow. Hurry up a bit!'

After reading the story, enter the details in the map below. This will help you to answer the questions with ease.

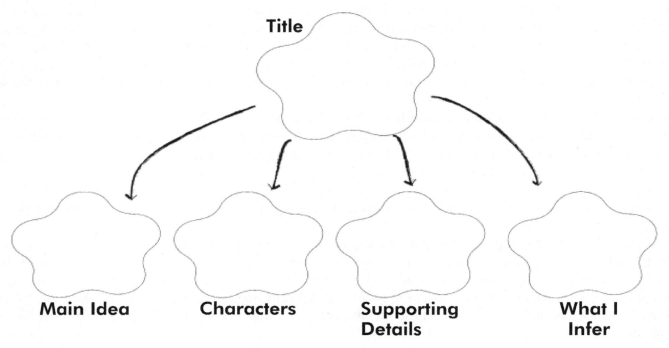

1. What event that occurred before the story begins, influences the way the character Iona acts in this story?

   Ⓐ The death of his son
   Ⓑ The winter storm
   Ⓒ The officer's harsh comments
   Ⓓ Iona's wife's sickness

2. Based on the plot of this story, what can you assume was The Lament mentioned in the title?

   Ⓐ The officer had to reach Viborg urgently.
   Ⓑ Grief made the cabby confused.
   Ⓒ The people were sad because the cabby was not driving carefully.
   Ⓓ The horse was lost.

Best Friend

Ever since they were kids, Julie and Max had been best friends. They went to kindergarten together. They went to summer camp together. They hung out together every weekend. But suddenly, things between the two had started to change.

Max had started playing on the football team and didn't have much time for Julie anymore. He was always busy, and he never seemed to make it to study hall, where the two used to swap stories about their favorite (or least favorite) teachers. In class, Julie noticed that Max never seemed to have his homework done on time anymore. She even noticed that he got a 'D' on his last paper. She knew something was going on with him – but what?

At first, Julie decided to play it cool and see how things went. She tried waiting in the hall for Max after class to see if she could ask if he was OK. But days went by, and he never had time to stop. He'd rush right past her in the hall, only to leave her feeling even worse about what was happening between them.

Even though she wasn't sure she could handle the situation herself, Julie didn't want to talk to her parents because she was afraid they would tell her not to hang out with Max anymore. She barely saw him as it was, so she knew it would just make things worse if her parents didn't approve of him. She didn't want to tell Max's parents either because she didn't want him to get in trouble. Still, it seemed like something needed to change.

Julie decided to go to one of her school counselors and let her know she was concerned. When she walked into Mrs. Smith's room, she was surprised to see that Max was already sitting there. "I'm sorry, I'll come back," Julie said.

"No, stay," said Max. "Maybe you can help."

Julie was surprised to find that Max had visited the counselor's office for the same reason she had: he was starting to feel overwhelmed with all of the things he was supposed to be doing as a student, an athlete, and a friend. He needed some guidance on how to determine what truly mattered and how to divide his time between all of the things that were important to him.

When she realized that Max was still the same old Max (just a little more stressed), Julie was relieved. She was also happy to know that he had come to a conclusion on his own, without her having to talk to someone else about it. She decided it was a sign they were both growing up.

After reading the story, enter the details in the map below. This will help you to answer the question with ease.

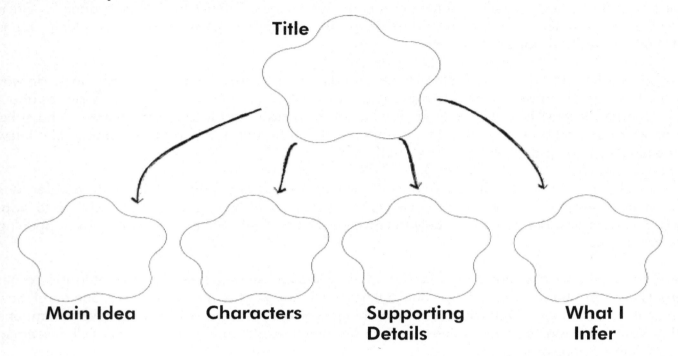

3. How does Max playing football affect his relationship with Julie in this story?

Ⓐ It brings the two of them closer together.
Ⓑ It gives the two something to talk about during study hall.
Ⓒ It makes Julie jealous.
Ⓓ It keeps the two of them from spending time together.

Tryouts

For years, Sam had dreamed of being the best tennis player in the world. He went to tennis practice every single morning and night. He spent every summer at tennis camp, and he gave up long week-ends at the beach to work on his game. Now, it seemed his hard work was finally paying off. He was invited to try out for the state tennis team!

Still, there was something that was bothering Sam. The tryouts for the tennis team were on the same day as his mom's birthday, and he knew his family was planning a huge surprise party for her. He didn't want to hurt his mom's feelings by missing the party, but he also didn't want to miss his one shot at being a champion tennis player just because the tryouts were on his mom's birthday. He was in a quandary; he didn't know what to do.

For days, Sam went to bed, worrying about the decision. If he went to the tryout, he worried he would seem selfish. If he stayed home, he would miss his one big shot at making the state team. In fact, despite the honor of being invited to try out, he hadn't even told his family about the opportunity. He was so stressed about deciding whether to go or not that he couldn't even think about sharing the news.

Weeks went by, and Sam was making no progress. Every day his coach asked him if he was ready for the tryout, and Sam couldn't even respond. Finally, Sam couldn't bear the stress any longer. He decided to talk to his grandfather about his predicament.
"You know, your mom wants you to be happy," he told Sam. "It would be a great birthday present for her to know you are making your dream come true."

Sam had never thought of it that way before, and after talking to his grandfather, he knew what he had to do. He immediately went home and sat down with his parents to let them know about the opportunity to try out for the state team. His parents were so excited that when he told them, apologetically, what day the tryouts were, they were so busy shrieking with excitement that he thought maybe they hadn't heard.
"But Mom, that means I'm going to miss your birthday," Sam said. "I am happy you are so nice about it, but I still feel really bad."
"Are you kidding?" his mom asked. "This is the best present I could ask for!"

After reading the story, enter the details in the map below. This will help you to answer the question with ease.

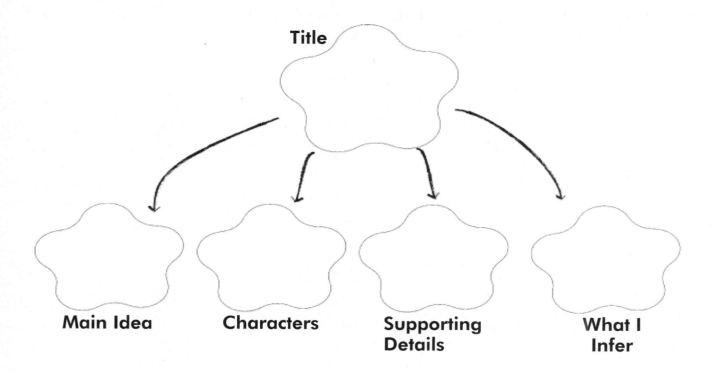

4. Why was Sam's tryout a great birthday present for his mother?

Ⓐ She was proud of her son.
Ⓑ She was excited about her birthday.
Ⓒ She loves birthday cake.
Ⓓ She feels younger every day.

Fairy Tales by A Brothers' Grimm (Excerpt)

A certain king once fell ill, and the doctor declared that only a sudden fright would restore him to health, but the king was not a man for anyone to play tricks on, except his fool. One day, when the fool was with him in his boat, he cleverly pushed the king into the water. Help had already been arranged, and the king was drawn ashore and put to bed. The fright, the bath, and the rest in bed cured the diseased king.

The king wanted to frighten the fool for his act, so he told him that he would be put to death. He directed the executioner privately not to use the ax but to let fall a single drop of water on the fool's neck. Amidst shouts and laughter, the fool was asked to rise and thank the king for his kindness. But the fool never moved; he was dead; killed by the master's joke.

5. Based on the relationships between the characters and the plot of this story, who is the only person who can play a trick on the king?

Ⓐ The courtiers
Ⓑ The prince
Ⓒ The fool
Ⓓ The doctor

"Bruno the Bear"
Excerpt from *The Bond of Love*

I will begin with Bruno, my wife's pet sloth bear. I got him for her by accident. Two years ago, we were passing through the cornfields near a small town in Iowa. People were driving away the wild pigs from the fields by shooting at them. Some were shot, and some escaped. We thought that everything was over when suddenly a black sloth bear came out panting in the hot sun.

Now I will not shoot a sloth bear wantedly, but unfortunately for the poor beast, one of my companions did not feel the same way about it and promptly shot the bear on the spot.

As we watched the fallen animal, we were surprised to see that the black fur on its back moved and left the prostrate body. Then we saw it was a baby bear that had been riding on its mother's back when the sudden shot had killed her. The little creature ran around its prostrate parent, making a pitiful noise. I ran up to it to attempt a capture. It scooted into the sugarcane field. Following it with my companions, I was at last able to grab it by the scruff of its neck while it snapped and tried to scratch me with its long, hooked claws.

We put it in one of the large jute-bags we had brought, and when I got back home, I duly presented it to my wife. She was delighted! She at once put a blue colored ribbon around its neck, and after discovering the cub was a 'boy,' she christened it Bruno.

Bruno soon took to drinking milk from a bottle. It was but a step further, and within a very few days, he started eating and drinking everything else. And everything is the right word, for he ate porridge made from any ingredients, vegetables, fruit, nuts, meat (especially pork), curry and rice regardless of condiments and chilies, bread, eggs, chocolates, sweets, pudding, ice-cream, etc. As for drink: milk, tea, coffee, lime juice, aerated water, buttermilk, beer, alcoholic liquor, and, in fact, anything liquid. It all went down with relish.

The bear became very attached to our two dogs and all the children living in and around our farm. He was left quite free in his younger days and spent his time playing, running into the kitchen, and going to sleep in our beds.

One day an accident befell him. I put down poison (barium carbonate) to kill the rats and mice that had got into my library. Bruno entered the library as he often did and ate some of the poison. Paralysis set into the extent that he could not stand on his feet. But he dragged himself on his stumps to my wife, who called me. I guessed what had happened.

Off I rushed him in the car to the vet's residence. A case of poisoning! Tame Bear—barium carbonate—what to do? Out came his medical books, and a feverish reference to index began: "What poison did you say, sir?" he asked, "Barium carbonate," I said.

"Ah yes—B—Ba—Barium Salts—Ah! Barium carbonate! Symptoms— paralysis—treatment—injections of . .. Just a minute, sir. I'll bring my syringe and the medicine." Said the doc. I dashed back to the car. Bruno was still floundering about on his stumps, but clearly, he was weakening rapidly; there was some vomiting, he was breathing heavily, with heaving flanks and gaping mouth. I was really scared and did not know what to do. I was feeling very guilty and was running in and out of the vet's house doing everything the doc asked me.

"Hold him, everybody!" In goes the hypodermic—Bruno squeals — 10 c.c. of the antidote enters his system without a drop being wasted. Ten minutes later: condition unchanged! Another 10 c.c. Injected! Ten minutes later: breathing less torturous— Bruno can move his arms and legs a little although he cannot stand yet. Thirty minutes later: Bruno gets up and has a great feed! He looks at us disdainfully, as much as to say, 'What's barium carbonate to a big black bear like me?' Bruno was still eating. I was really happy to see him recover.

The months rolled on, and Bruno had grown many times the size he was when he came. He had equaled the big dogs in height and had even outgrown them. But was just as sweet, just as mischievous, just as playful. And he was very fond of us all. Above all, he loved my wife, and she loved him too! And he could do a few tricks, too. At the command, 'Bruno, wrestle,' or 'Bruno, box,' he vigorously tackled anyone who came forward for a rough and tumble. Give him a stick and say 'Bruno, hold the gun,' and he pointed the stick at you. Ask him, 'Bruno, where's baby?' and he immediately produced and cradled affectionately a stump of wood which he had carefully concealed in his straw bed. But because of the neighborhoods' and our renters' children, poor Bruno, had to be kept chained most of the time.

Then my son and I advised my wife and friends advised her, too, to give Bruno to the zoo. He was getting too big to keep at home. After some weeks of such advice, she at last consented. Hastily, and before she could change her mind, a letter was written to the curator of the zoo. Did he want a tame bear for his collection? He replied, "Yes." The zoo sent a cage in a truck, a distance of hundred – eighty – seven miles, and Bruno was packed off. We all missed him greatly, but in a sense, we were relieved. My wife was inconsolable. She wept and fretted. For the first few days, she would not eat a thing. Then she wrote a number of letters to the curator. How was Bruno? Back came the replies, "Well, but fretting; he refuses food too."

After that, friends visiting the zoo were begged to make a point of seeing how Bruno was getting along. They reported that he was well but looked very thin and sad. All the keepers at the zoo said he was fretting. For three months, I managed to restrain my wife from visiting the zoo. Then she said one day, "I must see Bruno. Either you take me by car, or I will go myself by bus or train myself." So I took her by car. Friends had conjectured that the bear would not recognize her. I had thought so too. But while she was yet some yards from his cage, Bruno saw her and recognized her. He howled with happiness. She ran up to him, petted him through the bars, and he stood on his head in delight.

For the next three hours, she would not leave that cage. She gave him tea, lemonade, cakes, ice cream, and whatnot. Then 'closing time' came and we had to leave. My wife cried bitterly; Bruno cried bitterly; even the hardened curator and the keepers felt depressed. As for me, I had reconciled myself to what I knew was going to happen next.

"Oh please, sir," she asked the curator, "may I have my Bruno back"? Hesitantly, he answered, "Madam, he belongs to the zoo and is Government property now. I cannot give away Government property. But if my boss, the superintendent, agrees, certainly, you may have him back."

There followed the return journey home and a visit to the superintendent's office. A tearful pleading: "Bruno and I are both fretting for each other. Will you please give him back to me?" He was a kind-hearted man and consented. Not only that, but he wrote to the curator, telling him to lend us a cage for transporting the bear back home.

Back we went to the zoo again, armed with the superintendent's letter. Bruno was driven into a small cage and hoisted on top of the car; the cage was tied securely, and a slow and careful return journey back home was accomplished.

Once home, a squad of workers were engaged for special work around our yard. An island was made for Bruno. It was twenty feet long and fifteen feet wide and was surrounded by a dry moat, six feet wide and seven feet deep. A wooden box that once housed fowls was brought and put on the island for Bruno to sleep in at night. Straw was placed inside to keep him warm, and his 'baby,' the gnarled stump, along with his 'gun,' the piece of bamboo, both of which had been sentimentally preserved since he had been sent away to the zoo, were put back for him to play with. In a few days, the workers hoisted the cage on to the island, and Bruno was released. He was delighted; standing on his hind legs, he pointed his 'gun' and cradled his 'baby.' My wife spent hours sitting on a chair there while he sat on her lap. He was fifteen months old and pretty heavy too!

The way my wife reaches the island and leaves it is interesting. I have tied a rope to the overhanging branch of a maple tree with a loop at its end. Putting one foot in the loop, she kicks off with the other, to bridge the six-foot gap that constitutes the width of the surrounding moat. The return journey back is made the same way.

But who can say now that a sloth bear has no sense of affection, no memory, and no individual characteristics?

Name: _____   Date: _____

After reading the story, enter the details in the map below. This will help you to answer the question with ease.

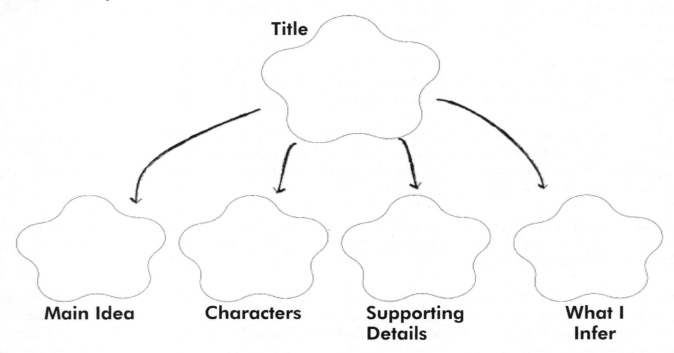

Title

Main Idea   **Characters**   **Supporting Details**   **What I Infer**

6. What event in the plot of this story led Bruno to be taken to the Vet's house?

Ⓐ He ate too much food.
Ⓑ He ate a rat poison called barium carbonate and was paralyzed.
Ⓒ He broke his leg trying to wrestle.
Ⓓ None of these.

THE OLD MAN AND THE DEVILS - A Gaelic Folk Tale
(Ed. Kate Douglas Wiggin)

A long time ago there was an old man who had a big lump on the right side of his face. One day he went into the mountain to cut wood when the rain began to pour and the wind to blow so very hard that, finding it impossible to return home, and filled with fear, he took refuge in the hollow of an old tree. While sitting there doubled up and unable to sleep, he heard the confused sound of many voices in the distance gradually approaching to where he was. He said to himself: "How strange! I thought I was all alone in the mountain, but I hear the voices of many people." So, taking courage, he peeped out and saw a great crowd of strange-looking beings. Some were red, and dressed in green clothes; others were black, and dressed in red clothes; some had only one eye; others had no mouth; indeed, it is quite impossible to describe their varied and strange looks. They kindled a fire so that it became as light as day. They sat down in two cross-rows, and began to drink wine and make merry just like human beings. They passed the wine cup around so often that many of them soon drank too much. One of the young devils got up and began to sing a merry song and to dance; so also many others; some danced well, others badly. One said: "We have had uncommon fun tonight, but I would like to see something new."

Then the old man, losing all fear, thought he would like to dance, and saying, "Let come what will, if I die for it, I will have a dance, too," crept out of the hollow tree and, with his cap slipped over his nose and his ax sticking in his belt, began to dance. The devils in great surprise jumped up, saying, "Who is this?" but the old man advancing and receding, swaying to and fro, and posturing this way and that way, the whole crowd laughed and enjoyed the fun, saying: "How well the old man dances! You must always come and join us in our sport; but, for fear you might not come, you must give us a pledge that you will." So the devils consulted together, and, agreeing that the lump on his face, which was a token of wealth, was what he valued most highly, demanded that it should be taken. The old man replied: "I have had this lump many years, and would not without good reason part with it; but you may have it, or an eye, or my nose either if you wish." So the devils laid hold of it, twisting and pulling, and took it off without giving him any pain, and put it away as a pledge that he would come back. Just then the day began to dawn, and the birds to sing, so the devils hurried away.

The old man felt his face and found it quite smooth, and not a trace of the lump left. He forgot all about cutting wood, and hastened home. His wife, seeing him, exclaimed in great surprise, "What has happened to you?" So he told her all that had befallen him.

Now, among the neighbors there was another old man who had a big lump on the left side of his face. Hearing all about how the first old man had got rid of his misfortune, he determined that he would also try the same plan. So he went and crept into the hollow tree, and waited for the devils to come. Sure enough, they came just as he was told, and they sat down, drank wine, and made merry just as they did before. The second old man, afraid and trembling, crept out of the hollow tree. The devils welcomed him, saying: "The old man has come; now let us see him dance." This old fellow was awkward, and did not dance as well as the other, so the devils cried out: "You dance badly, and are getting worse and worse; we will give you back the lump which we took from you as a pledge." Upon this, one of the devils brought the lump, and stuck it on the other side of his face; so the poor old fellow returned home with a lump on each side.

7. Based on information in the selection, what event can you assume happened between the first man returning without the lump on his face and the second man heading to the tree in hopes of having his lump removed?

Ⓐ The people in town began gossiping about how the first man lost his lump.
Ⓑ The old man's wife celebrated her husband losing his lump.
Ⓒ The second old man prayed he would lose his lump.
Ⓓ The devils decided to punish the next man who tried to dance with them.

MY SHADOW
by Robert Louis Stevenson

I have a little shadow that goes in and out with me,
And what can be the use of him is more than I can see.
He is very, very like me, from the heels up to the head;
And I see him jump before me, when I jump into my bed.
The funniest thing about him is the way he likes to grow—
Not at all like proper children, which is always very slow;
For he sometimes shoots up taller, like an India-rubber ball,
And he sometimes gets so little that there's none of him at all.

8. Part A
The narrator of this poem is a child. How does this character affect the plot of the poem?
Ⓐ
Ⓑ He is confused by his shadow, so he is constantly trying to avoid it.
Ⓒ He is amazed by his shadow, so plays with it to try to understand it.
   He is frightened by his shadow, so he tries to "lose" it.

Part B
When the poem talks about "Him/He" what literary element is being used?

Ⓐ oxymoron
Ⓑ simile
Ⓒ hyperbole
Ⓓ personification

Part C
What is the tone of this poem?

Ⓐ The people in town began gossiping about how the first man lost his lump.
Ⓑ The old man's wife celebrated her husband losing his lump.
Ⓒ The second old man prayed he would lose his lump.
Ⓓ The devils decided to punish the next man who tried to dance with them.

THE WONDERFUL HAIR by A. H. Wraitslaw

There was a man who was very poor, but so well supplied with children that he was utterly unable to maintain them, and one morning more than once prepared to kill them, in order not to see their misery in dying of hunger, but his wife prevented him.

One night a child came to him in his sleep, and said to him: "Man! I see that you are making up your mind to destroy and to kill your poor little children, and I know that you are distressed thereat; but in the morning you will find under your pillow a mirror, a red kerchief, and an embroidered pocket-handkerchief; take all three secretly and tell nobody; then go to such a hill; by it you will find a stream; go along it till you come to its fountain-head; there you will find a damsel as bright as the sun, with her hair hanging down over her back. Be on your guard, that the ferocious she-dragon do not coil around you; do not converse with her if she speaks; for if you converse with her, she will poison you, and turn you into a fish or something else, and will then devour you but if she bids you examine her head, examine it, and as you turn over her hair, look, and you will find one hair as red as blood; pull it out and run back again; then, if she suspects and begins to run after you, throw her first the embroidered pocket-handkerchief, then the kerchief, and, lastly, the mirror; then she will find occupation for herself. And sell that hair to some rich man; but don't let them cheat you, for that hair is worth countless wealth; and you will thus enrich yourself and maintain your children."

When the poor man awoke, he found everything under his pillow, just as the child had told him in his sleep; and then he went to the hill. When there, he found the stream, went on and on alongside of it, till he came to the fountain-head. Having looked about him to see where the damsel was, he espied her above a piece of water, like sunbeams threaded on a needle, and she was embroidering at a frame on stuff, the threads of which were young men's hair. As soon as he saw her, he made a reverence to her, and she stood on her feet and questioned him: "Whence are you, unknown young man?" But he held his tongue. She questioned him again: "Who are you? Why have you come?" and much else of all sorts; but he was as mute as a stone, making signs with his hands, as if he were deaf and wanted help. Then she told him to sit down on her skirt. He did not wait for any more orders, but sat down, and she bent down her head to him, that he might examine it. Turning over the hair of her head, as if to examine it, he was not long in finding that red hair, and separated it from the other hair, pulled it out, jumped off her skirt and ran away back as he best could. She noticed it, and ran at his heels full speed after him. He looked around, and seeing that she was about to overtake him, threw, as he was told, the embroidered pocket-handkerchief on the way, and when she saw the pocket-handkerchief she stooped and began to overhaul it in every direction, admiring the embroidery, till he had got a good way off. Then the damsel placed the pocket-handkerchief in her bosom, and ran after him again. When he saw that she was about to overtake him, he threw the red kerchief, and she again occupied herself, admiring and gazing, till the poor man had again got a good way off. Then the damsel became exasperated, and threw both the pocket-handkerchief and the kerchief on the way, and ran after him in pursuit. Again, when he saw that she was about to overtake him, he threw the mirror. When the damsel came to the mirror, the like of which she had never seen before, she lifted it up, and when she saw herself in it, not knowing that it was herself, but thinking that it was somebody else, she, as it were, fell in love with herself in the mirror, and the man got so far off that she was no longer able to overtake him. When she saw that she could not catch him, she turned back, and the man reached his home safe and sound. After arriving at his home, he showed his wife the hair, and told her all that had happened to him, but she began to jeer and laugh at him. But he paid no attention to her, and went to a town to sell the hair. A crowd of all sorts of people and merchants collected round him; one offered a sequin, another two, and so on, higher and higher, till they came to a hundred gold sequins. Just then the emperor heard of the hair, summoned the man into his presence, and said to him that he would give him a thousand sequins for it, and he sold it to him. What was the hair? The emperor split it in two from top to bottom, and found registered in it in writing many remarkable things, which happened in the olden time since the beginning of the world. Thus the man became rich and lived on with his wife and children. And that child, that came to him in his sleep, was an angel sent by the Lord God, whose will it was to aid the poor man, and to reveal secrets which had not been revealed till then.

9. How does the little child affect the plot of the story?

Ⓐ He makes his father feel guilty for wanting to kill his children.
Ⓑ He foreshadows the future events in the story.
Ⓒ He falsely predicts what will happen to his father later in the story.
Ⓓ His character does not have any influence on the plot.

HOW WISDOM BECAME THE PROPERTY OF THE HUMAN RACE
(West African Folktale)

THERE once lived, in Fanti-land, a man named Father Anansi. He possessed all the wisdom in the world. People came to him daily for advice and help.

One day the men of the country were unfortunate enough to offend Father Anansi, who immediately resolved to punish them. After much thought, he decided that the severest penalty he could inflict would be to hide all his wisdom from them. He set to work at once to gather again all that he had already given. When he had succeeded, as he thought, in collecting it, he placed all in one great pot. This he carefully sealed and determined to put it in a spot where no human being could reach it.

Now, Father Anansi had a son, whose name was Kweku Tsin. This boy began to suspect his father of some secret design, so he made up his mind to watch carefully.

The next day he saw his father quietly slip out of the house, with his precious pot hung around his neck. Kweku Tsin followed. Father Anansi went through the forest until he had left the village far behind. Then, selecting the highest and most inaccessible-looking tree, he began to climb. The heavy pot, hanging in front of him, made his ascent almost impossible. Again and again, he tried to reach the top of the tree, where he intended to hang the pot. There, he thought, Wisdom would indeed be beyond the reach of everyone but himself. He was unable, however, to carry out his desire. At each trial, the pot swung in his way.

For some time, Kweku Tsin watched his father's vain attempts. At last, unable to contain himself any longer, he cried out: "Father, why do you not hang the pot on your back? Then you could easily climb the tree."

LumosLearning.com

Father Anansi turned and said: "I thought I had all the world's wisdom in this pot. But I find you possess more than I do. All my wisdom was insufficient to show me what to do, yet you have been able to tell me." In his anger, he threw the pot down. It struck on a great rock and broke. The wisdom contained in it escaped and spread throughout the world.

10. What is the climax of this story?

Ⓐ When Kweku Tsin follows his father into the forest
Ⓑ When Kweku Tsin gives his father advice on how to carry the pot to the top of the tree
Ⓒ When Father Anansi threw the pot to the ground
Ⓓ When Father Anansi decided to hide the wisdom from the men

Summer Visit

Robert was considering what to do during his summer vacation. His grandparents had invited him to stay with them for a few weeks. He enjoyed spending time with them, but he didn't like the idea of being away from his friends for such a long time. Robert's uncle, Tom, had offered him a part-time job for the summer, but Robert didn't like the idea of being cooped up inside his uncle's office three days a week. Finally, Robert's parents had offered to send him to a soccer camp at the park on the other side of town. Robert enjoyed soccer, but he didn't know which of his friends would be attending the camp, so he was reluctant to agree to attend. With all the available options, Robert was having a very difficult time figuring out what he really wanted to do over the summer.

11. Part A.
What type of conflict is Robert experiencing?

Ⓐ Character versus character
Ⓑ Character versus self
Ⓒ Character versus society
Ⓓ Character versus nature

Part B
What should the next paragraph be about?

Ⓐ comparing the advantages of his options
Ⓑ a description of his school
Ⓒ Robert's parent's opinion of him
Ⓓ Robert's friends' summer plans

12. The _____ is the part of a story that can/will change everything causing the reader to get nervous/excited/scared.

Ⓐ resolution
Ⓑ exposition
Ⓒ falling action
Ⓓ climax

Addition

When I was in junior high school, my parents decided to build a new addition onto the back of our house. My sister and I were beyond excited because we thought this would give us a huge game room where we could hang out with all of our friends. Of course, we never expected the new addition to cause so many problems.

First, my parents could not agree on the size of the addition. My Dad wanted it to be a small room with just enough space for a home office; on the other hand, my Mom wanted the addition to be large enough to include space for a music and entertainment area. After many discussions back and forth, it was decided that the addition would be a combination of both their wishes. Consequently, the room consisted of a large seating area in the center of the room that faced a television and entertainment center. To the left of the couch and recliners was Dad's computer desk and home office; Mom's grand piano sat to the right.

For the remainder of my time in school, the addition was never empty. Between my sister's and my friends, Mom's music, and Dad's work, we always had something going on in that room. We were so grateful to have the extra space.

13. Part A
Which event occurred first in the story?

Ⓐ The author's parents argued over how to configure the space.
Ⓑ The author's parents decided to combine all the ideas into the new addition.
Ⓒ The author's parents could not agree on whether or not to build an addition.
Ⓓ The author's parents decided to build an addition.

13. Part B

Which sentence describes the effect of the parent's argument over how to use the room?

Ⓐ First, my parents could not agree on the size of the addition.

Ⓑ My Dad wanted it to be a small room with just enough space for a home office; on the other hand, my Mom wanted the addition to be large enough to include space for a music a

Ⓒ After many discussions back and forth, it was decided that the addition would be a combination of both their wishes.

Ⓓ Consequently, the room consisted of a large seating area in the center of the room that faced a television and entertainment center.

Summer Trip

"Juan!" Jacob called out excitedly to his best friend as he ran up to him in the hallway. "You are never going to believe what just happened in Mrs. Smith's class!"

"What, Jake?" Juan was a little unsure of what type of news his friend could have. Jacob had a tendency to get excited about the strangest things.

"She told us we get to go to Washington D.C., and New York City this summer!"

Juan stared at his friend in astonishment. He had always wanted to go to New York City. "No way!" he exclaimed.

"I'm serious! We get to travel as a class, stay in hotels, and visit the Capitol building as well as the White House."

"What about seeing a Broadway play?" Juan asked. "I have always wanted to see The Lion King on stage. My sister saw it when she was in high school, and she said it was amazing!"

"Who cares?" Jacob asked with an incredulous look on his face. "We might get to see the President in the White House!"

Juan just shook his head at his friend. "Uh. I don't think he just walks around the White House."

'

"You never know. But it won't matter if our parents do not agree to let us go."

Juan knew Jacob was right, and more than likely, his parents would not want him to go. They never trusted him to do anything without one of them going as well. Silence filled the air between the two friends for several seconds just before the warning bell sounded. Each was lost in his own thoughts, planning how they could convince their parents to let them go.

"Let's come up with a plan to ask them while we are at lunch." Juan suggested.

Jacob agreed immediately. "That's a great idea! I'll see you then."

14. Which event occurred third in the story?

Chapter 2

Lesson 6: When and Where?

Inferences from a text: After reading a text, an inference is an idea or conclusion that the reader has made or reached that was not in the text but is based on information that was in the text.

You can scan the QR code given below or use the url to access additional EdSearch resources including videos and mobile apps related to *When and Where?*

When and Where?

URL	QR Code
http://www.lumoslearning.com/a/rl73	

"Scouting for Boys"
(Excerpt)

"Hi! Stop Thief!" shouted old Blenkinsopp as he rushed out of his little store near the village. "He's stolen my sugar. Stop him."

Stop whom? There was nobody in sight running away, "Who stole it?" asked the policeman.

"I don't know, but a whole bag of sugar is missing. It was there only a few minutes ago." The policeman tried to track the thief, but it looked a pretty impossible job for him to single out the tracks of the thief from among dozens of other footprints about the store. However, he presently started off hopefully, at a jog-trot, away out into the bush. In some places, he went over the hard stony ground, but he never checked his pace, although no footmarks could be seen. People wondered how he could possibly find the trail. Still, he trotted on. Old Blenkinsopp was feeling the heat and the pace

At length, he suddenly stopped and cast around, having evidently lost the trail. Then a grin came on his face as he pointed with his thumb over his shoulder up the tree near which he was standing. There, concealed among the branches, they saw a young man with the missing bag of sugar.

How had the policeman spotted him? His sharp eyes had detected some grains of sugar sparkling in the dust. The bag leaked, leaving a slight trail of these grains. He followed that trail, and when it came to an end in the bush, he noticed a string of ants going up a tree. They were after the sugar, and so was he, and between them, they brought about the capture of the thief.

Old Blenkinsopp was so pleased that he promptly opened the bag and spilled a lot of the sugar on the ground as a reward to the ants.

He also appreciated the policeman for his cleverness in using his eyes to see the grains of sugar and the ants, and in using his wits to know why the ants were climbing the tree.

After reading the story, enter the details in the map below. This will help you to answer the question with ease.

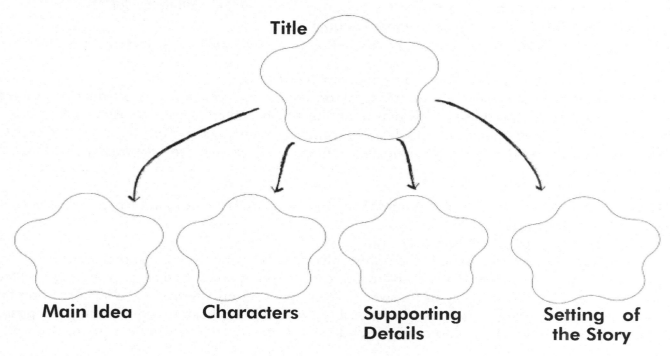

Title

Main Idea   **Characters**   **Supporting Details**   **Setting of the Story**

1. Based on the details in this story, where can you infer where the story begins (setting)?

   Ⓐ a store
   Ⓑ a house
   Ⓒ a bakery
   Ⓓ a police station

"The Lament"
by SRAVANI

It is twilight. Thick wet snow is slowly twirling around the newly lighted street lamps and lying in soft thin layers on roofs, on horses' backs, on people's shoulders and hats. The cab driver, Iona Potapov, is quite white and looks like a phantom: he is bent double as far as a human body can bend double; he is seated on his box; he never makes a move. If a whole snowdrift fell on him, it seems as if he would not find it necessary to shake it off. His little horse is also quite white, and remains motionless; its immobility, its angularity, and its straight wooden-looking legs, even close by, give it the appearance of a gingerbread horse worth a kopek. It is, no doubt, plunged in deep thought. If you were snatched from the plough, from your usual gray surroundings, and were thrown into this slough full of monstrous lights, unceasing noise and hurrying people, you too would find it difficult not to think.

Iona and his little horse have not moved from their place for a long while. They left their yard before dinner and, up to now, not a fare. The evening mist is descending over the town, the white lights of the lamps are replacing brighter rays, and the hubbub of the street is getting louder.

'Cabby for Viborg Way!' suddenly hears Iona. 'Cabby!'

Iona jumps and, through his snow-covered eyelashes, sees an officer in a greatcoat, with his hood over his head.

'Viborg way!' the officer repeats. 'Are you asleep, eh? Viborg way!'

With a nod of assent, Iona picks up the reins, in consequence of which layers of snow slip off the horse's back and neck. The officer seats himself in the sleigh, the cab driver smacks his lips to encourage his horse, stretches out his neck like a swan, sits up and, more from habit than necessity, brandishes his whip. The little horse also stretches its neck, bends its wooden-looking legs, and makes a move undecidedly.

'What are you doing, werewolf!' is the exclamation Iona hears from the dark mass moving to and fro, as soon as they have started.

'Where the devil are you going? To the r-r-right!'

'You do not know how to drive. Keep to the right!' calls the officer angrily. A coachman from a private carriage swears at him; a passerby, who has run across the road and rubbed his shoulder against the horse's nose, looks at him furiously as he sweeps the snow from his sleeve. Iona shifts about on his seat as if he was on needles, moves his elbows as if he were trying to keep his equilibrium, and gasps about like someone suffocating, who does not understand why and wherefore he is there.

'What scoundrels they all are!' jokes the officer; 'one would think they had all entered into an agreement to jostle you or fall under your horse.'

Iona looks around at the officer and moves his lips. He evidently wants to say something but the only sound that issues is a snuffle.

'What?' asks the officer.

Iona twists his mouth into a smile and, with an effort, says hoarsely:

'My son, Barin, died this week.' '

'Hm! What did he die of?'

Iona turns with his whole body towards his fare and says: 'And who knows! They say high fever. He was three

days in the hospital and then died… God's will be done.'

"Turn round! The devil!' sounds from the darkness. 'Have you popped off, old doggie, eh? Use your eyes!'

'Go on, go on,' says the officer, 'otherwise we shall not get there by tomorrow. Hurry up a bit!'

After reading the story, enter the details in the map below. This will help you to answer the questions with ease.

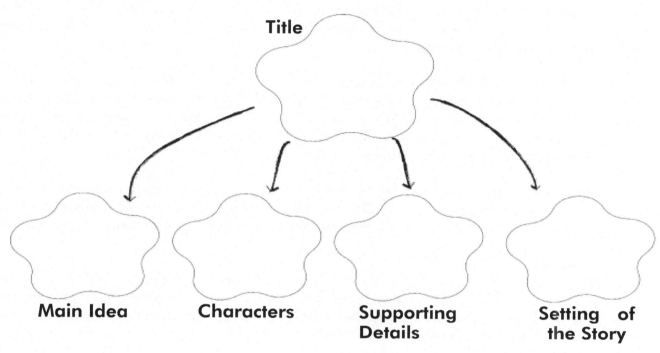

Title

Main Idea   **Characters**   **Supporting Details**   **Setting of the Story**

2. **Which detail in the passage tells us this story is set in the winter?**

Ⓐ It is twilight.
Ⓑ His little horse is also quite white, and remains motionless;
Ⓒ A thick wet snow is slowly twirling around the newly lighted street lamps and lying in soft thin layers on roofs, on horses' backs, on people's shoulders and hats.
Ⓓ The cab driver, Iona Potapov, is quite white and looks like a phantom: he is bent double as far as a human body can bend double;

3. **What details in the story tells us that the setting is in Russia?**

Ⓐ The name of the cab driver, Iona Potapov.
Ⓑ A police officer asks for a cab ride.
Ⓒ It is snowing heavily.
Ⓓ The name of the place the officer wants to go.

Best Friend

Ever since they were kids, Julie and Max had been best friends. They went to kindergarten together. They went to summer camp together. They hung out together every weekend. But suddenly, things between the two had started to change.

Max had started playing on the football team and didn't have much time for Julie anymore. He was always busy, and he never seemed to make it to study hall, where the two used to swap stories about their favorite (or least favorite) teachers. In class, Julie noticed that Max never seemed to have his homework done on time anymore. She even noticed that he got a 'D' on his last paper. She knew something was going on with him – but what?

At first, Julie decided to play it cool and see how things went. She tried waiting in the hall for Max after class to see if she could ask if he was OK. But days went by, and he never had time to stop. He'd rush right past her in the hall, only to leave her feeling even worse about what was happening between them.

Even though she wasn't sure she could handle the situation herself, Julie didn't want to talk to her parents because she was afraid they would tell her not to hang out with Max anymore. She barely saw him as it was, so she knew it would just make things worse if her parents didn't approve of him. She didn't want to tell Max's parents either because she didn't want him to get in trouble. Still, it seemed like something needed to change.

Julie decided to go to one of her school counselors and let her know she was concerned. When she walked into Mrs. Smith's room, she was surprised to see that Max was already sitting there.

"I'm sorry, I'll come back," Julie said.
"No, stay," said Max. "Maybe you can help."

Julie was surprised to find that Max had visited the counselor's office for the same reason she had: he was starting to feel overwhelmed with all of the things he was supposed to be doing as a student, an athlete, and a friend. He needed some guidance on how to determine what truly mattered and how to divide his time between all of the things that were important to him.

When she realized that Max was still the same old Max (just a little more stressed), Julie was relieved. She was also happy to know that he had come to a conclusion on his own, without her having to talk to someone else about it. She decided it was a sign they were both growing up.

After reading the story, enter the details in the map below. This will help you to answer the question with ease.

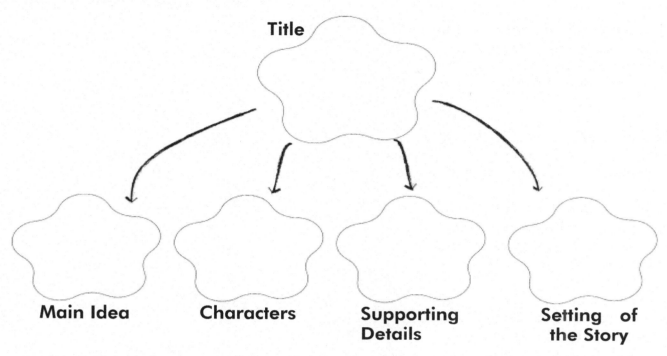

Title

Main Idea   Characters   Supporting
Details   Setting of
the Story

4. **How would the outcome of the selection be different if the final scene was set in the principal's office instead of the guidance counselor's office?**

Ⓐ Julie may not have been as sympathetic to Max because he would have been in trouble with the principal.

Ⓑ Max would have been embarrassed because Julie saw him in the principal's office.

Ⓒ The outcome of the selection wouldn't change if the setting changed.

Ⓓ The outcome would change with any setting/ending different than the counselor's office.

THE LAND OF NOD by Robert Louis Stevenson

From breakfast on through all the day
At home among my friends I stay,
But every night I go abroad
Afar into the Land of Nod.

All by myself I have to go,
With none to tell me what to do—
All alone beside the streams
And up the mountain-sides of dreams.

The strangest things are there for me,
Both things to eat and things to see,
And many frightening sights abroad
Till morning in the Land of Nod.

Try as I like to find the way,
I never can get back by day,
Nor can remember plain and clear
The curious music that I hear.

5. What is the setting of this poem?

   Ⓐ A child's bedroom
   Ⓑ A child's dreams
   Ⓒ The mountains
   Ⓓ The breakfast table

THE WONDERFUL HAIR by A. H. Wraitslaw

There was a man who was very poor, but so well supplied with children that he was utterly unable to maintain them, and one morning more than once prepared to kill them, in order not to see their misery in dying of hunger, but his wife prevented him. One night a child came to him in his sleep, and said to him: "Man! I see that you are making up your mind to destroy and to kill your poor little children, and I know that you are distressed thereat; but in the morning you will find under your pillow a mirror, a red kerchief, and an embroidered pocket-handkerchief; take all three secretly and tell no-body; then go to such a hill; by it you will find a stream; go along it till you come to its fountain-head; there you will find a damsel as bright as the sun, with her hair hanging down over her back. Be on your guard, that the ferocious she-dragon do not coil around you; do not converse with her if she speaks; for if you converse with her, she will poison you, and turn you into a fish or something else, and will then devour you but if she bids you examine her head, examine it, and as you turn over her hair, look, and you will find one hair as red as blood; pull it out and run back again; then, if she suspects and begins to run after you, throw her first the embroidered pocket-handkerchief, then the kerchief, and, lastly, the mirror; then she will find occupation for herself. And sell that hair to some rich man; but don't let them cheat you, for that hair is worth countless wealth; and you will thus enrich yourself and maintain your children."

When the poor man awoke, he found everything under his pillow, just as the child had told him in his sleep; and then he went to the hill. When there, he found the stream, went on and on alongside of it, till he came to the fountain-head. Having looked about him to see where the damsel was, he espied her above a piece of water, like sunbeams threaded on a needle, and she was embroidering at a frame on stuff, the threads of which were young men's hair. As soon as he saw her, he made a reverence to her, and she stood on her feet and questioned him: "Whence are you, unknown young man?" But he held his tongue. She questioned him again: "Who are you? Why have you come?" and much else of all sorts; but he was as mute as a stone, making signs with his hands, as if he were deaf and wanted help. Then she told him to sit down on her skirt. He did not wait for any more orders, but sat down, and she bent down her head to him, that he might examine it. Turning over the hair of her head, as if to examine it, he was not long in finding that red hair, and separated it from the other hair, pulled it out, jumped off her skirt and ran away back as he best could. She noticed it, and ran at his heels full speed after him. He looked around, and seeing that she was about to overtake him, threw, as he was told, the embroidered pocket-handkerchief on the way, and when she saw the pocket-handkerchief she stooped and began to overhaul it in every direction, admiring the embroi-dery, till he had got a good way off. Then the damsel placed the pocket-handkerchief in her bosom, and ran after him again. When he saw that she was about to overtake him, he threw the red kerchief, and she again occupied herself, admiring and gazing, till the poor man had again got a good way off. Then the damsel became exasperated, and threw both the pocket-handkerchief and the kerchief on the way, and ran after him in pursuit. Again, when he saw that she was about to overtake him, he threw the mirror. When the damsel came to the mirror, the like of which she had never seen before, she lifted it up, and when she saw herself in it, not knowing that it was herself, but thinking that it was somebody else, she, as it were, fell in love with herself in the mirror, and the man got so far off that she was no longer able to overtake him. When she saw that she could not catch him, she turned back, and the man reached his home safe and sound. After arriving at his home, he showed his wife the hair, and told her all that had happened to him, but she began to jeer and laugh at him. But he paid no attention to her, and went to a town to sell the hair. A crowd of all sorts of people and merchants collected round him; one offered a sequin, another two, and so on, higher and higher, till they came to a hundred gold sequins. Just then the emperor heard of the hair, summoned the man into his presence, and said to him that he would give him a thousand sequins for it, and he sold it to him. What was the hair? The emperor split it in two from top to bottom, and found registered in it in writing many remarkable things, which happened in the olden time since the beginning of the world. Thus the man became rich and lived on with his wife and children. And that child, that came to him in his sleep, was an angel sent by the Lord God, whose will it was to aid the poor man, and to reveal secrets which had not been revealed till then.

After reading the story, enter the details in the map below. This will help you to answer the question with ease.

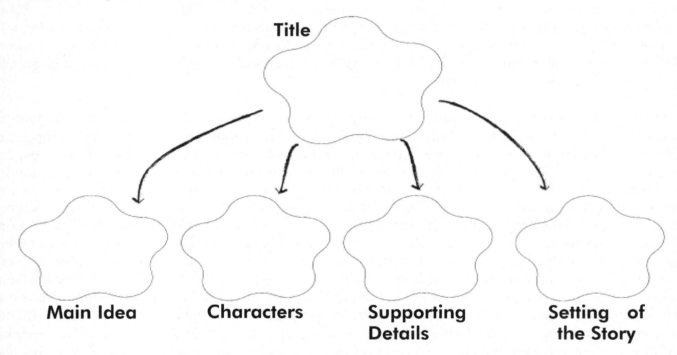

6. **What detail from this story does NOT help the reader see that it takes place in a rural (country) setting?**

   Ⓐ The characters live near a stream.
   Ⓑ He is going to sell hair in a local market.
   Ⓒ He has many children.
   Ⓓ He is to go into the woods/forest.

"The Smith and the Fairies" : A Gaelic Folk Tale (Ed. Kate Douglas Wiggin)

Years ago there lived in Crossbrig a smith of the name of MacEachern. This man had an only child, a boy of about thirteen or fourteen years of age, cheerful, strong, and healthy. All of a sudden he fell ill; took to his bed and moped whole days away. No one could tell what was the matter with him, and the boy himself could not, or would not, tell how he felt. He was wasting away fast; getting thin, old, and yellow; and his father and all his friends were afraid that he would die.

At last one day, after the boy had been lying in this condition for a long time, getting neither better nor worse, always confined to bed, but with an extraordinary appetite—one day, while sadly revolving these things, and standing idly at his forge, with no heart to work, the smith was agreeably surprised to see an old man, well known for his sagacity and knowledge of out-of-the-way things, walk into his workshop. Forthwith he told him the occurrence which had clouded his life.

The old man looked grave as he listened; and after sitting a long time pondering over all he had heard, gave his opinion thus: "It is not your son you have got. The boy has been carried away by the 'Daione Sith,' and they have left a Sibhreach in his place."
"Alas! and what then am I to do?" said the smith. "How am I ever to see my own son again?"
"I will tell you how," answered the old man. "But, first, to make sure that it is not your own son you have got, take as many empty egg-shells as you can get, go into his room, spread them out carefully before his sight, then proceed to draw water with them, carrying them two and two in your hands as if they were a great weight, and arrange them when full, with every sort of earnestness around the fire."

The smith accordingly gathered as many broken egg-shells as he could get, went into the room, and proceeded to carry out all his instructions.
He had not been long at work before there arose from the bed a shout of laughter, and the voice of the seeming sick boy exclaimed, "I am eight hundred years of age, and I have never seen the like of that before." The smith returned and told the old man.
"Well, now," said the sage to him, "did I not tell you that it was not your son you had: your son is in Borracheill in a digh there (that is, a round green hill frequented by fairies). Get rid as soon as possible of this intruder, and I think I may promise you your son. You must light a very large and bright fire before the bed on which this stranger is lying. He will ask you, 'What is the use of such a fire as that?' Answer him at once, 'You will see that presently!' and then seize him, and throw him into the middle of it. If it is your own son you have got, he will call out to you to save him; but if not, the thing will fly through the roof."
The smith again followed the old man's advice: kindled a large fire, answered the question put to him as he had been directed to do, and seizing the child flung him in without hesitation. The Sibhreach gave an awful yell, and sprang through the roof, where a hole had been left to let the smoke out.

On a certain night the old man told him the green round hill, where the fairies kept the boy, would be open, and on that date the smith, having provided himself with a Bible, a dirk, and a crowing cock, was to proceed to the hill. He would hear singing and dancing, and much merriment going on, he had been told, but he was to advance boldly; the Bible he carried would be a certain safeguard to him against any danger from the fairies. On entering the hill he was to stick the dirk in the threshold, to prevent the hill from closing upon him; "and then," continued the old man, "on entering you will see a spacious apartment before you, beautifully clean, and there, standing far within, working at a forge, you will also see your own son. When you are questioned, say you come to seek him, and will not go without him."

Not long after this, the time came round, and the smith sallied forth, prepared as instructed. Sure enough as he approached the hill, there was a light where light was seldom seen before. Soon after, a sound of piping, dancing, and joyous merriment reached the anxious father on the night wind.

Overcoming every impulse to fear, the smith approached the threshold steadily, stuck the dirk into it as directed, and entered. Protected by the Bible he carried on his breast, the fairies could not touch him; but they asked him, with a good deal of displeasure, what he wanted there. He answered, "I want my son, whom I see down there, and I will not go without him."

Upon hearing this the whole company before him gave a loud laugh, which wakened up the cock he carried dozing in his arms, who at once leaped up on his shoulders, clapped his wings lustily, and crowed loud and long.

The fairies, incensed, seized the smith and his son, and throwing them out of the hill, flung the dirk after them, and in an instant all was dark.

For a year and a day the boy never did a turn of work, and hardly ever spoke a word; but at last one day, sitting by his father and watching him finishing a sword he was making for some chief, and which he was very particular about, he suddenly exclaimed, "That is not the way to do it;" and taking the tools from his father's hands he set to work himself in his place, and soon fashioned a sword, the like of which was never seen in the country before.

From that day the young man wrought constantly with his father, and became the inventor of a peculiarly fine and well-tempered weapon, the making of which kept the two smiths, father and son, in constant employment, spread their fame far and wide, and gave them the means in abundance, as they before had the disposition, to live content with all the world and very happily with each other.

After reading the story, enter the details in the map below. This will help you to answer the question with ease.

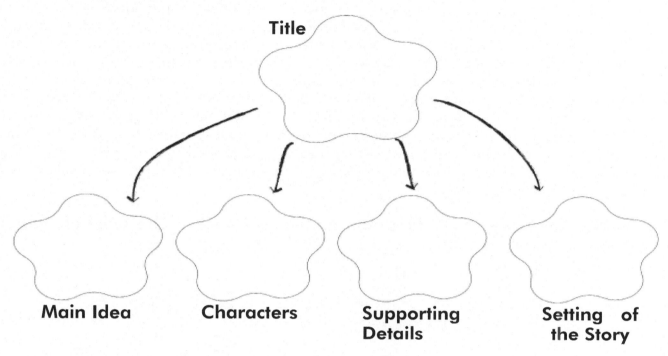

Title

Main Idea   Characters   Supporting Details   Setting of the Story

7. Which detail from the story is NOT a clue that the story is set in the past?

Ⓐ There are no longer smiths working today.
Ⓑ People in the story believe there are fairies in the woods.
Ⓒ The smith carries a Bible with him because he believes it will protect him.
Ⓓ The smith and his son make swords for people in town.

The Two Melons A Chinese Folk Tale (Ed. Kate Douglas Wiggin)

An honest and poor old woman was washing clothes at a pool when a bird that a hunter had disabled by a shot in the wing fell down into the water before her. She gently took up the bird, carried it home with her, dressed its wound, and fed it until it was well when it soared away. Some days later, it returned, put before her an oval seed, and departed again. The woman planted the seed in her yard, and when it came up, she recognized the leaf as that of a melon. She made a trellis for it, and gradually a fruit formed on it, and grew to great size.

Toward the end of the year, the old dame was unable to pay her debts, and her poverty so weighed upon her that she became ill. Sitting one day at her door, feverish and tired, she saw that the melon was ripe and looked luscious, so she determined to try its unknown quality. Taking a knife, she severed the melon from its stalk and was surprised to hear it chink in her hands. On cutting it in two, she found it full of silver and gold pieces, with which she paid her debts and bought supplies for many days.

Among her neighbors was a busybody who craftily found out how the old woman had so suddenly become rich. Thinking there was no good reason why she should not herself be equally fortunate, she washed clothes at the pool, keeping a sharp lookout for birds until she managed to hit and maim one of a flock that was flitting over the water. She then took the disabled bird home and treated it with care until its wing healed, and it flew away. Shortly afterward, it came back with a seed in its beak, laid it before her, and again took flight. The woman quickly planted the seed, saw it come up and spread its leaves, made a trellis for it, and had the gratification of seeing a melon form on its stalk. In the prospect of her future wealth, she ate rich food, bought fine garments, and got so deeply into debt that, before the end of the year, she was harried by duns. But the melon grew apace, and she was delighted to find that, as it ripened, it became of vast size and that when she shook it, there was a great rattling inside. At the end of the year, she cut it down, and divided it, expecting it to be a coffer of coins; but there crawled out of it two old, lame, hungry beggars, who told her they would remain and eat at her table as long as they lived.

After reading the story, enter the details in the map below. This will help you to answer the question with ease.

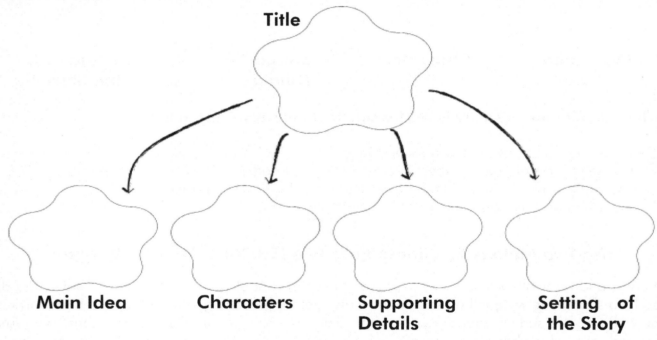

8. **Where and when can you infer this story takes place?**

 Ⓐ In the past in a bustling city
 Ⓑ In the past in a poor village
 Ⓒ In the present in a farming community
 Ⓓ In the present in a bustling city

Jane Eyre (Excerpt)
by Charlotte Bronte

The red-room was a square chamber, very seldom slept in, I might say never, indeed, unless when a chance influx of visitors at Gateshead Hall rendered it necessary to turn to account all the accommodation it contained: yet it was one of the largest and stateliest chambers in the mansion. A bed supported on massive pillars of mahogany, hung with curtains of deep red damask, stood out like a tabernacle in the centre; the two large windows, with their blinds always drawn down, were half shrouded in festoons and falls of similar drapery; the carpet was red; the table at the foot of the bed was covered with a crimson cloth; the walls were a soft fawn color with a blush of pink in it; the wardrobe, the toilet-table, the chairs were of darkly polished old mahogany. Out of these deep surrounding shades rose high, and glared white, the piled-up mattresses and pillows of the bed, spread with a snowy Marseilles counterpane. Scarcely less prominent was an ample cushioned easy-chair near the head of the bed, also white, with a footstool before it; and looking, as I thought, like a pale throne.

This room was chill because it seldom had a fire; it was silent, because remote from the nursery and kitchen; solemn because it was known to be so seldom entered. The house-maid alone came here on Saturdays, to wipe from the mirrors and the furniture a week's quiet dust: and Mrs. Reed herself, at far intervals, visited it to review the contents of a certain secret drawer in the wardrobe, where were stored divers parchments, her jewel-casket, and a miniature of her deceased husband; and in those last words lies the secret of the red-room--the spell which kept it so lonely in spite of its grandeur.

9. Where can you infer this story takes place?

   Ⓐ   In a hotel in the present
   Ⓑ   In a home in the future
   Ⓒ   In a large home in the past
   Ⓓ   In a country cottage in the present

10. Which line or lines from the excerpt best support the time in which this story is set?

   Ⓐ   This room was chilled, because it seldom had a fire; it was silent, because removed from the nursery and kitchen; solemn because it was known to be so seldom entered.
   Ⓑ   The red-room was a square chamber, very seldom slept in, I might say never, indeed, unless when a chance influx of visitors at Gateshead Hall rendered it necessary to turn to account all the accommodation it contained
   Ⓒ   A bed supported on massive pillars of mahogany, hung with curtains of deep red damask, stood out like a tabernacle in the centre; the two large windows, with their blinds always drawn down, were half shrouded in festoons and falls of similar drapery;
   Ⓓ   Scarcely less prominent was an ample cushioned easy-chair near the head of the bed, also white, with a footstool before it; and looking, as I thought, like a pale throne.

Excerpt from *The Wonderful Wizard of Oz*
L. Frank Baum

Dorothy lived in the midst of the great Kansas prairies, with Uncle Henry, who was a farmer, and Aunt Em, who was the farmer's wife. Their house was small, for the lumber to build it had to be carried by wagon many miles. There were four walls, a floor and a roof, which made one room; and this room contained a rusty looking cooking stove, a cupboard for the dishes, a table, three or four chairs, and the beds. Uncle Henry and Aunt Em had a big bed in one corner, and Dorothy a little bed in another corner. There was no garret at all, and no cellar-except a small hole dug in the ground, called a cyclone cellar, where the family could go in case one of those great whirlwinds arose, mighty enough to crush any building in its path. It was reached by a trap-door in the middle of the floor, from which a ladder led down into the small, dark hole.

When Dorothy stood in the doorway and looked around, she could see nothing but the great gray prairie on every side. Not a tree nor a house broke the broad sweep of flat country that reached the edge of the sky in all directions. The sun had baked the plowed land into a gray mass, with little cracks running through it. Even the grass was not green, for the sun had burned the tops of the long blades until they were the same gray color to be seen everywhere. Once the house had been painted, but the sun blistered the paint, and the rains washed it away, and now the house was as dull and gray as everything else.

When Aunt Em came there to live, she was a young, pretty wife. The sun and wind had changed her, too. They had taken the sparkle from her eyes and left them a sober gray; they had taken the red from her cheeks and lips, and they were gray also. She was thin and gaunt and never smiled now. When Dorothy, who was an orphan, first came to her, Aunt Em had been so startled by the child's laughter that she would scream and press her hand upon her heart whenever Dorothy's merry voice reached her ears; and she still looked at the little girl with wonder that she could find anything to laugh at.

Uncle Henry never laughed. He worked hard from morning till night and did not know what joy was. He was gray also, from his long beard to his rough boots, and he looked stern and solemn, and rarely spoke.

It was Toto that made Dorothy laugh, and saved her from growing as gray as her other surroundings. Toto was not gray; he was a little black dog, with long, silky hair and small black eyes that twinkled merrily on either side of his funny, wee nose. Toto played all day long, and Dorothy played with him and loved him dearly.

To-day, however, they were not playing. Uncle Henry sat upon the door-step and looked anxiously at the sky, which was even grayer than usual. Dorothy stood in the door with Toto in her arms and looked at the sky too. Aunt Em was washing the dishes.

From the far north, they heard a low wail of the wind, and Uncle Henry and Dorothy could see where the long grass bowed in waves before the coming storm. There now came a sharp whistling in the air from the south, and as they turned their eyes that way, they saw ripples in the grass coming from that direction also.

Suddenly Uncle Henry stood up.

"There's a cyclone coming, Em," he called to his wife; "I'll go look after the stock." Then he ran toward the sheds where the cows and horses were kept.

Aunt Em dropped her work and came to the door. One glance told her of the danger close at hand.

"Quick, Dorothy!" she screamed, "run for the cellar!"

Toto jumped out of Dorothy's arms and hid under the bed, and the girl started to get him. Aunt Em, badly frightened, threw open the trap-door in the floor and climbed down the ladder into the small, dark hole. Dorothy caught Toto at last and started to follow her aunt. When she was halfway across the room, there came a great shriek from the wind, and the house shook so hard that she lost her footing and sat down suddenly upon the floor.

11. Part A

Which line or lines from this excerpt support the conclusion that this story is set in the past?

Ⓐ When Dorothy stood in the doorway and looked around, she could see nothing but the great gray prairie on every side. Not a tree nor a house broke the broad sweep of flat country that reached the edge of the sky in all directions

Ⓑ Uncle Henry never laughed. He worked hard from morning till night and did not know what joy was.

Ⓒ Their house was small, for the lumber to build it had to be carried by wagon many miles.

Ⓓ Once the house had been painted, but the sun blistered the paint and the rains washed it away, and now the house was as dull and gray as everything else.

Part B

What changes in the setting support Uncle Henry's conclusion that a storm is coming?

Ⓐ There were no trees or houses in sight.

Ⓑ The heat of the sun had baked the plowed land and faded the paint on the house

Ⓒ They could hear the whistle of the wind.

Ⓓ The grass began to ripple in the direction from which the wind blew.

The Boys and the Frogs
by Marmaduke Park

Some boys, beside a pond or lake,
Were playing once at duck and drake;
When, doubtless to their heart's content,
Volleys of stones were quickly sent.
But there were some (there will be such)
Who did not seem amused so much;
These were the frogs, to whom the game,
In point of sport was not the same.
For scarce a stone arrived, 'tis said,
But gave some frog a broken head;
And scores in less than half an hour,
Perished beneath the dreadful shower.
At last, said one, "You silly folks, I say,
Do fling your stones another way;
Though sport to you, to throw them thus,
Remember, pray, 'tis death to us!"

12. Part A

The poem takes place next to a pond or lake, but WHEN does it occur?

Ⓐ in the morning
Ⓑ the reader is not sure
Ⓒ in the fall
Ⓓ in the spring

Part B

Based on the poem about how much time passes from the beginning to end?

Ⓐ a day
Ⓑ three hours
Ⓒ thirty minutes
Ⓓ an afternoon

"The Fox and the Stork"
From Aesop's Fables

At one time, the Fox and the Stork were on visiting terms and seemed very good friends. So the Fox invited the Stork to dinner, and for a joke, put nothing before her but some soup in a very shallow dish. This the Fox could easily lap up, but the Stork could only wet the end of her long bill in it and left the meal as hungry as when she began. "I am sorry, said the Fox, "the soup is not to your liking."

"Pray, do not apologize," said the Stork. "I hope you will return this visit and come and dine with me soon." So a day was appointed when the Fox should visit the Stork; but when they were seated at the table all that was for their dinner was contained in a very long-necked jar with a narrow mouth, in which the Fox could not insert his snout, so all he could manage to do was to lick the outside of the jar.

"I will not apologize for the dinner," said the Stork.

13. Part A
   What is the setting of this story?

Ⓐ The Fox and the Stork's homes
Ⓑ The 100 Acre Wood
Ⓒ A castle
Ⓓ A pond

   Part B
   Based on the events happening in the poem, when does it take place?

Ⓐ At breakfast
Ⓑ In the evening
Ⓒ Snack time
Ⓓ Tea time

Chapter 2

Lesson 7: Who or What?

You can scan the QR code given below or use the url to access additional EdSearch resources including videos and mobile apps related to *Who or What?*

Who or What?

URL	QR Code
http://www.lumoslearning.com/a/rl73	

"Bruno the Bear"
From *A Bond of Love*

I will begin with Bruno, my wife's pet sloth bear. I got him for her by accident. Two years ago, we were passing through the cornfields near a small town in Iowa. People were driving away the wild pigs from the fields by shooting at them. Some were shot, and some escaped. We thought that everything was over when suddenly a black sloth bear came out panting in the hot sun.

Now I will not shoot a sloth bear wantedly, but unfortunately for the poor beast, one of my companions did not feel the same way about it and promptly shot the bear on the spot.

As we watched the fallen animal, we were surprised to see that the black fur on its back moved and left the prostrate body. Then we saw it was a baby bear that had been riding on its mother's back when the sudden shot had killed her. The little creature ran around its prostrate parent, making a pitiful noise. I ran up to it to attempt a capture. It scooted into the sugarcane field. Following it with my companions, I was at last able to grab it by the scruff of its neck while it snapped and tried to scratch me with its long, hooked claws.

We put it in one of the large jute-bags we had brought, and when I got back home, I duly presented it to my wife. She was delighted! She at once put a blue colored ribbon around its neck, and after discovering the cub was a 'boy,' she christened it Bruno.

Bruno soon took to drinking milk from a bottle. It was but a step further, and within a very few days, he started eating and drinking everything else. And everything is the right word, for he ate porridge made from any ingredients, vegetables, fruit, nuts, meat (especially pork), curry and rice regardless of condiments and chilies, bread, eggs, chocolates, sweets, pudding, ice-cream, etc. As for drink: milk, tea, coffee, lime juice, aerated water, buttermilk, beer, alcoholic liquor, and, in fact, anything liquid. It all went down with relish.

The bear became very attached to our two dogs and all the children living in and around our farm. He was left quite free in his younger days and spent his time playing, running into the kitchen, and going to sleep in our beds.

One day an accident befell him. I put down poison (barium carbonate) to kill the rats and mice that had got into my library. Bruno entered the library as he often did and ate some of the poison. Paralysis set into the extent that he could not stand on his feet. But he dragged himself on his stumps to my wife, who called me. I guessed what had happened.

Off I rushed him in the car to the vet's residence. A case of poisoning! Tame Bear—barium carbonate—what to do? Out came his medical books, and a feverish reference to index began: "What poison did you say, sir?" he asked, "Barium carbonate," I said.

"Ah yes—B—Ba—Barium Salts—Ah! Barium carbonate! Symptoms— paralysis—treatment—injections of . .. Just a minute, sir. I'll bring my syringe and the medicine." Said the doc. I dashed back to the car. Bruno was still floundering about on his stumps, but clearly, he was weakening rapidly; there was some vomiting, he was breathing heavily, with heaving flanks and gaping mouth. I was really scared and did not know what to do. I was feeling very guilty and was running in and out of the vet's house doing everything the doc asked me.

"Hold him, everybody!" In goes the hypodermic—Bruno squeals — 10 c.c. of the antidote enters his system without a drop being wasted. Ten minutes later: condition unchanged! Another 10 c.c. Injected! Ten minutes later: breathing less torturous— Bruno can move his arms and legs a little although he cannot stand yet. Thirty minutes later: Bruno gets up and has a great feed! He looks at us disdainfully, as much as to say, 'What's barium carbonate to a big black bear like me?' Bruno was still eating. I was really happy to see him recover.

The months rolled on, and Bruno had grown many times the size he was when he came. He had equaled the big dogs in height and had even outgrown them. But was just as sweet, just as mischievous, just as playful. And he was very fond of us all. Above all, he loved my wife, and she loved him too! And he could do a few tricks, too. At the command, 'Bruno, wrestle,' or 'Bruno, box,' he vigorously tackled anyone who came forward for a rough and tumble. Give him a stick and say 'Bruno, hold the gun,' and he pointed the stick at you. Ask him, 'Bruno, where's baby?' and he immediately produced and cradled affectionately a stump of wood which he had carefully concealed in his straw bed. But because of the neighborhoods' and our renters' children, poor Bruno, had to be kept chained most of the time.

Then my son and I advised my wife and friends advised her, too, to give Bruno to the zoo. He was getting too big to keep at home. After some weeks of such advice, she at last consented. Hastily, and before she could change her mind, a letter was written to the curator of the zoo. Did he want a tame bear for his collection? He replied, "Yes." The zoo sent a cage in a truck, a distance of hundred – eighty – seven miles, and Bruno was packed off. We all missed him greatly, but in a sense, we were relieved. My wife was inconsolable. She wept and fretted. For the first few days, she would not eat a thing. Then she wrote a number of letters to the curator. How was Bruno? Back came the replies, "Well, but fretting; he refuses food too."

After that, friends visiting the zoo were begged to make a point of seeing how Bruno was getting along. They reported that he was well but looked very thin and sad. All the keepers at the zoo said he was fretting. For three months, I managed to restrain my wife from visiting the zoo. Then she said one day, "I must see Bruno. Either you take me by car, or I will go myself by bus or train myself." So I took her by car. Friends had conjectured that the bear would not recognize her. I had thought so too. But while she was yet some yards from his cage, Bruno saw her and recognized her. He howled with happiness. She ran up to him, petted him through the bars, and he stood on his head in delight.

For the next three hours, she would not leave that cage. She gave him tea, lemonade, cakes, ice cream, and whatnot. Then 'closing time' came and we had to leave. My wife cried bitterly; Bruno cried bitterly; even the hardened curator and the keepers felt depressed. As for me, I had reconciled myself to what I knew was going to happen next.

"Oh please, sir," she asked the curator, "may I have my Bruno back"? Hesitantly, he answered, "Madam, he belongs to the zoo and is Government property now. I cannot give away Government property. But if my boss, the superintendent, agrees, certainly, you may have him back."

There followed the return journey home and a visit to the superintendent's office. A tearful pleading: "Bruno and I are both fretting for each other. Will you please give him back to me?" He was a kind-hearted man and consented. Not only that, but he wrote to the curator, telling him to lend us a cage for transporting the bear back home.

Back we went to the zoo again, armed with the superintendent's letter. Bruno was driven into a small cage and hoisted on top of the car; the cage was tied securely, and a slow and careful return journey back home was accomplished.

Once home, a squad of workers were engaged for special work around our yard. An island was made for Bruno. It was twenty feet long and fifteen feet wide and was surrounded by a dry moat, six feet wide and seven feet deep. A wooden box that once housed fowls was brought and put on the island for Bruno to sleep in at night. Straw was placed inside to keep him warm, and his 'baby,' the gnarled stump, along with his 'gun,' the piece of bamboo, both of which had been sentimentally preserved since he had been sent away to the zoo, were put back for him to play with. In a few days, the workers hoisted the cage on to the island, and Bruno was released. He was delighted; standing on his hind legs, he pointed his 'gun' and cradled his 'baby.' My wife spent hours sitting on a chair there while he sat on her lap. He was fifteen months old and pretty heavy too!

The way my wife reaches the island and leaves it is interesting. I have tied a rope to the overhanging branch of a maple tree with a loop at its end. Putting one foot in the loop, she kicks off with the other, to bridge the six-foot gap that constitutes the width of the surrounding moat. The return journey back is made the same way.

But who can say now that a sloth bear has no sense of affection, no memory, and no individual characteristics?

After reading the story, enter the details in the map below. This will help you to answer the question with ease.

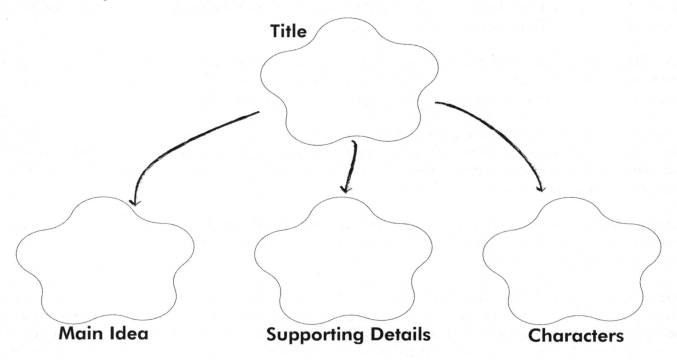

1. **What motivated the narrator to keep Bruno chained up?**

Ⓐ because he had grown big
Ⓑ because he was very playful and this scared some of the children in the neighborhood
Ⓒ because he was very dangerous
Ⓓ because he was a bear

Best Friend

Ever since they were kids, Julie and Max had been best friends. They went to kindergarten together. They went to summer camp together. They hung out together every weekend. But suddenly, things between the two had started to change.

Max started playing on the football team and didn't have much time for Julie anymore. He was always busy, and he never seemed to make it to study hall, where the two used to swap stories about their favorite (or least favorite) teachers. In class, Julie noticed that Max never seemed to have his homework done on time anymore. She even noticed that he got a 'D' on his last paper. She knew something was going on with him – but what?

At first, Julie decided to play it cool and see how things went. She tried waiting in the hall for Max after class to see if she could ask if he was OK. But days went by, and he never had time to stop. He'd rush right past her in the hall, only to leave her feeling even worse about what was happening between them.

Even though she wasn't sure she could handle the situation herself, Julie didn't want to talk to her parents because she was afraid they would tell her not to hang out with Max anymore. She barely saw him as it was, so she knew it would just make things worse if her parents didn't approve of him. She didn't want to tell Max's parents either because she didn't want him to get in trouble. Still, it seemed like something needed to change.

Julie decided to go to one of her school counselors and let her know she was concerned. When she walked into Mrs. Smith's room, she was surprised to see that Max was already sitting there.

"I'm sorry, I'll come back," Julie said.

"No, stay," said Max. "Maybe you can help."

Julie was surprised to find that Max had visited the counselor's office for the same reason she had: he was starting to feel overwhelmed with all of the things he was supposed to be doing as a student, an athlete, and a friend. He needed some guidance on how to determine what truly mattered and how to divide his time between all of the things that were important to him.

When she realized that Max was still the same old Max (just a little more stressed), Julie was relieved. She was also happy to know that he had come to a conclusion on his own, without her having to talk to someone else about it. She decided it was a sign they were both growing up.

After reading the story, enter the details in the map below. This will help you to answer the questions with ease.

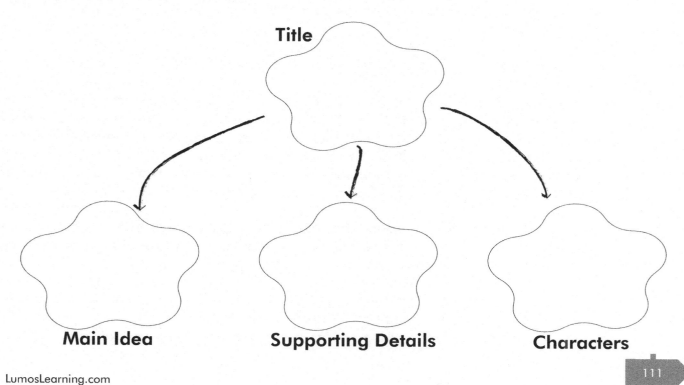

2. What events in the story did NOT contribute to the character of Max being overwhelmed?

Ⓐ work commitments
Ⓑ school commitments
Ⓒ sports commitments
Ⓓ parent's expectations

3. Which of the following is NOT an event in the story that leads Julie to become worried about Max?

Ⓐ He was getting bad grades.
Ⓑ He wasn't doing his homework.
Ⓒ He had lost weight.
Ⓓ He was too busy for her.

4. Who are the two main characters of the above story?

Ⓐ Max and the counselor
Ⓑ Max
Ⓒ Max and Julie
Ⓓ Julie and the counselor

"Scouting for Boys"
(Excerpt)

"Hi! Stop Thief!" shouted old Blenkinsopp as he rushed out of his little store near the village. "He's stolen my sugar. Stop him."

Stop whom? There was nobody in sight running away, "Who stole it?" asked the policeman.

"I don't know, but a whole bag of sugar is missing. It was there only a few minutes ago." The policeman tried to track the thief, but it looked a pretty impossible job for him to single out the tracks of the thief from among dozens of other footprints about the store. However, he presently started off hopefully, at a jog-trot, away out into the bush. In some places, he went over the hard stony ground, but he never checked his pace, although no footmarks could be seen. People wondered how he could possibly find the trail. Still, he trotted on. Old Blenkinsopp was feeling the heat and the pace

At length, he suddenly stopped and cast around, having evidently lost the trail. Then a grin came on his face as he pointed with his thumb over his shoulder up the tree near which he was standing. There, concealed among the branches, they saw a young man with the missing bag of sugar.

How had the policeman spotted him? His sharp eyes had detected some grains of sugar sparkling in the dust. The bag leaked, leaving a slight trail of these grains. He followed that trail, and when it came to an end in the bush, he noticed a string of ants going up a tree. They were after the sugar, and so was he, and between them, they brought about the capture of the thief.

Old Blenkinsopp was so pleased that he promptly opened the bag and spilled a lot of the sugar on the ground as a reward to the ants.

He also appreciated the policeman for his cleverness in using his eyes to see the grains of sugar and the ants, and in using his wits to know why the ants were climbing the tree.

After reading the story, enter the details in the map below. This will help you to answer the questions with ease.

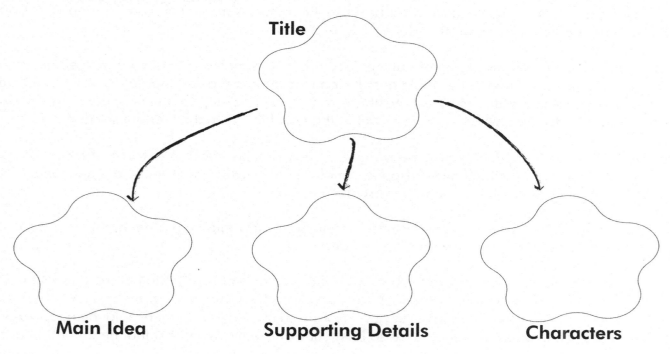

Title

Main Idea   **Supporting Details**   **Characters**

5. Why did the old man rush out of the store?

Ⓐ to stop the thief who had stolen his sugar
Ⓑ to catch the ants
Ⓒ to go for a walk
Ⓓ to leave the shop

6. What character, along with the policeman, helped to catch the thief?

Ⓐ the shopkeeper
Ⓑ the ants
Ⓒ the villagers
Ⓓ the shopkeeper's wife

Tryouts

For years, Sam had dreamed of being the best tennis player in the world. He went to tennis practice every single morning and night. He spent every summer at tennis camp, and he gave up long weekends at the beach to work on his game. Now, it seemed his hard work was finally paying off. He was invited to try out for the state tennis team!

Still, there was something that was bothering Sam. The tryouts for the tennis team were on the same day as his mom's birthday, and he knew his family was planning a huge surprise party for her. He didn't want to hurt his mom's feelings by missing the party, but he also didn't want to miss his one shot at being a champion tennis player just because the tryouts were on his mom's birthday. He was in a quandary; he didn't know what to do.

For days, Sam went to bed, worrying about the decision. If he went to the tryout, he worried he would seem selfish. If he stayed home, he would miss his one big shot at making the state team. In fact, despite the honor of being invited to try out, he hadn't even told his family about the opportunity. He was so stressed about deciding whether to go or not that he couldn't even think about sharing the news.

Weeks went by, and Sam was making no progress. Every day his coach asked him if he was ready for the tryout, and Sam couldn't even respond. Finally, Sam couldn't bear the stress any longer. He decided to talk to his grandfather about his predicament.

"You know, your mom wants you to be happy," he told Sam. "It would be a great birthday present for her to know you are making your dream come true."

Sam had never thought of it that way before, and after talking to his grandfather, he knew what he had to do. He immediately went home and sat down with his parents to let them know about the opportunity to try out for the state team. His parents were so excited that when he told them, apologetically, what day the tryouts were, they were so busy shrieking with excitement that he thought maybe they hadn't heard.

"But Mom, that means I'm going to miss your birthday," Sam said. "I am happy you are so nice about it, but I still feel really bad."

"Are you kidding?" his mom asked. "This is the best present I could ask for!"

After reading the story, enter the details in the map below. This will help you to answer the questions with ease.

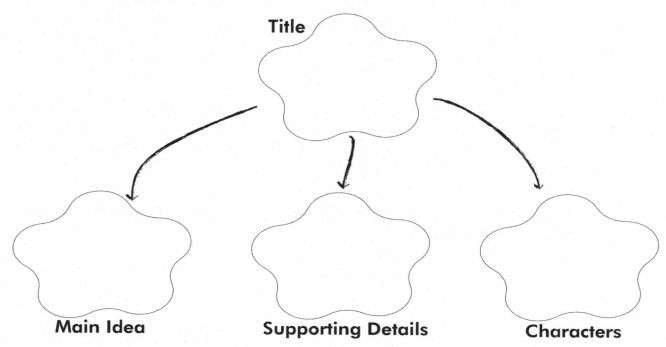

Title

Main Idea   Supporting Details   Characters

7. What character trait(s) did Sam NOT display in talking to his parents honestly about his tryout and his quandary?

Ⓐ Integrity – he understood the right thing to do in the situation
Ⓑ Honesty – he explained why he wanted to go and why he felt bad about it
Ⓒ Maturity – he was willing to talk to them even though he knew he might not like their answer
Ⓓ Being Proactive- he was hesitant and waited so long to ask for guidance.

8. Which of the following statements best characterizes Sam?

Ⓐ Sam is very selfish.
Ⓑ Sam does not care about what others feel. He just wants to do what he likes.
Ⓒ Sam is very concerned about others to the point where he would sacrifice his own happiness for someone else's.
Ⓓ Sam can't make decisions easily.

9. How does Sam's character change as the story progresses?

Ⓐ Sam goes from being selfish to caring.
Ⓑ Sam goes from being confident to self-doubting.
Ⓒ Sam goes from being concerned to confident.
Ⓓ Sam goes from being angry to happy.

Excerpt from *Tales of A Brothers' Grimm*

A certain king once fell ill, and the doctor declared that only a sudden fright would restore him to health, but the king was not a man for anyone to play tricks on, except his fool. One day, when the fool was with him in his boat, he cleverly pushed the king into the water. Help had already been arranged, and the king was drawn ashore and put to bed. The fright, the bath, and the rest in bed cured the diseased king.

The king wanted to frighten the fool for his act, so he told him that he would be put to death. He directed the executioner privately not to use the ax but to let fall a single drop of water on the fool's neck. Amidst shouts and laughter, the fool was asked to rise and thank the king for his kindness. But the fool never moved; he was dead; killed by the master's joke.

After reading the story, enter the details in the map below. This will help you to answer the question with ease.

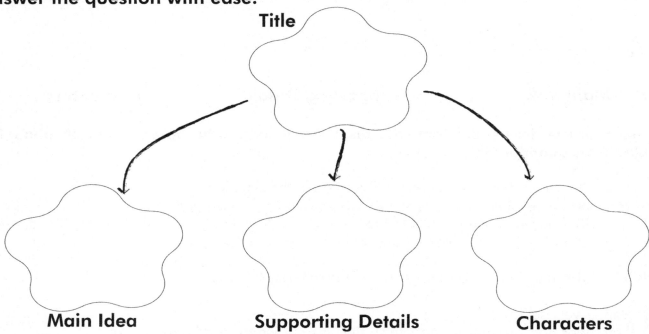

Title

Main Idea   **Supporting Details**   **Characters**

10. How was the king's view of jokes after the fool's death likely different than that of the fool when he was alive?

Ⓐ Both had the same view of jokes. Jokes were cruel and unkind.

Ⓑ The fool thought jokes were funny, but the king did not find them amusing.

Ⓒ The fool realized jokes can sometimes backfire, but the king always thought they would work out in his favor.

Ⓓ The king realized that jokes can sometimes not work out the way you intend for them to play out, but because the fool always had success with his jokes, the king did not consider the fact that his joke might backfire.

Emily and Jason

Emily and Jason spend every day together. Although both of them would have rather gone home with friends after school, they had no choice but to walk together. Emily could not stand the fact that Jason acted like such a know it all. He was only one year older than she was, but he acted like he knew everything. Of course, he never hesitated to tell on her every night at dinner either. Yesterday he complained because she did not clean the sink in the bathroom; last week, he ratted her out for not putting away the laundry. Emily could not wait for next year when she would be able to have the house to herself.

11. Part A

What type of relationship do Jason and Emily have?

Ⓐ Jason and Emily are neighbors.
Ⓑ Jason and Emily are classmates.
Ⓒ Jason and Emily walk to school every day.
Ⓓ Jason and Emily are siblings.

Part B

What evidence does the author use that allows the reader to infer Jason and Emily's relationship?

Ⓐ They walk home from school together and they eat dinner every night.
Ⓑ They walk home from school together and they argue all the time.
Ⓒ They share a bathroom and have the same chores.
Ⓓ They share a bathroom and walk home together every day.

Summer Trip

"Juan!" Jacob called out excitedly to his best friend as he ran up to him in the hallway. "You are never going to believe what just happened in Mrs. Smith's class!"

"What, Jake?" Juan was a little unsure of what type of news his friend could have. Jacob had a tendency to get excited about the strangest things.

"She told us we get to go to Washington D.C., and New York City this summer!"

Juan stared at his friend in astonishment. He had always wanted to go to New York City. "No way!" he exclaimed.

"I'm serious! We get to travel as a class, stay in hotels, and visit the Capitol building as well as the White House."

"What about seeing a Broadway play?" Juan asked. "I have always wanted to see The Lion King on stage. My sister saw it when she was in high school, and she said it was amazing!"

"Who cares?" Jacob asked with an incredulous look on his face. "We might get to see the President in the White House!"

Juan just shook his head at his friend. "Uh. I don't think he just walks around the White House."

"You never know. But it won't matter if our parents do not agree to let us go."

Juan knew Jacob was right, and more than likely, his parents would not want him to go. They never trusted him to do anything without one of them going as well. Silence filled the air between the two friends for several seconds just before the warning bell sounded. Each was lost in his own thoughts, planning how they could convince their parents to let them go.

"Let's come up with a plan to ask them while we are at lunch," Juan suggested.

Jacob agreed immediately. "That's a great idea! I'll see you then."

12. What suggestion could Juan offer his parents, so they agree to let him go on the trip? Circle the correct answer choice.

Ⓐ Jacob and Juan could room together.
Ⓑ Juan's parents could go as chaperones.
Ⓒ Jacob's brother could go as a chaperone.
Ⓓ He could detail all the wonderful sites the class would be able to explore.

13. How did Juan know Jacob might have amazing news?

Ⓐ Jacob ran up to him in the hallway talking excitedly.
Ⓑ Jacob just came from Mrs. Smith's class and she always does cool things.
Ⓒ Jacob's brother could go as a chaperone.
Ⓓ Juan was unsure what kind of news his friend would have.

Chapter 2

Lesson 8: A Matter of Attitude

Let us understand the concept with an example.

The Land of Nod
by Robert Louis Stevenson

From breakfast on through all the day
At home among my friends I stay,
But every night I go abroad
Afar into the Land of Nod.
All by myself I have to go,
With none to tell me what to do—
All alone beside the streams
And up the mountain-sides of dreams.
The strangest things are there for me,
Both things to eat and things to see,
And many frightening sights abroad
Till morning in the land of Nod.
Try as I like to find the way,
I never can get back by day,
Nor can remember plain and clear
The curious music that I hear.

Example of what you might write.

The poet uses figurative language. Figurative language is used to describe objects, actions and ideas in such a way that it appeals to our physical senses. In this poem, rhyme is used in the ending words of each pair of lines in the poem, which is pleasing to the ear and which creates phrases that are different and more interesting than expressing these thoughts in normal (non-rhyming) language. Another example of figurative language in this poem is the use of imagery. Words like "at home among my friends I stay," "all alone beside the streams." paint a mental picture. And still another example is the use of symbolism. The Land of Nod is not a physical location; it is a symbol of the mental and physical state of someone who is sleeping.

The literary genre (style of writing) of the poem is poetry but it also uses fantasy in the sense that the poet is dreaming in the Land of Nod; the things that appear in his dream are imagined; neither they nor he are real, actual experiences; he is not really beside a stream or seeing things to eat.

You can scan the QR code given below or use the url to access additional EdSearch resources including videos and mobile apps related to *A Matter of Attitude*

A Matter of Attitude

URL	QR Code
http://www.lumoslearning.com/a/rl74	

From THE HISTORY OF THE SEVEN FAMILIES OF THE LAKE PIPPLE-POPPLE. by Edward Lear

The Parrots lived upon the Soffsky-Poffsky trees, which were beautiful to behold, and covered with blue leaves; and they fed upon fruit, artichokes, and striped beetles.

The Storks walked in and out of the Lake Pipple-Popple and ate frogs for breakfast and buttered toast for tea, but on account of the extreme length of their legs, they could not sit down, and so they walked about continually. The Geese, having webs to their feet, caught quantities of flies, which they ate for dinner.

The Owls anxiously looked after mice, which they caught, and made into sago-puddings. The Guinea Pigs toddled about the gardens and ate lettuces and Cheshire cheese.

The Cats sate still in the sunshine and fed upon sponge biscuits. The Fishes lived in the lake and fed chiefly on boiled periwinkles. And all these seven families lived together in the utmost fun and felicity.

1. How do the author's descriptions of the animals' habitats affect the tone of the story?

Ⓐ   They make the animals appear hungry all the time.
Ⓑ   They make the animals seem greedy.
Ⓒ   They create a tone of nonsense and silliness.
Ⓓ   They show how diverse the animals are.

THE WONDERFUL HAIR by A. H. Wraitslaw

There was a man who was very poor, but so well supplied with children that he was utterly unable to maintain them, and one morning more than once prepared to kill them, in order not to see their misery in dying of hunger, but his wife prevented him. One night a child came to him in his sleep, and said to him: "Man! I see that you are making up your mind to destroy and to kill your poor little children, and I know that you are distressed thereat; but in the morning you will find under your pillow a mirror, a red kerchief, and an embroidered pocket-handkerchief; take all three secretly and tell no-body; then go to such a hill; by it, you will find a stream; go along it till you come to its fountain-head; there you will find a damsel as bright as the sun, with her hair hanging down over her back. Be on your guard, that the ferocious she-dragon do not coil around you; do not converse with her if she speaks; for if you converse with her, she will poison you, and turn you into a fish or something else, and will then devour you but if she bids you examine her head, examine it, and as you turn over her hair, look, and you will find one hair as red as blood; pull it out and run back again; then, if she suspects and begins to run after you, throw her first the embroidered pocket-handkerchief, then the kerchief, and, lastly, the mirror; then she will find occupation for herself. And sell that hair to some rich man; but don't let them cheat you, for that hair is worth countless wealth; and you will thus enrich yourself and maintain your children." When the poor man awoke, he found everything under his pillow, just as the child had told him in his sleep; and then he went to the hill. When there, he found the stream, went on and on alongside of it, till he came to the fountain-head. Having looked about him to see where the damsel was, he espied her above a piece of water, like sunbeams threaded on a needle, and she was embroidering at a frame on stuff, the threads of which were young men's hair. As soon as he saw her, he made a reverence to her, and she stood on her feet and questioned him: "Whence are you, unknown young man?" But he held his tongue. She questioned him again: "Who are you? Why have you come?" and much else of all sorts; but he was as mute as a stone, making signs with his hands, as if he were deaf and wanted help. Then she told him to sit down on her skirt. He did not wait for any more orders, but sat down, and she bent down her head to him, that he might examine it. Turning over the hair of her head, as if to examine it, he was not long in finding that red hair, and separated it from the other hair, pulled it out, jumped off her skirt and ran away back as he best could. She noticed it, and ran at his heels full speed after him. He looked around, and seeing that she was about to overtake him, threw, as he was told, the embroidered pocket-hand-kerchief on the way, and when she saw the pocket-handkerchief she stooped and began to overhaul it in every direction, admiring the embroidery, till he had got a good way off. Then the damsel placed the pocket-handkerchief in her bosom and ran after him again. When he saw that she was about to overtake him, he threw the red kerchief, and she again occupied herself, admiring and gazing, till the poor man had again got a good way off. Then the damsel became exasperated, and threw both the pocket-handkerchief and the kerchief on the way, and ran after him in pursuit. Again, when he saw that she was about to overtake him, he threw the mirror. When the damsel came to the mirror, the like of which she had never seen before, she lifted it up, and when she saw herself in it, not knowing that it was herself, but thinking that it was somebody else, she, as it were, fell in love with herself in the mirror, and the man got so far off that she was no longer able to overtake him. When she saw that she could not catch him, she turned back, and the man reached his home safe and sound. After arriving at his home, he showed his wife the hair and told her all that had happened to him, but she began to jeer and laugh at him. But he paid no attention to her and went to a town to sell the hair. A crowd of all sorts of people and merchants collected round him; one offered a sequin, another two, and so on, higher and higher, till they came to a hundred gold sequins. Just then, the emperor heard of the hair, summoned the man into his presence, and said to him that he would give him a thousand sequins for it, and he sold it to him. What was the hair? The emperor split it in two from top to bottom and found registered in it in writing many remarkable things, which happened in the olden time since the beginning of the world. Thus the man became rich and lived on with his wife and children. And that child, that came to him in his sleep was an angel sent by the Lord God, whose will it was to aid the poor man and to reveal secrets which had not been revealed till then.

2. What is the tone at the end of this story?

Ⓐ Serious
Ⓑ Joyful
Ⓒ Angry
Ⓓ Confused

"Base Details"
by Siegfried Sassoon

IF I were fierce, and bald, and short of breath,
I'd live with scarlet Majors at the Base,
And speed glum heroes up the line to death.

You'd see me with my puffy petulant face,
Guzzling and gulping in the best hotel,
Reading the Roll of Honour. 'Poor young chap,'
I'd say—'I used to know his father well;
Yes, we've lost heavily in this last scrap.'

And when the war is done and youth stone dead,
I'd toddle safely home and die—in bed.

3. What is the narrator's tone toward the officers at the base?

Ⓐ He respects the decisions they make about the war.
Ⓑ He looks forward to moving up the ranks and becoming an officer.
Ⓒ He is an officer and feels his decisions are well-thought out.
Ⓓ He believes the officers are fat and greedy and don't value the young soldiers.

4. From which line from the poem can you infer the narrator is disgusted with the officers?

Ⓐ I'd toddle safely home and die - in bed.
Ⓑ If I were fierce, and bald, and short of breath,
    I'd live with scarlet Majors at the base...
Ⓒ You'd see me with my puffy petulant face,
    Guzzling and gulping in the best hotel.
Ⓓ Yes, we've lost heavily in this last scrap.

From *The Moribund* by Guy de Maupassant

The warm autumn sun was beating down on the farmyard. Under the grass, which had been cropped close by the cows, the earth soaked by recent rains, was soft and sank in under the feet with a soggy noise, and the apple trees, loaded with apples, were dropping their pale green fruit in the dark green grass.

Four young heifers, tied in a line, were grazing, and at times, looking toward the house and lowing. The fowls made a colored patch on the dung-heap before the stable, scratching, moving about and cackling, while two roosters crowed continually, digging worms for their hens, whom they were calling with a loud clucking.

The wooden gate opened, and a man entered. He might have been forty years old, but he looked at least sixty, wrinkled, bent, walking slowly, impeded by the weight of heavy wooden shoes full of straw. His long arms hung down on both sides of his body. When he got near the farm, a yellow cur, tied at the foot of an enormous pear tree, beside a barrel which served as his kennel, began at first to wag his tail and then to bark for joy. The man cried:
"Down, Finot!"
The dog was quiet.

A peasant woman came out of the house. Her large, flat, bony body was outlined under a long woollen jacket drawn in at the waist. A gray skirt, too short, fell to the middle of her legs, which were encased in blue stockings. She, too, wore wooden shoes, filled with straw. The white cap, turned yellow, covered a few hairs which were plastered to the scalp, and her brown, thin, ugly, toothless face had that wild, animal expression which is often to be found on the faces of the peasants.

The man asked:
"How is he gettin' along?"
The woman answered:
"The priest said it's the end--that he will never live through the night."
Both of them went into the house.

After passing through the kitchen, they entered a low, dark room, barely lighted by one window, in front of which a piece of calico was hanging.

The big beams turned brown with age and smoke, crossed the room from one side to the other, supporting the thin floor of the garret, where an army of rats ran about day and night.

The moist, lumpy earthen floor looked greasy, and, at the back of the room, the bed made an indistinct white spot. A harsh, regular noise, a difficult, hoarse, wheezing breathing, like the gurgling of water from a broken pump, came from the darkened couch where an old man, the father of the peasant woman, was dying.

The man and the woman approached the dying man and looked at him with calm, resigned eyes. The son-in-law said:
"I guess it's all up with him this time; he will not last the night."
The woman answered:
"He's been gurglin' like that ever since midday." They were silent. The father's eyes were closed, his face was the color of the earth and so dry that it looked like wood. Through his open mouth came his harsh, rattling breath, and the gray linen sheet rose and fell with each respiration.

5. In the paragraph in bold, what is the author's tone toward the woman?

   Ⓐ sympathy
   Ⓑ repulsed
   Ⓒ anger
   Ⓓ longing

Excerpt from *Little Women*
By Louisa May Alcott

"Christmas won't be Christmas without any presents," grumbled Jo, lying on the rug.

"It's so dreadful to be poor!" sighed Meg, looking down at her old dress.

"I don't think it's fair for some girls to have plenty of pretty things, and other girls nothing at all," added little Amy, with an injured sniff.

"We've got Father and Mother, and each other," said Beth contentedly from her corner.

The four young faces on which the firelight shone brightened at the cheerful words, but darkened again as Jo said sadly, "We haven't got Father, and shall not have him for a long time." She didn't say "perhaps never," but each silently added it, thinking of Father far away, where the fighting was.

Nobody spoke for a minute; then Meg said in an altered tone, "You know the reason Mother proposed not having any presents this Christmas was because it is going to be a hard winter for everyone; and she thinks we ought not to spend money for pleasure, when our men are suffering so in the army. We can't do much, but we can make our little sacrifices, and ought to do it gladly. But I am afraid I don't." And Meg shook her head, as she thought regretfully of all the pretty things she wanted.

"But I don't think the little we should spend would do any good. We've each got a dollar, and the army wouldn't be much helped by our giving that. I agree not to expect anything from Mother or you, but I do want to buy UNDINE AND SINTRAM for myself. I've wanted it so long," said Jo, who was a bookworm.

"I planned to spend mine in new music," said Beth, with a little sigh, which no one heard but the hearth brush and kettle holder.

"I shall get a nice box of Faber's drawing pencils. I really need them," said Amy decidedly.

"Mother didn't say anything about our money, and she won't wish us to give up everything. Let's each buy what we want, and have a little fun. I'm sure we work hard enough to earn it," cried Jo, examining the heels of her shoes in a gentlemanly manner.

"I know I do--teaching those tiresome children nearly all day, when I'm longing to enjoy myself at home," began Meg, in the complaining tone again.

"You don't have half such a hard time as I do," said Jo. "How would you like to be shut up for hours with a nervous, fussy old lady, who keeps you trotting, is never satisfied, and worries you till you're ready to fly out the window or cry?"

"It's naughty to fret, but I do think washing dishes and keeping things tidy is the worst work in the world. It makes me cross, and my hands get so stiff, I can't practice well at all." And Beth looked at her rough hands with a sigh that anyone could hear that time.

"I don't believe any of you suffer as I do," cried Amy, "for you don't have to go to school with impertinent girls, who plague you if you don't know your lessons, and laugh at your dresses, and label your father if he isn't rich, and insult you when your nose isn't nice."

"If you mean libel, I'd say so, and not talk about labels, as if Papa was a pickle bottle," advised Jo, laughing.

"I know what I mean, and you needn't be satirical about it. It's proper to use good words and improve your vocabulary," returned Amy, with dignity.

"Don't peck at one another, children. Don't you wish we had the money Papa lost when we were little, Jo? Dear me! How happy and good we'd be if we had no worries!" said Meg, who could remember better times.

"You said the other day you thought we were a deal happier than the King children, for they were fighting and fretting all the time, in spite of their money."

"So I did, Beth. Well, I think we are. For though we do have to work, we make fun of ourselves, and are a pretty jolly set, as Jo would say."

"Jo does use such slang words!" observed Amy, with a reproving look at the long figure stretched on the rug.

Jo immediately sat up, put her hands in her pockets, and began to whistle.

"Don't, Jo. It's so boyish!"

"That's why I do it."

"I detest rude, unladylike girls!"

"I hate affected, niminy-piminy chits!"

"Birds in their little nests agree," sang Beth, the peacemaker, with such a funny face that both sharp voices softened to a laugh, and the "pecking" ended for that time.

"Really, girls, you are both to be blamed," said Meg, beginning to lecture in her elder-sisterly fashion. "You are old enough to leave off boyish tricks, and to behave better, Josephine. It didn't matter so much when you were a little girl, but now you are so tall, and turn up your hair, you should remember that you are a young lady."

"I'm not! And if turning up my hair makes me one, I'll wear it in two tails till I'm twenty," cried Jo, pulling off her net, and shaking down a chestnut mane. "I hate to think I've got to grow up and be Miss March, and wear long gowns, and look as prim as a China Aster! It's bad enough to be a girl, anyway, when I like boy's games and work and manners! I can't get over my disappointment in not being a boy. And it's worse than ever now, for I'm dying to go and fight with Papa. And I can only stay home and knit, like a poky old woman!"

And Jo shook the blue army sock till the needles rattled like castanets, and her ball bounded across the room.

6. Why does Beth compare her sisters to birds in a nest?

Ⓐ   Because they are "pecking" at each other, but not really hurting one another.
Ⓑ   Because they all need to learn to "fly" on their own and give their parents some relief.
Ⓒ   Because they are gifted musically and should sing together.
Ⓓ   Because they are always hungry and calling for someone to feed them.

7. From the passage above, what does the author want the reader to know about Jo?

Ⓐ That she enjoys buying and reading books
Ⓑ That she is selfish
Ⓒ That she knows exactly what she wants and how to get it.
Ⓓ That she is smarter than the other sisters

Excerpt from *War of the Worlds*
H.G. Wells

The Martians seem to have calculated their descent with amazing subtlety—their mathematical learning is evidently far in excess of ours—and to have carried out their preparations with a well-nigh perfect unanimity. Had our instruments permitted it, we might have seen the gathering trouble far back in the nineteenth century. Men like Schiaparelli watched the red planet—it is odd, by the way, that for countless centuries Mars has been the star of war—but failed to interpret the fluctuating appearances of the markings they mapped so well. All that time the Martians must have been getting ready.

8. In the excerpt above, what is the author's tone toward the Martians?

Ⓐ He is impressed by their intelligence and planning.
Ⓑ He finds them inferior to Earth's scientists.
Ⓒ He is afraid of what they will do.
Ⓓ He looks forward to learning from them.

9. In the excerpt above, what is the author's tone toward the scientists of Earth?

Ⓐ He forgives them for not seeing the building threat. Their instruments were too primitive. (forgiveness)
Ⓑ He blames them for not developing instruments to identify the building threat on Mars. (anger)
Ⓒ He believes they identified Mars as a source of war early on but didn't share what they knew. (distrustful)
Ⓓ He believes they could have been able to interpret the changes to the surface of the planet and determined what the Martians were planning. (annoyed)

"Dreams"
By Langston Hughes

Hold fast to dreams
For if dreams die
Life is a broken-winged bird
That cannot fly.

Hold fast to dreams
For when dreams go
Life is a barren field
Frozen with snow.

10. What point is the poet making with the comparison in the first stanza?

Ⓐ Without dreams, people cannot make progress in their lives.
Ⓑ Life without dreams is cold and barren.
Ⓒ Like a bird with a broken wing, life is fragile and must be protected.
Ⓓ Even if one cannot fly, he or she can still have a rewarding life.

O Captain! My Captain! By Walt Whitman

Read the poem and answer the questions below.

O Captain! my Captain! our fearful trip is done,
The ship has weather'd every rack, the prize we sought is won,
The port is near, the bells I hear, the people all exulting,
While follow eyes the steady keel, the vessel grim and daring;
   But O heart! heart! heart!
    O the bleeding drops of red,
     Where on the deck my Captain lies,
      Fallen cold and dead.

O Captain! my Captain! rise up and hear the bells;
Rise up--for you the flag is flung--for you the bugle trills,
For you bouquets and ribbon'd wreaths--for you the shores a-crowding,
For you they call, the swaying mass, their eager faces turning;
   Here Captain! dear father!
    This arm beneath your head!
     It is some dream that on the deck,
      You've fallen cold and dead.

My Captain does not answer, his lips are pale and still,
My father does not feel my arm, he has no pulse nor will,
My Captain does not answer, his lips are pale and still,
My father does not feel my arm, he has no pulse nor will,
The ship is anchor'd safe and sound, its voyage closed and done,
From fearful trip the victor ship comes in with object won;
    Exult O shores, and ring O bells!
     But I with mournful tread,
      Walk the deck my Captain lies,
       Fallen cold and dead.

11. What does the poet say has happened to the Captain? Write your answer in the box below.

12. Complete the following lines from the poem.

_____ Oh shores!

The prize we _____ is won

While follow eyes the steady_____.

Its _____ closed and done.

But I with _____ tread.

Chapter 2

Lesson 9: How it's Made and What it Means

Let us understand the concept with an example.

The Land of Nod
by Robert Louis Stevenson

From breakfast on through all the day
At home among my friends I stay,
But every night I go abroad
Afar into the Land of Nod.
All by myself I have to go,
With none to tell me what to do—
All alone beside the streams
And up the mountain-sides of dreams.
The strangest things are there for me,
Both things to eat and things to see,
And many frightening sights abroad
Till morning in the land of Nod.
Try as I like to find the way,
I never can get back by day,
Nor can remember plain and clear
The curious music that I hear.

Example of what you might write.

The stanzas in this poem follow the quatrain (4 lines per stanza) model. It allows the poet to combine like thoughts in four line stanzas and then to separate stanzas to allow different thoughts to be expressed in different stanzas. For example, the first stanza describes the poet's activities during the day, but includes a transition into the night and into sleep.

The second and third stanzas take place in a dream while the poet is asleep, and in the third stanza is a transition back to daytime (morning). The fourth stanza takes place during the day when the poet is awake and trying to remember details of the previous night's dream.

The form of the poem is descriptive; that is, it describes the world (a dream world in this case) that surrounds the subject of the poem (the poet in this case). The form also is partially lyric; that is, it only has one speaker (teller) expressing personal feelings.

You can scan the QR code given below or use the url to access additional EdSearch resources including videos and mobile apps related to How it's Made and What it Means.

How it's Made and What it Means

URL	QR Code
http://www.lumoslearning.com/a/rl75	

"Do Not Go Gentle into that Good Night"
Dylan Thomas

Do not go gentle into that good night,
Old age should burn and rave at close of day;
Rage, rage against the dying of the light.

Though wise men at their end know dark is right,
Because their words had forked no lightning they
Do not go gentle into that good night.

Good men, the last wave by, crying how bright
Their frail deeds might have danced in a green bay,
Rage, rage against the dying of the light.

Wild men who caught and sang the sun in flight,
And learn, too late, they grieved it on its way,
Do not go gentle into that good night.

Grave men, near death, who see with blinding sight
Blind eyes could blaze like meteors and be gay,
Rage, rage against the dying of the light.

And you, my father, there on the sad height,
Curse, bless me now with your fierce tears, I pray.
Do not go gentle into that good night.
Rage, rage against the dying of the light.

1. Which characteristic of this poem indicates it is a villanelle?

Ⓐ There are two rhyming patterns.
Ⓑ The poem is written in iambic meter.
Ⓒ The subject of the poem is death.
Ⓓ There is a chorus or refrain between every two stanzas.

2. Which answer does not use repetition to develop the tone of this poem?

Ⓐ The word rage is repeated to develop the idea that one can fight back against death.
Ⓑ The word men is repeated to remind the subject about whom he is writing.
Ⓒ The word gentle is repeated to remind the reader how to behave.
Ⓓ The word me is repeated to establish the focus of the poem.

3. How is end rhyme used to make connections between the stanzas?

Ⓐ Every other line rhymes.
Ⓑ Each stanza uses the same rhyme scheme.
Ⓒ The rhyme scheme changes every other stanza.
Ⓓ The last line of each stanza rhymes with the first line of the next stanza.

Ethan Frome
Edith Wharton

I HAD THE STORY, bit by bit, from various people, and, as generally happens in such cases, each time it was a different story.

If you know Starkfield, Massachusetts, you know the post-office. If you know the post-office you must have seen Ethan Frome drive up to it, drop the reins on his hollow-backed bay and drag himself across the brick pavement to the white colonnade; and you must have asked who he was.

It was there that, several years ago, I saw him for the first time; and the sight pulled me up sharp. Even then he was the most striking figure in Starkfield, though he was but the ruin of a man. It was not so much his great height that marked him, for the "natives" were easily singled out by their lank longitude from the stockier foreign breed: it was the careless powerful look he had, in spite of a lameness checking each step like the jerk of a chain. There was something bleak and unapproachable in his face, and he was so stiffened and grizzled that I took him for an old man and was surprised to hear that he was not more than fifty-two. I had this from Harmon Gow, who had driven the stage from Bettsbridge to Starkfield in pre-trolley days and knew the chronicle of all the families on his line.

"He's looked that way ever since he had his smash-up; and that's twenty four years ago come next February," Harmon threw out between reminiscent pauses.

The "smash-up" it was—I gathered from the same informant—which, besides drawing the red gash across Ethan Frome's forehead, had so shortened and warped his right side that it cost him a visible effort to take the few steps from his buggy to the post-office window. He used to drive in from his farm every day at about noon, and as that was my own hour for fetching my mail I often passed him in the porch or stood beside him while we waited on the motions of the distributing hand behind the grating. I noticed that, though he came so punctually, he seldom received anything but a copy of the Bettsbridge Eagle, which he put without a glance into his sagging pocket. At intervals, however, the post-master would hand him an envelope addressed to Mrs. Zenobia —or Mrs. Zeena-Frome, and usually bearing conspicuously in the upper left-hand corner the address of some manufacturer of patent medicine and the name of his specific. These documents my neighbour would also pocket without a glance, as if too much used to them to wonder at their number and variety, and would then turn away with a silent nod to the post-master.

4. What does this prologue to the story, Ethan Frome, suggest about the story that is about to be told?

Ⓐ That it is a true story.
Ⓑ That the story is based in part on rumors heard about town.
Ⓒ That the narrator is not certain of the accuracy of all of the details she is about to present.
Ⓓ That the narrator has known the subject of the story for a long time.

5. Why might the author have included this prologue?

Ⓐ To relieve herself of any responsibility for the story's accuracy.
Ⓑ To explain how she became familiar with the story she is about to tell.
Ⓒ To explain the importance of accuracy in the story that will follow.
Ⓓ To hint at how the story will end.

Excerpt from Romeo and Juliet
By William Shakespeare

PROLOGUE

Two households, both alike in dignity,
In fair Verona, where we lay our scene,
From ancient grudge break to new mutiny,
Where civil blood makes civil hands unclean.
From forth the fatal loins of these two foes
A pair of star-cross'd lovers take their life;
Whose misadventured piteous overthrows
Do with their death bury their parents' strife.
The fearful passage of their death-mark'd love,
And the continuance of their parents' rage,
Which, but their children's end, nought could remove,
Is now the two hours' traffic of our stage;
The which if you with patient ears attend,
What here shall miss, our toil shall strive to mend.

SCENE I. Verona. A public place.

Enter SAMPSON and GREGORY, of the house of Capulet, armed with swords and bucklers
SAMPSON
Gregory, o' my word, we'll not carry coals.
GREGORY
No, for then we should be colliers.
SAMPSON
I mean, an we be in choler, we'll draw.
GREGORY
Ay, while you live, draw your neck out o' the collar.
SAMPSON
I strike quickly, being moved.
GREGORY
But thou art not quickly moved to strike.

SAMPSON
A dog of the house of Montague moves me.
GREGORY
To move is to stir; and to be valiant is to stand:
therefore, if thou art moved, thou runn'st away.
SAMPSON
A dog of that house shall move me to stand: I will
take the wall of any man or maid of Montague's.
GREGORY
That shows thee a weak slave; for the weakest goes
to the wall.
SAMPSON
True; and therefore women, being the weaker vessels,
are ever thrust to the wall: therefore I will push
Montague's men from the wall, and thrust his maids
to the wall.
GREGORY
The quarrel is between our masters and us their men.
SAMPSON
'Tis all one, I will show myself a tyrant: when I
have fought with the men, I will be cruel with the
maids, and cut off their heads.
GREGORY
The heads of the maids?
SAMPSON
Ay, the heads of the maids, or their maidenheads;
take it in what sense thou wilt.
GREGORY
They must take it in sense that feel it.
SAMPSON
Me they shall feel while I am able to stand: and
'tis known I am a pretty piece of flesh.
GREGORY
'Tis well thou art not fish; if thou hadst, thou
hadst been poor John. Draw thy tool! here comes
two of the house of the Montagues.
SAMPSON
My naked weapon is out: quarrel, I will back thee.
GREGORY
How! turn thy back and run?
SAMPSON
Fear me not.
GREGORY
No, marry; I fear thee!

SAMPSON
Let us take the law of our sides; let them begin.
GREGORY
I will frown as I pass by, and let them take it as
they list.
SAMPSON
Nay, as they dare. I will bite my thumb at them;
which is a disgrace to them, if they bear it.
Enter ABRAHAM and BALTHASAR

6. What is the difference between the format of the prologue and the rest of this excerpt?

Ⓐ   The prologue is written in verse, the rest in prose.
Ⓑ   The prologue is written in prose, the rest in verse.
Ⓒ   The prologue uses iambic tetrameter and the rest of the excerpt uses iambic pentameter.
Ⓓ   There is a difference in the spacing of the lines for easier reading.

"Stopping by Woods on a Snowy Evening"
By Robert Frost

Whose woods these are I think I know.
His house is in the village though;
He will not see me stopping here
To watch his woods fill up with snow.

My little horse must think it queer
To stop without a farmhouse near
Between the woods and frozen lake
The darkest evening of the year.

He gives his harness bells a shake
To ask if there is some mistake.
The only other sound's the sweep
Of easy wind and downy flake.

The woods are lovely, dark and deep.
But I have promises to keep,
And miles to go before I sleep,
And miles to go before I sleep.

Source: The Random House Book of Poetry for Children (1983). Retrieved 13, July, 2013.http://www.poetryfoundation.org/poem/171621.

7. What is the rhyme scheme of the first two stanzas?

Ⓐ aabb
   aabb

Ⓑ aabb
   bbaa

Ⓒ abcd
   abcd

Ⓓ aaba
   bbcb

"...He gives his harness bells a shake
As if to ask if there is some mistake..."

8. What is the effect of this use of personification?

Ⓐ The author likes to use horses in his poetry to show the time in history that the poem was written.
Ⓑ To show the reader that the horse and the man are very close.
Ⓒ The horse's communication emphasizes how odd it would be to stop in the woods at that time.
Ⓓ The horse shakes because he is cold and wants the man to hurry.

9. What is the rhyme scheme of this poem?

A) abaa
   abba
   aaba
   cccc

B) aaba
   bbcb
   ccdc
   dddd

C) abcd
   abcd
   abcd
   abcd

D) abaad
   abaab
   abcdeb
   abdec

"The Road Not Taken"
BY ROBERT FROST

Two roads diverged in a yellow wood,
And sorry I could not travel both
And be one traveler, long I stood
And looked down one as far as I could
To where it bent in the undergrowth;

Then took the other, as just as fair,
And having perhaps the better claim,
Because it was grassy and wanted wear;
Though as for that the passing there
Had worn them really about the same,

And both that morning equally lay
In leaves no step had trodden black.
Oh, I kept the first for another day!
Yet knowing how way leads on to way,
I doubted if I should ever come back.

I shall be telling this with a sigh
Somewhere ages and ages hence:
Two roads diverged in a wood, and I—
I took the one less traveled by,
And that has made all the difference.

10. Which line in the last stanza indicates a time in the future?

Ⓐ no step had trodden black
Ⓑ two roads diverged
Ⓒ yellow wood
Ⓓ somewhere ages and ages hence

Lines Written In A Young Lady's Album

'Tis not in youth, when life is new, when but to live is sweet,
When Pleasure strews her starlike flow'rs beneath our careless feet,
When Hope, that has not been deferred, first waves its golden wings,
And crowds the distant future with a thousand lovely things; -

When if a transient grief o'ershades the spirit for a while,
The momentary tear that falls is followed by a smile;
Or if a pensive mood, at times, across the bosom steals,
It scarcely sighs, so gentle is the pensiveness it feels

It is not then the, restless soul will seek for one with whom
To share whatever lot it bears, its gladness or its gloom, -
Some trusting, tried, and gentle heart, some true and faithful breast,
Whereon its pinions it may fold, and claim a place of rest.

But oh! when comes the icy chill that freezes o'er the heart,
When, one by one, the joys we shared, the hopes we held, depart;
When friends, like autumn's withered leaves, have fallen by our side,

And life, so pleasant once, becomes a desert wild and wide; -
As for her olive branch the dove swept o'er the sullen wave,
That rolled above the olden world - its death-robe and its grave! -
So will the spirit search the earth for some kind, gentle one,
With it to share her destiny, and make it all her own!

11.Identify the rhyming pattern in the poem and write it in the box below.

12. If you were to write a poem about feelings such as the one above, what would you write about and explain in the box below.

Landing of the Pilgrims
-by Felicia D. Hemans , public domain

The breaking waves dashed high

On a stern and rock-bound coast,

And the woods against a stormy sky

Their giant branches tossed;

And the heavy night hung dark

The hills and waters o'er,

When a band of exiles moored their bark

On the wild New England shore

Not as the conqueror comes,

They, the truehearted, came;

Not with the roll of the stirring drums

And the trumpet that sings of fame;

Not as the flying come,

In silence and in fear,

They shook the depths of the desert gloom

With their hymns of lofty cheer

What sought they thus afar?

Bright jewels of the mine?

The wealth of seas, the spoils of war?

They sought a faith's pure shrine!

Ay, call it holy ground —

The soil where they first trod;

They have left unstained what there they found:

Freedom to worship God!

Name: _____   Date: _____

13. What is described in the first stanza of the poem? Write your answer in the box below.

14. In the second stanza to whom is the poet contrasting the Pilgrims to make her point? Write your answer in the box below.

Chapter 2

Lesson 10: What a Character!

Before answering the questions, it is important to understand the meaning of Summary and Characters.

Summary: to restate the main points or events in an argument or proposal of an idea, usually in a brief, concise manner.

Character(s)

The actions and thoughts and emotions of the main (major) character(s) have the most influence, are the most important, to the plot. There may be other less important characters (known as minor or secondary characters) in the story, but they will have less influence on the plot.

Answering below questions will help you Summarize the text

Who is the main character?
What did the character want?
What was the problem?
How did the character try to solve the problem?
What was the resolution?

You can scan the QR code given below or use the url to access additional EdSearch resources including videos and mobile apps related to *What a Character!*

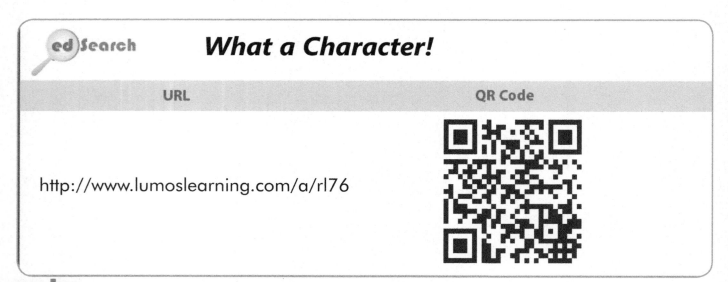

THE EMPEROR'S NEW CLOTHES
by Hans Christian Anderson

Many years ago there was an Emperor, who was so excessively fond of new clothes that he spent all his money on them. He cared nothing about his soldiers, nor for the theatre, nor for driving in the woods except for the sake of showing off his new clothes. He had a costume for every hour in the day, and instead of saying, as one does about any other king or emperor, 'He is in his council chamber,' here one always said, 'The Emperor is in his dressing-room.'

Life was very gay in the great town where he lived; hosts of strangers came to visit it every day and among them one day two swindlers. They gave themselves out as weavers and said that they knew how to weave the most beautiful stuff imaginable. Not only were the colors and patterns unusually fine, but the clothes that were made of the stuff had the peculiar quality of becoming invisible to every person who was not fit for the office he held, or if he was impossibly dull.

Those must be splendid clothes,' thought the Emperor. 'By wearing them, I should be able to discover which men in my kingdom are unfitted for their posts. I shall distinguish the wise men from the fools. Yes, I certainly must order some of that stuff to be woven for me.

He paid the two swindlers a lot of money in advance so that they might begin their work at once.

They did put up two looms and pretended to weave, but they had nothing whatever upon their shuttles. At the outset, they asked for a quantity of the finest silk and the purest gold thread, all of which they put into their own bags while they worked away at the empty looms far into the night. I should like to know how those weavers are getting on with the stuff,' thought the Emperor; but he felt a little queer when he reflected that anyone who was stupid or unfit for his post would not be able to see it. He certainly thought that he need have no fears for himself, but still, he thought he would send somebody else first to see how it was getting on. Everybody in the town knew what wonderful power the stuff possessed, and everyone was anxious to see how stupid his neighbor was.

I will send my faithful old minister to the weavers,' thought the Emperor. 'He will be best able to see how the stuff looks, for he is a clever man, and no one fulfills his duties better than he does!'

So the good old minister went into the room where the two swindlers sat working at the empty loom.

Heaven preserve us!' thought the old minister, opening his eyes very wide. 'Why, I can't see a thing!' But he took care not to say so. Both the swindlers begged him to be good enough to step a little nearer and asked if he did not think it a good pattern and beautiful coloring. They pointed to the empty loom, and the poor old minister stared as hard as he could, but he could not see anything, for of course there was nothing to see. Good heavens!' thought he, 'is it possible that I am a fool. I have never thought so, and nobody must know it. Am I not fit for my post? It will never do to say that I cannot see the stuff.

Well, sir, you don't say anything about the stuff,' said the one who was pretending to weave. Oh, it is beautiful! quite charming!' said the old minister, looking through his spectacles; 'this pattern and these colors! I will certainly tell the Emperor that the stuff pleases me very much.

We are delighted to hear you say so,' said the swindlers, and then they named all the colors and described the peculiar pattern. The old minister paid great attention to what they said, so as to be able to repeat it when he got home to the Emperor.

Then the swindlers went on to demand more money, more silk, and more gold, to be able to proceed with the weaving; but they put it all into their own pockets—not a single strand was ever put into the loom, but they went on as before weaving at the empty loom.

The Emperor soon sent another faithful official to see how the stuff was getting on, and if it would soon be ready. The same thing happened to him as to the minister; he looked and looked, but as there was only the empty loom, he could see nothing at all.

Is not this a beautiful piece of stuff?' said both the swindlers, showing and explaining the beautiful pattern and colors which were not there to be seen.

I know I am not a fool!' thought the man, 'so it must be that I am unfit for my good post! It is very strange, though! However, one must not let it appear!' So he praised the stuff he did not see and assured them of his delight in the beautiful colors and the originality of the design. 'It is absolutely charming!' he said to the Emperor. Everybody in the town was talking about this splendid stuff.

Now the Emperor thought he would like to see it while it was still on the loom. So, accompanied by a number of selected courtiers, among whom were the two faithful officials who had already seen the imaginary stuff, he went to visit the crafty impostors, who were working away as hard as ever they could at the empty loom.

It is magnificent!' said both the honest officials. 'Only see, your Majesty, what a design! What colors!' And they pointed to the empty loom, for they thought no doubt the others could see the stuff.

What!' thought the Emperor; 'I see nothing at all! This is terrible! Am I a fool? Am I not fit to be Emperor? Why, nothing worse could happen to me! Oh, it is beautiful!' said the Emperor. 'It has my highest approval!' and he nodded his satisfaction as he gazed at the empty loom. Nothing would induce him to say that he could not see anything.

The whole suite gazed and gazed, but saw nothing more than all the others. However, they all exclaimed with his Majesty, 'It is very beautiful!' and they advised him to wear a suit made of this wonderful cloth on the occasion of a great procession which was just about to take place. 'It is magnificent! gorgeous! excellent!' went from mouth to mouth; they were all equally delighted with it.

The Emperor gave each of the rogues an order of knighthood to be worn in their buttonholes and the title of 'Gentlemen weavers.'

The swindlers sat up the whole night before the day on which the procession was to take place, burning sixteen candles; so that people might see how anxious they were to get the Emperor's new clothes ready. They pretended to take the stuff off the loom. They cut it out in the air with a huge pair of scissors, and they stitched away with needles without any thread in them. At last, they said: 'Now the Emperor's new clothes are ready! The Emperor, with his grandest courtiers, went to them himself, and both the swindlers raised one arm in the air, as if they were holding something, and said: 'See, these are the trousers, this is the coat, here is the mantle!' and so on. 'It is as light as a spider's web. One might think one had nothing on, but that is the very beauty of it!'

Yes!' said all the courtiers, but they could not see anything, for there was nothing to see.

Will your imperial majesty be graciously pleased to take off your clothes,' said the impostors, 'so that we may put on the new ones, along here before the great mirror?' The Emperor took off all his clothes, and the impostors pretended to give him one article of dress after the other of the new ones which they had pretended to make. They pretended to fasten something round his waist and to tie on something; this was the train, and the Emperor turned round and round in front of the mirror.

How well his majesty looks in the new clothes! How becoming they are!' cried all the people around. 'What a design, and what colors! They are the most gorgeous robes!' The canopy is waiting outside, which is to be carried over your majesty in the procession,' said the master of the ceremonies.

Well, I am quite ready,' said the Emperor. 'Don't the clothes fit well?' and then he turned around again in front of the mirror so that he should seem to be looking at his grand things.

The chamberlains who were to carry the train stooped and pretended to lift it from the ground with both hands, and they walked along with their hands in the air. They dared not let it appear that they could not see anything.

Then the Emperor walked along in the procession under the gorgeous canopy, and everybody in the streets and at the windows exclaimed, 'How beautiful the Emperor's new clothes are! What a splendid train! And they fit to perfection!' Nobody would let it appear that he could see nothing, for then he would not be fit for his post, or else he was a fool. None of the Emperor's clothes had been so successful before. But he has got nothing on,' said a little child.

Oh, listen to the innocent,' said its father; and one person whispered to the other what the child had said. 'He has nothing on; a child says he has nothing on! But he has nothing on!' at last cried all the people. The Emperor writhed, for he knew it was true, but he thought 'the procession must go on now,' so held himself stiffer than ever, and the chamberlains held up the invisible train.

After reading the story, enter the details in the map below. This will help you to answer the questions with ease.

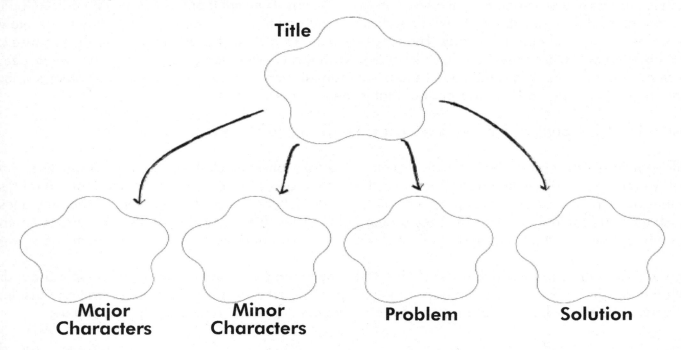

1. Which excerpt from the text provides the reason the Emperor agreed to buy clothes from the swindlers?

Ⓐ Not only were the colors and patterns unusually fine, but the clothes that were made of the stuff had the peculiar quality of becoming invisible to every person who was not fit for the office he held, or if he was impossibly dull.

Ⓑ Life was very gay in the great town where he lived; hosts of strangers came to visit it every day, and among them one day two swindlers. They gave themselves out as weavers, and said that they knew how to weave the most beautiful stuff imaginable.

Ⓒ At the outset they asked for a quantity of the finest silk and the purest gold thread, all of which they put into their own bags, while they worked away at the empty looms far into the night.

Ⓓ 'I know I am not a fool!' thought the man, 'so it must be that I am unfit for my good post! It is very strange, though! However, one must not let it appear!' So he praised the stuff he did not see, and assured them of his delight in the beautiful colors and the originality of the design.

2. What character trait do the Emperor and his minister share?

Ⓐ They are both insecure about their qualifications.
Ⓑ They both want to fool the public
Ⓒ They both want the Emperor to have the most wonderful clothing available.
Ⓓ Both men are able to imagine things that are not visible.

3. Why does the Emperor continue with the procession after the child reviews the truth?

Ⓐ He doesn't believe the child.
Ⓑ He doesn't want to admit to his subjects that the swindlers had tricked him.
Ⓒ He is concerned that there are people in the audience who can see the clothes.
Ⓓ He has paid for his new clothes and wants to continue showing them off.

Huckleberry Finn (Excerpt)
By Mark Twain

In this excerpt from Chapter Five, Huck's father arrives unexpectedly.

I HAD shut the door to. Then I turned around and there he was. I used to be scared of him all the time, he beat me so much. I reckoned I was scared now, too; but in a minute I see I was mistaken -- that is, after the first jolt, as you may say, when my breath sort of hitched, he being so unexpected; but right away after I see I warn't scared of him worth bothring about.

He was most fifty, and he looked it. His hair was long and tangled and greasy, and hung down, and you could see his eyes shining through like he was behind vines. It was all black, no gray; so was his long, mixed-up whiskers. There warn't no color in his face, where his face showed; it was white; not like another man's white, but a white to make a body sick, a white to make a body's flesh crawl -- a tree-toad white, a fish-belly white. As for his clothes -- just rags, that was all. He had one ankle resting on t'other knee; the boot on that foot was busted, and two of his toes stuck through, and he worked them now and then. His hat was laying on the floor -- an old black slouch with the top caved in, like a lid.

I stood a-looking at him; he set there a-looking at me, with his chair tilted back a little. I set the candle down. I noticed the window was up; so he had climbed in by the shed. He kept a-looking me all over. By and by he says:

"Starchy clothes -- very. You think you're a good deal of a big-bug, don't you?"

"Maybe I am, maybe I ain't," I says.

"Don't you give me none o' your lip," says he. "You've put on considerable many frills since I been away. I'll take you down a peg before I get done with you. You're educated, too, they say -- can read and write. You think you're better'n your father, now, don't you, because he can't? I'll take it out of you. Who told you you might meddle with such hifalut'n foolishness, hey? -- who told you you could?"

"The widow. She told me."

"The widow, hey? -- and who told the widow she could put in her shovel about a thing that ain't none of her business?"

"Nobody never told her."

"Well, I'll learn her how to meddle. And looky here -- you drop that school, you hear? I'll learn people to bring up a boy to put on airs over his own father and let on to be better'n what he is. You lemme catch you fooling around that school again, you hear? Your mother couldn't read, and she couldn't write, nuther, before she died. None of the family couldn't before they died. I can't; and here you're a-swelling yourself up like this. I ain't the man to stand it -- you hear? Say, lemme hear you read."

I took up a book and begun something about General Washington and the wars. When I'd read about a half a minute, he fetched the book a whack with his hand and knocked it across the house. He says:

"It's so. You can do it. I had my doubts when you told me. Now looky here; you stop that putting on frills. I won't have it. I'll lay for you, my smarty; and if I catch you about that school I'll tan you good. First you know you'll get religion, too. I never see such a son.

He took up a little blue and yaller picture of some cows and a boy, and says:

"What's this?"

"It's something they give me for learning my lessons good."

He tore it up, and says:

"I'll give you something better -- I'll give you a cowhide.

He set there mumbling for a minute, and then he says:

"*Ain't* you a sweet-scented dandy, though? A bed; and bedclothes; and a look'n'-glass; and a piece of carpet on the floor -- and your own father got to sleep with the hogs in the tanyard. I never see such a son. I bet I'll take some o' these frills out o' you before I'm done with you. Why, there ain't no end to your airs -- they say you're rich. Hey? -- how's that?"

"They lie -- that's how."

"Looky here -- mind how you talk to me; I'm a-standing about all I can stand now -- so don't gimme no sass. I've been in town two days, and I hain't heard nothing but about you bein' rich. I heard about it away down the river, too. That's why I come. You git me that money to-morrow -- I want it."

"I hain't got no money."

"It's a lie. Judge Thatcher's got it. You git it. I want it."

"I hain't got no money, I tell you. You ask Judge Thatcher; he'll tell you the same."

"All right. I'll ask him; and I'll make him pungle, too, or I'll know the reason why. Say, how much you got in your pocket? I want it."

"I hain't got only a dollar, and I want that to -- "

"It don't make no difference what you want it for -- you just shell it out."

After reading the story, enter the details in the map below. This will help you to answer the questions with ease.

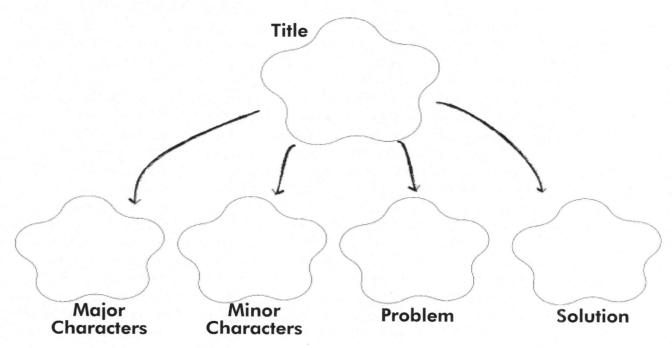

4. Why might Huck be afraid of his father?

Ⓐ His father has beaten him in the past.
Ⓑ Huck hasn't been attending school and is afraid his father will be angry.
Ⓒ He is afraid his father will hurt his friends.
Ⓓ His father has threatened to take him away from his friends.

5. What does Huck's father want hm to do after he demonstrates his reading ability?

Ⓐ He tells Huck he's proud of him and then asks for Huck's money.
Ⓑ He hits the book out of Huck's hands and flings it across the room, then tells Huck to stop showing off.
Ⓒ He tells Huck to stop attending school.
Ⓓ He asks Huck to teach him how to read.

The Call of the Wild
Excerpt by Jack London

Buck lived at a big house in the sun-kissed Santa Clara Valley. Judge Miller's place, it was called. It stood back from the road, half-hidden among the trees, through which glimpses could be caught of the wide cool veranda that ran around its four sides. The house was approached by graveled driveways, which wound about through wide-spreading lawns and under the interlacing boughs of tall poplars. At the rear, things were on even a more spacious scale than at the front. There were great stables, where a dozen grooms and boys held forth, rows of vine-clad servants' cottages, an endless and orderly array of out-houses, long grape arbors, green pastures, orchards, and berry patches. Then there was the pumping plant for the artesian well and the big cement tank where Judge Miller's boys took their morning plunge and kept cool in the hot afternoon. And over this great demesne, Buck ruled. Here he was born, and here he had lived the four years of his life. It was true, there were other dogs, There could not but be other dogs on so vast a place, but they did not count. They came and went, resided in the populous kennels, or lived obscurely in the recesses of the house after the fashion of Toots, the Japanese pug, or Ysabel, the Mexican hairless,--strange creatures that rarely put nose out of doors or set foot to the ground. On the other hand, there were the fox terriers, a score of them at least, who yelped fearful promises at Toots and Ysabel looking out of the windows at them and protected by a legion of housemaids armed with brooms and mops. But Buck was neither house-dog nor kennel-dog. The whole realm was his. He plunged into the swimming tank or went hunting with the Judge's sons; he escorted Mollie and Alice, the Judge's daughters, on long twilight or early morning rambles; on wintry nights he lay at the Judge's feet before the roaring library fire; he carried the Judge's grandsons on his back, or rolled them in the grass, and guarded their footsteps through wild adventures down to the fountain in the stable yard, and even beyond, where the paddocks were, and the berry patches. Among the terriers he stalked imperiously, and Toots and Ysabel he utterly ignored, for he was king,--king over all creeping, crawling, flying things of Judge Miller's place, humans included.

After reading the story, enter the details in the map below. This will help you to answer the questions with ease.

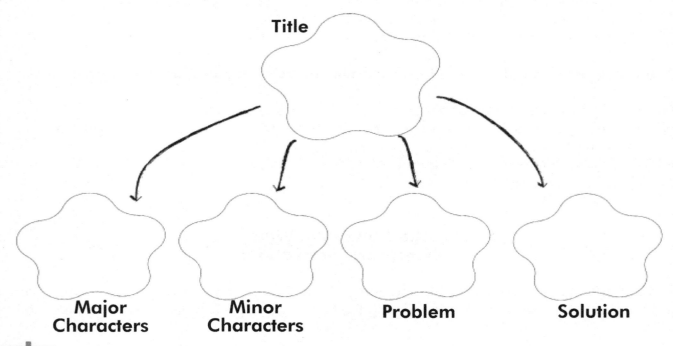

6. Why does Buck "utterly ignore" Toots and Ysabel?

(A) Their names are strange.
(B) The other two dogs don't act the way he feels a dog should behave.
(C) He's not allowed inside, so he thinks it is odd that they are.
(D) The other two dogs tease him.

7. What made Buck proud of being "neither a house-dog or a kennel-dog?"

(A) The judge told him so.
(B) Buck chose that life.
(C) Buck was part of family events.
(D) Buck had been with the Miller's longer than other dogs.

8. The quote "...strange creatures that rarely put nose out of doors or set foot to ground..." tells the reader what about Toots and Ysabel?

(A) Their names are odd, and so are they.
(B) They are too little to be outside.
(C) They are "babied" in the house and behave like people.
(D) There are too many dogs outside already.

9. What is Buck's mood in this excerpt?

(A) weary and wishful
(B) relaxed and relieved
(C) joyful and jaded
(D) desperate and dejected

10. Based on the excerpts from *The Call of the Wild*, all of these can describe Buck EXCEPT_____?

(A) honorable
(B) persistent
(C) grateful
(D) aggressive

O Captain! My Captain! By Walt Whitman
Read the poem and answer the questions below.

O Captain! my Captain! our fearful trip is done,
The ship has weather'd every rack, the prize we sought is won,
The port is near, the bells I hear, the people all exulting,
While follow eyes the steady keel, the vessel grim and daring;
   But O heart! heart! heart!
    O the bleeding drops of red,
     Where on the deck my Captain lies,
      Fallen cold and dead.

O Captain! my Captain! rise up and hear the bells;
Rise up--for you the flag is flung--for you the bugle trills,
For you bouquets and ribbon'd wreaths--for you the shores a-crowding,
For you they call, the swaying mass, their eager faces turning;
   Here Captain! dear father!
    This arm beneath your head!
     It is some dream that on the deck,
      You've fallen cold and dead.

My Captain does not answer, his lips are pale and still,
My father does not feel my arm, he has no pulse nor will,
The ship is anchor'd safe and sound, its voyage closed and done,
From fearful trip the victor ship comes in with object won;
   Exult O shores, and ring O bells!
    But I with mournful tread,
     Walk the deck my Captain lies,
      Fallen cold and dead.

11. Tell how the vocabulary in this poem helps you to visualize the scene. Write your answer in the box below.

Landing of the Pilgrims
-by Felicia D. Hemans , public domain

The breaking waves dashed high
On a stern and rock-bound coast,
And the woods against a stormy sky
Their giant branches tossed;
And the heavy night hung dark
The hills and waters o'er,
When a band of exiles moored their bark
On the wild New England shore

Not as the conqueror comes,
They, the truehearted, came;
Not with the roll of the stirring drums
And the trumpet that sings of fame;
Not as the flying come,
In silence and in fear,
They shook the depths of the desert gloom
With their hymns of lofty cheer

What sought they thus afar?
Bright jewels of the mine?
The wealth of seas, the spoils of war?
They sought a faith's pure shrine!
Ay, call it holy ground —
The soil where they first trod;
They have left unstained what there they found:
Freedom to worship God!

12. The poet wrote the poem to accomplish what? Write your answer in the box below.

Chapter 2

Lesson 11: Finding Patterns - Comparing and Contrasting

Let us understand the concept with an example.

Here are descriptions of the last few seconds of a basketball game, presented as if you were reading about it in a newspaper, seeing it broadcast live on TV, or listening to a live radio broadcast.

Article in a newspaper

There would be a headline and a still photo from the game. There might also be a web address for further information and the writer's contact information. In the article would be a written description of the last few seconds of the game including the slam dunk by Hendricks that won the game.

Broadcast live on TV
Imagine this as a continuous stream of live action pictures with live commentary by the sportscaster.

Sportscaster's commentary:
"Rebound Jackson, pass to Jacovik, closing seconds, pass to Hendricks…a slam dunk, there's the buzzer, AND THE TIGERS WIN IT!! What a comeback! One for the record books! And what a slam dunk – did you ever see anything like it?"

Broadcast on the radio
Sportscaster's commentary: "Rebound Jackson, he fakes a dribble, passes to his right to Jacovik, Jacovik drives to the right of the key, closely guarded by Sosnowska, fakes a jump shot and passes to Hendricks slanting into the center of the key…slam dunk by Hendricks, there's the buzzer, THE TIGERS WIN IT!! Hendricks must have leaped four feet in the air, and sailed most of the way from the foul line to the basket! An amazing slam dunk! What athleticism!"

Your assignment: Make a comparison of the differences in techniques used by the three types of media mentioned above and the effects these techniques have on the way the story is presented by each media type.

What you might write should be influenced by your personal observations and opinions from reading sports news in a newspaper, watching a live broadcast of a sporting event, or listening to live coverage on the radio.

Here is an example of what you might write.

The newspaper reporter is facing a disadvantage compared with the sportscasters. The reporter is writing after the event, and through his/her creative use of words, will try to create interest and emotions with details about the game, but will not match the excitement experienced by someone watching or listening to a live broadcast. On the other hand, the reporter has more time to create a write-up of the game, because his deadline is not the moment the game ends, and he/she is only limited by the amount of space available for the article. Therefore, the reporter can add details that the sportscasters may not have had time to do, and can write related articles such as articles about the league that the Tigers play in, and tables of stats that readers can take the time to study. The reporter can also add one or more still photos to enhance the article.

In the past, before television was available, if you could not attend the game or listen on the radio, the newspaper was the only other source of information. Today, however, with rebroadcast options and VCR capabilities, you can see the game live after the event is over.

For those Tiger fans unable to attend the game, the television sportscaster probably has the best advantage in attracting the attention of Tiger fans. He/she has the advantage of live video coverage of the game while also injecting his/her commentary. He can also conduct live interviews of coaches and players during pregame and postgame time periods. Also, he can capture crowd noise and any entertainment provided by the venue. Like the newspaper reporter and radio broadcaster, he/she has to research the teams and the players and the stats relating to the teams.

In my opinion, the second most interesting media coverage is the radio broadcast. While it lacks the excitement of video, it has the excitement of live action commentary, with time for pregame and postgame interviews.

One characteristic of the broadcasting jobs is the ability to think on your feet and react professionally to unexpected situations that can occur during live coverage of a game. This is more pressure that a newspaper reporter will likely have.

You can scan the QR code given below or use the url to access additional EdSearch resources including videos and mobile apps related to *Finding Patterns - Comparing and Contrasting.*

ed)Search ***Finding Patterns - Comparing and Contrasting***

URL	QR Code
http://www.lumoslearning.com/a/rl77	

THE WONDERFUL HAIR by A. H. Wraitslaw

There was a man who was very poor, but so well supplied with children that he was utterly unable to maintain them, and one morning more than once prepared to kill them, in order not to see their misery in dying of hunger, but his wife prevented him. One night a child came to him in his sleep, and said to him: "Man! I see that you are making up your mind to destroy and to kill your poor little children, and I know that you are distressed thereat; but in the morning you will find under your pillow a mirror, a red kerchief, and an embroidered pocket-handkerchief; take all three secretly and tell no-body; then go to such a hill; by it you will find a stream; go along it till you come to its fountain-head; there you will find a damsel as bright as the sun, with her hair hanging down over her back. Be on your guard, that the ferocious she-dragon do not coil around you; do not converse with her if she speaks; for if you converse with her, she will poison you, and turn you into a fish or something else, and will then devour you but if she bids you examine her head, examine it, and as you turn over her hair, look, and you will find one hair as red as blood; pull it out and run back again; then, if she suspects and begins to run after you, throw her first the embroidered pocket-handkerchief, then the kerchief, and, lastly, the mirror; then she will find occupation for herself. And sell that hair to some rich man; but don't let them cheat you, for that hair is worth countless wealth; and you will thus enrich yourself and maintain your children."

When the poor man awoke, he found everything under his pillow, just as the child had told him in his sleep; and then he went to the hill. When there, he found the stream, went on and on alongside of it, till he came to the fountain-head. Having looked about him to see where the damsel was, he espied her above a piece of water, like sunbeams threaded on a needle, and she was embroidering at a frame on stuff, the threads of which were young men's hair. As soon as he saw her, he made a reverence to her, and she stood on her feet and questioned him: "Whence are you, unknown young man?" But he held his tongue. She questioned him again: "Who are you? Why have you come?" and much else of all sorts; but he was as mute as a stone, making signs with his hands, as if he were deaf and wanted help. Then she told him to sit down on her skirt. He did not wait for any more orders, but sat down, and she bent down her head to him, that he might examine it. Turning over the hair of her head, as if to examine it, he was not long in finding that red hair, and separated it from the other hair, pulled it out, jumped off her skirt and ran away back as he best could. She noticed it, and ran at his heels full speed after him. He looked around, and seeing that she was about to overtake him, threw, as he was told, the embroidered pocket-handkerchief on the way, and when she saw the pocket-handkerchief she stooped and began to overhaul it in every direction, admiring the embroi-dery, till he had got a good way off. Then the damsel placed the pocket-handkerchief in her bosom, and ran after him again.

When he saw that she was about to overtake him, he threw the red kerchief, and she again occu-pied herself, admiring and gazing, till the poor man had again got a good way off. Then the damsel became exasperated, and threw both the pocket-handkerchief and the kerchief on the way, and ran after him in pursuit. Again, when he saw that she was about to overtake him, he threw the mirror. When the damsel came to the mirror, the like of which she had never seen before, she lifted it up, and when she saw herself in it, not knowing that it was herself, but thinking that it was somebody else, she, as it were, fell in love with herself in the mirror, and the man got so far off that she was no longer able to overtake him. When she saw that she could not catch him, she turned back, and the man reached his home safe and sound. After arriving at his home, he showed his wife the hair, and told her all that had happened to him, but she began to jeer and laugh at him.

But he paid no attention to her, and went to a town to sell the hair. A crowd of all sorts of people and merchants collected round him; one offered a sequin, another two, and so on, higher and higher, till they came to a hundred gold sequins. Just then the emperor heard of the hair, summoned the man into his presence, and said to him that he would give him a thousand sequins for it, and he sold it to him. What was the hair? The emperor split it in two from top to bottom, and found registered in it in writing many remarkable things, which happened in the olden time since the beginning of the world. Thus the man became rich and lived on with his wife and children. And that child, that came to him in his sleep, was an angel sent by the Lord God, whose will it was to aid the poor man, and to reveal secrets which had not been revealed till then.

1. How is the outcome of this selection different than what the little boy predicted when he spoke to his father through a dream?

Ⓐ   The father is not able to earn a great deal of money by selling the damsel's hair.
Ⓑ   The damsel comes after the father and attacks him.
Ⓒ   The boy's prediction is accurate. There is no difference.
Ⓓ   The father is not happy with the boy's instructions.

"The Smith and the Fairies": A Gaelic Folk Tale (Ed. Kate Douglas Wiggin)

Years ago there lived in Crossbrig a smith of the name of MacEachern. This man had an only child, a boy of about thirteen or fourteen years of age, cheerful, strong, and healthy. All of a sudden he fell ill; took to his bed and moped whole days away. No one could tell what was the matter with him, and the boy himself could not, or would not, tell how he felt. He was wasting away fast; getting thin, old, and yellow; and his father and all his friends were afraid that he would die.

At last one day, after the boy had been lying in this condition for a long time, getting neither better nor worse, always confined to bed, but with an extraordinary appetite—one day, while sadly revolving these things, and standing idly at his forge, with no heart to work, the smith was agreeably surprised to see an old man, well known for his sagacity and knowledge of out-of-the-way things, walk into his workshop. Forthwith he told him the occurrence which had clouded his life.

The old man looked grave as he listened; and after sitting a long time pondering over all he had heard, gave his opinion thus: "It is not your son you have got. The boy has been carried away by the 'Daione Sith,' and they have left a Sibhreach in his place."
"Alas! and what then am I to do?" said the smith. "How am I ever to see my own son again?"
"I will tell you how," answered the old man. "But, first, to make sure that it is not your own son you have got, take as many empty egg-shells as you can get, go into his room, spread them out carefully before his sight, then proceed to draw water with them, carrying them two and two in your hands as if they were a great weight, and arrange them when full, with every sort of earnestness around the fire." The smith accordingly gathered as many broken egg-shells as he could get, went into the room, and proceeded to carry out all his instructions.

He had not been long at work before there arose from the bed a shout of laughter, and the voice of the seeming sick boy exclaimed, "I am eight hundred years of age, and I have never seen the like of that before." The smith returned and told the old man.

"Well, now," said the sage to him, "did I not tell you that it was not your son you had: your son is in Borracheill in a digh there (that is, a round green hill frequented by fairies). Get rid as soon as possible of this intruder, and I think I may promise you your son. You must light a very large and bright fire before the bed on which this stranger is lying. He will ask you, 'What is the use of such a fire as that?' Answer him at once, 'You will see that presently!' and then seize him, and throw him into the middle of it. If it is your own son you have got, he will call out to you to save him; but if not, the thing will fly through the roof."

The smith again followed the old man's advice: kindled a large fire, answered the question put to him as he had been directed to do, and seizing the child flung him in without hesitation. The Sibhreach gave an awful yell, and sprang through the roof, where a hole had been left to let the smoke out.

On a certain night the old man told him the green round hill, where the fairies kept the boy, would be open, and on that date the smith, having provided himself with a Bible, a dirk, and a crowing cock, was to proceed to the hill. He would hear singing and dancing, and much merriment going on, he had been told, but he was to advance boldly; the Bible he carried would be a certain safeguard to him against any danger from the fairies. On entering the hill he was to stick the dirk in the threshold, to prevent the hill from closing upon him; "and then," continued the old man, "on entering you will see a spacious apartment before you, beautifully clean, and there, standing far within, working at a forge, you will also see your own son. When you are questioned, say you come to seek him, and will not go without him."

Not long after this, the time came round, and the smith sallied forth, prepared as instructed. Sure enough as he approached the hill, there was a light where light was seldom seen before. Soon after, a sound of piping, dancing, and joyous merriment reached the anxious father on the night wind.

Overcoming every impulse to fear, the smith approached the threshold steadily, stuck the dirk into it as directed, and entered. Protected by the Bible he carried on his breast, the fairies could not touch him; but they asked him, with a good deal of displeasure, what he wanted there. He answered, "I want my son, whom I see down there, and I will not go without him."

Upon hearing this the whole company before him gave a loud laugh, which wakened up the cock he carried dozing in his arms, who at once leaped up on his shoulders, clapped his wings lustily, and crowed loud and long.

The fairies, incensed, seized the smith and his son, and throwing them out of the hill, flung the dirk after them, and in an instant all was dark.

For a year and a day the boy never did a turn of work, and hardly ever spoke a word; but at last one day, sitting by his father and watching him finishing a sword he was making for some chief, and which he was very particular about, he suddenly exclaimed, "That is not the way to do it;" and taking the tools from his father's hands he set to work himself in his place, and soon fashioned a sword, the like of which was never seen in the country before.

From that day the young man wrought constantly with his father, and became the inventor of a peculiarly fine and well-tempered weapon, the making of which kept the two smiths, father and son, in constant employment, spread their fame far and wide, and gave them the means in abundance, as they before had the disposition, to live content with all the world and very happily with each other.

2. How is the fairy pretend version of the smith's son different than the smith's actual son?

Ⓐ The fairy is a humorous trickster, while the real son is quiet and serious.
Ⓑ The fairy is cruel to the father, while the real son is kind to his father.
Ⓒ The fairy and the son are exactly alike.
Ⓓ The fairy and the father are alike.

The Two Melons A Chinese Folk Tale (Ed. Kate Douglas Wiggin)

An honest and poor old woman was washing clothes at a pool, when a bird that a hunter had disabled by a shot in the wing, fell down into the water before her. She gently took up the bird, carried it home with her, dressed its wound, and fed it until it was well, when it soared away. Some days later it returned, put before her an oval seed, and departed again. The woman planted the seed in her yard and when it came up she recognized the leaf as that of a melon. She made a trellis for it, and gradually a fruit formed on it, and grew to great size.

Toward the end of the year, the old dame was unable to pay her debts, and her poverty so weighed upon her that she became ill. Sitting one day at her door, feverish and tired, she saw that the melon was ripe, and looked luscious; so she determined to try its unknown quality. Taking a knife, she severed the melon from its stalk, and was surprised to hear it chink in her hands. On cutting it in two, she found it full of silver and gold pieces, with which she paid her debts and bought supplies for many days.

Among her neighbors was a busybody who craftily found out how the old woman had so suddenly become rich. Thinking there was no good reason why she should not herself be equally fortunate, she washed clothes at the pool, keeping a sharp lookout for birds until she managed to hit and maim one of a flock that was flitting over the water. She then took the disabled bird home, and treated it with care till its wing healed and it flew away. Shortly afterward it came back with a seed in its beak, laid it before her, and again took flight. The woman quickly planted the seed, saw it come up and spread its leaves, made a trellis for it, and had the gratification of seeing a melon form on its stalk. In prospect of her future wealth, she ate rich food, bought fine garments, and got so deeply into debt that, before the end of the year, she was harried by duns. But the melon grew apace, and she was delighted to find that, as it ripened, it became of vast size, and that when she shook it there was a great rattling inside. At the end of the year she cut it down, and divided it, expecting it to be a coffer of coins; but there crawled out of it two old, lame, hungry beggars, who told her they would remain and eat at her table as long as they lived.

3. How are the busybody neighbor and the honest old woman different?

Ⓐ They are not different. They are both poor and hungry.
Ⓑ The honest old woman acts out of selflessness while the busybody neighbor acts out of self-interest.
Ⓒ The honest old woman is much poorer than the busybody neighbor.
Ⓓ The honest old woman minds her own business while the busybody neighbor is concerned with everyone else's business.

4. How would this story be different if the busybody neighbor was the first to receive a melon seed?

Ⓐ She would have gotten a garden full of melons to eat and the old, honest woman would be left with a garden full of beggars.
Ⓑ Both the busybody neighbor and the old, honest woman would no longer be poor.
Ⓒ There would be no difference. The busybody neighbor would have still gotten a garden of beggars because of the way she went about getting her melon seed.
Ⓓ The busybody would tell everyone about the melon.

"Love Between Brothers and Sisters"
by Isaac Watts

Whatever brawls disturb the street,
There should be peace at home;
Where sisters dwell and brothers meet,
Quarrels should never come.

Birds in their little nests agree;
And 'tis a shameful sight,
When children of one family
Fall out and chide and fight.

5. Which statement contrasts with the author's viewpoint in this poem?

Ⓐ Brothers and sisters should try their hardest to love one another.
Ⓑ Nothing good can come from siblings arguing with one another.
Ⓒ There's no harm in siblings occasionally not getting along with one another.
Ⓓ It is natural for siblings to have arguments.

TO MAKE AN AMBLONGUS PIE.
by Edward Lear

Take 4 pounds (say 4½ pounds) of fresh Amblongusses, and put them in a small pipkin.

Cover them with water, and boil them for 8 hours incessantly; after which, add 2 pints of new milk, and proceed to boil for 4 hours more.

When you have ascertained that the Amblongusses are quite soft, take them out, and place them in a wide pan, taking care to shake them well previously.

Grate some nutmeg over the surface, and cover them carefully with powdered gingerbread, curry-powder, and a sufficient quantity of Cayenne pepper.

Remove the pan into the next room, and place it on the floor. Bring it back again, and let it simmer for three-quarters of an hour. Shake the pan violently till all the Amblongusses have become of a pale purple color.

Then, having prepared the paste, insert the whole carefully, adding at the same time a small pigeon, 2 slices of beef, 4 cauliflowers, and any number of oysters.

Watch patiently till the crust begins to rise, and add a pinch of salt from time to time.

Serve up in a clean dish, and throw the whole out of the window as fast as possible.

6. How is this recipe different than a typical recipe?

Ⓐ This recipe is nonsense while real recipes are intended to be made.
Ⓑ The directions in this recipe are out of order while real recipes present the directions in the order they are intended to be followed in.
Ⓒ This recipe uses exotic ingredients while typical recipes use common ingredients.
Ⓓ This recipe is much more time consuming than a typical recipe.

Best Friend

Max had started playing on the football team and didn't have much time for Julie anymore. He was always busy, and he never seemed to make it to study hall, where the two used to swap stories about their favorite (or least favorite) teachers. In class, Julie noticed that Max never seemed to have his homework done on time anymore. She even noticed that he got a 'D' on his last paper. She knew something was going on with him – but what?

At first, Julie decided to play it cool and see how things went. She tried waiting in the hall for Max after class to see if she could ask if he was OK. But days went by, and he never had time to stop. He'd rush right past her in the hall, only to leave her feeling even worse about what was happening between them.

Even though she wasn't sure she could handle the situation herself, Julie didn't want to talk to her parents because she was afraid they would tell her not to hang out with Max anymore. She barely saw him as it was, so she knew it would just make things worse if her parents didn't approve of him. She didn't want to tell Max's parents either because she didn't want him to get in trouble. Still, it seemed like something needed to change. Julie decided to go to one of her school counselors and let her know she was concerned.

When she walked into Mrs. Smith's room, she was surprised to see that Max was already sitting there. "I'm sorry, I'll come back," Julie said.

"No, stay," said Max. "Maybe you can help."

Julie was surprised to find that Max had visited the counselor's office for the same reason she had: He was starting to feel overwhelmed with all of the things he was supposed to be doing as a student, an athlete, and a friend. He needed some guidance on how to determine what truly mattered and how to divide his time between all of the things that were important to him. When she realized that Max was still the same old Max (just a little more stressed), Julie was relieved. She was also happy to know that he had come to a conclusion on his own, without her having to talk to someone else about it. She decided it was a sign they were both growing up.

7. Even though Julie and Max are interested in different things once they enter high school, what remains the same about the two of them?

Ⓐ They both care about each other.
Ⓑ They are both interested in sports.
Ⓒ They both want to do well in school.
Ⓓ They both need help in their classes.

A VALENTINE TO CATHERINE
by Evaleen Stein

If you will be my True-Love,
I'll tell you what I'll do,
I'll ask a little bluebird
To sing a song to you.

When first you see a violet
And softly pricking through
The garden-bed come crocuses
And golden tulips, too,

Then watch! for he'll be coming,
The little bird of blue;
He'll sing, "I love you, Sweetheart,
It's true, true, true!"

8. How is this Valentine poem unlike the valentines people exchange on Valentine's Day today?

Ⓐ The poem and valentines show love for the people they are given to.
Ⓑ The poem and valentines have "I love you" written in them.
Ⓒ The poem uses a bird to convey a valentine message.
Ⓓ There is no difference in either types of cards.

From "The Strike of the Fireworks" by Carolyn Wells

'Twas the night before the Fourth of July, the people slept serene;
The fireworks were stored in the old town hall that stood on the village green.
The steeple clock tolled the midnight hour, and at its final stroke,
The fire in the queer old-fashioned stove lifted its voice and spoke;
"The earth and air have naught to do, the water, too, may play,
And only fire is made to work on Independence Day.

9. How is the scene described in this stanza of the poem typical of a Fourth of July celebration?

Ⓐ The people in town go to bed early on the Fourth of July.
Ⓑ There is a fireworks celebration held in the town on the Fourth of July.
Ⓒ There is a bonfire on the Fourth of July.
Ⓓ There is a town clock that strikes midnight.

"Base Details"
Siegfried Sassoon

IF I were fierce, and bald, and short of breath,
I'd live with scarlet Majors at the Base,
And speed glum heroes up the line to death.

You'd see me with my puffy petulant face,
Guzzling and gulping in the best hotel,
Reading the Roll of Honour. 'Poor young chap,'
I'd say—'I used to know his father well;
Yes, we've lost heavily in this last scrap.'

And when the war is done and youth stone dead,
I'd toddle safely home and die—in bed.

10. Which statement is NOT inferred by this poem?

Ⓐ He is young and may still be fighting in the war.
Ⓑ He is on the opposite side of the war.
Ⓒ People have died in the war.
Ⓓ The speaker doesn't like the man he describes in the poem

Excerpt from Little Women
By Louisa May Alcott

"Christmas won't be Christmas without any presents," grumbled Jo, lying on the rug.

"It's so dreadful to be poor!" sighed Meg, looking down at her old dress.

"I don't think it's fair for some girls to have plenty of pretty things, and other girls nothing at all," added little Amy, with an injured sniff.

"We've got Father and Mother, and each other," said Beth contentedly from her corner.

The four young faces on which the firelight shone brightened at the cheerful words, but darkened again as Jo said sadly, "We haven't got Father, and shall not have him for a long time." She didn't say "perhaps never," but each silently added it, thinking of Father far away, where the fighting was.

Nobody spoke for a minute; then Meg said in an altered tone, "You know the reason Mother proposed not having any presents this Christmas was because it is going to be a hard winter for everyone; and she thinks we ought not to spend money for pleasure, when our men are suffering so in the army. We can't do much, but we can make our little sacrifices, and ought to do it gladly. But I am afraid I don't." And Meg shook her head, as she thought regretfully of all the pretty things she wanted.

"But I don't think the little we should spend would do any good. We've each got a dollar, and the army wouldn't be much helped by our giving that. I agree not to expect anything from Mother or you, but I do want to buy UNDINE AND SINTRAM for myself. I've wanted it so long," said Jo, who was a bookworm.

"I planned to spend mine in new music," said Beth, with a little sigh, which no one heard but the hearth brush and kettle holder.

"I shall get a nice box of Faber's drawing pencils. I really need them," said Amy decidedly.

"Mother didn't say anything about our money, and she won't wish us to give up everything. Let's each buy what we want, and have a little fun. I'm sure we work hard enough to earn it," cried Jo, examining the heels of her shoes in a gentlemanly manner.

"I know I do--teaching those tiresome children nearly all day, when I'm longing to enjoy myself at home," began Meg, in the complaining tone again.

"You don't have half such a hard time as I do," said Jo. "How would you like to be shut up for hours with a nervous, fussy old lady, who keeps you trotting, is never satisfied, and worries you till you you're ready to fly out the window or cry?"

"It's naughty to fret, but I do think washing dishes and keeping things tidy is the worst work in the world. It makes me cross, and my hands get so stiff, I can't practice well at all." And Beth looked at her rough hands with a sigh that anyone could hear that time.

"I don't believe any of you suffer as I do," cried Amy, "for you don't have to go to school with impertinent girls, who plague you if you don't know your lessons, and laugh at your dresses, and label your father if he isn't rich, and insult you when your nose isn't nice."

"If you mean libel, I'd say so, and not talk about labels, as if Papa was a pickle bottle," advised Jo, laughing.

"I know what I mean, and you needn't be satirical about it. It's proper to use good words and improve your vocabulary," returned Amy, with dignity.

"Don't peck at one another, children. Don't you wish we had the money Papa lost when we were little, Jo? Dear me! How happy and good we'd be if we had no worries!" said Meg, who could remember better times.

"You said the other day you thought we were a deal happier than the King children, for they were fighting and fretting all the time, in spite of their money."

"So I did, Beth. Well, I think we are. For though we do have to work, we make fun of ourselves, and are a pretty jolly set, as Jo would say."

"Jo does use such slang words!" observed Amy, with a reproving look at the long figure stretched on the rug.

Jo immediately sat up, put her hands in her pockets, and began to whistle.

"Don't, Jo. It's so boyish!"

"That's why I do it."

"I detest rude, unladylike girls!"

"I hate affected, niminy-piminy chits!"

"Birds in their little nests agree," sang Beth, the peacemaker, with such a funny face that both sharp voices softened to a laugh, and the "pecking" ended for that time.

"Really, girls, you are both to be blamed," said Meg, beginning to lecture in her elder-sisterly fashion."You are old enough to leave off boyish tricks, and to behave better, Josephine. It didn't matter so much when you were a little girl, but now you are so tall, and turn up your hair, you should remember that you are a young lady."

"I'm not! And if turning up my hair makes me one, I'll wear it in two tails till I'm twenty," cried Jo, pulling off her net, and shaking down a chestnut mane. "I hate to think I've got to grow up and be Miss March, and wear long gowns, and look as prim as a China Aster! It's bad enough to be a girl, anyway, when I like boy's games and work and manners! I can't get over my disappointment in not being a boy. And it's worse than ever now, for I'm dying to go and fight with Papa. And I can only stay home and knit, like a poky old woman!"

And Jo shook the blue army sock till the needles rattled like castanets, and her ball bounded across the room.

11. Part A
In what way is Jo different from other girls of her age?

Ⓐ She likes to whistle.
Ⓑ She can knit.
Ⓒ She refuses to wear her hair up.
Ⓓ She is poor.

Part B
What do all of the girls have in common?

Ⓐ They all believe they deserve to be wealthy.
Ⓑ They are all unhappy with their responsibilities.
Ⓒ They all behave boyishly.
Ⓓ They all remember a time when their family had more money

Excerpt from The Wonderful Wizard of Oz

L. Frank Baum

Dorothy lived in the midst of the great Kansas prairies, with Uncle Henry, who was a farmer, and Aunt Em, who was the farmer's wife. Their house was small, for the lumber to build it had to be carried by wagon many miles. There were four walls, a floor and a roof, which made one room; and this room contained a rusty looking cooking stove, a cupboard for the dishes, a table, three or four chairs, and the beds. Uncle Henry and Aunt Em had a big bed in one corner, and Dorothy a little bed in another corner. There was no garret at all, and no cellar-except a small hole, dug in the ground, called a cyclone cellar, where the family could go in case one of those great whirlwinds arose, mighty enough to crush any building in its path. It was reached by a trap-door in the middle of the floor, from which a ladder led down into the small, dark hole.

When Dorothy stood in the doorway and looked around, she could see nothing but the great gray prairie on every side. Not a tree nor a house broke the broad sweep of flat country that reached the edge of the sky in all directions. The sun had baked the plowed land into a gray mass, with little cracks running through it. Even the grass was not green, for the sun had burned the tops of the long blades until they were the same gray color to be seen everywhere. Once the house had been painted, but the sun blistered the paint and the rains washed it away, and now the house was as dull and gray as everything else.

When Aunt Em came there to live she was a young, pretty wife. The sun and wind had changed her, too. They had taken the sparkle from her eyes and left them a sober gray; they had taken the red from her cheeks and lips, and they were gray also. She was thin and gaunt, and never smiled, now. When Dorothy, who was an orphan, first came to her, Aunt Em had been so startled by the child's laughter that she would scream and press her hand upon her heart whenever Dorothy's merry voice reached her ears; and she still looked at the little girl with wonder that she could find anything to laugh at.

Uncle Henry never laughed. He worked hard from morning till night and did not know what joy was. He was gray also, from his long beard to his rough boots, and he looked stern and solemn, and rarely spoke.

It was Toto that made Dorothy laugh, and saved her from growing as gray as her other surroundings. Toto was not gray; he was a little black dog, with long, silky hair and small black eyes that twinkled merrily on either side of his funny, wee nose. Toto played all day long, and Dorothy played with him, and loved him dearly.

To-day, however, they were not playing. Uncle Henry sat upon the door-step and looked anxiously at the sky, which was even grayer than usual. Dorothy stood in the door with Toto in her arms, and looked at the sky too. Aunt Em was washing the dishes.

From the far north they heard a low wail of the wind, and Uncle Henry and Dorothy could see where the long grass bowed in waves before the coming storm. There now came a sharp whistling in the air from the south, and as they turned their eyes that way they saw ripples in the grass coming from that direction also.

Suddenly Uncle Henry stood up.

"There's a cyclone coming, Em," he called to his wife; "I'll go look after the stock." Then he ran toward the sheds where the cows and horses were kept.

Aunt Em dropped her work and came to the door. One glance told her of the danger close at hand.

"Quick, Dorothy!" she screamed; "run for the cellar!"

Toto jumped out of Dorothy's arms and hid under the bed, and the girl started to get him. Aunt Em, badly frightened, threw open the trap-door in the floor and climbed down the ladder into the small, dark hole. Dorothy caught Toto at last, and started to follow her aunt. When she was half way across the room there came a great shriek from the wind, and the house shook so hard that she lost her footing and sat down suddenly upon the floor.

12. Part A

How is Aunt Em different from how she was when she first married Uncle Henry?

Ⓐ She is more cautious about the weather.
Ⓑ She doesn't smile as often as she used to.
Ⓒ She no longer enjoys the company of children.
Ⓓ She wears only gray clothing.

Part B
What behavior of Dorothy's did Aunt Em find almost frightening?

Ⓐ Dorothy's laughter.
Ⓑ Dorothy's love for her dog, Toto.
Ⓒ Dorothy's lack of caution during a storm.
Ⓓ Dorothy's laziness.

Chapter 2

Lesson 12: Based on a True Story - History and Fiction

Let us understand the concept with an example.

Battle of Gettysburg[1]

The Battle of Gettysburg was fought on July 1–3, 1863, in and around the town of Gettysburg, Pennsylvania, by Union and Confederate forces during the American Civil War. The battle involved the largest number of casualties of the entire war and is often described as the war's turning point. Union Major General George Meade's Army of the Potomac defeated attacks by Confederate General Robert E. Lee's Army of Northern Virginia, ending Lee's attempt to invade the North.

After his success at Chancellorsville in Virginia in May 1863, Lee led his army through the Shenandoah Valley to begin his second invasion of the North—the Gettysburg Campaign. With his army in high spirits, Lee intended to shift the focus of the summer campaign from war-ravaged northern Virginia and hoped to influence Northern politicians to give up their prosecution of the war by penetrating as far as Harrisburg, Pennsylvania, or even Philadelphia. Prodded by President Abraham Lincoln, Major General Joseph Hooker moved his army in pursuit, but was relieved of command just three days before the battle and replaced by Meade.

Elements of the two armies initially collided at Gettysburg on July 1, 1863, as Lee urgently concentrated his forces there, his objective being to engage the Union army and destroy it. Low ridges to the northwest of town were defended initially by a Union cavalry division under Brigadier General John Buford, and soon reinforced with two corps of Union infantry. However, two large Confederate corps assaulted them from the northwest and north, collapsing the hastily developed Union lines, sending the defenders retreating through the streets of the town to the hills just to the south.

On the second day of battle, most of both armies had assembled. The Union line was laid out in a defensive formation resembling a fishhook. In the late afternoon of July 2, Lee launched a heavy assault on the Union left flank, and fierce fighting raged at Little Round Top, the Wheatfield, Devil's Den, and the Peach Orchard. On the Union right, Confederate demonstrations escalated into full-scale assaults on Culp's Hill and Cemetery Hill. All across the battlefield, despite significant losses, the Union defenders held their lines.

On the third day of battle, fighting resumed on Culp's Hill, and cavalry (soldiers on horses) battles raged to the east and south, but the main event was a dramatic infantry assault by 12,500 Confederates against the center of the Union line on Cemetery Ridge, known as Pickett's Charge. The charge was repulsed by Union rifle and artillery fire, at great loss to the Confederate army.

Lee led his army on a torturous retreat back to Virginia. Between 46,000 and 51,000 soldiers from both armies were casualties in the three-day battle, the most costly in US history.

A Partial (fictional) Eyewitness Account of the Battle of Gettysburg

July 5th, 1863
To: John Edelson, Editor, Philadelphia Clarion
From: Joseph Smith, Feature Writer

Dear John:

Here is my personal account of what I saw in this battle. I am sure you will agree with my biases and conclusions since we are of the same mind about this war.

It is July 5th, and the fighting here in Gettysburg looks like it is over. The Confederate troops were beaten and have retreated south from the area. The destruction is everywhere and life in this village will not return to normal for a long time. Not only have buildings been burned and damaged, but the bodies of dead soldiers are everywhere, raising concerns about disease and an invasion by animals and insects on the bodies, as well as finding enough men and equipment to remove and bury them and the weapons and wagons and garbage left behind.

Over the course of the three day battle, I changed my location and hid inside three different buildings, one of which had been converted to a hospital for wounded Union soldiers. The wounds suffered by the soldiers brought to that hospital made me sick to my stomach, not to mention the stench from the dying and dead. I witnessed several of the battles – such fierceness, such noise and smoke everywhere. Otherwise decent men turned into warriors, fighting for their cause and their lives.

Why did it come to this? Is it worth the sacrifice on both sides? Why can't we work out compromises to avoid the killing of our own citizens? I do not want another assignment covering this war. This was enough.

Sincerely,
Joseph
[1]Source: https://en.wikipedia.org/wiki/Battle_of_Gettysburg

Your assignment: Compare the two accounts of this battle for their similarities and differences, including the degree of objectivity each account shows.

The first account appears to be an attempt to accurately describe the events that took place over the three days of the battle, including General Lee's strategy. The author does not make any judgments, just reports facts. The reporter's account does not give many details of the battles themselves, but gives a personal account of what he saw during several battles and also in the aftermath of the battles. He also makes judgments about the war itself, which, if his letter is published in the newspaper, may influence readers to do more to make compromises and avoid wars.

You can scan the QR code given below or use the url to access additional EdSearch resources including videos and mobile apps related to *Based on a True Story - History and Fiction.*

 **Based on a True Story - History and Fiction**

URL	QR Code
http://www.lumoslearning.com/a/rl79	

"Paul Revere's Ride" (Excerpt)
Henry Wadsworth Longfellow

Listen my children and you shall hear
Of the midnight ride of Paul Revere,
On the eighteenth of April, in Seventy-five;
Hardly a man is now alive
Who remembers that famous day and year.
He said to his friend, "If the British march
By land or sea from the town to-night,
Hang a lantern aloft in the belfry arch
Of the North Church tower as a signal light,--
One if by land, and two if by sea;
And I on the opposite shore will be,
Ready to ride and spread the alarm
Through every Middlesex village and farm,
For the country folk to be up and to arm."
Then he said "Good-night!" and with muffled oar
Silently rowed to the Charlestown shore,
Just as the moon rose over the bay,
Where swinging wide at her moorings lay
The Somerset, British man-of-war;
A phantom ship, with each mast and spar
Across the moon like a prison bar,
And a huge black hulk, that was magnified
By its own reflection in the tide.

It was twelve by the village clock
When he crossed the bridge into Medford town.
He heard the crowing of the cock,
And the barking of the farmer's dog,
And felt the damp of the river fog,
That rises after the sun goes down.
It was one by the village clock,
When he galloped into Lexington.
He saw the gilded weathercock
Swim in the moonlight as he passed,
And the meeting-house windows, black and bare,
Gaze at him with a spectral glare,
As if they already stood aghast
At the bloody work they would look upon.
It was two by the village clock,
When he came to the bridge in Concord town.
He heard the bleating of the flock,

And the twitter of birds among the trees,
And felt the breath of the morning breeze
Blowing over the meadow brown.
And one was safe and asleep in his bed
Who at the bridge would be first to fall,
Who that day would be lying dead,
Pierced by a British musket ball.
You know the rest. In the books you have read
How the British Regulars fired and fled,---
How the farmers gave them ball for ball,
From behind each fence and farmyard wall,
Chasing the redcoats down the lane,
Then crossing the fields to emerge again
Under the trees at the turn of the road,
And only pausing to fire and load.

The Real Story of Revere's Ride
From the Paul Revere House official Website
In 1774 and the Spring of 1775 Paul Revere was employed by the Boston Committee of Correspondence and the Massachusetts Committee of Safety as an express rider to carry news, messages, and copies of resolutions as far away as New York and Philadelphia.

On the evening of April 18, 1775, Paul Revere was sent for by Dr. Joseph Warren and instructed to ride to Lexington, Massachusetts, to warn Samuel Adams and John Hancock that British troops were marching to arrest them. After being rowed across the Charles River to Charlestown by two associates, Paul Revere borrowed a horse from his friend Deacon John Larkin. While in Charlestown, he verified that the local "Sons of Liberty" committee had seen his pre-arranged signals. (Two lanterns had been hung briefly in the bell-tower of Christ Church in Boston, indicating that troops would row "by sea" across the Charles River to Cambridge, rather than marching "by land" out Boston Neck. Revere had arranged for these signals the previous weekend, as he was afraid that he might be prevented from leaving Boston).

On the way to Lexington, Revere "alarmed" the country-side, stopping at each house, and arrived in Lexington about midnight. As he approached the house where Adams and Hancock were staying, a sentry asked that he not make so much noise. "Noise!" cried Revere, "You'll have noise enough before long. The regulars are coming out!" After delivering his message, Revere was joined by a second rider, William Dawes, who had been sent on the same errand by a different route. Deciding on their own to continue on to Concord, Massachusetts, where weapons and supplies were hidden, Revere and Dawes were joined by a third rider, Dr. Samuel Prescott. Soon after, all three were arrested by a British patrol. Prescott escaped almost immediately, and Dawes soon after. Revere was held for some time and then released. Left without a horse, Revere returned to Lexington in time to witness part of the battle on the Lexington Green.

1. According to the poem, what was the purpose of Revere's ride?

Ⓐ   To alert everyone in the county that the British were approaching.
Ⓑ   To warn Samuel Adams and John Hancock that the British were approaching.
Ⓒ   To make it back to Boston in time for the battle.
Ⓓ   To reach Lexington before the British troops to awaken the members of the militia.

2. According to the non-fiction passage, what was the purpose of Revere's ride?

Ⓐ   To alert everyone in the county that the British were approaching.
Ⓑ   To warn Samuel Adams and John Hancock that the British were approaching.
Ⓒ   To make it back to Boston in time for the battle.
Ⓓ   To reach Lexington before the British troops to awaken the members of the militia.

3. What information from the non-fiction passage does the poem exclude?

Ⓐ   The description of the signals in the church steeple.
Ⓑ   That Revere was arrested and held by the British.
Ⓒ   That Revere reached the town of Lexington.
Ⓓ   That the British soldiers were coming by sea.

4. Which excerpt from the non-fiction passage conflicts most with the poem?

Ⓐ   Left without a horse, Revere returned to Lexington in time to witness part of the battle on the Lexington Green.
Ⓑ   Paul Revere borrowed a horse from his friend, Deacon John Larkin.
Ⓒ   Two lanterns had been hung briefly in the bell-tower of Christ Church in Boston, indicating that troops would row "by sea" across the Charles River to Cambridge, rather than marching "by land" out Boston Neck.
Ⓓ   On the way to Lexington, Revere "alarmed" the country-side, stopping at each house, and ar rived in Lexington about midnight.

5. About whom might Longfellow have just as accurately written this poem?

Ⓐ   Samuel Adams
Ⓑ   John Larkin
Ⓒ   Samuel Prescott
Ⓓ   William Dawes

THE BAND OF THE TITANIC
By Florence Earle Coates
"These are the immortal,—the fearless"—*Upanishads*

UP, lads! they say we've struck a berg, though there's no danger yet,—
Our noble liner was not built to wreck!—
But women may have felt a shock they're needing to forget,
And when there's trouble, men should be on deck.

Come!—now's the time! They're wanting us to brighten them a bit;
Play up, my lads—as lively as you can!
Give them a merry English air! they want no counterfeit
Like that down-hearted tune you just began!...

I think the Captain's worried, lads: maybe the thing's gone wrong;
Well, we will show them all is right with us!
Of Drake and the Armadas now we'll play them such a song
Shall make them of the hero emulous.

When boats are being lowered, lads, your place and mine are here,—
Oh, we were never needed more than now!
When others go, it is for us those left behind to cheer,
And I am glad, my lads, that we know how!

If it is Death that's calling us, we'll make a brave response;
Play up, play up!—ye may not play again;
The prize that Nelson won at last, the chance that comes but once,
Is ours, my lads!—the chance to die like men!

From The Worcester Evening Gazette
April 20, 1912
New York, April 19. [1]Of all the heroes who went to their death when the Titanic dived to its ocean grave, none, in the opinion of Miss Hilda Slater, a passenger in the last boat to pull off, deserved greater credit than the members of the vessel's orchestra. According to Miss Slater, the orchestra played until the last. When the vessel took its final plunge the strains of a lively air, mingled gruesomely with the cries of those who realized that they were face to face with death.

"It was terrible," said Miss Slater, who had come from her home in England to visit a brother, an architect in this city. "From the moment the vessel struck, or as soon as the members of the orchestra could be collected, there was a steady round of lively airs. It did much to keep up the spirits of everyone and probably served as much as the efforts of the officers trying to prevent panic."

1

When the ship struck the iceberg, Miss Slater went on deck. She was ordered to go back to bed, which she did on being assured there was no danger. A half-hour later, she heard confusion on deck and heard someone cry, "Order everyone to don life belts."

After dressing again, Miss. Slater returned to the deck and was ordered to the boat deck aloft.

"When I got there," she said, "I found an indescribable scene. A number of the steerage men passengers had attempted to seize one of the boats, and there was a brisk revolver fire: many men fell under it. The prompt and drastic action of the officers restored order."

"There were many touching scenes as the boats put off. I saw Col. John Jacob Astor hand his young wife into a boat tenderly and then asked an officer whether he might also go. When permission was refused, he stepped back and coolly took out his cigarette case. "Good-bye, dearie" he called gaily, as he lighted a cigarette and leaned over the rail. "I'll join you later." Another man, a Frenchman, I think, approached one of the boats about to be lowered. He had with him, two little boys. An officer waved him back sternly. "Bless you," he said, "I don't want to go, but for God's sake take the boys. Their mother is waiting for them in New York." The boys were taken aboard."
From The Worcester Evening Gazette
April 20, 1912
New York, April 19- Mrs. John Murray Brown of Acton, Mass, who with her sister, Mrs. Robert C. Cornell and Mrs. E.D. Appleton, was saved, was in the last life-boat to get safely away from the Titanic.

"The band played marching from deck to deck, and as the ship went under, I could still hear the music." Mrs. Brown said. "The musicians were up to their knees in water when last I saw them. We offered assistance to Capt. Smith, but he refused."

"Mrs. Astor was in the life-boat with my sister, Mrs. Cornell. I heard Col. Astor tell her he would wait with the men. Our boat was almost dragged down by the suction."

6. Based on the two newspaper articles, what information from the poem can be confirmed as fact?

Ⓐ   The band played because they were cold.
Ⓑ   The musicians had no intentions of trying to save themselves.
Ⓒ   The musicians played so that women would forget the horror of the sinking.
Ⓓ   The band played as people were loaded into the lifeboats.

7. What detail from the newspaper articles supports the attitude assigned to the musicians in the last stanza of the poem?

Ⓐ "The band played marching from deck to deck, and as the ship went under I could still hear the music. Mrs. Brown said."

Ⓑ "The musicians were up to their knees in water when last I saw them."

Ⓒ "From the moment the vessel struck, or as soon as the members of the orchestra could be collected, there was a steady round of lively airs. It did much to keep up the spirits of everyone and probably served as much as the efforts of the officers trying to prevent panic."

Ⓓ "Another man, a Frenchman, I think, approached one of the boats about to be lowered. He had with him two little boys. An officer waved him back sternly."

8. What detail from the newspaper articles supports the information in the second stanza of the poem?

Ⓐ When the vessel took its final plunge, the strains of a lively air mingled gruesomely with the cries of those who realized that they were face to face with death.

Ⓑ "The band played marching from deck to deck, and as the ship went under I could still hear the music." Mrs. Brown said.

Ⓒ Of all the heroes who went to their death when the Titanic dived to its ocean grave, none, in the opinion of Miss. Hilda Slater, a passenger in the last boat to pull off, deserved greater credit than the members of the vessel's orchestra.

Ⓓ When the ship struck the iceberg, Miss Slater went on deck. She was ordered to go back to bed, which she did on being assured there was no danger.

9. What do both the poem and newspaper articles suggest the ship's band did for the victims and survivors?

Ⓐ Provided entertainment while the passengers awaited rescue

Ⓑ Helped organize the lifeboats so that only women and children had places

Ⓒ Helped people from becoming hysterical while the lifeboats were lowered

Ⓓ Helped lower the lifeboats into the water

10. Why would readers consider Mrs. Brown and Miss Slater accurate reporters of what was happening on board the Titanic just before the ship sank?

Ⓐ They were personal friends of the members of the band.

Ⓑ They were on the ship until it sank and were rescued from the water.

Ⓒ They were on lifeboats as the ship was sinking.

Ⓓ Their stories offer identical details.

End of Reading: Literature

Answer Key and
Detailed Explanations

Chapter 2: Reading: Literature

Lesson 1: Prove It! (With Evidence from the Text)

Question No.	Answer	Detailed Explanations
1	B	Answer choice two is the best answer. This answer is the best one because it shows that there were so many footprints that the policeman could not figure out exactly which prints belonged to the thief and which prints belonged to other customers. The first answer is incorrect because if the prints were marked, there would be no point in searching for the thief. The third answer choice can't be correct because the story clearly tells the reader that there are several footprints. The last answer choice does not make sense. Why would someone clean the footprints when a crime had been committed?
2	C	Answer choice three is correct. The first two choices are not mentioned in the story, so they cannot be the correct choice. The last answer choice is not the best. Although his mom is encouraging, she did not help him make the decision.
3	D	Answer choice four is the correct answer. Sam was very concerned about what his parents would think if he missed the party. This shows he considers other's feelings and is a sign he was raised well by his parents.
4	C	Answer choice three is correct. The answer is in the passage and can be found in the third paragraph. The first two choices are not mentioned in the story, and although they make sense for today, this passage does not indicate that was an option. The last choice is in the story, a ride in the boat, but what is expected to cure the king is a sudden fright (something unexpected), not a ride in a boat.
5	C	Answer choice three is correct. The last few lines of the poem tells the reader that the pig had a ring on the end of his nose, and that he is willing to sell it for a shilling (type of money).
6 Part A	A	Answer choice one is correct. In the last part of the poem, the frog tells the boys that the rocks hit them in the head.

Question No.	Answer	Detailed Explanations
6 Part B	D	Answer choice four is correct. Answer choices one and two are things boys might do, but the poem does not mention them doing so in this piece. Answer choice three seems possible because the frogs complain of getting hit on the head, and claiming it "'tis death to us." However, the boys are not TRYING to kill the frogs. They are throwing stones in the water.
7	A	Answer choice one is correct. In the sixth line of the poem, there are quotation marks that indicate someone is talking. "The wolf once met...and began 'Your servant'...." section tells the reader that the wolf began speaking, therefore the best answer is choice number one.
8	B	The evidence is given therefore B is the correct choice.
9		The secret of the poem is about losing loved ones. The lines from the poem that relates to this feeling of the poet are - But oh! When comes the icy chill that freezes o'er the heart, When, one by one, the joys we shared, the hopes we held, depart; When friends, like autumn's withered leaves, have fallen by our side, And life, so pleasant once, becomes a desert wild and wide.

Lesson 2: Use Those Clues - Make an Inference

Question No.	Answer	Detailed Explanations
1	C	Answer choice three is correct. The quote indicates that the cabby was not paying attention, lost in thought, or asleep when the policemen called to him. It is meant to explain how the day had been slow, boring and cold, and he was somewhat startled and had a hard time getting his senses together to drive the policeman.
2	D	Answer choice four is correct. The bear behaved very differently when he went to the zoo. He would not eat and he lost weight. He was a happy bear before going to the zoo. His changed behavior was a clue that he was depressed.
3	A	Answer choice one is correct. They were very good friends/best friends. The passage explains their interactions with each other, indicating they were more than acquaintances or neighbors.
4	B	Answer choice two is the best answer. Because the dog was well fed, unlike the wolf, his master must have cared for the dog.
5	C	Answer choice three is the correct answer. The wolf is hungry, while the dog is plump (fat) with living a good life free of want. The wolf is always in need of a good meal.
6	B	Answer choice number one is true, but it is not the best answer because it does not explain fully how the dog lives. Answer choice number two is the best answer because the dog is well fed and does not want or need anything whereas the wolf is hungry and worries about getting food. Answer choice number three is incorrect because the dog is not greedy, he doesn't take from another, he just doesn't have to worry about his needs being met. Answer choice four is not the best answer because the poem does not mention sharing.
7	B	Answer choice two is correct. The frogs pleaded that the boys pay attention. This implies that the boys did not know they were hurting the frogs.
8	A	Answer choice one is correct. The captain came back, but he was in a wheelchair. Also, he said he had a leg that was nearly "blown off." These facts explain why he came back home.

Question No.	Answer	Detailed Explanations
9	B	Answer choice two is correct. The story is told from a third person's point of view. All could be "seen," but we did not know what every one was thinking, so it is not omniscient.
10	D	Answer choice four is the correct answer. Sam was very concerned about what his parents would think if he missed the party. He also knew that it was important to put in a lot of hard work if he wanted to excel as a tennis player. This shows he considers other's feelings and is a sign he was raised well by his parents.

Name: _____ Date: _____

Lesson 3: And the Point of This is...?

Question No.	Answer	Detailed Explanations
1	B	Answer choice two is the correct answer. The bear would not eat, and he was getting too thin. Then the wife came to see him, and he ate again.
2	B	Answer choice two is the correct answer. The bear and the wife were so close that both of them were not happy/healthy when they were separated.
3	B	Answer choice two is the best answer. Central idea means center or main idea. The question asks about what is the main point of this story. This portion tells of the pet eating, accidentally, rat poison nearly dying before the vet could get him the antidote shot.
4	C	Answer choice three is correct. All answer choices apply somewhere in the passage. However, the third answer choice is the best summary of the second paragraph.
5	A	Answer choice number one is the BEST answer of the provided choices. Sam did have trouble with tennis, but that is not the focus of the passage. Sam's mother was part of the story, but the passage was about more than just his mother. And, Sam did NOT ruin his mother's birthday.
6	A	The first answer choice is the best answer. The little boy is enjoying watching his shadow as he walks, skips and plays. The boy is referring to his shadow as if it is another person, but we know that it is not. The sun and the time of day affect how one sees his shadow, and this poem is hinting at that. Answer choice number three is similar to one, but the tone of the poem does not indicate confusion (which has a negative connotation), but just of fun.
7	D	Answer choice four is the best answer. To summarize something, all the information has to be included (minus small details), so the last answer is the most accurate of what is in the passage.
8	C	Answer choice three is correct. The paragraph explains how the boy returns, stays silent for a year and then suddenly becomes alert and speaks again. He watches his father making a sword and feels his father is not making it correctly, and this causes him to return to talking and working.

Question No.	Answer	Detailed Explanations
9	C	Answer choice number three is the correct answer. The paragraph states that the father was offended and he set out to punish the men. He does so by hiding his wisdom from them.
10	B	Answer choice number two is the correct answer. His father was trying to keep the wisdom from everyone but himself. His son followed him out of the village and watched Kewku Tsin try to climb a tree to keep wisdom away from everyone. His son saw a solution that his father did not causing the father to realize he did NOT have all the wisdom. This angered him.
11	B	Answer choice two is the BEST answer. All of the other answer choices are in fact true, but the second description is the most accurate. The last answer choice does not mention the fireplace or wardrobe.
12	D	Answer choice number one is incorrect because other than "deceased husband" there is no mention of a Mr. Reed. Answer choice number two is not the best answer because cleaning is what the maid does, regardless of who is or is not in the room. This would not be a concern of Mrs. Reed. Answer number three is not the best answer. The room is beautifully described, but Mrs. Reed would not be concerned about messing up the furniture because she has a maid. Answer choice number four is the best answer. The fact that Mrs. Reed does not spend time in the room , as pretty as it is, only reinforces the point that she avoids the room.

Lesson 4: What is it All About?

Question No.	Answer	Detailed Explanations
1	A	Answer choice one is the correct answer. The entire story is about the angst a young man feels when he worries about disappointing his mom. Family values and doing what is important is the theme.
2	C	The story is about how Sam's open communication with his grandfather and later with his mother, helped in solving his dilemma and also strengthened his relationships with them. Hence, answer choice three is correct.
3	C	Answer choice three is the best answer. The poem discusses how feeling sorry for oneself is not good because everyone has their problems. And often, they are worse than yours.
4	C	Answer one is incorrect because the boy was not disobedient. He did as his father asked. Answer two is incorrect because there was no mention of anyone going to Heaven, just a new/different life. Answer three is the best choice because the boy respected and obeyed his father, when he did not want to. However, the end result is not what the father had hoped for. The story tells about acquiring a spirit, but it does not specifically mention dying.
5	A	Answer one is the best choice. The young man felt he needed to be excused from the fast, but his father would not listen to his son. The father could have still asked his son to remain with his fast, after hearing his son's concerns. But, the father would not even hear what his son had to say. Answer two is incorrect because the strictness of the father was NOT effective to the father's hopes. Answer choice three is not the best answer because the word "always" is used. Any choice that uses "always," or other absolutes are usually not good answer choices. Answer choice four is incorrect because the boy did not take his father for granted, or take advantage of him. This is not a reasonable theme of this story.

Question No.	Answer	Detailed Explanations
6	B	Answer choice one is not the best answer. Yes, people should watch out for falling objects, but that is not the point of this poem. Answer choice two is the best. The acorn, although small, had a big impact on this story. Answer choice three is not the best answer because Mother Nature is not questioned in the passage. The fourth answer choice is not the best choice because not EVERY seed becomes a beautiful plant. Some don't grow at all, others sprout into weeds. Try to avoid answer choices that use absolutes such as "always" or "every."
7	C	Answer one is not the best choice. Even though the first old man danced without being self-conscious, this is not the main point of the story. Answer two is not the best choice because the old men did not negotiate with the Devil, he was offered without asking for anything. Answer three is the best choice. The first man benefitted from his time in the woods. He did not ask for the lump to be removed nor did he expect something good to happen. He was happily participating and because of this he was blessed to have the lump removed. Changing his appearance helped the first old man, but did not help the second one (had a lump added), so changing appearance does not bring someone ONLY misery.
8	B	Answer choice one is not the best choice. In this answer choice the word "nod" refers to moving ones head. In the story it is about going to sleep/dreaming (nodding off to sleep). Answer choice two is the best selection. The poem describes different places he has to go, alone, while dreaming. Also, he cannot find those places by day (when he is awake), nor can he quite remember the music (what happened in the dreams). Answer choice three might be true, but it is not the best answer. Not everything mentioned in the Land of Nod was exciting. The last answer choice is not the best answer because the poem does not indicate that the person can control where he visits.

Question No.	Answer	Detailed Explanations
9	C	Answer choice one is not the best answer. Yes, it took extreme force to crack the nut open, but that Devil just happened to be in the nut. Answer choice number two is not the best answer. The young boy did play a trick on the Devil, but it is commonly believed in literature that any way the Devil is controlled is an acceptable act. And, the act of the trick was just part of the story, not the focus of the story. Answer choice number three is the best answer because the message from this story, all of the elements, indicate that even though the nut was tiny, something dangerous or bad could still be there. The boy asked for help, but this was not the message this story tries to convey.
10	B	Answer choice number one is not the best answer. Obviously it is wrong for a parent to want to hurt their children, but in THIS story, there was no indication that anyone was worried about this. Answer choice two is the best answer because the family was indeed benefited by the father's actions. Answer choice three is not the best answer because this story did not mention protecting the children, only providing food for them. Answer choice four is not the best answer because the father is the main character in the story. Without him, there is no story, so he DID influence on the plot.
11		This answer implies that there are many reasons to fight; when the excerpt gives reasons people THINK they are at war, there is only one reason: money.
12 Part A	C	Answer choice three is the correct answer. The wolf is hungry, while the dog is plump (fat) with living a good life free of want. The wolf is always in need of a good meal.
12 Part B	B	Answer choice number one is true, but it is not the best answer because it does not explain fully how the dog lives. Answer choice number two is the best answer because the dog is well fed and does not want or need anything whereas the wolf is hungry and worries about getting food. Answer choice number three is incorrect because the dog is not greedy, he doesn't take from another, and he just doesn't have to worry about his needs being met. Answer choice four is not the best answer because the poem does not mention sharing.

Lesson 5: One Thing Leads to Another

Question No.	Answer	Detailed Explanations
1	A	Answer choice one is the correct answer. The cab driver indicates that his son was ill and then died. The story describes him sitting very still and somewhat dazed.
2	B	Answer choice number two is the correct answer. The cab driver's son died, and due to that he was grief stricken and sad. He was confused and not sure where to go with the policeman. He was sad (lamented) about the death of his child.
3	D	Answer choice four is the best answer. Playing a sport or any extra-curricular activity takes up time. Practices and games take hours after school, so the answer is that the two kids could not spend as much time together as they usually did.
4	A	Answer choice one is the correct choice. Sam's gift to his mom (according to her) was the fact the he was able to tryout for the state team. She is not focused on her birthday as much as she is on her son's achievement. She is proud of him, and wants him to do well.
5	C	Answer choice number three is the correct answer. The first line of the story states that no one "except his fool" could play tricks on the king.
6	B	Answer choice number two is the best answer. The story says "one day an accident befell him." This means Bruno made a mistake, or had something happened to him. In this case, he ate poison intended for rats.
7	A	Answer choice one is the correct choice. The first man came back to the village with no lump where he previously had one. After some time another man went to the tree. It is a logical conclusion to believe that the second man was attempting to get the same help the first man did. That is the only "real" reason he'd go in to the trees.
8 Part A	B	Answer choice two is the best answer. The little boy is the narrator of the poem, and this innocence of not understanding the shadow completely adds to the mood of this poem. The main character (the boy) adds to the meaning/feeling of the poem because he is young, and everyone can relate to watching and playing with their shadow.

Question No.	Answer	Detailed Explanations
8 Part B	D	The poem uses personification by referring to the shadow as if the shadow is a real human and can make willful decisions. The other three choices are other elements, but not the one employed for "Him."
8 Part C	B	Answer two is the best choice. The choice of words, rhythm and rhyme scheme help the poem to be enjoyable to read. Also, this poem is relatable for everyone, as all remember being a child and trying to move in such a way to play with our shadow.
9	B	Answer choice two is the correct answer. In the first line of the second paragraph it states "just as the boy told him" this hints to the reader that the boy knows more than others in the story. His foreshadowing is important, and that makes the boy important in the story.
10	C	Answer choice three is the correct answer. The climax of a story is the changing point. This is the point that all the mystery or energy builds to. This is where the major character (protagonist) makes a decision that changes the direction of the story.
11 Part A	B	Answer choice two is the correct answer. Robert is having an internal issue (inside). He is struggling with himself. No one or thing is causing him to struggle. The issues are his own decision/opinion.
11 Part B	A	Answer choice one is the best choice. After the first paragraph lists the summer options for Robert, the following paragraphs should explain the positives and negatives of each option. The second answer choice is not reasonable because nothing in the first paragraph mentions school. The third answer choice is not appropriate because his parent's opinion of Robert has nothing to do with what his summer options are. They do not play into Robert's decision. The last answer choice is also inappropriate because like his parents' opinions, his friends summer plans have nothing to do with what Robert's options are.
12	D	Answer choice four is correct. The climax is the turning part of the story. This is where the hero defeats the antagonist; where everything that has been building in the story comes to the deciding point.

Question No.	Answer	Detailed Explanations
13 Part A	D	Answer choice four is the best answer. This is found in the first paragraph, stated clearly.
13 Part B	D	Answer choice number four is the best choice. The question asks the reader the consequence of the parents' disagreement. Answer choice three is true, but it is not a "result" of the disagreement/discussion.
14		The reader could come to this conclusion if he read back through the story and numbered the events.

Lesson 6: When and Where?

Question No.	Answer	Detailed Explanations
1	A	Answer choice one is the correct answer. The first line in the story tells the reader where it is taking place.
2	C	Answer choice three is the correct answer. Snow is not common everywhere, but where it does on a regular basis, it is a winter form of precipitation.
3	A	Correct answer is the first choice. The other three answers are too general to make a determination of setting. However, the story first states the name of the cab driver, and it is a Russian name.
4	A	Answer choice one is the best answer. The principal's office is usually a place students go when there is behavior issues. So, if Julie saw Max there she might assume he was in trouble, and that would support her idea that he had changed and was not the same friend she'd had. They likely would not have reconciled.
5	B	Answer choice two is the correct answer. "Nod" represents sleep (nodding off), so it implies that the person in the poem is dreaming in his sleep.
6	C	Answer choice three is the best answer. Regardless where a family lives, the number of children does not affect that.
7	C	Answer choice number three is the correct answer. Making swords, fairies, and blacksmiths, indicate a time other than present day. People have been carrying Bibles and will continue to carry them. This has no bearing on time or setting.
8	B	Answer choice two is the best answer. While there are still cities where poor people wash their clothes in a river or pool, the fact that there was a hunter in the area indicates a rural village setting.
9	C	Answer choice number three is the best answer. The description describes a large (size) room/home and a fire is needed to warm the place (past). Cottage is not mentioned, nor a hotel, and the fire indicates that the time is not in the future.
10	A	Answer choice one is the best because it indicates that the fireplace has the only source of heat. More modern homes have furnaces. The remaining three answers describe the room and furniture. The first answer choice gives more of an idea about how the remaining part of the home is situated. These other rooms indicate the time frame of the story. Current homes are not designed that way.

Question No.	Answer	Detailed Explanations
11.Part A	C	Answer choice three is the best answer. The fact that lumber had to be brought in on a wagon (horse drawn) tells the reader that this was written before the motor vehicle was invented.
11 Part B	D	Answer choice four is the best answer." From the far north they heard a low wail of the wind, and Uncle Henry and Dorothy could see where the long grass bowed in waves before the coming storm. There now came a sharp whistling in the air from the south, and as they turned their eyes that way they saw ripples in the grass coming from that direction also." Describes the weather and changing atmosphere. This tells the reader that indeed a storm is blowing in.
12 Part A	B	The first lines of the poem tell the reader that this occurs by a pond or a lake, but there is NO mention of time of day or year.
12 Part B	C	Answer choice three is the correct answer. The poem states that in "less than half an hour" scores (many) of frogs were dead.
13 Part A	A	In the poem both the Fox and the Stork have dinner at one another's, so they are visiting each other's homes.
13 Part B	B	Answer choice two is the BEST answer. Dinner can mean either late night or the evening meal, but the other choices do not apply to a "dinner."

Lesson 7: Who or What?

Question No.	Answer	Detailed Explanations
1	B	Answer choice two is the correct answer. The passage states, "But because of the neighborhoods' and our renters' children, poor Bruno, had to be kept chained most of the time." explains why the answer is the correct answer.
2	D	Answer choice number four is the best answer. All three of the other choices in the passage are mentioned as being things causing Max stress.
3	C	Answer choice number three is the answer. The other three options are mentioned in the story. There is no discussion of Max's appearance.
4	C	Answer choice three is the correct answer. Max and Julie are the only two that talk. There is casual mention of the counselor at the end, but he/she is not a major part of the story.
5	A	Answer choice one is the correct answer. The shopkeeper runs out shouting for someone to stop the thief. This tells the reader he left to catch the person who stole his sugar from the store.
6	B	Answer choice two is the correct answer. The policeman was able to find the "thief" by looking at the line of ants. Ants often are looking for sugar.
7	D	Answer choice four is the correct answer. Sam let the quandary bother him for a long time. He let it affect his mood and second-guess himself. Had he sought assistance earlier, he could have avoided a lot of stress.
8	C	Answer choice three is the BEST answer. Choice four is possible, but the third choice best describes Sam in this passage. The first two answer choices are not reasonable for the story.
9	C	Answer choice three is the best answer. In the beginning of the story he is concerned about the decision he needs to make and how it will affect others. Then, after getting guidance, he is confident and happy that he gets to share his good news with his mom.
10	D	Answer choice four is the correct answer. The fool's jokes were generally harmless, just fun. The king's joke turned out to be a sad event. So, the king likely had a different view on playing a prank on someone. He might have had a greater appreciation for his fool than he did prior to the fool dying.

Question No.	Answer	Detailed Explanations
11 Part A	D	The best answer choice is the last one. The passage explains a relationship. They live together. One of them is older than the other and is bossy. The first two answers cannot be correct because they indicate that Emily and Jason do not live together. The passage states that they do live together. The third answer choice is not mentioned. They walk home from school, but there is nothing to indicate they walk together in the morning.
11 Part B	A	Answer choice number one is the best answer choice. The other options are possible, but based on the passage, the first answer choice is the BEST. There is no mention of having the same chores, walking every day, or sharing a bathroom.
12	B	Answer choice number two is the best answer. The passage mentions that the parents usually wanted to be with their children on trips like such as this. The other answer choices aren't reasonable in helping ease the parents' concerns. So, the best answer is getting their parents to go as chaperones.
13	A	Answer choice one is the best one. Talking excitedly would indicate that someone had something unusual or good to share.

Lesson 8: A Matter of Attitude

Question No.	Answer	Detailed Explanations
1	C	Answer choice three is the best answer. The words to describe their habitats are fun and non-sensical (Sofsky-Popsky and Pipple Popple). This helps sets the tone of silly. There is no indication of greed or really of constant hunger. And whether the animals are diverse or not does not answer the question about tone.
2	B	Answer choice two is the best answer. "Thus the man became rich and lived on with his wife and children. And that child, that came to him in his sleep, was an angel sent by the Lord God, whose will it was to aid the poor man, and to reveal secrets which had not been revealed till then." describes a happy, relieved, and JOYFUL feeling. There is no anger, or confusion in this passage's end, nor any seriousness.
3	D	Answer choice four is the best answer. The line "speed glum heroes up the line" tells the reader that the narrator feels that the major is not considerate of the enlisted men he is in charge of. The comment about being "out of breath" hints that the man is overweight, likely not a trait the younger men have.
4	C	Answer choice three is the best answer. Guzzling and gulping are words that hint at greed. Also, the "best hotel" is annoying to the narrator when young men are at war on the front lines.
5	B	Answer choice two is correct. The reader knows the author is repulsed because of the word choice. The author uses words that are not flattering to the woman. The descriptions of her body frame in the coat as well as the negative comment about the length of her skirt tell the reader that she is not attractive (the opposite of repulse). Also, the author mentions the bad teeth. This does not paint a pretty picture for the reader.
6	A	Answer choice one is the best choice. The author is comparing the sisters to little birds in a nest (metaphor). The author is trying to illustrate how siblings pick on one another by comparing them to birds in a nest who literally peck their siblings.
7	A	Answer choice one is the correct answer. Jo wants to buy a book, and the author calling her a "bookworm" helps indicate this.

Question No.	Answer	Detailed Explanations
8	A	Answer choice one is the best answer. The author describes the Martians as organized and thoughtful. So, the tone is one of admiration.
9	A	Answer choice one is the correct answer.
10	A	Answer choice one is the best answer. If a person does not have dreams there is no reason to work hard to achieve other things.
11		The post says that the captain is dead. Despite the celebrations on land and the successful voyage, the poet reveals that his Captain's dead body is lying on the deck. In the second stanza, the poet wishes that the dead man could witness the elation. Everyone adored the captain, and the poet admits that his death feels like a horrible dream.
12		Correct order of answers - Box 1:Exult Box 2:sought Box 3:keel Box 4:voyage Box 5:mournful

Lesson 9: How it's Made and What it Means

Question No.	Answer	Detailed Explanations
1	A	Part of the definition of a villanelle is that it has two rhyming patterns. This poem has two rhyming patterns so answer choice number one is the answer to select.
2	D	In poetry repetition is used to stress an idea, sound or feeling. The word me is not repeated, so answer choice number four is the best answer.
3	D	The correct answer is answer choice four. The way this poem is structured in rhyme helps lead the reader from one stanza to the next. This helps with pacing and feeling connected.
4	C	Answer choice number three is the best answer. When the author states she got the story "bit by bit" from various people, and that it was slightly different each time, she is hinting that she has pieced the story together, and the accuracy is not necessarily the way it actually happened.
5	B	Answer choice two is the best answer. If the author had explained how she learned of the story, it would help the reader analyze the accuracy of the story and the person telling the story. It would give the story as told more credit.
6	A	Answer choice number one is the best answer. The prologue is written to rhyme, like a poem. The remaining portion of the passage is written in the format of a play (prose=anything not poetic).
7	D	Answer D is correct. Rhyming patterns are based on words that rhyme at the end of each line in a stanza. The rhyming pattern in the first stanza is aaba, using the rhyming words at the end of the lines know, though, here, snow. The second stanza rhyming pattern is bbcb , using the words queer (which rhymed with the third line in stanza one), near, lake and year. The pattern becomes aaba, bbcb.
8	C	Answer choice three is the best choice. The man in this poem is traveling late at night and he stops for seemingly no reason. A horse that is accustomed to traveling the same paths/roads would realize something was out of the ordinary. His shaking of bells would be an indication of the horse "asking" why they are stopped.
9	B	The second choice is the correct answer. When analyzing a poem each sound is assigned a letter. Any time that sound appears it is assigned the same letter. When a new sound presents itself, the next letter in the alphabet is assigned. The scheme can be simple, aabb, or very complex, aaba,bbcd etc.
10	D	Answer choice four is the correct answer. This line indicates that the author hopes to be telling this story a long time from now.

Question No.	Answer	Detailed Explanations
11		Rhyming patterns are based on words that rhyme at the end of each line in a stanza. The rhyming pattern in the poem is aabb. The first and the second line ends with the rhyming words. The third and the fourth line ends with the rhyming words.
12		The student needs to decide what kind of poem using feelings he/she would write about and why.
13		In the first stanza, the student should note that it is about the night that the Pilgrims arrived on the shore with details of what the waves, coast, woods, hills, and shore.
14		The second stanza shows the contrast of conquerors to Pilgrims.

Lesson 10: What a Character!

Question No.	Answer	Detailed Explanations
1	A	Answer choice one is the correct answer. The passage explains that the swindlers (dishonest people) told the Emperor that if a person was wise, and worthy of their job/status, they would be able to see the fabric/costumes. But, the men never intended to make any clothes. No one was willing to admit that they saw no clothes because they did not want to appear to be unworthy. It took a child, who did not know to hide what he saw, to point out the obvious. The remaining three answers describe the swindlers (2 and 3) and what an official thought upon seeing the "clothes." They do not answer the question: **why** did the Emperor agree to hire the men (swindlers).
2	A	Answer choice one is the best answer. The king is insecure about himself and that is why he hired the swindlers. He only cares about looks and he wanted a "trick" to help him with his work/people. The minister would be considered wise and trustworthy, so if he could not see the fabric, he would be out of a job. Not seeing the fabric made him feel as though maybe he really wasn't good enough for the job. Choice two is incorrect because the minister never indicated he wanted to fool the public. Choice three is incorrect because only the Emperor was worried about clothes. And answer four is incorrect. The Emperor thought the minister could see things not visible. The Emperor never claimed to.
3	B	Answer choice two is the best answer. The passage states that the Emperor knows he has no clothes on. He continues though because he does not want to admit he was wrong, and that he was tricked by the swindlers. Answer choice one is incorrect because he did believe him, he knew it to be true. Answer choices two and three are incorrect because no one can see what is not there, and he can't show off nothing.

Question No.	Answer	Detailed Explanations
4	A	Answer choice one is the correct answer. The beginning of the passage Huck mentions his father used to hit him. Then, when he sees his father, he realizes he should not be afraid of him anymore. Answer choice two is incorrect because his father WANTS him to STOP going to school. The remaining answer choices deal with his friends. His father is only interested in Huck not being "better than his dad" and any money Huck might have on him.
5	C	Answer choice three is the correct answer. First, Huck's father slaps the book from Buck's hands, but then he tells him to stay away from the school. Answer choice four is incorrect because he does not ask to learn to read. He seems proud that neither he nor Huck's mom could read or write. Answer choice one is incorrect because Huck's father is NOT proud of him. He does demand Huck give him money, but he is not proud. Answer choice two is partially correct, but not the best answer. Huck's father does hit the book from his hand, but the question asked is what does Huck's father ask/tell him to do. Not what does Huck's dad do.
6	B	Answer choice two is the best answer. His attitude towards them is one of shame. They don't come outside at all, and he finds that odd. Answer choice three is incorrect because he is allowed inside (Judge's feet), and answer four is not reasonable. No dogs tease him.
7	C	Answer choice three is the correct answer. He did not want to be a house dog. He does not respect those dogs who do nothing dog-like. He does not want to be a kennel dog because those dogs are working dogs. He enjoys being part of the family, being around the family, and he is proud of his place. He is trusted with being involved/caring for the family.
8	C	Answer choice three is correct. Buck feels that it is strange that they rarely put nose out of doors (go outside) or put their feet to the ground (someone holds/carries them all the time). The three remaining answers may be true, but they do not hint at Buck's opinions of the two inside dogs.

Question No.	Answer	Detailed Explanations
9	B	Answer choice two is the correct answer. After a long, long trip he is relaxing and getting well. He mentions being surprised that the other dogs are not jealous. This indicates being relieved that he does not have to worry about dog fights or any other issues with jealousy.
10	D	The last answer choice is the answer choice that does NOT describe Buck. He is honorable in his actions (the Jude's), he is persistent (went for long walks and kept others company) and he is grateful (for Thornton and Skeet). Nothing in these passages indicate aggression.
11		The answers may vary but should include the fact that the poet uses vocabulary such as the ship, port is near, people exulting, hear the bells, flag is flung, bouquets and wreaths, shores a -crowding, fallen cold and dead, and ship anchored.
12		The poet is trying to tell why the Pilgrims came over. It is not for wealth, but to be able to worship freely.

Lesson 11: Finding Patterns - Comparing and Contrasting

Question No.	Answer	Detailed Explanations
1	C	Answer choice three is the best answer. The dream predicted what the man should do, and when he did this, his life improved.
2	A	Answer choice one is the correct answer. The boy was very serious and quiet. He hardly spoke or did anything.
3	B	Answer choice two is the best answer. One woman is decent and good, the other woman only does things to benefit herself. The last answer choice is true, but it is not as good a characterization as the second choice.
4	C	Answer choice three is the correct answer. The women had different attitudes towards life. Thus, the difference would not exist regardless of the order of the events.
5	C	Answer choice three is the best answer. All answers might be correct depending on who holds the opinion, but the author's opinion in this poem is that it is not good for siblings to argue. So, the answer choice three is not in agreement with the author's view.
6	A	Answer choice one is the correct answer. The ingredients are non-sensical, and the directions are silly. It is not a true recipe, as nothing would be produced by completing the steps.
7	A	Answer choice one is the best answer. They have gone different ways to a degree, however they both still are concerned about each other.
8	C	Answer choice three is the correct answer. This poem says that a bird will give the message of love. Modern valentine cards and poems usually mention hearts and candy. Answers one and two are characteristics of modern valentines. Answer choice four is not applicable to the question. There is a difference.
9	B	Answer choice two is the best answer. The question asks what the poem and the holiday have in common. Both have fireworks.
10	B	All other answers could be inferred by the poem.
11 Part A	A	Answer choice one is the best answer. She is not the only poor child, other girls might not wear their hair up, but few girls whistle as it is considered "boyish."

Question No.	Answer	Detailed Explanations
11 Part B	B	Answer choice two is the correct answer. In this passage all of the girls take turns complaining of what they have to endure in life. They don't all remember having money, and there is no indication to their belief about they being wealthy.
12 Part A	B	Answer choice two is the correct answer. The passage describes how Auntie Em has changed and she seems to be not as happy as when she was younger.
12 Part B	A	Answer choice one is the correct answer. The passage describes how Aunt Em changed after marrying. It emphasizes how Dorothy's young merry voice startled Aunt Em when she heard the laughter.

Lesson 12: Based on a True Story - History and Fiction

Question No.	Answer	Detailed Explanations
1	A	The first answer choice is the best choice. The first line of the second stanza tells the reader what Revere was planning to do.
2	B	Answer choice two. The first line of the second paragraph states why Revere was riding.
3	B	Answer choice two is the best choice. The poem and the passage cover the same historical event. The poem is more entertaining and gives the same information, but leaves out Revere's arrest.
4	A	Answer choice one is the best choice. Left without a horse is not in the poem, and it would not be because the poem is intended to celebrate the heroics of Revere.
5	D	The fourth answer choice is the correct one. Dawes and Revere were together almost the entire ride.
6	D	Answer choice four is the best choice. Factual information from survivors reported that the band played until the very last, but does not explain why.
7	C	The last stanza of the poem expresses the commitment the band had to helping in any way they could. Answer choice number three is the best answer.
8	B	Answer choice two is the best choice. The band played on and on trying to boost the spirits of those on the deck of the boat.
9	C	Answer choice three is the best answer. The poem, in particular, mentions why the band is needed by explaining different situations of chaos.
10	C	Answer choice three is the correct answer. Both women saw the boat go down, one even mentioned nearly being sucked under by the ship, so they would know what happened at the last minute.

Chapter 3 - Reading: Informational Text

The objective of the Reading Informational Text standards is to ensure that the student is able to read and comprehend informational texts (such as history/social studies, science, and technical texts) related to Grade 7.

To help students master the necessary skills, information to help the student understand the concepts related to the standard is given. Along with this, we encourage the student to go through the resources available online on EdSearch to gain an in depth understanding of these concepts. The EdSearch page for each lesson can be accessed with the help of the url or the QR code provided.

A small map is provided after each passage or text in which the student can enter the details as understood from the literary text. Doing this will help the student to refer to key points that help in answering the questions with ease.

Chapter 3

Lesson 1: Key Ideas and Details

Let us understand the concept with an example.

Example: You have been assigned to read the following article, and write text that meets what the standard requires.

Scientists tell us that changes in our climate are happening. Average temperatures around the world are getting higher. The planet's average surface temperature has risen about 2.0 degrees Fahrenheit since the late 19th century. The warmest year on record was 2016; eight months were the warmest on record. The number of warm days in a year has increased while the number of cold days has decreased. This is called global warming.

Because of the rise in temperature, the ice caps in Greenland and Antarctica are melting and are have caused sea levels to rise 8" in the last 100 years; glaciers are shrinking; ocean water temperatures are rising. Carbon dioxide levels in the air have risen from an average of 300 ppm (parts per million) to 400 ppm, the highest levels ever. Carbon dioxide forms a blanket above the earth that traps heat, an additional contributor to global warming.

Studies by scientists point out that global warming is having bad effects on humans, animals and plants. Carbon dioxide reduces air quality which is not healthy for humans and animals to breathe. Water is essential for living creatures; without enough water they die. Global warming decreases the amount of water on the planet. Some creatures cannot adapt quickly to changes in climates and will die, and those that migrate can be forced to change their migration patterns.

Why is this happening? Ninety seven percent of global scientists think this is happening because of things we humans are doing. Our use of fuels from fossils, such as oil and coal, are major causes, and our manufacturing activities are another cause. We need your help to convince our government and companies that use chemicals to manufacture their products to agree to rules that minimize the release of harmful chemicals into the air. Please click on the link below to sign up to help us combat the trend in global warming (assume that the author provides a link to a signup form).

Your assignment:

Part 1. To analyze the text and summarize its main ideas, and quote from the text-specific statements that support what you list as the main ideas.

Part 2. What do you infer from the text (draw a conclusion or opinion from the text that is not stated in the text)?

Here is an example of what you might write.

Part 1:

Main idea #1: Our climate is changing. Average temperatures around the world are getting higher. Proof: The planet's average surface temperature has risen about 2.0 degrees Fahrenheit since the late 19th century. The warmest year on record was 2016; eight months were the warmest on record. The number of warm days in a year has increased while the number of cold days has decreased. This is called global warming.

Main idea #2: The rise in temperature is resulting in changes we can see.

Proof: The ice caps in Greenland and Antarctica are melting and are have caused sea levels to rise 8" in the last 100 years; glaciers are shrinking; ocean water temperatures are rising. Carbon dioxide levels in the air have risen from an average of 300 ppm (parts per million) to 400 ppm, the highest levels ever.

Main idea #3: These changes in climate are having harmful effects on humans, plants and animals. Proof: Carbon dioxide reduces air quality which is not healthy for humans and animals to breathe. Water is essential for living creatures; without enough water they die. Global warming decreases the amount of water on the planet. Some creatures cannot adapt quickly to changes in climates and will die, and those that migrate can be forced to change their migration patterns.

Main idea #4: Most scientists agree that human activities are the most important causes of global warming. Examples: using fossil fuels like oil and coal in the manufacture of products or producing gasoline to fuel vehicles.

Main idea #5: Take action to help combat the trend in global warming.
Proof: a link to a website that gives more information on this topic.

Part 2:
I am inferring that if we do not reverse the trend in global warming, available fresh water will become increasingly scarce, temperatures will become increasingly warm, and large numbers of humans, plants and animals will die. Also, in the short term, flooding will occur as melting glaciers and ice caps increase the amounts of ocean water.

You can scan the QR code given below or use the url to access additional EdSearch resources including videos and mobile apps related to *Key Ideas and Details*.

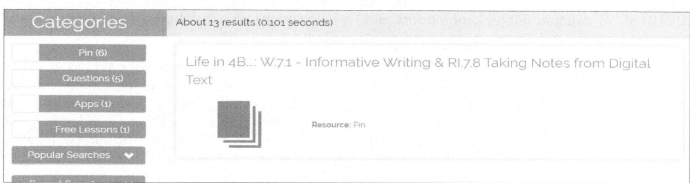

From <u>Guiseppi Verdi</u> by Thomas Trapper

Whenever the organ man came into the village of Roncole, in Italy (where Verdi was born, October 10, 1813), Verdi could not be kept indoors. But he followed the wonderful organ and the wonderful man who played it, all day long, as happy as he could be.

When Giuseppe was seven years old, his father, though only a poor innkeeper, bought him a spinet, a sort of small piano. So faithfully did the little boy practice that the spinet was soon quite worn out and new jacks, or hammers, had to be made for it. This was done by Stephen Cavaletti, who wrote a message on one of the jacks telling that he made them anew and covered them with leather, and fixed the pedal, doing all for nothing, because the little boy, Giuseppe Verdi, showed such willingness to practice and to learn. Thus the good Stephen thought this was pay enough.

1. Which sentence from the passage best explains how Verdi felt about his first spinet?

Ⓐ "But he followed the wonderful organ and wonderful man who played it all day long, as happy as he could be."

Ⓑ "So faithfully did the little boy practice that the spinet was soon quite worn out and new jacks, or hammers, had to be made for it."

Ⓒ "…because the little boy, Guiseppi Verdi, showed such willingness to practice and to learn."

Ⓓ "Thus the good Stephen thought this was pay enough."

Skunk Chow

Skunks are omnivores. They can be found eating nuts, berries, roots, leaves, grasses, and even some types of fungi (mushroom-like plants). For animals, they enjoy dining on rodents such as mice and rats, insects, earthworms, frogs, lizards, toads, and birds. Sometimes when they are unable to find live animals to eat, they become scavengers eating dead animals left behind. When they live close to people's homes, skunks sometimes will even get into trash cans, eating garbage.

When skunks eat, they do not limit themselves to small meals. They like to "pig out" on whatever food they can find. When there is a large amount of food available, skunks get very fat very quickly. http://en.wikipedia.org/wiki/Skunk

2. If you had to answer the question "Can skunks control their appetites?" which sentence would you use to support your answer?

Ⓐ "They can be found eating nuts, berries, roots, leaves, grasses, and even some types of fungi (mushroom-like plants)."

Ⓑ "For animals, they enjoy dining on rodents such as mice and rats, insects, earth worms, frogs, lizards, toads, and birds."

Ⓒ "When they live close to people's homes, skunks sometimes will even get into trash cans, eating garbage."

Ⓓ "They like to 'pig out' on whatever food they can find. When there is a large amount of food, skunks get fat very quickly."

3. If the author removed the sentence telling you skunks were omnivores, could you still infer that skunks are omnivores?

Ⓐ No, because the author does not tell me what an omnivore is or what it eats.

Ⓑ No, because the author does not provide enough information about the types of food a skunk eats.

Ⓒ Yes, because the author shows that a skunk eats both plants and animals.

Ⓓ Yes, because the author says that skunks are also scavengers.

Scientists in South Korea have developed a type of artificial skin that will allow robots to feel slight vibrations. This skin, developed by weaving together extremely small nano hairs made of polymer or plastic, is more sensitive than human skin. When vibration is applied to this artificial skin, the nano hairs bend against each other to generate an electrical current. Sensors within the skin evaluate the current, and using that information determine the source of the vibration.

Researchers are excited about the potential for this new development. The artificial skin could be used to cover prosthetic limbs to help those who have lost a limb experience more realistic sensations and function more naturally.

http://en.wikipedia.org/wiki/Neuroplasticity

4. Which sentence best explains why scientists are developing the artificial skin?

Ⓐ "The artificial skin could be used to cover prosthetic limbs to help those who have lost a limb experience more realistic sensations and function more naturally."

Ⓑ "Sensors within the skin evaluate the current and using that information determine the source of the vibration."

Ⓒ "This skin, developed by weaving together extremely small nano hairs made of polymer or plastic is more sensitive than human skin."

Ⓓ "Scientists in South Korea have developed a type of skin that will allow robots to feel slight vibrations."

Diabetic Help

Researchers at pharmaceutical company Eli Lilly and an association that places assistance dogs in Indianapolis, IN, are working together on an exciting new project that will study how dogs are able to detect low blood sugar in their diabetic owners. Diabetics suffer from a condition by which the pancreas does not produce enough insulin to maintain a healthy level of blood glucose. If a diabetic person's blood glucose level drops too low, he or she may become unconscious or even go into a coma.

One dog who has had a lot of success in identifying low blood sugar is a two-year-old named Pete. Pete, like all dogs, has a sense of smell 10,000 times more sensitive than that of humans. Pete's owner is a scientist with Eli Lilly, and she is trying to figure out what is inside a dog's nose that makes it possible to smell low blood sugar. If the researcher can figure out how to reproduce that kind of sensitivity, more diabetic people can be protected from the consequences of low blood sugar.

Until the researchers isolate what is inside Pete's nose, the Indiana Canine Assistance Network will continue to train dogs like Pete. It's a slow and expensive process, though. In the last ten years, the organization has trained 100 dogs, and the training has cost $25,000 or more for each dog. http://www.diabetesadvocacy.com/diabetes_news.htm

5. Which sentence from this article best explains how dogs can help diabetic owners?

Ⓐ "In the last ten years, the organization has trained 100 dogs, and the training has cost $25,000 or more for each dog."
Ⓑ "If the researcher can figure out how to reproduce that kind of sensitivity, more diabetic people can be protected from the consequences of low blood sugar."
Ⓒ "Pete's owner is a scientist with Eli Lilly, and she is trying to figure out what is inside a dog's nose that makes it possible to smell low blood sugar."
Ⓓ "If a diabetic person's glucose drops too low he or she may become unconscious or even drop into a coma."

6. Based on the sentence, "if the researcher can figure out how to reproduce that sensitivity, more diabetic people can be protected from the consequences of low blood sugar," you can infer that...

Ⓐ The researcher wants to come up with technology that can help detect low blood sugar similar to how dogs can detect low blood sugar.
Ⓑ The researcher wants to breed more dogs with the same sensitivity to low blood sugar as Pete.
Ⓒ The researcher wants to train more dogs to detect low blood sugar levels in diabetic patients.
Ⓓ The researcher wants to reproduce the same sensitivity in herself so she can detect low blood sugar levels in diabetic patients.

7. Which sentence from the passage best explains why scientists want to reproduce the sensitivity rather than simply training dogs to recognize the sensitivity?

Ⓐ "It's a slow and expensive process though."

Ⓑ "Until the researchers isolate what is inside Pete's nose, the Indiana Canine Assistance Net work will continue to train dogs like Pete."

Ⓒ "If the researcher can figure out how to reproduce that kind of sensitivity, more diabetic people can be protected from the consequences of low blood sugar."

Ⓓ "One dog who has had a lot of success in identifying low blood sugar is a two year old named Pete."

Class Rules and Expectations
7th Grade-Reading

1. NO HUNTING! Be nice.
2. No gum allowed.
3. You must be in your seat when the bell rings. If you are not, you are tardy and appropriate consequences will be enforced.
4. Students start the class...not the bell.
5. Make-up work is the student's responsibility.
6. No rude gestures or comments. If you cannot say something nice, do not say anything at all.
7. Have all of your materials with you and ready at the beginning of class.
8. There are no dumb questions...ask if you do not understand.
9. Respect others. This includes teachers as well as students.
10. Keep your hands and feet to yourself.
11. Every student will learn and have fun.

8. Which rule explains what happens if a student is late to class?

Ⓐ Rule 3
Ⓑ Rule 4
Ⓒ Rule 5
Ⓓ Rule 8

The Assassination of President Lincoln
April 14, 1865

Shortly after 10 p.m. on April 14, 1865, actor, John Wilkes Booth entered the presidential box at Ford's Theatre in Washington D.C. and fatally shot President Abraham Lincoln. As Lincoln slumped forward in his seat, Booth leapt onto the stage and escaped through the back door. A doctor in the audience rushed over to examine the paralyzed president. Lincoln was then carried across the street to Petersen's Boarding House, where he died early the next morning.

Lincoln was the first president assassinated in U.S. history. Why did Booth do it? He thought it would aid the South, which had just surrendered to Federal forces. It had nearly the opposite effect, ending Lincoln's plans for a rather generous peace. Booth did not act alone. This "wanted" poster appeared everywhere, offering a reward for the arrest of Booth and his accomplices. The conspirators were all captured, and Booth was shot while trying to escape from Union soldiers.

The whole country grieved the death of President Lincoln. As the nine-car funeral train carried President Lincoln home for burial in Springfield, Illinois, people showed up at train stations all along the way to pay their respects.

"The Assassination of President Lincoln." The Assassination of President Lincoln. N.p., n.d. Web. 15 July 2013.

9. Which sentence best explains why Booth shot Lincoln?

- (A) "He thought it would aid the South, which had just surrendered to Federal forces."
- (B) "It had nearly the opposite effect, ending Lincoln's plans for a rather generous peace."
- (C) "This "wanted" poster appeared everywhere, offering a reward for the arrest of Booth and his accomplices."
- (D) "The conspirators were all captured, and Booth was shot while trying to escape from Union soldiers."

10. Which detail in the first sentence helps you infer how Booth was able to get access to the theater?

- (A) It was 10 p.m.
- (B) He was an actor.
- (C) He was going to the presidential box.
- (D) It was on April 14.

11. Which sentence best SHOWS how Lincoln's death affected people across the country?

- (A) Lincoln was the first president assassinated in U.S. history.
- (B) Booth did not act alone.
- (C) The conspirators were all captured.
- (D) … people showed up at train stations all along the way to pay their respects.

Chapter 3

Lesson 2: Get Right to the Point

Let us understand the concept with an example.

Over the course of history in the United States, necessity and economics have combined to change the way we transport cargo, consisting of either living creatures (people, animals and plants) and nonliving items. When the colonies were first settled, walking or riding horses or using horses, oxen or mules with carriages, stagecoaches and wagons were the common forms of transportation on land. But these were relatively slow, limited in the number of passengers or cargo they could carry, and cumbersome when having to deal with natural forces like streams, mountains, forests, heavy snow, heavy rain and the resulting mud. And horses required a lot of care – food, water, shelter, horseshoes, harnesses and saddles.

But then someone invented the steam engine. Steam-driven locomotives, which used plentiful coal and water, could transport many more people and cargo than animals pulling wagons, and at a greater speed over a long distance. All that was needed were rails (instead of roads), both of which required a lot of initial effort, but once built, required much less effort to maintain. And later on, the hauling power of trains was increased with the introduction of the diesel engine, which had the further advantage of not needing a fireman to keep shoveling coal into the boiler of the steam train. Yes, maintenance was required, but it was worth it because of the long lifespan of the engine and the rails. Steam engines also drove factory machines and fire engines, an improvement over bucket brigades. In 1903, the demonstration of the first heavier than air flight by the Wright brothers ushered in the age of flight. While early aircraft were severely limited in the number of people or amount of cargo they could carry, the development of more powerful gasoline engines increased the cargo carrying capacity, speed and distance an aircraft could fly. And the introduction of the jet engine increased these capabilities even more. Also, the gasoline engine was an important factor in making automobiles more useful than a horse, oxen or mules for transporting cargo. An advantage of aircraft was the speed with which cargo could be transported, for purposes of conducting business meetings, peaceful trade or warfare, and rescue missions.

Your assignment: Apply the requirements of this standard to the text.

Here is what you might write.

The central ideas are: necessity drives invention and economics drives invention. The text infers that from the early days of the colonies until today, there were people with ambition and motivation. These ingredients led people to invent things to meet their needs, such as for food, medical treatments or convenience and to influence the economy by creating rewards such as income or property.

Examples of necessities were improvements in firefighting equipment using steam and gasoline engines, and the use of these and jet engines to rapidly deliver rescuers and their equipment to locations where needed, including remote locations unreachable by road. Vehicles such as ambulances became more efficient, able to transport patients and medical personnel more quickly.

Economics drove the inventions of equipment that was faster, more powerful, more versatile and more efficient and cheaper to operate than its predecessors. These inventions made manufacturing more efficient, which meant increased output of products at lower and lower costs. Same with the transportation of goods and services.

You can scan the QR code given below or use the url to access additional EdSearch resources including videos and mobile apps related to *Get Right to the Point*.

Get Right to the Point

URL	QR Code
http://www.lumoslearning.com/a/ri72	

Fall Leaves
USDA Forest Service

We almost always think of trees as being green, but there is one time of year when their leaves turn a myriad orange, red, yellow, and brown: the beautiful and chilly days of fall. Those living in the Eastern or Northern United States come to anticipate the change in color starting in September or October every single year. But what causes the leaves to change color, and why?

Just like many animals that hibernate for the winter, trees experience a unique change during the winter months. During summer, for instance, plants use the process of photosynthesis to transform carbon dioxide found in the air into organic compounds like sugars using energy from the sun. During the winter, however, there is less light to go around, and their ability to create food from the photosynthesis process is limited.

What does that have to do with a leaf's color? The substance that allows trees to turn carbon dioxide into food (chlorophyll) is also the cause of the leaf's green sheen. As the photosynthesis process wanes in the colder months due to the lack of sun, so does its greenish hue, allowing other elements present in the leaf to show through. Believe it or not, the yellows and oranges that appear in fall have actually been there all year in the form of nutrients like carotene (also found in carrots). The intense green color of the chlorophyll had simply overshadowed them. But what about the reds and browns? And what causes the leaves to fall away after they change color?

The bright reds and purples in each leaf come from a strong antioxidant that many trees create on their own because of their protective qualities. The antioxidant helps protect the trees from the sun, lower their freezing levels, and protect them from frost. As winter comes, so does the need for the antioxidant (similar to the way a dog gets more fur during winter to stay warmer).

As for the leaves falling, that is another story. At the base of each leaf, there is a layer of cells that carry food and water from the leaf to the tree during the summer months to keep it fed. In the fall, that layer actually starts to harden, preventing the passage of nutrients. Because of this, the nutrients and waste that previously passed from the leaf into the tree become trapped in the leaf with no fresh water to clean it. Not only does this cause the leaf to turn brown, eventually it causes the cells within it to harden so much that the leaf tears and blows away. Thus the pile of leaves you enjoyed jumping in as a child.

Because each tree, and each leaf, contains a unique amount of nutrients depending on how well-nourished it was over the spring and summer, the way each leaf breaks down during the winter months is also quite different. The result is the unique and complex facet of colors we see in each neighborhood or forest each fall.

http://www.sciencemadesimple.com/leaves.htm

After reading the story, enter the details in the map below. This will help you to answer the questions with ease.

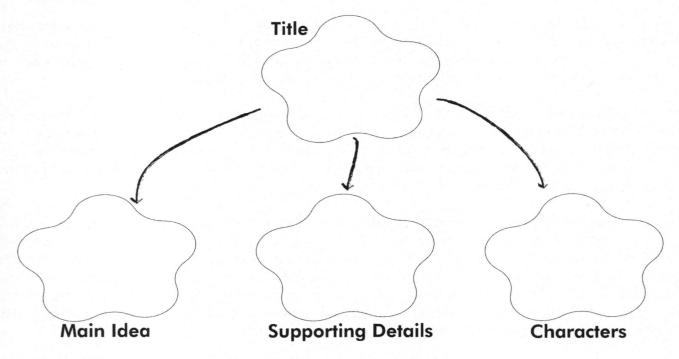

Title

Main Idea   **Supporting Details**   **Characters**

1. **What is the main theme of the above passage?**

   Ⓐ Fall weather
   Ⓑ What happens to the leaves during fall
   Ⓒ The life cycle of a tree during fall
   Ⓓ Weather during fall

2. **What is the purpose of this excerpt? Circle the correct answer choice.**

   Ⓐ to explain why leaves change colors and drop from trees.
   Ⓑ to describe the colors of leaves in the fall
   Ⓒ to tell the reader about the North East part of the country
   Ⓓ to define chlorophyll

History of Olympics
From *Ancient Olympics Guide*

Even though the modern Olympic Games are held every four years, they bear little resemblance to the athletic contests held at Olympia in Greece in ancient times.

The games were open to competitors from all Greece, and the contests included chariot racing, horse racing, running, wrestling, boxing, and the pentathlon, a contest involving jumping, quoit- throwing, javelin throwing, running and wrestling.

Scholars date the earliest contests at 776 B.C., more than two and a half thousand years ago. The first trophies that were won consisted not of gold medals and cups but of simple crowns of olive leaves. Women and slaves were admitted neither as contestants nor as spectators. The classical games ceased to be held probably about A.D.393.

Much of the credit for the revival of the Games held at Athens in 1896 goes to Baron Pierre de Coubertin, a French classical scholar, who greatly admired the sporting ideals of the ancient Greeks. As an educationist and lover of amateurism, he looked upon physical exercise as an essential feature of balanced education. Forty-two events were contested and new disciplines such as cycling, hurdling, the high jump, shooting and gymnastics were introduced.

One of the most popular events of the modern Olympics is the marathon. This very tiring twenty-six mile foot race over an open course is the supreme test of the runners' endurance. The marathon was not a part of the ancient Olympics although it originated in Greece. And, finally, a more recent development in the Olympics is the introduction of the winter games, which were started in 1924. They are held separately from the summer games but in the same year. The Winter Olympics provide competition in skiing, speed and figure skating, ice hockey, and rifle shooting. Such cold weather sports could never have developed in the warm climate of Greece.

After reading the story, enter the details in the map below. This will help you to answer the question with ease.

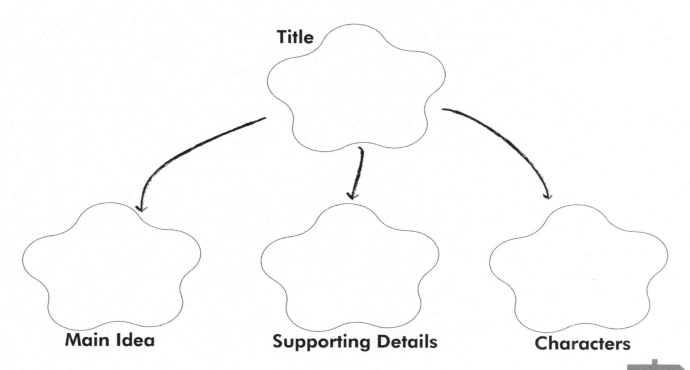

3. Choose a suitable alternate title for this passage.

- Ⓐ The Winter Sports
- Ⓑ The Games' Growth
- Ⓒ How the Olympics Evolved
- Ⓓ Popular Sports

Egyptian Pyramids

Today, we have high-tech cranes and other machines to help us create massive skyscrapers and other modern works of architecture. Still, some of the most breathtaking architecture in the world, such as the ancient pyramids of Egypt, were created before those high-tech machines even existed. So how did those ancient civilizations create them?

Believe it or not, though they are one of the most studied and admired relics in history, there is no evidence to tell historians exactly how the Ancient Egyptians built the pyramids. Thus, they have been left to create their own theories as to how Egyptians created such amazing and awe-inspiring works of art.

According to one theory, the Egyptians placed logs under the large stone blocks in order to roll or transport them to the pyramid building location. Large groups of men would work to push or pull them into place (although historians also disagree on whether these men were slaves or skilled artisans). Still more, once the men moved the blocks to the pyramid location, they needed to lift them to ever-increasing heights to reach the top levels of the pyramid as it grew. Without modern cranes, many scientists have been baffled as to how they were able to do it. Some believe they used a ramp system that would allow them to roll the blocks upward around or through the pyramids; others believe they must have used a combination of pulleys and lifts. Still, most agree that once they did, they used a mixture of gravel and limestone to help fill any crevices and hold the mound together.

With such a primitive yet impressive building process, it's obvious that the pyramids must have taken a great deal of time to build. With an estimated 2 million blocks weighing an average of 2.5 million tons each, the Great Pyramid of Giza, for instance, is estimated to have taken some 20 years to build. At 481 feet tall, it held the record of tallest building for 3,800 years – not bad for a building created almost entirely by hand.

Even though scientists don't know exactly how the Egyptians did it, they do know that the method the Egyptians used to build pyramids changed over time. In the early days, the pyramids were made completely of stone, with limestone used to create the main body and higher quality limestone being used for the smooth outer casing. Later on, the pyramids were made mostly of mud brick with a limestone casing. Though they were likely much easier to build, they didn't stand up nearly as well over time, leaving archaeologists with even fewer clues about their creation.

http://en.wikipedia.org/wiki/Egyptian_pyramid_construction_techniques

After reading the story, enter the details in the map below. This will help you to answer the questions with ease.

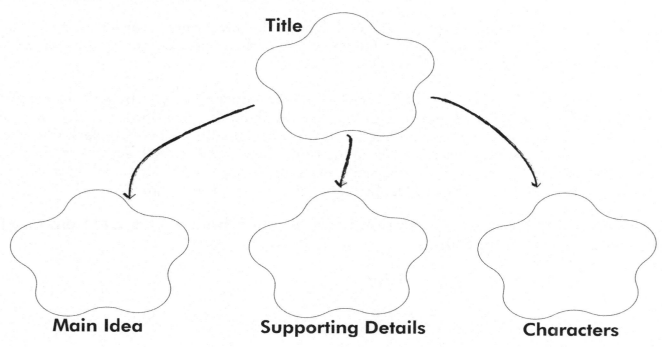

Title

Main Idea   Supporting Details   Characters

4. What is the main idea of this selection?

Ⓐ The Egyptians had a very advanced way of building the pyramids.
Ⓑ The Ancient Egyptians built the pyramids by hand.
Ⓒ To this day, historians are not entirely sure how the Egyptians built the pyramids.

5. What is the theme of this excerpt?

Ⓐ how the Egyptian army was used to build the pyramids.
Ⓑ several theories about how the Egyptian pyramids were built.
Ⓒ how the boulders were carved for the Egyptian pyramids.
Ⓓ how the Egyptians used architecture to build the pyramids

From <u>Guiseppi Verdi</u>
by Thomas Trapper

Whenever the organ man came into the village of Roncole, in Italy (where Verdi was born, October 10, 1813), Verdi could not be kept indoors. But he followed the wonderful organ and the wonderful man who played it, all day long, as happy as he could be.

When Guiseppi was seven years old, his father, though only a poor innkeeper, bought him a spinet, a sort of small piano. So faithfully did the little boy practice that the spinet was soon quite worn out and new jacks, or hammers, had to be made for it. This was done by Stephen Cavaletti, who wrote a message on one of the jacks telling that he made them anew and covered them with leather, and fixed the pedal, doing all for nothing, because the little boy, Guiseppi Verdi, showed such willingness to practice and to learn. Thus the good Stephen thought this was pay enough.

After reading the story, enter the details in the map below. This will help you to answer the question with ease.

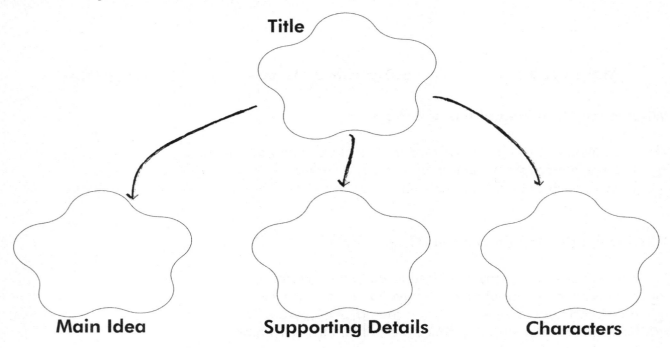

Title

Main Idea   **Supporting Details**   **Characters**

6. What is the main idea the writer wants the reader to draw from these paragraphs?

    Ⓐ Verdi was drawn and committed to music from an early age.
    Ⓑ Verdi was hard on his spinet because he played it every day.
    Ⓒ Verdi practiced the spinet for too many hours each day.
    Ⓓ Verdi lived in Italy when he was a child.

Gettysburg Address

Four score and seven years ago, our fathers brought forth on this continent, a new nation, conceived in liberty and dedicated to the proposition that all men are created equal.

Now we are engaged in a great civil war, testing whether that nation or any nation so conceived and so dedicated, can long endure. We are met on a great battlefield of that war. We have come to dedicate a portion of that field as a final resting place for those who here gave their lives that that nation might live. It is altogether fitting and proper that we should do this.

But in a larger sense, we cannot dedicate - we cannot consecrate - we cannot hallow - this ground. The brave men, living and dead, who struggled here, have consecrated it, far above our poor power to add or detract. The world will little note, nor long remember, what we say here, but it can never forget what they did here. It is for us the living, rather, to be dedicated here to the unfinished work which they who fought here have thus far so nobly advanced. It is rather for us to be here dedicated to the great task remaining before us - that from these honored dead we take increased devotion to that cause for which they gave the last full measure of devotion - that we here highly resolve that these dead shall not have died in vain - that this nation, under God, shall have a new birth of freedom - and that government of the people, by the people, for the people, shall not perish from the earth.

President Abraham Lincoln - November 19, 1863

After reading the story, enter the details in the map below. This will help you to answer the question with ease.

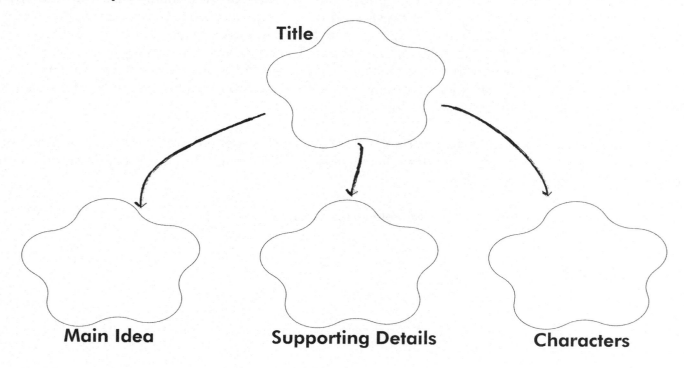

7. What is Lincoln's purpose in delivering this speech?

Ⓐ To encourage people to not give up on the country being united as one country
Ⓑ To encourage people to end the war and honor the dead
Ⓒ To convince the south to surrender so that it would end more quickly
Ⓓ To build a new cemetery at this location

The bread-and-butter of the film industry is the action movie. Each summer, audiences can expect to see car chases, gunfights, and explosions, and studios can expect to see millions and millions of dollars in return. Though most viewers and critics see these movies as "fluff" entertainment, there is one director who puts as much heart and soul into his "fluff" as any number of talented directors put into their "serious" movies. His name is John Woo. Even though you may not have heard about him, he is widely considered to be the best contemporary director of action films working anywhere.

John Woo, after many years of hard work, has become known as the world's best action film director. His action sequences have become the stuff of legend and are now the basis from which all other action movies are judged. More importantly, along with the bloodshed, Woo has proven that he can create real characters with real emotions that the audience can sympathize with.

He's a bold visual stylist who stages a kinetic scene of over-the-top gunplay with fluid camera movements, extremely long takes, and perfectly timed choreography of movement. Woo's on the spot improvising that also delivered one of the most amazing gun-blazing sequences when in the middle of the movie, a full-blooded gunfight erupts, but is played out in balletic slow-motion to "Somewhere Over The Rainbow," heard through child's headphones. The song was put in to represent the child's innocence, and also to show how that innocence is being corrupted by the violence around him. Woo gets upset when he hears about violence, and when he is angry and directing, he thinks, "let's hit the villain with more bullets, let's beat him up just a little bit more."

Woo considers himself to be an artist, as he does once in a while get emotional while filming one of his movies. This goes to show that he relates his movies well to real life, and has an understanding of what it takes to become a great director.

http://www.hollywoodauditions.com/news/celebrities/directors.htm

After reading the story, enter the details in the map below. This will help you to answer the question with ease.

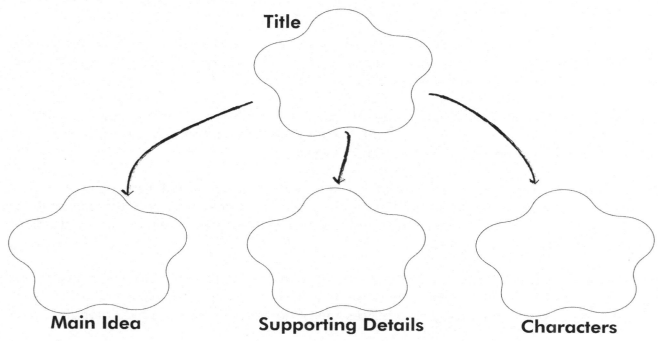

Title

Main Idea   **Supporting Details**   **Characters**

8. What is an appropriate title for this article?

Ⓐ John Woo Puts the Action in Action!
Ⓑ A History of Action Movies
Ⓒ The Director who Hates Violence
Ⓓ Somewhere over the Rainbow

The Great Round World and What's Going On In It
magazine article -- Anonymous author

Did you ever see a house move?

If you have not, you have missed a very funny sight.

Imagine driving along a country road, and meeting a three-story house making a journey along the highway to new quarters.

There is a good deal of this to be seen just now at Katonah, New York.

A year or so ago the Croton water-shed water, which is in use in New York City, was found to be impure.

A commission was appointed to go and examine the Croton Water-Shed. This meant that they were to examine the little streams, and brooks, and rivers, and lakes, which supplied the water to our aqueduct, and see what the trouble was.

They found that along the banks of these streams and lakes, in villages and out in the country, a great many dwelling-houses and shanties had been built, the occupants of which were in the habit of throwing all sorts of rubbish into the water, making it unfit for drinking.

In consequence of this, all of the houses were ordered to be torn down or moved away, and one small village of shanties was destroyed. Among others, the inhabitants of Katonah were ordered to move, that the banks of the stream might be cleared of dwellings.

Katonah has a railroad depot, and a post office, and thinks a good deal of itself.
When the Water-Shed Commission said that it must move or be destroyed, the residents of Katonah gathered together, and decided that rather than be wiped off the face of the map, it would pick up its houses and move itself.

So a new Katonah was established, about a quarter of a mile away from the old one, and just outside the Water-Shed on which it was forbidden to build, for fear of spoiling the water for New York.
For several months past there has been a procession of houses moving from old Katonah to new.

http://www.gutenberg.org/files/15326/15326.txt

After reading the story, enter the details in the map below. This will help you to answer the question with ease.

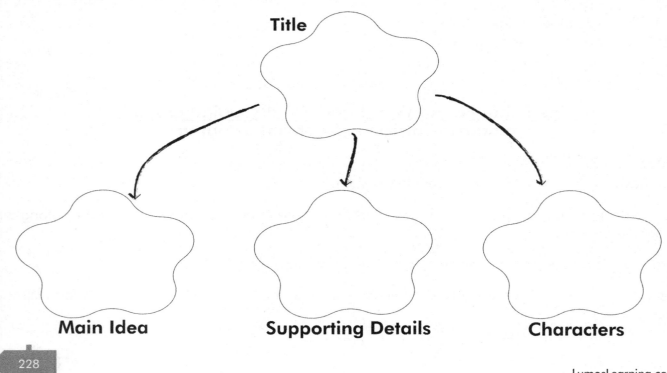

Title

Main Idea   **Supporting Details**   **Characters**

9. What is the main idea of this article?

Ⓐ The water in Kantonah is polluted.
Ⓑ Many people are moving their homes because the water in Kantonah is polluted.
Ⓒ Everyone should have the experience of seeing a house being moved.
Ⓓ The people of Kantonah are angry because of the quality of their drinking water.

The Great Round World and What's Going On In It
magazine article -- Anonymous author

The news comes from Hamburg that the strike of the dock laborers is over.

The strikers have been beaten because of their lack of money.

In No. 7 of The Great Round World, you will find an account of the strike, and if you will also refer to No. 10, you will see that it was thought that the strikers could not hold out very much longer.

The money the strikers expected to receive from other labor unions to help them was so slow in coming that the men and their families were in want, and no man is likely to stand out for the benefit of others when his own children are suffering from cold and hunger.

The men have gone back to their old employers and asked for work. The pity of it all is, however, that during the strike, others have been taken on in their places, and the employers have now no work to give them.

After holding out since the end of October, and refusing the masters' offer to give them $1.10 a day, and let all future troubles be settled by arbitration, the strikers have had to give in without gaining a single point. It is very sad.

After reading the story, enter the details in the map below. This will help you to answer the question with ease.

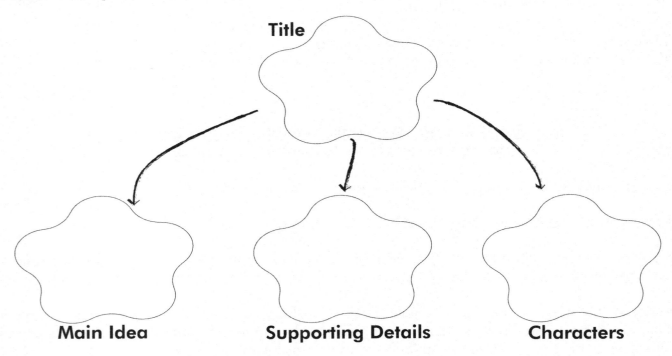

Title

Main Idea   **Supporting Details**   **Characters**

10. What is this short article mostly about?

Ⓐ Where to find more information about the Hamburg workers' strike
Ⓑ The end result of the Hamburg workers' strike
Ⓒ The causes of the Hamburg workers' strike
Ⓓ The Hamburg unions

What You Need to Be a Baseball Card Collector

The main thing you need to start a baseball card collection is cards, of course! Baseball cards are usually sold in packs of four or more cards. Large chain stores like Walmart and Target, as well as drug stores, are the easiest places to find packs of baseball cards. You can also find cards at special baseball card shops. You should plan on spending around $2.99 for each pack of baseball cards you purchase. Once you've started your collection by buying packs of cards, you'll probably find that there are one or two specific cards you want that you haven't been able to get in packs. The best places to get single cards are the baseball card shows held at malls or convention centers or on the Internet. You can also trade cards with another baseball card collector. A lot of times, a friend has the card you're looking for. Because you might also have a card he or she wants, trading is a great way to build the collection that you want. Plus, it doesn't cost you a cent!

http://answers.yahoo.com/question/index?qid=20100526011332AA7fhAF

After reading the story, enter the details in the map below. This will help you to answer the question with ease.

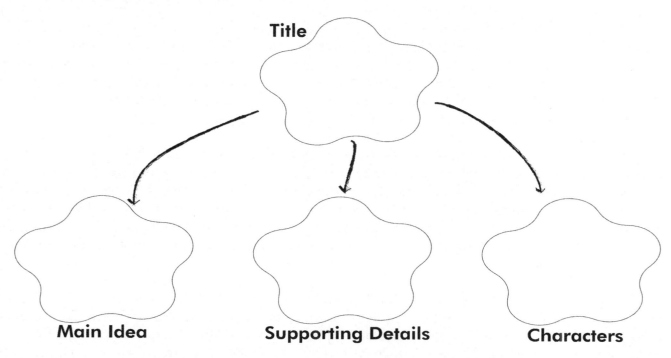

Title

Main Idea

Supporting Details

Characters

11. What message does the author want the reader to walk away from this paragraph with?

Ⓐ A new baseball card collector should plan on having lots of money and time to start his collection.

Ⓑ A new baseball card collector must be very organized.

Ⓒ Baseball card collecting is easy and inexpensive.

Ⓓ The best way to get baseball cards is to trade them.

ARCHIMEDES
from Stories of Invention by Edward E. Hale

Archimedes was born in Syracuse in the year 287 B. C. and was killed there in the year 212 B. C. He is said to have been a relation of Hiero, King of Syracuse; but he seems to have held no formal office known to the politicians. Like many other such men, however, from his time down to Ericsson, he came to the front when he was needed, and served Syracuse better than her speech-makers. While he was yet a young man, he went to Alexandria to study; and he was there the pupil of Euclid, the same Euclid whose Geometry is the basis of all the geometry of to-day.

While Archimedes is distinctly called, on very high authority, "the first mathematician of antiquity," and while we have nine books which are attributed to him, we do not have--and this is a great misfortune--any ancient biography of him. He lived seventy-five years, for most of that time probably in Syracuse itself, and it would be hard to say how much Syracuse owed to his science. At the end of his life he saved Syracuse from the Romans for three years, during a siege in which, by his ingenuity, he kept back Marcellus and his army. At the end of this siege he was killed by a Roman soldier when the Romans entered the city.

The books of his which we have are on the "Sphere and Cylinder," "The Measure of the Circle," "Conoids and Spheroids," "On Spirals," "Equiponderants and Centres of Gravity," "The Quadrature of the Parabola," "On Bodies floating in Liquids," "The Psammites," and "A Collection of Lemmas." The books which are lost are "On the Crown of Hiero;" "Cochleon, or Water-Screw;" "Helicon, or Endless Screw;"

"Trispaston, or Combination of Wheels and Axles;" "Machines employed at the Siege of Syracuse;" "Burning Mirror;" "Machines moved by Air and Water;" and "Material Sphere."

12. Part A
Why are Archimedes' works included in the book Stories of Invention? (Hint: See title)

Ⓐ   He was a good friend of the people publishing the books.
Ⓑ   Many of the titles of his books are about machines and tools used in new and different ways.
Ⓒ   All books in his time were about inventions, so that was the only kind to write.
Ⓓ   He loved machines and liked making new ones.

Part B
What type of career might a person who reads Archimedes have?

Carnivorous Plant

Venus Fly Traps are difficult to locate because they are endangered. This means that even in the places where they grow the best, you'll find fewer and fewer plants. For a long time, people would go to these areas and dig up Venus Fly Traps to take home because they are so different and rare. Over time, the number of plants growing in the wild has gotten smaller. Now it's illegal to pick a Venus Fly Trap from the wild. In fact, if you do try and take one home, you could have to pay a fine of up to $2000! Because people still love to look at these unique plants, the Carolina Beach Park in North Carolina has created a safe preserve to grow, protect, and show off Venus Fly Traps.

13. What is the best summary of this paragraph? Circle the correct answer choice.

Ⓐ Venus Fly Traps are beautiful plants
Ⓑ Venus Fly Traps need special nutrients to grow and reproduce
Ⓒ Venus Fly Traps are endangered plants and there are laws to ensure their preservation
Ⓓ Venus Fly Traps are used to prepare delicious food items

Chapter 3

Lesson 3: Relationship Between People and Events

Let us understand the concept with an example.

Global Warming

For many years, scientists have been studying the effects of temperature on living organisms on planet Earth. In the last few years, there has been an increase in the earth's atmospheric and oceanic temperatures, which has been called global warming. Global warming has been recognized as a very important environmental phenomenon that can have dramatic and devastating effects on the environment of planet Earth.

Scientists in one group, we'll call it Group A, believe the theory that global warming is caused by the increase in certain gases (such as carbon dioxide) in the atmosphere that occurs when warmth from the sun is trapped in the Earth's atmosphere by a layer of gases (such as carbon dioxide) and water vapor. They refer to this as the "greenhouse effect." This group believes that human activities, such as manufacturing, deforestation and pollution are the primary contributors to the greenhouse effect.

Group A provides the following key details to support their theory: An IPCC (United Nations' Intergovernmental Panel on Climate Change) report, based on the work of some 2,500 scientists in more than 130 countries, concluded that humans have caused all or most of the current planetary warming. Human-caused global warming is often called anthropogenic climate change. Industrialization, deforestation, and pollution have greatly increased atmospheric concentrations of water vapor, carbon dioxide, methane, and nitrous oxide, all greenhouse gases that help trap heat near Earth's surface. Humans are pouring carbon dioxide into the atmosphere much faster than plants and oceans can absorb it.

Also, that 97% of the climate scientists surveyed believe "global average temperatures have increased" during the past century; and 97% think human activity is a significant contributing factor in changing mean global temperatures.

Scientists in another group, we'll call it Group B, believe the theory that global warming is not just a recent phenomenon, but is a natural phenomenon that has been occurring for thousands of years as part of a cycle of warming and cooling of the earth's atmosphere, and that human activity is only a minor contributor.

Group B provides the following key details to support their theory: 31,000 scientists reject global warming and say "no convincing evidence" that humans can or will cause global warming. This claim originates from an organization which published an online petition that they claim 31,000

234

scientists have signed.

Also, they mention that some experts point out that natural cycles in the Earth's orbit can alter the planet's exposure to sunlight, which may explain the current trend. Earth has indeed experienced warming and cooling cycles roughly every hundred thousand years due to these orbital shifts, but such changes have occurred over the span of several centuries.

Lastly, they claim that in 2009, hackers unearthed hundreds of emails stored at a university that exposed private conversations among some top-level climate scientists discussing whether certain data that did not support Group A's theory should be released to the public. The email exchanges also refer to statistical tricks used to illustrate climate change trends, according to a report in one major newspaper. Climate change skeptics have heralded the emails as an attempt to fool the public into accepting Group A's theory.

Your assignment: Explain the relationship between Group A and Group B based on the Global Warming article.

This is what you might write.

Group A's theory states that "global warming is caused by the increase of certain gases (such as carbon dioxide) in the atmosphere that occurs when warmth from the sun is trapped in the Earth's atmosphere by a layer of gases (such as carbon dioxide) and water vapor." They cite studies measuring the increase of carbon dioxide and other pollutant gases in the atmosphere over a period of years. They cite one study within the United Nations that supports the theory "that human activities, such as manufacturing, deforestation and pollution are the primary contributors to the greenhouse effect."

As a result of their conclusions, there has been an increased awareness worldwide of the negative effects of global warming, and many governmental and private organizations have spent time and money investigating ways to reduce global emissions. I have personally read literature and seen TV programs promoting the views of Group A. This is an example of how individuals (scientists in Group A) influence events.

Group B's theory states that "global warming is not just a recent phenomenon, but is a natural phenomenon that has been occurring for thousands of years as part of a cycle of warming and cooling of the earth's atmosphere, and that human activity is only a minor contributor." This idea has led Group B to oppose the efforts of Group A as an unnecessary expenditure of time and money, since natural phenomena will cause a change to global warming naturally, without human intervention.

You can scan the QR code given below or use the url to access additional EdSearch resources including videos and mobile apps related to *Relationship Between People and Events.*

 **Relationship Between People and Events**

URL	QR Code
http://www.lumoslearning.com/a/ri73	

1. Which sentence below contains a conjunction indicating a possible relationship?

Ⓐ Due to the large number of offers, Mike had to increase his giveaway time limit.
Ⓑ Kelsey is coming to dinner and a movie with me tonight.
Ⓒ The oven did not cook right because the brownies were not completely done.
Ⓓ The promise of a better life brought many immigrants to America.

2. Which set of words lets the reader know a passage will include sequencing?

Ⓐ Finally, before, after that
Ⓑ Consequently, as a result, therefore
Ⓒ And, if, or
Ⓓ Neither, because of that, and

3. Which set of words lets the reader know a passage will include cause and effect?

Ⓐ Finally, before, after that
Ⓑ Consequently, as a result, therefore
Ⓒ And, if, or
Ⓓ Neither, because of that, and

The Assassination of President Lincoln
April 14, 1865

Shortly after 10 p.m. on April 14, 1865, actor, John Wilkes Booth entered the presidential box at Ford's Theatre in Washington D.C. and fatally shot President Abraham Lincoln. **As Lincoln slumped forward in his seat, Booth leapt onto the stage and escaped through the back door.** A doctor in the audience rushed over to examine the paralyzed president. Lincoln was then carried across the street to Petersen's Boarding House, where he died early the next morning.

Lincoln was the first president assassinated in U.S. history. Why did Booth do it? He thought it would aid the South, which had just surrendered to Federal forces. It had nearly the opposite effect, ending Lincoln's plans for a rather generous peace. Booth did not act alone. This "wanted" poster appeared everywhere, offering a reward for the arrest of Booth and his accomplices. The conspirators were all captured, and Booth was shot while trying to escape from Union soldiers.

The whole country grieved the death of President Lincoln. As the nine-car funeral train carried President Lincoln home for burial in Springfield, Illinois, people showed up at train stations all along the way to pay their respects.

"The Assassination of President Lincoln." The Assassination of President Lincoln. N.p., n.d. Web. 15 July 2013.

4. In the bolded sentence above, what does the word "as" tell the reader?

Ⓐ   A doctor looked at the President.
Ⓑ   Booth waited after shooting Lincoln.
Ⓒ   The president slumped so he was shot.
Ⓓ   Two events occurred at very nearly the same time.

5. What happens second in the passage?

Ⓐ   Booth shot Lincoln
Ⓑ   Booth entered the theater
Ⓒ   Lincoln slumped
Ⓓ   The doctor came to Lincoln's aid.

6. What is the correct statement about the passage?

Ⓐ   Because Lincoln was untrustworthy, Booth shot him.
Ⓑ   The country grieved Lincoln, and this is why they waited for the carriage with his body to go by.
Ⓒ   The country grieved Lincoln, so they lined up at the train station to pay their respects.
Ⓓ   There were no doctors in the theater so Lincoln could not be saved.

7. What best describes the bolded sentence? Circle the correct answer choice.

Ⓐ   flashback
Ⓑ   sequence of events
Ⓒ   compare contrast
Ⓓ   cause and effect

8. What happened last in the SECOND paragraph?

Chapter 3

Lesson 4: Getting Technical

Let us understand the concept with an example.

Here are definitions of the words "technical," "figurative" and "connotative" with examples of their usage. In the examples, key words whose meanings you need to determine are shown in bold type.

Technical language (jargon) is connected with one specific subject or used in one specific activity or job. Examples of technical jargon relating to computers are: "motherboard," "chip," "backing up," "crash." Applied to aircraft and flying: "pitch," "yaw," "ailerons," "altimeter."

Examples:

1. The fog limited their visibility as they flew over the mountains; the copilot was continuously looking at the **altimeter** to make sure they were not going to crash into them.

Comment: Mountains are high, they are flying over them, and to avoid crashing into them it seems logical that an altimeter (the first three letters are the same as in altitude) is a measure of height. The tone is one of awareness and need to focus on a potentially dangerous situation.

2. When the computer appeared to **crash**, the first question the technician asked was: "When was the last time you **backed up** your data?"

Comment: Crash indicates that something unexpected or uncontrollable happened (it sets a tone of panic), and because data is stored in the computer and access to the data is provided by it, the crash may have damaged or destroyed the data and/or prevented access to it by a user. "Backing up" implies that a copy of the data has been made and stored on another device so that the copy can be accessed by a user.

Figurative language is a language where the meaning is different from the literal (primary or strict or dictionary) meaning. Another way of defining this term is using language that has other meaning than its normal definition.

Examples: writers use similes or metaphors to compare different objects, such as: her face was as red as a fire engine; the birds soared and swooped in a ballet of movement; she was busy as a bee; he has a heart of stone. She is literally not a fire engine, the birds are not ballet dancers, she is not a bee and his heart is not made of stone.

Connotative language suggests an associated or secondary meaning of a word or expression in addition to its primary meaning.

Examples: A puppy connotes cuteness, warmth and affection. A flyer advertising a cottage "with a view of the mountains or ocean" connotes feelings of peace and awe at the beauty of nature. A tornado or hurricane warning connotes a tone of danger and triggers those in its path to take action to find a suitable shelter.

You can scan the QR code given below or use the url to access additional EdSearch resources including videos and mobile apps related to *Getting Technical*.

Getting Technical

URL	QR Code
http://www.lumoslearning.com/a/ri74	

Scientists in South Korea have developed a type of artificial skin that will allow robots to feel slight vibrations. This skin, developed by weaving together extremely small nano hairs made of polymer or plastic, is more sensitive than human skin. When vibration is applied to this artificial skin, the nano hairs bend against each other to generate an electrical current. Sensors within the skin evaluate the current, and using that information determine the source of the vibration.

Researchers are excited about the potential for this new development. The artificial skin could be used to cover prosthetic limbs to help those who have lost a limb experience more realistic sensations and function more naturally.

http://en.wikipedia.org/wiki/Neuroplasticity

1. What can we assume about the nano hairs described in this article?

Ⓐ   They are not made of natural or organic material.
Ⓑ   They are made of the same material as human hair.
Ⓒ   They generate electricity.
Ⓓ   They were invented by South Korean scientists.

2. Based on this article, we can assume that prosthetic means...

Ⓐ   Natural
Ⓑ   Computerized
Ⓒ   Artificial
Ⓓ   Electrical

3. What is a sensor?

Ⓐ   A device used to transmit a message
Ⓑ   A means by which the body perceives an external stimulus; one of the faculties of sight, smell, hearing, taste, and touch.
Ⓒ   A device that detects or measures a physical property and records, indicates, or otherwise responds to it.
Ⓓ   An artificial limb used by those who have suffered an accident or disease.

An Advertisement for SIMPLE LESSONS IN THE STUDY OF NATURE By I.G. OAKLEY (from <u>The Great Round World and What's Going On In It</u> magazine)

This is a handy little book, which many a teacher who is looking for means to offer children genuine nature study may be thankful to get hold of.

Nature lessons, to be entitled to that name, must deal with what can be handled and scrutinized at leisure by the child, pulled apart, and even wasted. This can be done with the objects discussed in this book; they are under the feet of childhood—**grass, feathers, a fallen leaf, a budding twig, or twisted shell**; these things cannot be far out of the way, even within the stony limits of a city.

Nor are the lessons haphazard dashes at the nearest living thing; on the contrary, they are virtually fundamental, whether with respect to their relation to some of the classified sciences, or with reference to the development of thought and power of expression in the child himself.

The illustrations are few, and scarcely more than figures; it is not meant to be a pretty picture-book, yet is most clearly and beautifully printed and arranged, for its material is to be that out of which pictures are made. It will be found full of suggestions of practical value to teachers who are carrying the miscellaneous work of ungraded schools, and who have the unspeakable privilege of dealing with their pupils untrammeled by cast-iron methods and account-keeping examination records.

Sample copy, 50 Cents, post-paid

WILLIAM BEVERLEY HARISON
3 & 5 W. 18th St. • • • New York City

4. What category do the items in bold all fit into?

    Ⓐ   They are all animals.
    Ⓑ   They are all located in the author's backyard.
    Ⓒ   They are all items a child is likely to walk on when outside.
    Ⓓ   They are all plants.

<u>The Great Round World and What's Going On In It</u>
magazine article -- Anonymous author

Did you ever see a house move?
If you have not, you have missed a very funny sight.

Imagine driving along a country road, and meeting a three-story house making a journey along the highway to new quarters.
There is a good deal of this to be seen just now at Katonah, New York.
A year or so ago the Croton water-shed water, which is in use in New York City, was found to be impure.

A commission was appointed to go and examine the Croton Water-Shed. This meant that they were to examine the little streams, and brooks, and rivers, and lakes, which supplied the water to our aqueduct, and see what the trouble was.

They found that along the banks of these streams and lakes, in villages and out in the country, a great many dwelling-houses and shanties had been built, the occupants of which were in the habit of throwing all sorts of rubbish into the water, making it unfit for drinking.

As a consequence of this, all of the houses were ordered to be torn down or moved away, and one small village of shanties was destroyed. Among others, the inhabitants of Katonah were ordered to move, that the banks of the stream might be cleared of dwellings.

Katonah has a railroad depot, and a post office, and thinks a good deal of itself.

When the Water-Shed Commission said that it must move or be destroyed, the residents of Katonah gathered together, and decided that rather than be wiped off the face of the map, it would pick up its houses and move itself.

So a new Katonah was established, about a quarter of a mile away from the old one, and just outside the Water-Shed on which it was forbidden to build, for fear of spoiling the water for New York. For several months past there has been a procession of houses moving from old Katonah to new.

5. When water is described as impure, it can be assumed that...

   Ⓐ it is brown-colored.
   Ⓑ it is unsafe to drink.
   Ⓒ it is coming from a polluted river.
   Ⓓ it is from a stream.

The Great Round World and What's Going On In It
magazine article -- Anonymous author

The news comes from Hamburg that the strike of the dock laborers is over.
The strikers have been beaten because of their lack of money.
In No. 7 of The Great Round World you will find an account of the strike, and if you will also refer to No. 10, you will see that it was thought that the strikers could not hold out very much longer.

The money the strikers expected to receive from other labor unions to help them was so slow in coming that the men and their families were in want, and no man is likely to stand out for the benefit of others when his own children are suffering from cold and hunger.

The men have gone back to their old employers and asked for work. The pity of it all is, however, that during the strike others have been taken on in their places, and the employers have now no work to give them.

After holding out since the end of October, and refusing the masters' offer to give them $1.10 a day, and let all future troubles be settled by arbitration, the strikers have had to give in without gaining a single point. It is very sad.

6. What does a strike mean in reference to workers?

Ⓐ   A place where people in Hamburg work
Ⓑ   A protest where workers refuse to go to work until their needs are met
Ⓒ   A long list of people who are out of work.
Ⓓ   A missed hit in baseball

Skunk Chow

Skunks are <u>omnivores</u>. They can be found eating nuts, berries, roots, leaves, grasses, and even some types of fungi (mushroom-like plants). For animals, they enjoy dining on rodents such as mice and rats, insects, earthworms, frogs, lizards, toads, and birds. Sometimes when they are unable to find live animals to eat, they become scavengers eating dead animals left behind. When they live close to people's homes, skunks sometimes will even get into trash cans, eating garbage.

When skunks eat, they do not limit themselves to small meals. They like to "pig out" on whatever food they can find. When there is a large amount of food available, skunks get very fat very quickly.

http://en.wikipedia.org/wiki/Skunk

7. Based on information in the selection, what does the underlined term mean?

Ⓐ   An animal that eats only plants
Ⓑ   An animal that eats nuts and berries
Ⓒ   An animal that eats plants and meat
Ⓓ   An animal that is usually awake only at night

Skunk Chow

Skunks are omnivores. They can be found eating nuts, berries, roots, leaves, grasses, and even some types of fungi (mushroom-like plants). For animals, they enjoy dining on rodents such as mice and rats, insects, earthworms, frogs, lizards, toads, and birds. Sometimes when they are unable to find live animals to eat, they become <u>scavengers</u> eating dead animals left behind. When they live close to people's homes, skunks sometimes will even get into trash cans, eating garbage.

When skunks eat, they do not limit themselves to small meals. They like to "pig out" on whatever food they can find. When there is a large amount of food available, skunks get very fat very quickly.

http://en.wikipedia.org/wiki/Skunk

8. Based on information in the selection, what does the underlined term mean?

Ⓐ   An animal that eats other animals.
Ⓑ   An animal that overeats.
Ⓒ   An animal that eats meat from carcasses left by other animals.
Ⓓ   An animal that eats human garbage.

Advertisement from <u>The Great Round World and What's Going On In It</u> magazine -- Anonymous author

Photographs in relief.

A new plan in regard to photographs has been invented.

It is to take a photograph, similar to the one that is to be embossed, and, after cutting it in a certain way, press the portions outward so that it shall stand in relief.

An open mask of the same shape as the photograph is then used, and the two photographs are dampened and pressed tightly together until the face and figure stand out from the card, and the picture looks as if it had been carved in wood.

This is a very ingenious invention, but the work is very difficult, and can only be done by people who are regularly trained to do it.

9. What is the meaning of relief as it is used in this selection?

Ⓐ   To feel as if a weight has been taken off your shoulders
Ⓑ   Embossed
Ⓒ   Sticking outward from the paper
Ⓓ   Sunk into the paper

The Great Round World and What's Going On In It
magazine article -- Anonymous author

At last, beyond any further question, Major William McKinley has been elected President of the United States.

The last formality was complied with when, on February 11th, at one o'clock, the **Senate** of the United States, headed by the Vice-President, filed into the **House of Representatives** to count the vote of the Electoral College, cast in the manner described in The Great Round World, No. 13.

As the Senators entered the House of Representatives, all the Congressmen rose and remained standing while their visitors filed in, two by two.

The little procession was preceded by the officers of the Senate, who carried the ballot boxes.

The work of counting was then commenced by the tellers, and ere long, it was officially announced that William McKinley was the choice of the people for President of the United States.

10. What do the bold terms in this selection have in common?

Ⓐ They are all places William McKinley has worked.
Ⓑ They are all parts of the U.S. government.
Ⓒ They are people who work for the President of the U.S.
Ⓓ The Supreme Court

Class Rules and Expectations

7th Grade-Reading

Class Rules and Expectations

7th Grade-Reading

1. NO HUNTING! Be nice.

2. No gum allowed.

3. You must be in your seat when the bell rings. If you are not, you are tardy and appropriate consequences will be enforced.

4. Students start the class…not the bell.

5. Make-up work is the student's responsibility.

6. No rude gestures or comments. If you cannot say something nice, do not say anything at all.

7. Have all of your materials with you and ready at the beginning of class.

8. There are no dumb questions...ask if you do not understand.

10. Respect others. This included teachers as well as students.

11. Keep your hands and feet to yourself.

13. Every student will learn and have fun.

11.Part.A
Which of the answer choices is NOT an example of number six?

Ⓐ sticking tongue out
Ⓑ rolling eyes at another
Ⓒ waving and smiling
Ⓓ covering ears when someone is sharing

11.Part.B
What does number one mean by "No Hunting?"

Ⓐ Don't look for trouble, or to cause trouble.
Ⓑ The teacher does not agree with hunting.
Ⓒ Students need to be prepared and not have to hunt for their supplies.
Ⓓ The teacher is trying to be cute.

In the Class Novel section of your Reader's Notebook:

· Make a list of the most important characters in Someone Was Watching.

· Make a list of the most important characters in the AR book you're reading.

· Compare a character from each novel. Describe how the characters are alike. Be specific.

For example:

I'm reading a novel called Mockingjay. Katniss (the main character) is like Chris because they are both trying to protect someone they love. Katniss is trying to make the world a safer place and is not sure who she can trust. Chris is searching for the truth about his sister's disappearance, and is not sure who he can trust.

12.Part.A
What does the document tell the reader to be specific about?

Ⓐ Comparing characters
Ⓑ Describing how the characters are alike and different
Ⓒ Comparing characters and describing how they are alike
Ⓓ Contrasting the characters traits

12.Part.B
What is the reader supposed to do with the characters from Someone Was Watching?

Ⓐ make a list of books read
Ⓑ make a list of important characters
Ⓒ make a list characters in their own novel
Ⓓ make a list of items left to do

Chapter 3

Lesson 5: How is it Built? Analyzing structure

Let us understand the concept with an example.

Text structure: Text structure refers to how the information within a written text is organized. The examples below include several different text structures.

Compare-Contrast Structure

This type of text examines the similarities and differences between two or more people, events, concepts, ideas, etc.

Example: Square dancing consists of squares with four couples lining up so each couple forms the side of a square, and everyone faces toward the center of the square. A caller calls out the steps that the dancers follow. In contrast, country-western line dancing requires dancers to form straight lines with all dancers in the lines facing the same direction. The DJ calls out the name of the dance, and the dancers follow the steps that they have been taught for that dance, in time to the music.

Cause-Effect Structure

This structure presents a relationship between the cause of an event, idea, or concept and the effects of carrying out that event, idea, or concept.

Example: Several days of heavy rain will probably cause some areas to be flooded.

Sequence Structure

This text structure gives readers a chronology of events or a list of steps in a procedure.
Example: How did I end up being the mayor of a large eastern city? I grew up in a small town in the mid-west. I went to college in the east as a political science major with a minor in project management. While there I met my future wife, who was from a large eastern city. We moved there and I worked my way up through the dominant political party, organizing and participating in the campaigns of other politicians. This experience acquainted various party members with me and my ideas, and when it came time to select a mayoral candidate, they picked me.

Example: Recipe for making a cake. Step 1..., Step 2..., Step 3...

Problem-Solution Structure

This type of structure sets up a problem or problems, explains the solution, and then discusses the effects of the solution.

Example: Years ago, a serious disease called polio was prevalent in this country. Through research, a researcher discovered a cure for the disease. As a result, a vaccine was developed, and the disease was wiped out.

Descriptive Structure

This type of text structure features a detailed description of something intended to give the reader a mental picture.

Example: There is now a better phone available than the Flip-Phone. It is called a smartphone. It is a little larger than the Flip-Phone, about 3" wide and 4" long, which allows for a larger screen than a Flip-Phone. There is a border around the screen which comes in a choice of colors. There is an on/off button under the screen, and push buttons on the side to control volume, and ring or vibrate settings. There is no cover to open or close to use the phone. The screen is a touch screen with many icons that when touched, offer many different capabilities, from interacting with emails and text messages to selecting applications called apps.

Question-Answer Structure

This text structure starts by posing a question then goes on to answer that question.

Example: Here is what an online FAQ (frequently asked questions) structure looks like:

Q. Is the green light glowing when you turn the unit on?

A. If not, check to make sure the unit is plugged in. If so, plug it into a different electrical outlet. If still not glowing, go to the next step.

Example: Questionnaire

Q1. Do you agree with the present immigration policy?

A1 _ Yes _ No _ Unsure

Example: How major sections contribute to the whole and to the development of the ideas.

Main idea: Over the course of history in the United States, necessity and economics have combined to change the way we transport cargo, either living creatures (people, animals and plants) and non-living items.

Text that supports the statement in the main idea, in chronological order:

Beginning: When the colonies were first settled, walking or riding horses or using horses with carriages, stagecoaches and wagons were the common forms of transportation on land.

Disadvantages of this kind of transportation: But these were relatively slow, limited in the number of passengers or cargo they could carry, and cumbersome when having to deal with natural forces like streams, mountains, forests, heavy snow, heavy rain and the resulting mud. And horses required a lot of care – food, water, shelter, horseshoes, harnesses and saddles.

Next phase: But then someone invented the steam engine.

Advantages: Steam-driven locomotives, which used plentiful coal and water, could transport many more people and cargo than horses and wagons, and at a greater speed over a long distance. All that was needed were rails (instead of roads), both of which required a lot of initial effort, but once built, required much less effort to maintain.

Next phase and advantages: And later on, the hauling power of trains was increased with the introduction of the diesel engine, which had the further advantage of not needing a fireman to keep shoveling coal into the boiler of the steam train. Yes, maintenance was required, but it was worth it because of the long lifespan of the engine and the rails. Steam engines also drove factory machines and fire engines, and improvement over bucket brigades.

Next phase and advantages: In 1903, the demonstration of the first heavier than air flight by the Wright brothers ushered in the age of flight. While early aircraft were severely limited by the number of people or amount of cargo they could carry, the development of the gasoline engine increased the cargo carrying capacity, speed and distance an aircraft could fly. And the introduction of the jet engine increased these capabilities even more. Also, the gasoline engine was an important factor in making automobiles more useful than a horse, oxen or mules for transporting cargo. An advantage of aircraft was the speed with which cargo could be transported, for purposes of conducting business meetings, peaceful trade or warfare, and rescue missions.

You can scan the QR code given below or use the url to access additional EdSearch resources including videos and mobile apps related to *How is it Built? Analyzing structure*.

 **How is it Built? Analyzing structure**

URL	QR Code
http://www.lumoslearning.com/a/ri75	

Bushmen

With so much technology around us each day, it is hard to imagine that anyone in the world would live without television, let alone a cell phone or radio. Still, there are a few cultures that maintain an extremely primitive lifestyle, nearly untouched by the modern world. One of those is commonly known as the Bushmen of Kalahari.

The Bushmen, also known as the "Basarwa" or "San" is found throughout southern Africa in regions of the Kalahari Desert. Nomadic hunters and gatherers by nature, they roam the region living in small kinship groups and, relatively isolated from the rest of society, have developed an extremely unique culture not otherwise seen or understood by modern man.

Unlike English, which is built on a complex system of sounds and letters, the Bushmen speak an extremely unique language made exclusively of clicking sounds. The sounds are created with a sucking action from the tongue, and even the click language itself can vary widely from tribe to tribe, making it extremely difficult to communicate with non-Bush people.

In addition to language, the Bushmen have a very different way of living. Similar to Eskimos, groups of Bushmen will live in "kinship" societies. Led by their elders, they travel together, with women in the group gathering food while men hunt for it. Children, on the other hand, have no duties other than playing. In fact, leisure is an extremely important part of the Bushmen society. Dance, music, and humor are essential, with a focus on family rather than technology or development. Because of this, some people associate the Bush culture with a backward kind of living or low status.

Because of the increased speed of advancement and urban development, the Bushmen culture is in danger. Some have already been forced to switch from hunting to farming due to modernization programs in their countries. Others have been forced to move to certain areas of their countries so that modernization can continue to occur there. With so much development, it's clear that though the Bushmen culture is very rich, it is also in danger of extinction. It is unclear how long the Bush culture will continue.

http://en.wikibooks.org/wiki/Cultural_Anthropology/Print_version'

1. How are the paragraphs in this selection organized?

Ⓐ by topic
Ⓑ from broad ideas to narrow ideas
Ⓒ chronologically
Ⓓ compare and contrast

Baseball Card Collecting

Looking for a new hobby? Do you like baseball? If you answered "yes" to these two questions, baseball card collecting might be a fun pastime for you to begin! Ever since candy and gum manufacturers started putting cards with pictures of popular baseball players into the packages in the 1800s to encourage young people to buy their sweets, kids have been collecting baseball cards. Now, more than 200 years later, baseball card collecting has become a popular hobby for children and adults alike.

What You Need to Be a Baseball Card Collector

The main thing you need to start a baseball card collection is cards, of course! Baseball cards are usually sold in packs of four or more cards. Large chain stores like Walmart and Target, as well as drug stores, are the easiest places to find packs of baseball cards. You can also find cards at special baseball card shops. You should plan on spending around $2.99 for each pack of baseball cards you purchase. Once you've started your collection by buying packs of cards, you'll probably find that there are one or two specific cards you want that you haven't been able to get in packs. The best places to get single cards are the baseball card shows held at malls or convention centers or on the Internet. You can also trade cards with another baseball card collector. A lot of times, a friend has the card you're looking for. Because you might also have a card he or she wants, trading is a great way to build the collection that you want. Plus, it doesn't cost you a cent!

As a baseball card collector, you'll not only need cards, but also a place to put them. Baseball cards can become very valuable. You may get a card in a pack today that is worth ten or twenty times the price you paid for it years down the line. The price that you can sell a baseball card is based on the condition that it is in. For this reason, you want to be sure to have a safe place to store your cards where they won't get damaged. There are lots of different options for storing baseball cards. If you have just a few important cards that you want to protect, you can purchase sleeves to store them in. Sleeves are firm plastic wrappers that are slightly larger than a card. You simply slip the card into the opening on the sleeve, and it is protected from wetness and bending. If you have several cards to store, consider buying boxes or albums. At baseball card shops, you can buy boxes that are specially designed to store baseball cards. For serious baseball card collectors with very valuable cards, cases that lock are the ideal spot to store your cards.

Once you've collected cards for a while, you'll want a way to keep track of what cards you have in your collection. Those with small collections can use a notebook where they write down the players' names and dates of the cards they have. For those with larger collections, the computer is the best place to keep track of their collections. While you can create your own database of cards using a software program on your computer, there are also special baseball card software programs that make it much easier. Beckett, the company that publishes a most popular guide to baseball card values, sells a computer program with the names of cards already loaded into it. You simply need to go in and click on the names of cards to record those that are part of your collection.

Types of Baseball Cards You Can Collect

There are four main companies that produce baseball cards: Topps, Upper Deck, Fleer, and Donruss/Playoff. The most popular and easiest cards to find in stores are those made by Topps and Upper Deck. Each of these companies sells sets of cards. You can either purchase a full set from a baseball card store or show, or you can put together a set by buying enough packs of cards to collect each card in the set. The basic set put out each year by each company is made up of 500 or more cards. Cards feature posed pictures of Major League Baseball players as well as action shots. Within the basic set, there are several subsets that each has a special theme. For example, a card set might have a special subset of homerun heroes within the larger basic set they sell that year. If you buy individual packs of baseball cards to build your set, you'll have a chance at getting insert cards. These are special cards that are printed in limited quantities and are inserted into packs. Insert cards are usually worth more money than basic cards because there are fewer of them produced each year.

For serious baseball collectors, there are premium and specialty cards available. Premium cards come in sets and are printed by the main baseball card companies. These cards are more expensive but feature extra perks. For example, parallel sets of premium cards are the same as the basic set but are fancier. They might have bolder colors or special borders. In addition to premium sets, serious baseball card collectors like to collect rookie cards. A rookie card is a player's first baseball card. The year that the player is placed on a team's roster, he becomes a rookie. Rookie cards become very valuable when the player goes on to have a successful career. Autographed baseball cards are another great find for devoted baseball card collectors. There are two types of autographed cards: those with autographs signed on the actual card and those with autographs cut from other sources that are glued onto the card. This second type is known as cut autos. Cut autos are usually created for players who are no longer living.

A new type of baseball card has just come out in the last few years and may totally change card collecting in the future. Digital baseball cards are now available. These cards don't come printed on paper like traditional baseball cards. Instead, they are purchased and stored on the Internet. One of the major companies, Topps, has already had great success with its line of computer based cards called eTopps.

Whatever type of cards you choose to collect, you're sure to find hours of enjoyment in with your new hobby.

http://en.wikibooks.org/wiki/Cultural_Anthropology/Print_version'

2. **If you wanted to find information about how to start a baseball card collection, which section of this selection would you want to read?**

   Ⓐ what you need to be a baseball card collector
   Ⓑ types of baseball cards you can collect
   Ⓒ what companies make baseball cards
   Ⓓ looking for a new hobby

Table of Contents for <u>Flowers of the Farm</u>

3. Based on this table of contents, what can you tell about how this book is organized?

Ⓐ The book is organized by types of flowers.
Ⓑ The book is organized by locations where the flowers can be found.
Ⓒ The book is organized chronologically.
Ⓓ The book is organized by location and type of flower found on the farm.

All about Skunks

Skunks are animals that people both love and hate. To look at them you'd think they are cuddly little critters. They have cute faces that look almost like those of cats and long black and white fur that seems like it would be soft to pet. You might even think, "Flower on the movie <u>Bambi</u> is sweet and Pepe LePew on cartoons doesn't seem so bad. Certainly I could walk up to a skunk and play with it." Yet getting too close to a skunk is a mistake…a big stinky mistake. Though they may look cute and sweet, they hardly smell so! Skunks produce one of the most powerful odors of all animals.

Black and White with a Long Bushy Tail

Skunks are easy to spot because almost all of them look the same. Most of the 12 species or types of skunks have black, bushy fur with a white stripe running down their long tails. There are a few types of skunks that have brown, grey or red fur and one that has what looks like spots instead of a stripe (but is actually an uneven stripe), but for the most part all skunks look pretty much the same. While their appearances may be very much alike, their sizes can be quite different. A skunk can be anywhere from 15.6 inches long to 37 inches long and can weigh between 1.1 pounds and 18 pounds. Skunks are mostly found in Canada, the United States and Mexico though there are a few kinds that live in the Philippines and Indonesia.

Life as a Skunk

For the most part, skunks like to live by themselves. It's not very often that you'll see a group of skunks together. Usually they only travel in groups when the weather is cold. This way they can sleep close together to stay warm.

Skunks are also nocturnal animals. This means that they sleep during the day and are active when it is dark outside. Skunks cannot see very well, but they have excellent senses of smell and hearing. It's not surprising that skunks would rather move around during the night knowing that sight is not their best sense. In fact, most skunks are killed when they happen to wander on to roads and are hit by cars. They cannot see where they are at very well and walk into these dangerous areas.

Skunk Chow

Skunks are omnivores meaning that they eat both plants and animals. They can be found eating nuts, berries, roots, leaves, grasses, and even some types of fungi (mushroom-like plants). For animals, they enjoy dining on rodents such as mice and rats, insects, earthworms, frogs, lizards, toads and birds. Sometimes when they are unable to find live animals to eat, they become scavengers eating dead animals left behind. When they live close to people's homes, skunks sometimes will even get into trash cans eating garbage.

When skunks eat, they do not limit themselves to small meals. They like to "pig out" on whatever food they can find. When there is a large amount of food available skunks get very fat very quickly.

Oooh, that Smell!

What's the first thing you think of when you see a skunk? If you answered "stink" then you're like most people. Many of us connect skunks with their smell. In fact, the name "skunk" comes from the Algonquin Indian word "seganuku" which means "one who squirts". The stinky odor that you smell when skunks are around comes from a liquid that they can spray from two spots near their tails. This "skunk juice" is a mixture of sulfur chemicals. Sulfur is a mineral that smells a lot like rotten eggs which is why skunk spray is so stinky. Watch out if you get any of this juice on you because it is not easy to get off! Skunk spray is very difficult to remove from clothes, skin, and hair. Though lots of pet owners swear that you can get a skunk's smell out of a dog's hair by washing him in tomato juice, the best way to remove the scent is by washing the stinky area with a mixture of hydrogen peroxide, baking soda, and dishwashing soap. This mixture changes the chemicals in the skunk spray so that it no longer stinks.

Not only does skunk juice smell bad, but it also stings. A person who happens to get this fluid on his skin will feel like he's been stung by a bee. The burning feeling caused by skunk spray is so strong that if you were to get it in your eyes you might become blind for a short period of time!
Even though it might seem to people who have been sprayed by skunks that the reason for their stinky smell is to annoy us, there is actually a much more important reason why these animals make and squirt their juice. Skunks use their spray to protect themselves from predators (other animals who are

trying to attack them). When the average skunk believes that another animal is about to hurt him he will warn it to get away by first stomping his front legs or running forwards and then backwards. Some types of skunks will also hiss or stand up on their front legs. If the predator does not back away, the skunk shoots a cloud of his smelly juice into the air in front of the other animal so that it will have to walk through it to get to him. Skunks are able to spray their juice up to 15 feet. When the predator comes near the cloud of spray he usually is so bothered by the smell that he leaves the skunk alone. The odor from the spray is so powerful that it even keeps bears from attacking skunks!

While skunks are able to use this smelly liquid to protect themselves, they try not to use it too often. They only have enough juice in their bodies at a time to spray 5 or 6 times. It takes a skunk's body at least 2 weeks to make more juice. Luckily, once a predator has been sprayed once by a skunk he doesn't usually forget the event. Many animals will stay away from skunks because they remember their horrible smell. As soon as they see a white stripe on a black body they will run away!

Beyond the Stink

Skunks aren't just stinky animals. They can be very helpful to people. Because they enjoy eating insects and rats sometimes people will purposely put skunks in their yards, on their farms or in their barns to help keep the number of pesky critters down. Some people even enjoy keeping skunks as pets!

http://www.pbs.org/wnet/nature/is-that-skunk-do-skunks-make-good-pets/4569/

4. If you wanted to find information about how to get the smell of skunk spray out of your dog's fur, which section should you read?

Ⓐ Black and White with a Long Bushy Tail
Ⓑ Life as a Skunk
Ⓒ Skunk Chow
Ⓓ Oooh, that Smell!

5. What does each heading in this selection tell the reader?

Ⓐ An interesting fact about skunks
Ⓑ What the selection is about
Ⓒ The title of another article about skunks
Ⓓ The main idea of the paragraphs below the heading

The Great Round World and What's Going On In It
magazine article -- Anonymous author

Blondin, the celebrated tight-rope walker, has just died in London, at the age of seventy-three.

The performance which made him famous was the crossing of Niagara Falls on the tight-rope.

Blondin was a Frenchman, his father having been one of Napoleon's soldiers.

A story is told of him that when he was five years old, he saw an acrobat performing on a tight-rope.

He was so pleased with what he saw, that when he got home, he stretched a rope between two posts, and, as soon as his mother was out of the way, took his father's fishing-rod, and, using it as a balancing pole, made his first appearance as a tight-rope walker.

He was trained for an acrobat and tight-rope walking and came to this country with a troupe of pantomimes.

While here, he visited Niagara Falls, and the idea at once struck him that, if he dared to cross those terrible waters on a rope, his fortune would be made. He made up his mind to try it, and stayed in the village of Niagara for weeks until he had learned just how it would be possible for him to perform the feat.

Then he set about getting the scheme well-advertised and securing plenty of money for himself if he succeeded in accomplishing it.

On August 17th, 1859, he made the trip across the Falls in the presence of 50,000 spectators.

His rope was 175 feet above the waters.

He was not satisfied with merely walking across; he crossed again blindfolded and then carrying a man on his back, and once again wheeling a barrow before him.

In the summer of 1860, he crossed once more in the presence of the Prince of Wales and carried a man on his back, whom he set down on the rope six times, while he rested.

6. How is this selection organized?

Ⓐ Chronological Order
Ⓑ Order of Importance
Ⓒ Causes and Effects
Ⓓ Comparison-Contrast

Advertisement from <u>The Great Round World and What's Going On In It</u> magazine -- Anonymous author

FOUR FAMOUS BOOKS

Every boy and girl is interested in what is going on about them. The authors of this series have gathered together the most interesting kind of information and have told it in a most entertaining way.

Copies will be sent post-paid to any address upon receipt of the price named.

1. Foods and Beverages, by E.A. Beal, M.D. Contains reading lessons on the various kinds of Foods and their hygienic values; on Grains, Fruits, and useful Plants, with elementary botanical instruction relating thereto; and on other common subjects of interest and importance to all, old and young. 281 pages. Cloth, 60 cents.

2. Every-Day Occupations, by H. Warren Clifford, S.D. Quantities of useful facts entertainingly told, relating to work and workers. How Leather is Tanned; How Silk is Made; The Mysteries of Glass-Making, of Cotton Manufacture, of Cloth-Making, of Ship and House Building; The Secrets of the Dyer's Art and the Potter's Skill—all and more are described and explained in detail with wonderful clearness. 330 pages. Cloth, 60 cents.

3. Man and Materials, by Wm. G. Parker, M.E. Shows how man has raised himself from savagery to civilization by utilizing the raw material of the earth. This brings for the first time the wonderful natural resources of the United States to the notice of American children. The progress of the Metal-Working arts simply described and very attractively illustrated. 323 pages. Cloth, 60 cents.

4. Modern Industries and Commerce, by Robert Louis, Ph.D. Treats of commerce and the different means of conveyance used in different eras. Highways, Canals. Tunnels, Railroads, and the Steam Engine are discussed in an entertaining way. Other subjects are Paper Manufacture, Newspapers, Electric Light, Atlantic Cable, the Telephone, and the principal newer commercial applications of Electricity, etc. 329 pages. Cloth, 60 cents.

7. How does the way the author has structured this advertisement help the reader understand the information in it?

Ⓐ The headings organize the topics in the selection.
Ⓑ The book titles help the reader locate information about specific books.
Ⓒ The ad is organized from the most interesting to the least interesting book which helps the reader know which books are best to purchase.
Ⓓ The author numbers the items.

The Great Barrier Reef

Located off the northeastern coast of Australia is the most complex and diverse ecosystem in the world. The Great Barrier Reef is comprised of more than 3,000 individual coral reefs and is home to a plethora of species of plants and animals.

Geology of Great Barrier Reef

Formation of the Great Barrier Reef began millions of years ago. Volcanic activity created what is known as the Coral Sea Basin and a series of raised islands surrounding the basin. As the sea level changed over time, so did life living in the basin and on the islands. Over time coral reefs grew, died and were buried under sediment from volcanic eruptions. This layer of rich sediment built up over time, forming shelves. The earliest individual coral located on in the raised area now known as the Great Barrier Reef is thought to have formed a half-million years ago. Around 600,000 years ago, complete corals began forming in the area, and the origin of the oldest of those still living today dates back 20,000 years. Sea levels in the area continued to rise until approximately 6,000 years ago. At that point, the water level evened out, creating the ideal conditions for the formation of a fusion of coral and other plant and animal life. The shallow grounds created by years of volcanic activity and sedimentary build up combined with the warm waters and high levels of sunlight provide the perfect environment for the Great Barrier Reef to form and thrive

Life in the Great Barrier Reef

Within the Great Barrier Reef, there are several habitats. Consistent throughout the entire 1616-mile formation are coral reefs. What we consider a piece of coral is actually a collection of several individual coral polyps. Each coral is actually a number of polyps. Coral polyps are living creatures that encase themselves in hard, protective shells made of calcium carbonate. These shells band together, forming colonies. The colonies together are known as reefs. Within the Great Barrier Reef, there are millions of coral featuring a multitude of colors and textures. There are more than 400 species of hard and soft corals living in the Reef.

Housed within the reefs is a vastly diverse collection of animal life, many of which are endangered. Within its waters, the Great Barrier Reef provides homes to 5,000 species of mollusks and 125 species of sharks, stingrays, and skates. In addition, there are more than 1,500 species of fish, including the colorful clown fish. Thirty species of whales, dolphins, and porpoises live in the Great Barrier Reef, including humpback whales which use its warm, shallow waters as breeding grounds before journeying to Hawaii to give birth. Six endangered species of marine turtles also use the area to reproduce. The loggerhead turtle, one of the most highly protected endangered species, lives and breeds in the Great Barrier Reef. Over the last 40 years, the number of these turtles has decreased so rapidly that there are only 3% of the number of the creatures alive today. Housed around this extremely diverse collection of animal life are 2,195 species of plants. Above water 215 species of birds live on the Great Barrier Reef.

Environmental Threats

Because of the diversity, complexity, and uniqueness of the ecosystem, the Great Barrier Reef was placed under the protection of the Australian federal parks system, was named a World Heritage Site in 1981, and has been called one of the Seven Natural Wonders of the World. Still, life in the Reef is at risk.

Coral Bleaching

One of the greatest threats to the Great Barrier Reef is climate change, also known as global warming. Three times over the last ten years, the water in the seas surrounding the Great Barrier Reef has risen 1 or more degrees Celsius. While this may not seem that significant, any temperature increase threatens the coral reefs. When the water becomes warmer , the coral become stressed. This stress causes them to force Zooxanthellae, algae living in coral shells essential to the sustenance of the coral polyp, out of their shells. Without this algae, the coral is unable to use photosynthesis to form its color, which is why the phenomenon is known as "coral bleaching". Once the algae are absent, the coral's white skeleton shows and the coral begins dying, stops reproducing and becomes vulnerable to disease. The Great Barrier Reef experienced episodes of coral bleaching in 1998, 2002 and 2006. Scientists estimate that the 2002 temperature increase caused 60 to 95% of the Reef's coral to become bleached. Because water temperatures are likely to continue to rise, researchers predict that episodes of coral bleaching will continue to occur. Therefore, the Great Barrier Reef Marine Park Authority has formed a response plan aimed at detecting and responding to future occurrences.

Crown of Thorns Starfish

Another natural threat to the Great Barrier Reef is the Crown of Thorns Starfish. This creature which is a naturally occurring species feeds on coral. While a small number of starfish pose no major threat to the vast collection of coral reefs, when they rapidly multiply, they place the Reef at risk. Eradicating these creatures (by forcing them to migrate out of the area) takes anywhere between 1 and 15 years.

Over the last 40 years there have been three major outbreaks of Crown of Thorn Starfish. During those periods large portions of the coral reefs were damaged. These outbreaks combined with episodes of coral bleaching have had dramatic impacts on the coral forming the foundation of the Great Barrier Reef as well as threatening marine and bird species living in the Reef.

Human Impact

Not all of the destruction of the Great Barrier Reef has come from natural sources. Human actions have also negatively impacted the area. Water pollution has threatened life in the Reef. A series of rivers feed the sea where the Reef is located. These rivers have flooded farm lands upstream siphoning large amounts of pesticides used on cattle and sugar cane farms surrounding the rivers. These waters then empty into the seas polluting the waters that the ecosystem.

In addition, land development poses risks to the Great Barrier Reef. Because of its beauty and diversity, the area attracts a huge number of visitors. Though the Reef is protected by the Australian Parks Authority, the tourism industry has built up commercial areas on the lands surrounding the area.

This coastal development threatens the delicate ecosystem adjacent to it.

Beyond this, boats have damaged the Reef. Fishing boats have stripped the area of a number of key species of fish including the Giant Triton. While fishing of certain types of fish has been limited, the boats legitimately fishing in the area pose a potential threat to the entire collection of life located in the Great Barrier Reef. Because the boats carry large amounts of oil necessary for their operation, they always hold the possibility of creating a hazardous situation by spilling the oil into the area's waters.

8. How is this selection organized?

- Ⓐ Using headings
- Ⓑ Using subheadings
- Ⓒ Using graphics
- Ⓓ Using topics

9. If the writer wanted to add the example of people dumping their beach garbage into the reef to the selection, what section would it best fit into?

- Ⓐ Geology of Great Barrier Reef
- Ⓑ Life in the Great Barrier Reef
- Ⓒ Coral Bleaching
- Ⓓ Human Impact

Summer Safety Tips for your Pets

Never leave your pets in a parked car.

In the heat of summer, there is no safe amount of time to leave your pet in a parked car. Even if you leave the engine running and the air conditioning on, the temperature inside the vehicle can go up very quickly. According to the Humane Society, on an 85 degree day, the temperature in a car with the windows slightly open can go up to 102 degrees in ten minutes or less. In less than an hour, that temperature can go up to 120 degrees or more! Your pet could suffer permanent organ damage or worse from exposure to high temperatures. If you plan to go somewhere where your pet is not allowed inside, leave him home!

Pets feel humidity too.

Unlike humans, animals don't sweat from pores all over their bodies. Animals pant or breathe rapidly to eliminate heat and moisture from their bodies. If there is a lot of moisture in the air, panting is less effective, and the pet could become overheated and have no way to release that heat. A dehumidifier or air conditioner will remove moisture from the air and make your pet's natural cooling mechanism more effective.

Fans don't help animals very much.

When a human stands in front of a fan, the air current rushes over his or her skin and helps evaporate the moisture from sweating. Evaporation helps a human feel cooler. Dogs only sweat from the pads on the bottoms of their feet. Standing in front of a fan doesn't help a dog, since there isn't a large amount of evaporation going on.

Limit exercise on hot days.

Do you feel like running when the temperature is high? Why not? Generally, exercising in extreme heat makes you thirsty and very tired. Too much exercise could lead to heat stroke, a dangerous condition when your body isn't able to cool down. Your pets can suffer the same consequences. When it is extremely hot outside, try to exercise your pet only in the morning or evening when the temperature is cooler, and cut down the amount of time your pet spends running around.

http://www.petfinder.com/dogs/dog-care/leaving-pet-parked-car-deadly/

10. How is this article organized?

Ⓐ By subtopic
Ⓑ Chronologically
Ⓒ By order of importance
Ⓓ Alphabetically

Cycling Tours of Brooklyn

Brooklyn is an exciting borough of New York City and offers much to see and do. Visitors can enjoy many different shops and restaurants, as well as parks, museums, and outside festivals. A great way to visit Brooklyn is by bicycle and "Get up and Ride," a cycling tour company, offers two different options.

The Classic Tour

Distance – 10 miles

Duration – 3 to 3.5 hours

Stops include – Greenpoint, Brooklyn Heights, and the Brooklyn Navy Yard

Food and Drink – Stop in the Dekalb Marketplace

Special features – Cyclists end the day with a ferry ride to Manhattan

Cost - $65

The Best of Brooklyn Tour

Distance – 15 miles

Duration - 5 hours

Stops – All of the stops on the classic tour, plus Clinton Hill and Fort Green

Food and Drink – Stop in Dekalb Marketplace

Special Features – Cyclists end with a ferry ride to Manhattan

Cost - $95

The tours can accommodate groups of up to eight people. Bicycles and safety equipment are provided. Tours run Tuesday through Saturday and leave from Brooklyn Heights.

11. Based on the way it is formatted, this document is most likely a(n)_____. Circle the correct answer choice.

Ⓐ Encyclopedia entry
Ⓑ Outline for an essay
Ⓒ Advertisement
Ⓓ Table of contents

12. What comparison can the reader make when looking at both tours? Circle the correct answer choice.

Ⓐ The author makes point to point out comparisons between the features
Ⓑ Identical categories are presented for both tours.
Ⓒ The author lists the stops and indicates which tour covers those areas.
Ⓓ General information is presented first.

Chapter 3

Lesson 6: What's the Author's Angle?

You can scan the QR code given below or use the url to access additional EdSearch resources including videos and mobile apps related to *What's the Author's Angle?*

What's the Author's Angle?

URL	QR Code
http://www.lumoslearning.com/a/ri76	

From <u>Guiseppi Verdi</u> by Thomas Trapper

Whenever the organ man came into the village of Roncole, in Italy (where Verdi was born, October 10, 1813), Verdi could not be kept indoors. But he followed the wonderful organ and the wonderful man who played it, all day long, as happy as he could be.

When Giuseppe was seven years old, his father, though only a poor innkeeper, bought him a spinet, a sort of small piano. So faithfully did the little boy practice that the spinet was soon quite worn out and new jacks, or hammers, had to be made for it. This was done by Stephen Cavaletti, who wrote a message on one of the jacks telling that he made them anew and covered them with leather, and fixed the pedal, doing all for nothing, because the little boy, Giuseppe Verdi, showed such willingness to practice and to learn. Thus the good Stephen thought this was pay enough.

1. Based on these paragraphs, what can you infer the author's view of Verdi is?

- Ⓐ He is amazed by Verdi's talent.
- Ⓑ He thinks Verdi started playing an instrument at too young of an age.
- Ⓒ He is jealous of Verdi's talent.
- Ⓓ He is unsure what to make of Verdi's talent.

<u>The Great Round World and What's Going On In It</u> (magazine article)

The Czar of Russia is quite ill, and everyone feels sorry that he should be sick now when his advice and assistance is so badly needed to settle the worrying Turkish question, which has so troubled Europe.

The young Czar Nicholas, who was crowned with so much pomp and glory at Moscow last August, seems unable to carry on the government of Russia.

Many people say he is too weak to govern, and that there are going to be troubles and revolts in Russia.

The truth of the matter seems to be, that the young Czar is a gentle, kind-hearted man, who will not govern Russia in the stern, cruel way that his forefathers have done, and who is therefore thought to be weak and incapable.

While he is making a part of his people love him for his goodness, by far the larger half, who have, under the old rule, been able to make money and gain great power, are furious against him.

Poor young Nicholas is not only hated by the people who were most friendly to his father, but by the Nihilists, who look upon him as their natural enemy, and, between the two parties, it is said that the Czar goes about in constant fear of his life.

Nicholas never wanted to be a ruler. Those who know him say that he has become grave and sad in the few months since he came to the throne.

It is said that he is of too gentle a disposition to be able to keep his ministers in order and that they quarrel fiercely in his presence, and show very little respect for him.

According to all accounts, his health is giving way under the constant worry, and it is reported that he received a shock a few weeks ago, which so completely upset him, that it brought on his present illness.

He was walking in his gardens, and wishing to speak to one of the men who were at work; he signaled to him to come to him. The gardener, proud of his sovereign's notice, ran towards him at full speed. But a sentry, who had not noticed the Czar's signal, fearing that the man was going to harm the Emperor, fired his gun at him, and he fell dead at the Czar's feet.

Nicholas was terribly overcome by the dreadful mistake.

Some people say that his present illness is due to anxiety about the Czarina, who is also ill, and again others say that the wound which Nicholas received when he was traveling in Japan is the cause.

He was struck by a crazy Japanese, and would have been killed, had not Prince George of Greece, the son of the present King of Greece, who was with him, warded off the blow. As it was, the blow was heavy enough to form a lump on the young man's skull, which has caused him great pain, and which some people declare is troubling him now.

Whatever the cause, the Czar is ill, and in no state to attend to anything but his own affairs. It is a sad pity just at this moment when Europe needs him so badly.

2. What is the author's view of Czar Nicholas?

Ⓐ   The author does not have much respect for Nicholas.
Ⓑ   The author feels sympathy and pity for Nicholas.
Ⓒ   The author thinks that Nicholas has no business being a Czar.
Ⓓ   The author thinks Russia is worse off now that Czar Nicholas is its ruler.

Advertisement from <u>The Great Round World and What's Going On In It</u> magazine -- Anonymous author

School and College Text-Books
AT WHOLESALE PRICES
At my New Store (FEBRUARY 1ST)
3 & 5 West 18th Street, The St. Ann Building

With the greatly increased facilities, I can now offer to my customers the convenience of an assortment of text books and supplies more complete than any other in any store in this city. Books will be classified according to subject. Teachers and students are invited to call and refer to the shelves when in search of information; every convenience and assistance will be rendered to them.

Reading Charts, miscellaneous Reference Charts, Maps, Globes, Blackboards, and School Supplies at net prices singly or in quantity.

All books removed from old store (more or less damaged by removal) will be closed out at low prices.

Mail orders promptly attended to
All books, etc., subject to approval
William Beverley Harrison, 3 & 5 West 18th Street
FORMERLY 59 FIFTH AVENUE

3. What is the author's point of view in this ad?

Ⓐ His new store is even better than his old store.
Ⓑ His store has some of the books teachers and students need.
Ⓒ His books are now available by mail order.
Ⓓ His store has moved to a new location.

An Advertisement for SIMPLE LESSONS IN THE STUDY OF NATURE By I.G. OAKLEY from <u>The Great Round World and What's Going On In It</u> magazine -- Anonymous author

This is a handy little book, which many a teacher who is looking for means to offer children genuine nature study may be thankful to get hold of.

Nature lessons, to be entitled to that name, must deal with what can be handled and scrutinized at leisure by the child, pulled apart, and even wasted. This can be done with the objects discussed in this book; they are under the feet of childhood—grass, feathers, a fallen leaf, a budding twig, or twisted shell; these things cannot be far out of the way, even within the stony limits of a city.

Nor are the lessons haphazard dashes at the nearest living thing; on the contrary, they are virtually fundamental, whether with respect to their relation to some of the classified sciences, or with reference to the development of thought and power of expression in the child himself.

The illustrations are few, and scarcely more than figures; it is not meant to be a pretty picture-book, yet is most clearly and beautifully printed and arranged, for its material is to be that out of which pictures are made. It will be found full of suggestions of practical value to teachers who are carrying the miscellaneous work of ungraded schools, and who have the unspeakable privilege of dealing with their pupils untrammeled by cast-iron methods and account-keeping examination records.

Sample copy, 50 Cents, post-paid
WILLIAM BEVERLEY HARISON
3 & 5 W. 18th St. • • • New York City

4. Which statement about this book would the author of this ad be least likely to agree with?

Ⓐ   The book is educational.
Ⓑ   The book offers kids great lessons about nature.
Ⓒ   The book is like a children's picture book.
Ⓓ   The book features items in nature a child would be likely to find on his or her own.

Advertisement from <u>The Great Round World and What's Going On In It</u> magazine -- Anonymous author

Photographs in relief.

A new plan in regard to photographs has been invented.
It is to take a photograph, similar to the one that is to be embossed, and, after cutting it in a certain way, press the portions outward so that it shall stand in relief.

An open mask of the same shape as the photograph is then used, and the two photographs are dampened and pressed tightly together until the face and figure stand out from the card, and the picture looks as if it had been carved in wood.
This is a very ingenious invention, but the work is very difficult, and can only be done by people who are regularly trained to do it.

5. How does the author feel about this new invention?

Ⓐ   He thinks it will be too difficult to use.
Ⓑ   It will cause less people to visit photographers.
Ⓒ   He thinks this is an incredible invention.
Ⓓ   It's too much like the embosser.

The Great Round World and What's Going On In It
magazine article -- Anonymous author

The news comes from Hamburg that the strike of the dock laborers is over.
The strikers have been beaten because of their lack of money.
In No. 7 of The Great Round World you will find an account of the strike, and if you will also refer to No. 10, you will see that it was thought that the strikers could not hold out very much longer.

The money the strikers expected to receive from other labor unions to help them was so slow in coming that the men and their families were in want, and no man is likely to stand out for the benefit of others when his own children are suffering from cold and hunger.

The men have gone back to their old employers and asked for work. The pity of it all is, however, that during the strike others have been taken on in their places, and the employers have now no work to give them.

After holding out since the end of October, and refusing the masters' offer to give them $1.10 a day, and let all future troubles be settled by arbitration, the strikers have had to give in without gaining a single point. It is very sad.

6. Who would the author of this article be most likely to support?

Ⓐ The business owners of Hamburg
Ⓑ The workers who were on strike
Ⓒ The workers who refused to strike

The Great Round World and What's Going On In It
magazine article -- Anonymous author

Did you ever see a house move?
If you have not, you have missed a very funny sight.

Imagine driving along a country road, and meeting a three-story house making a journey along the highway to new quarters.

There is a good deal of this to be seen just now at Katonah, New York.

A year or so ago the Croton water-shed water, which is in use in New York City, was found to be impure.

A commission was appointed to go and examine the Croton Water-Shed. This meant that they were to examine the little streams, and brooks, and rivers, and lakes, which supplied the water to our aqueduct, and see what the trouble was.

In consequence of this, all of the houses were ordered to be torn down or moved away, and one small village of shanties was destroyed. Among others, the inhabitants of Katonah were ordered to move, that the banks of the stream might be cleared of dwellings.

Katonah has a railroad depot, and a post office, and thinks a good deal of itself.

When the Water-Shed Commission said that it must move or be destroyed, the residents of Katonah gathered together, and decided that rather than be wiped off the face of the map, it would pick up its houses and move itself.

So a new Katonah was established, about a quarter of a mile away from the old one, and just outside the Water-Shed on which it was forbidden to build, for fear of spoiling the water for New York. For several months past there has been a procession of houses moving from old Katonah to new.

7. What is the author's point of view in this article?

Ⓐ   The people of Kantonah were silly to move their homes.
Ⓑ   Houses should be moved regardless of the circumstances.
Ⓒ   The Kantonah residents were trying to maintain control by choosing when and where they moved them.
Ⓓ   The Kantonah government should pay to move people's homes.

Baseball Card Collecting

Looking for a new hobby? Do you like baseball? If you answered "yes" to these two questions, then baseball card collecting might be a fun pastime for you to begin! Ever since candy and gum manufacturers started putting cards with pictures of popular baseball players into the packages in the 1800's to encourage young people to buy their sweets, kids have been collecting baseball cards. Now, more than 200 years later, baseball card collecting has become a popular hobby for children and adults alike.

8. Based on this paragraph, which statement describes the author's view of baseball card collecting?

Ⓐ   The author thinks baseball card collecting is an expensive hobby.
Ⓑ   The author thinks baseball card collecting is a worthwhile hobby.
Ⓒ   The author thinks everyone in the world should become a baseball card collector.
Ⓓ   Baseball card collecting leads people to eat too much candy.

Advertisement from <u>The Great Round World and What's Going On In It</u> magazine -- Anonymous author

FOUR FAMOUS BOOKS

Every boy and girl is interested in what is going on about them. The authors of this series have gathered together the most interesting kind of information and have told it in a most entertaining way.

Copies will be sent post-paid to any address upon receipt of price named.

1. Foods and Beverages, by E.A. Beal, M.D. Contains reading lessons on the various kinds of Foods and their hygienic values; on Grains, Fruits, and useful Plants, with elementary botanical instruction relating thereto; and on other common subjects of interest and importance to all, old and young. 281 pages. Cloth, 60 cents.

2. Every-Day Occupations, by H. Warren Clifford, S.D. Quantities of useful facts entertainingly told, relating to work and workers. How Leather is Tanned; How Silk is Made; The Mysteries of Glass-Making, of Cotton Manufacture, of Cloth-Making, of Ship and House Building; The Secrets of the Dyer's Art and the Potter's Skill—all and more are described and explained in detail with wonderful clearness. 330 pages. Cloth, 60 cents.

3. Man and Materials, by Wm. G. Parker, M.E. Shows how man has raised himself from savagery to civilization by utilizing the raw material of the earth. This brings for the first time the wonderful natural resources of the United States to the notice of American children. The progress of the Metal-Working arts simply described and very attractively illustrated. 323 pages. Cloth, 60 cents.

4. Modern Industries and Commerce, by Robert Louis, Ph.D. Treats of commerce and the different means of conveyance used in different eras. Highways, Canals. Tunnels, Railroads, and the Steam Engine are discussed in an entertaining way. Other subjects are Paper Manufacture, Newspapers, Electric Light, Atlantic Cable, the Telephone, and the principal newer commercial applications of Electricity, etc. 329 pages. Cloth, 60 cents.

9. **Which statement about the books in this advertisement would the author be least likely to agree with?**

   Ⓐ The books are educational for children.
   Ⓑ There are interesting facts and descriptions in these books.
   Ⓒ Most children would not find these books very useful.
   Ⓓ Children are likely to be entertained by the information in these books.

Advertisement from <u>The Great Round World and What's Going On In It</u> magazine -- Anonymous author

Klemm's Practice Relief Maps Advertisement

LIST OF MAPS.

Small size, 9-1/2 x 11	{Plain,	5	cents	each
	{With Waterproofed surface	10	cents	each

Europe, Asia, Africa; North America, South America, East Central States, New England, Middle Atlantic States, South Atlantic States, Palestine, Australia.

Large size, 10 x 15	{Plain,	10	cents	each
	{With Waterproofed surface	15	cents	each

United States, British Isles, Roman Empire, Western Europe, North America, South America, Asia.

(POSTAGE ON SINGLE MAPS, 5 CENTS.)
"I would advise Sunday school teachers to use, in connection with the lessons of 1897, Klemm's Relief Map of the Roman Empire. Every scholar who can draw should have a copy of it. Being blank, it can be beautifully colored: waters, blue; mountains, brown; valleys, green; deserts, yellow; cities marked with pin-holes; and the journeys of Paul can be traced upon it."—Mrs. Wilbur F. Crafts, *President International Union of Primary Sabbath-School Teachers of the United States.*

DESCRIPTION OF THE MAPS.
These maps are made in two forms, both with beautifully executed relief (embossed)—the cheaper ones of plain stiff paper similar to drawing paper (these are to be substituted for and used as outline map blanks), the others covered with a durable waterproof surface, that can be quickly cleaned with a damp sponge, adapted to receive a succession of markings and cleansings. Oceans, lakes, and rivers, as well as land, appear in the same color, white, so as to facilitate the use of the map as a *geographical slate.*
WILLIAM BEVERLEY HARISON
3 & 5 W. 18th St. • • • New York City

10. What strategy does the author of this advertisement use to try to convince readers his point of view is shared by others?

   Ⓐ He describes the maps in detail.
   Ⓑ He uses a testimonial from someone who uses the maps.
   Ⓒ He lists the costs of the maps at the beginning of the ad.
   Ⓓ He lists all the different types of maps that can be purchased from Klemm's.

Diabetic Help

Researchers at pharmaceutical company Eli Lilly and an association that places assistance dogs in Indianapolis, IN, are working together on an exciting new project that will study how dogs are able to detect low blood sugar in their diabetic owners. Diabetics suffer from a condition by which the pancreas does not produce enough insulin to maintain a healthy level of blood glucose. **If a diabetic person's blood glucose level drops too low, he or she may become unconscious or even go into a coma.**

One dog who has had a lot of success in identifying low blood sugar is a two-year-old named Pete. Pete, like all dogs, has a sense of smell 10,000 times more sensitive than that of humans. Pete's owner is a scientist with Eli Lilly, and she is trying to figure out what is inside a dog's nose that makes it possible to smell low blood sugar. If the researcher can figure out how to reproduce that kind of sensitivity, more diabetic people can be protected from the consequences of low blood sugar.

Until the researchers isolate what is inside Pete's nose, the Indiana Canine Assistance Network will continue to train dogs like Pete. It's a slow and expensive process, though. In the last ten years, the organization has trained 100 dogs, and the training has cost $25,000 or more for each dog.

http://www.diabetesadvocacy.com/diabetes_news.htm

11. Part A
Why would the author include the section about Pete?

Ⓐ The author owns Pete and is proud.
Ⓑ Pete is the only dog that can do this, so it must be shared.
Ⓒ By giving an example, the reader gets a personal connection.
Ⓓ The explanation is meant to make the reader feel bad for someone with diabetes.

Part B
What might be a reason the author mentions the cost of training?

Ⓐ To express how much time is needed for training
Ⓑ To make people want to buy stock in Lilly pharmaceuticals
Ⓒ To brag at how valuable the dogs are
Ⓓ So the reader will understand why everyone with diabetes does not have a dog like Pete

Part C
What is the purpose of the bolded statement?

Ⓐ To emphasise the seriousness of the disease
Ⓑ To scare the reader into giving money to the researchers
Ⓒ To explain why Pete is so valuable
Ⓓ To make diabetics feel important

12. Why is it important for a reader to understand the view point or beliefs of an author? Circle the correct answer choice.

Ⓐ To keep the author's thoughts from the reader
Ⓑ To make sure the author is telling the correct information
Ⓒ To keep the author from changing his/her mind
Ⓓ The author's opinion is not important

13. In which of the following types of writing are author's beliefs NOT important? Circle the correct answer choice.

Ⓐ Political speech
Ⓑ Advertisement
Ⓒ News report
Ⓓ Job resume

Chapter 3

Lesson 7: Comparing Media

Let us understand the concept with an example.

Here are descriptions of the last few seconds of a basketball game, presented as if you were reading about it in a newspaper, seeing it broadcast live on TV, listening to a live radio broadcast, or watching a video recording of it online with a link to more details. You can assume that for each type of media, the sportscaster would have broadcast information about the teams and players in the pregame show, postgame show or during time outs; the sportswriter would have written similar information in the newspaper article. This is one area that they all would have in common.

Article in a newspaper

There would be a headline and a still photo from the game. There might also be a web address for further information and the writer's contact information. In the article would be a written description of the last few seconds of the game and the slam dunk by Hendricks.

Broadcast live on TV

Imagine this as a continuous stream of live action pictures with live commentary by the sportscaster.

Sportscaster's commentary: "Rebound Jackson, pass to Jacovik, closing seconds, pass to Hendricks...a slam dunk, there's the buzzer, AND THE TIGERS WIN IT!! What a come-back! One for the record books! And what a slam dunk — did you ever see anything like it?"

Broadcast on the radio

Sportscaster's commentary: "Rebound Jackson, he fakes a dribble, passes to his right to Jacovik, Jacovik drives to the right of the key, closely guarded by Sosnowska, fakes a jump shot and passes to Hendricks driving in...slam dunk by Hendricks, there's the buzzer, THE TIGERS WIN IT!! Hendricks must have leaped four feet in the air, and sailed most of the way from the foul line to the basket! An amazing slam dunk! What athleticism!"

Broadcast as a multimedia video recording with audio, viewed online with a link to more details. Assume that the video and audio were recorded from the live TV broadcast. The difference is that there is a link with additional information, such as a biography of Hendricks, stats on the Tigers season, their schedule with scores and future opponents, and other relevant information.

Compare and contrast a text to an audio, video, or multimedia version of the text, analyzing each medium's portrayal of the subject

The newspaper article would create some level of emotion about the game; the diehard fans would either feel happy or sad depending on the result. But the level of emotion would not match diehard fans watching the game on TV or listening on the radio or watching the video. The reasons why? The newspaper article covered an event that was finished, and the end result was communicated in the article. But for those watching the game in live coverage, the level of suspense was high; the end result was not known in those last few seconds, and emotions ran high. Not only that, the voice of the sportscaster and noise from the crowd further enhanced the viewer's emotions.

Note the differences in the spoken words between the TV sportscaster and the radio sportscaster. The TV text is shorter; viewers can see the action for themselves; there is less need to describe every action. The radio announcer has to describe the action in enough detail for the audience to picture in their minds what is happening in the game.

You can scan the QR code given below or use the url to access additional EdSearch resources including videos and mobile apps related to *Comparing Media*.

ed Search	**Comparing Media**
URL	**QR Code**
http://www.lumoslearning.com/a/ri77	

Fall Leaves
USDA Forest Service

We almost always think of trees as being green, but there is one time of year when their leaves turn a myriad orange, red, yellow, and brown: the beautiful and chilly days of fall. Those living in the Eastern or Northern United States come to anticipate the change in color starting in September or October every single year. But what causes the leaves to change color, and why? Just like many animals that hibernate for the winter, trees experience a unique change during the winter months. During summer, for instance, plants use the process of photosynthesis to transform carbon dioxide found in the air into organic compounds like sugars using energy from the sun. During the winter, however, there is less light to go around, and their ability to create food from the photosynthesis process is limited. What does that have to do with a leaf's color? The substance that allows trees to turn carbon dioxide into food (chlorophyll) is also the cause of the leaf's green sheen. As the photosynthesis process wanes in the colder months due to the lack of sun, so does its greenish hue, allowing other elements present in the leaf to show through. Believe it or not, the yellows and oranges that appear in fall have actually been there all year in the form of nutrients like carotene (also found in carrots). The intense green color of the chlorophyll had simply overshadowed them. But what about the reds and browns? And what causes the leaves to fall away after they change color? The bright reds and purples in each leaf come from a strong antioxidant that many trees create on their own because of their protective qualities. The antioxidant helps protect the trees from the sun, lower their freezing levels, and protect them from frost. As winter comes, so does the need for the antioxidant (similar to the way a dog gets more fur during winter to stay warmer). As for the leaves falling, that is another story. At the base of each leaf, there is a layer of cells that carry food and water from the leaf to the tree during the summer months to keep it fed. In the fall, that layer actually starts to harden, preventing the passage of nutrients. Because of this, the nutrients and waste that previously passed from the leaf into the tree become trapped in the leaf with no fresh water to clean it. Not only does this cause the leaf to turn brown, eventually, but it also causes the cells within it to harden so much that the leaf tears and blows away. Thus the pile of leaves you enjoyed jumping in as a child.

Because each tree, and each leaf, contains a unique amount of nutrients depending on how well-nourished it was over the spring and summer, the way each leaf breaks down during the winter months is also quite different. The result is the unique and complex facet of colors we see in each neighborhood or forest each fall.

http://www.sciencemadesimple.com/leaves.htm

1. **If this passage was turned into a video documentary, what would it include to help you understand how the leaves change color?**

   Ⓐ Time-lapse video of the leaves changing color
   Ⓑ Paintings by artists depicting fall leaves
   Ⓒ Pictures of animals that hibernate during the winter
   Ⓓ Subtitles of the text on the screen

2. **You've been asked to turn this passage into a slide show presentation. Which graphic would you use to help explain the process of leaves changing color?**

   Ⓐ A picture of leaves that have changed color
   Ⓑ A picture of animals hibernating
   Ⓒ A diagram of the process leaves go through when changing color
   Ⓓ A diagram explaining when leaves change color around the world

3. **A naturalist is presenting this information to a class of students. Which visual aid could she bring to help students understand the information in the passage?**

   Ⓐ A picture of leaves that have changed color
   Ⓑ A pile of leaves of different colors
   Ⓒ A photograph of a pile of leaves
   Ⓓ A diagram explaining the process

History of Olympics
From *Ancient Olympics Guide*

Even though the modern Olympic Games are held every four years, they bear little resemblance to the athletic contests held at Olympia in Greece in ancient times. The games were open to competitors from all Greece, and the contests included chariot racing, horse racing, running, wrestling, boxing, and the pentathlon, a contest involving jumping, quoit throwing, javelin throwing, running and wrestling. Scholars date the earliest contests at 776 B.C., more than two and a half thousand years ago. The first trophies that were won consisted not of gold medals and cups but of simple crowns of olive leaves. Women and slaves were admitted neither as contestants nor as spectators. The classical games ceased to be held probably about A.D.393.

Much of the credit for the revival of the Games held at Athens in 1896 goes to Baron Pierre de Coubertin, a French classical scholar, who greatly admired the sporting ideals of the ancient Greeks. As an educationist and lover of amateurism, he looked upon physical exercise as an essential feature of a balanced education. Forty-two events were contested, and new disciplines such as cycling, hurdling, high jump, shooting, and gymnastics were introduced. One of the most popular events of the modern Olympics is the marathon. This very tiring twenty-six-mile foot race over an open course is the supreme test of the runners' endurance. The marathon was not a part of the ancient Olympics, although it originated in Greece. And, finally, a more recent development in the Olympics is the introduction of the winter games, which were started in 1924. They are held separately from the summer games but in the same year. The Winter Olympics provide competition in skiing, speed and figure skating, ice hockey, and rifle shooting. Such cold weather sports could never have developed in the warm climate of Greece

4. The History Channel is making a documentary based on this passage. What would be most helpful for them to include?

Ⓐ Footage from recent Olympic games
Ⓑ Video of the original Olympic games
Ⓒ Images showing the different Olympic sports from the beginning until now.
Ⓓ Interviews with current Olympic athletes

5. A gym teacher wants students to understand this passage better. What can the teacher do to make this passage more interactive?

Ⓐ Play a video about the Olympics
Ⓑ Have students play some of the sports
Ⓒ Show students pictures of the Olympics
Ⓓ Bring in an Olympic athlete to talk to students

6. A news station has turned this piece into a special news report. When should they air it?

Ⓐ Around the next summer or winter Olympic games
Ⓑ Right before the Super Bowl
Ⓒ Sometime in the summer
Ⓓ Sometime in the winter

Egyptian Pyramids

Today, we have high-tech cranes and other machines to help us create massive skyscrapers and other modern works of architecture. Still, some of the most breathtaking architecture in the world, such as the ancient pyramids of Egypt, were created before those high-tech machines even existed. So how did those ancient civilizations create them?

Believe it or not, though they are one of the most studied and admired relics in history, there is no evidence to tell historians exactly how the Ancient Egyptians built the pyramids. Thus, they have been left to create their own theories as to how Egyptians created such amazing and awe-inspiring works of art.

According to one theory, the Egyptians placed logs under the large stone blocks in order to roll or transport them to the pyramid building location. Large groups of men would work to push or pull them into place (although historians also disagree on whether these men were slaves or skilled artisans). Still more, once the men moved the blocks to the pyramid location, they needed to lift them to ever-increasing heights to reach the top levels of the pyramid as it grew. Without modern cranes, many scientists have been baffled as to how they were able to do it. Some believe they used a ramp system that would allow them to roll the blocks upward around or through the pyramids; others believe they must have used a combination of pulleys and lifts. Still, most agree that once they did, they used a mixture of gravel and limestone to help fill any crevices and hold the mound together.
With such a primitive yet impressive building process, it's obvious that the pyramids must have taken a great deal of time to build. With an estimated 2 million blocks weighing an average of 2.5 million tons each, the Great Pyramid of Giza, for instance, is estimated to have taken some 20 years to build. At 481 feet tall, it held the record of tallest building for 3,800 years – not bad for a building created almost entirely by hand.

Even though scientists don't know exactly how the Egyptians did it, they do know that the method the Egyptians used to build pyramids changed over time. In the early days, the pyramids were made completely of stone, with limestone used to create the main body and higher quality limestone being used for the smooth outer casing. Later on, the pyramids were made mostly of mud brick with a limestone casing. Though they were likely much easier to build, they didn't stand up nearly as well over time, leaving archaeologists with even fewer clues about their creation.

http://en.wikipedia.org/wiki/Egyptian_pyramid_construction_techniques

7. This passage is being displayed as part of a museum exhibit. What would it most likely be accompanied by?

Ⓐ Pictures of modern-day construction trucks
Ⓑ Pictures of Egyptians building the pyramids
Ⓒ Relics from Ancient Egypt
Ⓓ Items from Egyptian kings

8. If creating a documentary based on this passage, what would the director most likely use in the opening sequence related to the opening of the passage?

Ⓐ Illustrations of modern-day skyscrapers
Ⓑ Illustrations of the pyramids
Ⓒ Illustrations of Egyptian kings
Ⓓ Illustrations of modern-day houses

9. If this passage was turned into a play, what would it most likely be about?

Ⓐ A specific modern-day construction worker
Ⓑ A factual account of how pyramids were built
Ⓒ A specific pyramid-builder or group of pyramids
Ⓓ An interpretive dance of the building of pyramids

From <u>Guiseppi Verdi</u>
by Thomas Trapper

Whenever the organ man came into the village of Roncole, in Italy (where Verdi was born, October 10, 1813), Verdi could not be kept indoors. But he followed the wonderful organ and the wonderful man who played it, all day long, as happy as he could be.

When Guiseppi was seven years old, his father, though only a poor innkeeper, bought him a spinet, a sort of small piano. So faithfully did the little boy practice that the spinet was soon quite worn out and new jacks, or hammers, had to be made for it. This was done by Stephen Cavaletti, who wrote a message on one of the jacks telling that he made them anew and covered them with leather, and fixed the pedal, doing all for nothing, because the little boy, Guiseppi Verdi, showed such willingness to practice and to learn. Thus the good Stephen thought this was pay enough.

10. If turned into a media production, this passage would most likely be...?

Ⓐ A story on the local news
Ⓑ A play at the local theater
Ⓒ A slideshow presentation
Ⓓ A song about Verdi

Human Spaceflight

In just 20 years, the human exploration into space has made incredible strides.

In 1961, Soviet Cosmonaut Yuri Gagarin became the first human being to travel into space. On April 12 of that year, his Vostok spacecraft orbited the Earth once, then using a parachute that deployed 2.5 km above the planet and guided his re-entry.

The Vostok spacecraft was a sphere just 2.3 m in diameter with room for just one crew member. The entire mission took only 108 minutes, less than two hours.

Less than a month later, American Alan Shepard became the first American in space. His Mercury spaceship entered space but did not orbit the earth. The flight lasted just fifteen minutes, but unlike Gagarin, whose ship was automatically programmed, Shepard navigated the entire voyage.

Twenty years later, the United States launched the first Space Shuttle, a vehicle designed and intended to be reusable for multiple flights. Unlike the early spacecraft that used parachutes to "splashdown" in the ocean upon re-entry, the space shuttle landed much like an airplane on a runway and could be refurbished and sent back into space on subsequent missions.

While the early space missions were measured in terms of minutes spent in space, the space shuttle was capable of staying in orbit for days. The longest flight was achieved by the Columbia Space Shuttle, which made a total of 28 flights, the longest of which was over 17 days.

While the space shuttle program ended in 2011, that does not mean the end of human exploration of space. Since the 1990s, several private American companies have developed viable space exploration vehicles, and several organizations are exploring the notion of space tourism, which is not part of the mission of the US government-funded program. Joint missions between the United States and countries such as Russia have continued the long tradition of exploring the frontier beyond the earth's atmosphere.

http://www.cnn.com/2013/07/01/world/human-spaceflight-fast-facts

11. Part A
What is not a difference between space flight in the 1960s and space travel in the 1980s?

Ⓐ Space flights in the 1980s lasted days as opposed to hours or minutes.
Ⓑ Space-traveling vehicles in the 1980s were reusable.
Ⓒ Space flights in the 1980s were navigated by crews on the ship.
Ⓓ Space crafts in the 1980s carried at least one human passenger

Part B
What is one way Yuri Gagarin's mission was different from Alan Shepard's?

Ⓐ Yuri Gagarin's mission was more than seven times longer than Shepard's.
Ⓑ Yuri Gagarin's navigated the space ship on his own.
Ⓒ Alan Shepard's spaceship landed on a runway.
Ⓓ Yuri Gagarin's spaceship used a parachute to "splashdown."

Part C
What is one way space flight in the future may be different from that of the pioneers in the 1960s and 1980s?

Ⓐ Future space flight may involve reusable spacecrafts.
Ⓑ In the past, the people who traveled into space were all from the Soviet Union or Russia.
Ⓒ In the future, space travel may be funded by private companies rather than the government.
Ⓓ In the future, women may travel into space.

From Guiseppi Verdi

by Thomas Trapper

Whenever the organ man came into the village of Roncole, in Italy (where Verdi was born, October 10, 1813), Verdi could not be kept indoors. But he followed the wonderful organ and the wonderful man who played it, all day long, as happy as he could be.

When Guiseppi was seven years old, his father, though only a poor innkeeper, bought him a spinet, a sort of small piano. So faithfully did the little boy practice that the spinet was soon quite worn out and new jacks, or hammers, had to be made for it. This was done by Stephen Cavaletti, who wrote a message on one of the jacks telling that he made them anew and covered them with leather, and fixed the pedal, doing all for nothing, because the little boy, Guiseppi Verdi, showed such willingness to practice and to learn. Thus the good Stephen thought this was pay enough.

12. If turned into a media production, this passage would most likely be...?

Ⓐ A story on the local news
Ⓑ A play at the local theater
Ⓒ A slideshow presentation
Ⓓ A song about Verdi

Chapter 3

Lesson 8: What's the Author's Point?

Let us understand the concept with an example.

The Obesity Epidemic

In the United States population, 30% of adults and 17% of children are obese, according to the American Heart Association. And by 2020, 83% of men and 72% of women are expected to be overweight or obese, according to research presented to the Heart Association's scientific meeting in 2011. More than one-third (36.5%) of U.S. adults have obesity, states the Centers for Disease Control and Prevention.

Being obese has negative health and health expense disadvantages. According to the Centers for Disease Control and Prevention:

- Obesity-related conditions include heart disease, stroke, type 2 diabetes, high blood pressure, arthritis and certain types of cancer, some of the leading causes of preventable death.
- The estimated annual medical cost of obesity in the U.S. was $147 billion in 2008 U.S. dollars; the medical costs for people who are obese were $1,429 higher than those of normal weight.

What is causing so many people to be obese? More sedentary lifestyles are one factor. Sitting and watching television, driving instead of walking, not exercising enough. Nutrition is another. So much of our food is processed, which means fat and sugar are added. Also, we frequently eat portions larger than our bodies need, and we often snack between meals.

What can people do about reducing their obesity?

- Exercise: The Centers for Disease Control (CDC) recommends 2.5 hours of moderate aerobic exercise per week, along with 2 days of strength training. Americans are clearly not abiding by these minimum recommendations. But diet can have more effect on weight loss than exercise, although both are important solutions.
- Nutrition: Controlling the intake of carbohydrates is one important action. Also, eating less processed food, less refined grains and bread and more vegetables are also important. You need to add lean protein to every meal and every snack, along with moderate amounts of healthy fats.

Your assignment: Write text that meets the requirements of the standard.

Here is what you might write.

The authors state the argument that there is an obesity epidemic today among adults and children in America. They cite statistics from the American Heart Association and the Centers for Disease Control and Prevention as proof. Because these two organizations are reputable and trustworthy, I believe that their arguments are relevant and accurate.

The authors also state that being obese has negative health and health expense disadvantages, and list diseases associated with obesity and the medical costs incurred by obese people. These facts were also provided by the Centers for Disease Control and Prevention. I checked with two family doctors and both agreed with the list of diseases.

Therefore, I support these facts as accurate.

The authors also speculate on the causes of the obesity epidemic, citing a more sedentary lifestyle, insufficient exercise and dietary factors. I have observed many fellow students, and the lifestyles of most fit these three causes of obesity. My parents also subscribe to a newsletter edited by a nutritionist, and it cites the same conclusions about the causes of obesity.

Lastly, the authors state what can be done to reduce obesity, citing suggestions for exercise and nutrition. These suggestions are also in line with the newsletter and with the recommendations of two trainers at my parent's physical fitness center

You can scan the QR code given below or use the url to access additional EdSearch resources including videos and mobile apps related to *What's the Author's Point?*

 **What's the Author's Point?**

URL	QR Code
http://www.lumoslearning.com/a/ri78	

Fall Leaves
USDA Forest Service

We almost always think of trees as being green, but there is one time of year when their leaves turn a myriad orange, red, yellow, and brown: the beautiful and chilly days of fall. Those living in the Eastern or Northern United States come to anticipate the change in color every year starting in September or October. What causes the leaves to change color, and why?

Just like many animals that hibernate for the winter, trees experience a unique change during the winter months. During summer, plants use the process of photosynthesis to transform carbon dioxide found in the air into organic compounds like sugars using energy from the sun. During the winter, however, there is less light to go around, and their ability to create food from the photosynthesis process is limited. What does that have to do with a leaf's color? The substance that allows trees to turn carbon dioxide into food (chlorophyll) is also the cause of the leaf's green sheen. As the photosynthesis process wanes in the colder months due to the lack of sun, so does its greenish hue, allowing other elements present in the leaf to show through. Believe it or not, the yellows and oranges that appear in fall have actually been there all year in the form of nutrients like carotene (also found in carrots). The intense green color of the chlorophyll had simply overshadowed them.

But what about the reds and browns? And what causes the leaves to fall away after they change color? The bright reds and purples in each leaf come from a strong antioxidant that many trees create on their own because of their protective qualities. The antioxidant helps protect the trees from the sun, lower their freezing levels, and protect them from frost. As winter comes, so does the need for the antioxidant (similar to the way a dog gets more fur during winter to stay warm).

As for the leaves falling, that is another story. At the base of each leaf, there is a layer of cells that carry food and water from the leaf to the tree during the summer months to keep it fed. In the fall, that layer actually starts to harden, preventing the passage of nutrients. Because of this, the nutrients and waste that previously passed from the leaf into the tree become trapped in the leaf with no fresh water to clean it. Not only does this cause the leaf to turn brown, eventually it causes the cells within it to harden so much that the leaf tears and blows away. Thus the pile of leaves you enjoyed jumping in as a child.

Because each tree, and each leaf, contains a unique amount of nutrients depending on how well-nourished it was over the spring and summer, the way each leaf breaks down during the winter months is also quite different. The result is the unique and complex facet of colors we see in neighborhoods and forests each fall.

1. For the information in this selection to be considered reliable, it would need to be written by....

  Ⓐ a journalist
  Ⓑ a student
  Ⓒ a scientist
  Ⓓ an environmental activist

Egyptian Pyramids

Today, we have high-tech cranes and other machines to help us create massive skyscrapers and other modern works of architecture. Still, some of the most breathtaking architecture in the world, such as the ancient pyramids of Egypt, were created before those high-tech machines even existed. So how did those ancient civilizations create them?

Believe it or not, though they are one of the most studied and admired relics in history, there is no evidence to tell historians exactly how the Ancient Egyptians built the pyramids. Thus, they have been left to create their own theories as to how Egyptians created such amazing and awe-inspiring works of art.

According to one theory, the Egyptians placed logs under the large stone blocks in order to roll or transport them to the pyramid building location. Large groups of men would work to push or pull them into place (although historians also disagree on whether these men were slaves or skilled artisans). Still more, once the men moved the blocks to the pyramid location, they needed to lift them to ever-increasing heights to reach the top levels of the pyramid as it grew. Without modern cranes, many scientists have been baffled as to how they were able to do it. Some believe they used a ramp system that would allow them to roll the blocks upward around or through the pyramids; others believe they must have used a combination of pulleys and lifts. Still, most agree that once they did, they used a mixture of gravel and limestone to help fill any crevices and hold the mound together.

With such a primitive yet impressive building process, it's obvious that the pyramids must have taken a great deal of time to build. With an estimated 2 million blocks weighing an average of 2.5 million tons each, the Great Pyramid of Giza, for instance, is estimated to have taken some 20 years to build. At 481 feet tall, it held the record of tallest building for 3,800 years — not bad for a building created almost entirely by hand.

Even though scientists don't know exactly how the Egyptians did it, they do know that the method the Egyptians used to build pyramids changed over time. In the early days, the pyramids were made completely of stone, with limestone used to create the main body and higher quality limestone being used for the smooth outer casing. Later on, the pyramids were made mostly of mud brick with a limestone casing. Though they were likely much easier to build, they didn't stand up nearly as well over time, leaving archaeologists with even fewer clues about their creation.

2. How could you verify whether or not the information in this selection is accurate?

Ⓐ by interviewing the author of the essay
Ⓑ by reading an encyclopedia entry on the Egyptian pyramids
Ⓒ by talking with an Egyptian historian
Ⓓ by going to Egypt

From <u>The Great Round World and What's Going On In It</u> magazine

The Czar of Russia is quite ill, and everyone feels sorry that he should be sick now when his advice and assistance is so badly needed to settle the worrying Turkish question, which has so troubled Europe.

The young Czar Nicholas, who was crowned with so much pomp and glory at Moscow last August, seems unable to carry on the government of Russia.
Many people say he is too weak to govern, and that there are going to be troubles and revolts in Russia.

The truth of the matter seems to be, that the young Czar is a gentle, kind-hearted man, who will not govern Russia in the stern, cruel way that his forefathers have done, and who is therefore thought to be weak and incapable.

While he is making a part of his people love him for his goodness, by far the larger half, who have, under the old rule, been able to make money and gain great power, are furious against him.

Poor young Nicholas is not only hated by the people who were most friendly to his father, but by the Nihilists, who look upon him as their natural enemy, and, between the two parties, it is said that the Czar goes about in constant fear of his life.

Nicholas never wanted to be a ruler. Those who know him say that he has become grave and sad in the few months since he came to the throne.
It is said that he is of too gentle a disposition to be able to keep his ministers in order and that they quarrel fiercely in his presence, and show very little respect for him.

According to all accounts, his health is giving way under the constant worry, and it is reported that he received a shock a few weeks ago, which so completely upset him, that it brought on his present illness.

He was walking in his gardens, and wishing to speak to one of the men who were at work; he signaled to him to come to him. The gardener, proud of his sovereign's notice, ran towards him at full speed. But a sentry, who had not noticed the Czar's signal, fearing that the man was going to harm the Emperor, fired his gun at him, and he fell dead at the Czar's feet.

Nicholas was terribly overcome by the dreadful mistake.

Some people say that his present illness is due to anxiety about the Czarina, who is also ill, and again others say that the wound which Nicholas received when he was traveling in Japan is the cause.

He was struck by a crazy Japanese, and would have been killed, had not Prince George of Greece, the son of the present King of Greece, who was with him, warded off the blow. As it was, the blow was heavy enough to form a lump on the young man's skull, which has caused him great pain, and which some people declare is troubling him now.

Whatever the cause, the Czar is ill, and in no state to attend to anything but his own affairs. It is a sad pity just at this moment when Europe needs him so badly.

3. **Which statement from this selection is a fact?**

Ⓐ Many people say he is too weak to govern, and that there are going to be troubles and revolts in Russia.
Ⓑ The truth of the matter seems to be, that the young Czar is a gentle, kind-hearted man, who will not govern Russia in the stern, cruel way that his forefathers have done, and who is there fore thought to be weak and incapable.
Ⓒ According to all accounts, his health is giving way.
Ⓓ Nicholas was terribly overcome by the dreadful mistake.

4. **What would be the best source to use to determine whether the eighth paragraph of this selection is factual or is an opinion?**

Ⓐ An eyewitness article on the event.
Ⓑ A newspaper article by someone who dislikes the Czar.
Ⓒ An interview with the author of this article.
Ⓓ Nicholas was terribly overcome by the dreadful mistake.

Advertisement from <u>The Great Round World and What's Going On In It</u> magazine -- Anonymous author

School and College Text-Books
AT WHOLESALE PRICES
At my New Store (FEBRUARY 1ST)
3 & 5 West 18th Street The St. Ann Building

With the greatly increased facilities, I can now offer to my customers the convenience of an assort-ment of text books and supplies more complete than any other in any store in this city. Books will be classified according to subject. Teachers and students are invited to call and refer to the shelves when in search of information; every convenience and assistance will be rendered to them.

Reading Charts, miscellaneous Reference Charts, Maps, Globes, Blackboards, and School Supplies at net prices singly or in quantity.
All books removed from old store (more or less damaged by removal) will be closed out at low prices.

Mail orders promptly attended to
All books, etc., subject to approval
William Beverley Harrison, 3 & 5 West 18th Street
FORMERLY 59 FIFTH AVENUE

5. Which statement from this ad is NOT a fact?

(A) I can now offer to my customers the convenience of an assortment of text-books and supplies more complete than any other in any store in this city.

(B) Teachers and students are invited to call and refer to the shelves when in search of information.

(C) All books removed from old store (more or less damaged by removal) will be closed out at low prices.

(D) Mail orders promptly attended to.

An Advertisement for SIMPLE LESSONS IN THE STUDY OF NATURE By I.G. OAK-LEY from The Great Round World and What's Going On In It magazine -- Anonymous author

This is a handy little book, which many a teacher who is looking for means to offer children genuine nature study may be thankful to get hold of.

Nature lessons, to be entitled to that name, must deal with what can be handled and scrutinized at leisure by the child, pulled apart, and even wasted. This can be done with the objects discussed in this book; they are under the feet of childhood—grass, feathers, a fallen leaf, a budding twig, or twisted shell; **these things cannot be far out of the way, even within the stony limits of a city.**

Nor are the lessons haphazard dashes at the nearest living thing; on the contrary, they are virtually fundamental, whether with respect to their relation to some of the classified sciences, or with reference to the development of thought and power of expression in the child himself.

The illustrations are few, and scarcely more than figures; it is not meant to be a pretty picture-book, yet is most clearly and beautifully printed and arranged, for its material is to be that out of which pictures are made. It will be found full of suggestions of practical value to teachers who are carrying the miscellaneous work of ungraded schools, and who have the unspeakable privilege of dealing with their pupils untrammeled by cast-iron methods and account-keeping examination records.

Sample copy, 50 Cents, post-paid

WILLIAM BEVERLEY HARISON
3 & 5 W. 18th St. • • • New York City

6. How could you determine whether or not the statement in bold is true?

(A) Purchase the book

(B) Call the author and ask him if this statement is a fact or an opinion

(C) Buy the book and follow the lessons in your own backyard

(D) Buy the book and follow the lessons in several different settings

The Great Round World and What's Going On In It
magazine article -- Anonymous author

Did you ever see a house move?

If you have not, you have missed a very funny sight.
Imagine driving along a country road, and meeting a three-story house making a journey along the highway to new quarters.
There is a good deal of this to be seen just now at Katonah, New York.
A year or so ago the Croton water-shed water, which is in use in New York City, was found to be impure.

A commission was appointed to go and examine the Croton Water-Shed. This meant that they were to examine the little streams, and brooks, and rivers, and lakes, which supplied the water to our aqueduct, and see what the trouble was.

They found that along the banks of these streams and lakes, in villages and out in the country, a great many dwelling-houses and shanties had been built, the occupants of which were in the habit of throwing all sorts of rubbish into the water, making it unfit for drinking.

In consequence of this, all of the houses were ordered to be torn down or moved away, and one small village of shanties was destroyed. Among others, the inhabitants of Katonah were ordered to move, that the banks of the stream might be cleared of dwellings.

Katonah has a railroad depot, and a post office, and thinks a good deal of itself.

When the Water-Shed Commission said that it must move or be destroyed, the residents of Katonah gathered together, and decided that rather than be wiped off the face of the map, it would pick up its houses and move itself.

So a new Katonah was established, about a quarter of a mile away from the old one, and just outside the Water-Shed on which it was forbidden to build, for fear of spoiling the water for New York.

For several months past there has been a procession of houses moving from old Katonah to new.

7. Which statement from this article contains an opinion?

Ⓐ Katonah has a railroad depot, and a post-office.
Ⓑ When the Water-Shed Commission said that it must move or be destroyed, the residents of Katonah gathered together, and decided that rather than be wiped off the face of the map, it would pick up its houses and move itself.
Ⓒ Did you ever see a house move? If you have not, you have missed a very funny sight.
Ⓓ A year or so ago the Croton water-shed water, which is in use in New York City, was found to be impure.

<u>The Great Round World and What's Going On In It</u>
magazine article -- Anonymous author

The news comes from Hamburg that the strike of the dock laborers is over.

The strikers have been beaten because of their lack of money.

In No. 7 of The Great Round World, you will find an account of the strike, and if you will also refer to No. 10, you will see that it was thought that the strikers could not hold out very much longer.

The money the strikers expected to receive from other labor unions to help them was so slow in coming that the men and their families were in want, and no man is likely to stand out for the benefit of others when his own children are suffering from cold and hunger.

The men have gone back to their old employers and asked for work. The pity of it all is, however, that during the strike others have been taken on in their places, and the employers have now no work to give them.

After holding out since the end of October, and refusing the masters' offer to give them $1.10 a day, and let all future troubles be settled by arbitration, the strikers have had to give in without gaining a single point. It is very sad.

8. According to this selection, if readers want to gather more information to determine whether or not the labor strike should have taken place, where should they look?

Ⓐ   In newspapers from Hamburg
Ⓑ   In past issues of the magazine this article was published in
Ⓒ   In an encyclopedia
Ⓓ   In other magazines

<u>The Great Round World and What's Going On In It</u>
magazine article -- Anonymous author

Blondin, the celebrated tight-rope walker, has just died in London, at the age of seventy-three.

The performance which made him famous was the crossing of Niagara Falls on the tight-rope.

Blondin was a Frenchman, his father having been one of Napoleon's soldiers.

A story is told of him that when he was five years old, he saw an acrobat performing on a tight-rope.

He was so pleased with what he saw, that when he got home, he stretched a rope between two posts, and, as soon as his mother was out of the way, took his father's fishing-rod, and, using it as a balancing pole, made his first appearance as a tight-rope walker.

He was trained for an acrobat and tight-rope walking and came to this country with a troupe of pantomimes.

While here, he visited Niagara Falls, and the idea at once struck him that, if he dared to cross those terrible waters on a rope, his fortune would be made. He made up his mind to try it, and stayed in the village of Niagara for weeks until he had learned just how it would be possible for him to perform the feat.

Then he set about getting the scheme well-advertised and securing plenty of money for himself if he succeeded in accomplishing it.

On August 17th, 1859, he made the trip across the Falls in the presence of 50,000 spectators. His rope was 175 feet above the waters.

He was not satisfied with merely walking across; he crossed again blindfolded and then carrying a man on his back, and once again wheeling a barrow before him.

In the summer of 1860, he crossed once more in the presence of the Prince of Wales and carried a man on his back, whom he set down on the rope six times, while he rested.

9. Which of the following does the author express in this article?

Ⓐ His opinions about Blondin
Ⓑ Factual information about Blondin
Ⓒ Both his opinions of Blondin and factual information
Ⓓ Blondin's input

Advertisement from <u>The Great Round World and What's Going On In It</u> magazine -- Anonymous author

FOUR FAMOUS BOOKS

Every boy and girl is interested in what is going on about them. The authors of this series have gathered together the most interesting kind of information and have told it in a most entertaining way.

Copies will be sent post-paid to any address upon receipt of price named.
1. Foods and Beverages, by E.A. Beal, M.D. Contains reading lessons on the various kinds of Foods and their hygienic values; on Grains, Fruits, and useful Plants, with elementary botanical instruction relating thereto; and on other common subjects of interest and importance to all, old and young.

281 pages. Cloth, 60 cents.

2. Every-Day Occupations, by H. Warren Clifford, S.D. Quantities of useful facts entertainingly told, relating to work and workers. How Leather is Tanned; How Silk is Made; The Mysteries of Glass-Making, of Cotton Manufacture, of Cloth-Making, of Ship and House Building; The Secrets of the Dyer's Art and the Potter's Skill—all and more are described and explained in detail with wonderful clearness. 330 pages. Cloth, 60 cents.

3. Man and Materials, by Wm. G. Parker, M.E. Shows how man has raised himself from savagery to civilization by utilizing the raw material of the earth. Brings for the first time the wonderful natural resources of the United States to the notice of American children. The progress of the Metal-Working arts simply described and very attractively illustrated. 323 pages. Cloth, 60 cents.

4. Modern Industries and Commerce, by Robert Louis, Ph.D. Treats of commerce and the different means of conveyance used in different eras. Highways, Canals. Tunnels, Railroads, and the Steam Engine are discussed in an entertaining way. Other subjects are Paper Manufacture, Newspapers, Electric Light, Atlantic Cable, the Telephone, and the principal newer commercial applications of Electricity, etc. 329 pages. Cloth, 60 cents.

10. Which of the following does the author express in this advertisement?

- Ⓐ his opinions about the books.
- Ⓑ factual information about the books
- Ⓒ both factual information about the books and the author's opinion of the books
- Ⓓ readers' viewpoints

Dear Mr. Smith,

Yesterday I visited your company's movie theater on Fourth Avenue to see the new film Return of the Giant Superhero. I have looked forward to seeing this movie for several weeks, as the advertisements on television and the previews at other movies made it seem like the most exciting movie of the year.

Because the movie is in 3-D, the ticket price was quite high at $17. I gladly paid this price, however, because I expected it to be a once in a lifetime experience, just as it was described on the poster in the lobby of your theater.

As you probably know, Return of the Giant Superhero is definitely not a once in a lifetime experience, and viewing it in your theater did nothing to improve how mediocre this movie is. First of all, I was disappointed to see that you screened the film in the smallest of your six theaters. Although only 16 of the 50 seats in the theater were filled, this is a movie intended for a large auditorium and the largest screen possible. I'm sure I would have enjoyed the film much more if I had watched it in a larger room.

Second, nothing makes a movie-experience even more fun than freshly popped popcorn. I am happy to hand over $5 for a bag of fresh, hot popcorn, but when the popcorn is ice-cold and stale to the point of being chewy, it can only make the customer's movie experience less than perfect.

Finally, it seems that you let just about anyone into the movies these days. For the price of a ticket, anyone can walk into the theater and spend the entire two hours talking on his phone, ruining the movie for the rest of us.

In conclusion, because the movie Return of the Giant Superhero was not as good as I expected it to be, and because I had to watch it in a small theater, while eating stale popcorn and listening to someone talk on his cell phone, I would like a refund for the price of my ticket, the popcorn, and the money I spent on transportation to visit your theater.

Thank you,

James Jones

11. Part A
What is a fact from the letter above?

Ⓐ Nothing makes a movie-experience even more fun than freshly popped popcorn.
Ⓑ Only 16 of the 50 seats were filled.
Ⓒ Because the movie is in 3-D, the ticket price was quite high at $17.
Ⓓ As you probably know, Return of the Giant Superhero is definitely not a once in a lifetime experience, and viewing it in your theater did nothing to improve how mediocre this movie is.

Part B
What is this writer's main claim?

Ⓐ The experience of watching a great movie was ruined because of this substandard theater.
Ⓑ This movie was terrible, but the theater was acceptable.
Ⓒ The movie was not very good and the experience at the theater was terrible.
Ⓓ The theater should reimburse the writer for the price of the popcorn.

Cycling Tours of Brooklyn

Brooklyn is an exciting borough of New York City and offers much to see and do. Visitors can enjoy many different shops and restaurants, as well as parks, museums, and outside festivals. A great way to visit Brooklyn is by bicycle and "Get up and Ride," a cycling tour company, offers two different options.

The Classic Tour

Distance – 10 miles

Duration – 3 to 3.5 hours

Stops include – Greenpoint, Brooklyn Heights, and the Brooklyn Navy Yard

Food and Drink – Stop in the Dekalb Marketplace

Special features – Cyclists end the day with a ferry ride to Manhattan

Cost - $65

The Best of Brooklyn Tour

Distance – 15 miles

Duration - 5 hours

Stops – All of the stops on the classic tour, plus Clinton Hill and Fort Green

Food and Drink – Stop in Dekalb Marketplace

Special Features – Cyclists end with a ferry ride to Manhattan

Cost - $95

The tours can accommodate groups of up to eight people. Bicycles and safety equipment are provided. Tours run Tuesday through Saturday and leave from Brooklyn Heights.

12. Part A
Which statement is a fact from the advertisement above?

Ⓐ Tours leave from Brooklyn Heights.
Ⓑ Brooklyn is exciting.
Ⓒ Visitors will enjoy the shops and restaurants in Brooklyn.
Ⓓ A good way to see Brooklyn is on a bicycle tour.

Part B
Which part of the text to be made in Italics?

Ⓐ The tour operator.
Ⓑ A cab driver in Brooklyn.
Ⓒ Someone who has gone on the Classic Tour.
Ⓓ Someone who has gone on the Best of Brooklyn Tour

13. What does the writer of this advertisement assume about the readers? Circle the correct answer choice.

Ⓐ They have visited Brooklyn before.
Ⓑ They live in Manhattan.
Ⓒ They own bicycles.
Ⓓ They know how to ride a bicycle.

Chapter 3

Lesson 9: Equal? Alike? Different? Comparing Authors

Let us understand the concept with an example.

Global Warming

For many years, scientists have been studying the effects of temperature on living organisms on planet Earth. In the last few years, there has been an increase in the earth's atmospheric and oceanic temperatures, which has been called global warming. Global warming has been recognized as a very important environmental phenomenon that can have dramatic and devastating effects on the environment of planet Earth.

Group A believes the theory that global warming is caused by the increase of certain gases (such as carbon dioxide) in the atmosphere that occurs when warmth from the sun is trapped in the Earth's atmosphere by a layer of gases (such as carbon dioxide) and water vapor. They refer to this as the "greenhouse effect." This group believes that human activities, such as manufacturing, deforestation and pollution are the primary contributors to the greenhouse effect.

Group A provides the following key details to support their theory: An IPCC (United Nations' Intergovernmental Panel on Climate Change) report, based on the work of some 2,500 scientists in more than 130 countries, concluded that humans have caused all or most of the current planetary warming. Human-caused global warming is often called anthropogenic climate change. Industrialization, deforestation, and pollution have greatly increased atmospheric concentrations of water vapor, carbon dioxide, methane, and nitrous oxide, all greenhouse gases that help trap heat near Earth's surface. Humans are pouring carbon dioxide into the atmosphere much faster than plants and oceans can absorb it.

Also, that 97% of the climate scientists surveyed believe "global average temperatures have increased" during the past century; and 97% think human activity is a significant contributing factor in changing mean global temperatures.

Group B believes the theory that global warming is not just a recent phenomenon, but is a natural phenomenon that has been occurring for thousands of years as part of a cycle of warming and cooling of the earth's atmosphere, and that human activity is only a minor contributor.

Group B provides the following key details to support their theory: 31,000 scientists reject global warming and say "no convincing evidence" that humans can or will cause global warming. This claim originates from an organization which published an online petition that they claim 31,000 scientists have signed.

Also, they mention that some experts point out that natural cycles in the Earth's orbit can alter the planet's exposure to sunlight, which may explain the current trend. Earth has indeed experienced warming and cooling cycles roughly every hundred thousand years due to these orbital shifts, but such changes have occurred over the span of several centuries.

Lastly, they claim that in 2009, hackers unearthed hundreds of emails stored at a university that exposed private conversations among some top-level climate scientists discussing whether certain data that did not support Group A's theory should be released to the public. The email exchanges also refer to statistical tricks used to illustrate climate change trends, according to a report in one major newspaper. Climate change skeptics have heralded the emails as an attempt to fool the public into accepting Group A's theory.

Your assignment: Comment on how Group A and Group B differ in the evidence they use and its interpretation to support their theories about the causes of global warming.

This is what you might write.

Both groups agree that the atmosphere is warming around the globe (planet earth). However, each group has a different theory about the causes of global warming, and each group believes its theory is correct and the other group's theory is not correct.

Specifically, Group A's theory states that "global warming is caused by the increase of certain gases (such as carbon dioxide) in the atmosphere that occurs when warmth from the sun is trapped in the Earth's atmosphere by a layer of gases (such as carbon dioxide) and water vapor." They call this the "greenhouse effect." They believe that human activities, such as manufacturing, deforestation and pollution are the primary contributors to the greenhouse effect. In support of this theory they cite a report from a United Nations panel, which used input from 2500 scientists from 103 countries.

Group B's theory states that "global warming is not just a recent phenomenon, but is a natural phenomenon that has been occurring for thousands of years as part of a cycle of warming and cooling of the earth's atmosphere, and that human activity is only a minor contributor." They cite a petition signed by 31,000 scientists that states there is no evidence that human activities have or will cause global warming. They also point out emails among scientists that discuss whether that data that does not support Group A's theory should be released to the public, which is challenging the integrity of these scientists.

You can scan the QR code given below or use the url to access additional EdSearch resources including videos and mobile apps related to *Equal? Alike? Different? Comparing Authors.*

 **Equal? Alike? Different? Comparing Authors**

URL	QR Code
http://www.lumoslearning.com/a/ri79	

PASSAGE A:

When I was in the fourth grade, no one liked me because my brother was arrested, and that made everyone think that I might do something illegal too. It hurt my feelings to have to sit through school every day and not talk to anyone. When it was time to work in groups, I would have to sit with a group of kids that I knew hated me. Sometimes they would say something mean or move a chair away when it looked like I might sit with them. It was worse during lunch and on the bus when kids would yell things about my brother and ask me if I visited him in prison. After a while, I didn't want to go to school anymore, and I pretended to be sick every day, so I could stay home. Telling my parents and my teachers didn't change anything. After a while, my parents decided to let me change schools. The first year at my new school was bad because I didn't know anyone and was afraid to talk to people because of everything that happened at the old school. After a while, I made a few friends, and I started to feel better about talking to people. Now I have a few friends, and I don't feel like people are bullying me anymore.

PASSAGE B:

According to Dr. Norman Anderson, CEO of the American Psychological Association, bullying is any kind of aggressive behavior in which someone intentionally tries to harm or cause discomfort to another person. Bullying can be in the form of physical contact but is just as frequently demonstrated in cruel remarks, intentional exclusion of the victim, or in recent years, cyberbullying, in which the aggressor lashes out to the victim via e-mail, social networking, or text messaging.

There is no single, identifiable cause of bullying. Bullying often occurs as a result of influences from peer groups, family groups, communities, or even the media. It is, therefore, important to engage all of these groups if any anti-bullying effort is to be successful.

For many years, the primary means employed by schools to deal with the student to student bullying has been to punish the aggressor. Research has shown that disciplinary consequences alone will not significantly curb bullying in academic settings. Faculty and administrators must be trained to identify early warning signs that students are either bullies or being bullied, and onlookers, students who are not bullies themselves, but do nothing to inhibit bullying they witness, must be empowered with interpersonal skills training to help them intervene when they witness bullying within their peer groups.

1. According to the author of Passage B, what strategy would most likely have helped the author of Passage A?

Ⓐ Disciplinary consequences for the bullies
Ⓑ Changing schools
Ⓒ Training "onlookers" to intervene when they witness bullying
Ⓓ Counseling for the bullying victim

2. What information from Passage B best explains this line from Passage A:

Telling my parents and my teachers didn't change anything.

Ⓐ Faculty and administrators must be trained to identify early warning signs that students are either bullies or being bullied.
Ⓑ Bullying often occurs as a result of influences from peer groups, family groups, community, or even the media.
Ⓒ Bullying can be in the form of physical contact, but is just as frequently demonstrated in cruel remarks, intentional exclusion of the victim, or in recent years, cyber bullying, in which the aggressor lashes out to the victim via e-mail, social networking, or text messaging.
Ⓓ For many years, the primary means employed by schools to deal with student to student bullying has been to punish the aggressor.

3. Which passage was most likely written by a middle school student?

Ⓐ Passage A
Ⓑ Passage B
Ⓒ Both passages
Ⓓ There is not enough information to determine the authors.

4. Which passage explains what is meant by bullying?

Ⓐ Passage A
Ⓑ Passage B
Ⓒ Both passages
Ⓓ Neither passage

5. Which form of bullying described in Passage B was experienced by the author of Passage A?

Ⓐ Physical contact
Ⓑ Intentional exclusion
Ⓒ Bullying by way of social media
Ⓓ Cyber-bullying

Success

One should guard against preaching to young people success in the customary form as the main aim in life. The most important motive for work in school and in life is pleasure in work, pleasure in a result, and the knowledge of the value of the result to the community.
- Albert Einstein

The way to learn to do things is to do things. The way to learn a trade is to work at it. Success teaches how to succeed. Begin with the determination to succeed, and the work is half-done already.
- Henry Ford

"What Constitutes Success"
By Bessie Stanley (1905)

He has achieved success who has lived well,
laughed often and loved much;
who has gained the respect of intelligent men
and the love of little children;
who has filled his niche and accomplished his task;
who has left the world better than he found it,
whether by an improved poppy, a perfect poem, or a rescued soul;
who has never lacked appreciation of earth's beauty
or failed to express it;
who has always looked for the best in others
and given them the best he had;
whose life was an inspiration;
whose memory a benediction.

6. Which of the other two authors likely shared Einstein's idea of what constitutes success?

Ⓐ Henry Ford
Ⓑ Bessie Stanley
Ⓒ Both authors
Ⓓ Neither author

7. Which of the authors most likely subscribed to what Einstein referred to as "success in the customary form?"

Ⓐ Albert Einstein
Ⓑ Bessie Stanley
Ⓒ Henry Ford
Ⓓ None of the authors.

Steve Jobs, the CEO of Apple Computer, once said, "Being the richest man in the cemetery doesn't matter to me...Going to bed at night saying I've done something wonderful...that's what matters to me."

8. Which of the expressions about success above most closely align with Jobs' idea?

- Ⓐ Albert Einstein
- Ⓑ Henry Ford
- Ⓒ Bessie Stanley
- Ⓓ Both B and C.

9. Which of the authors above aligns themselves with the desire to succeed through industrial work for the common man?

- Ⓐ Albert Einstein
- Ⓑ Henry Ford
- Ⓒ Bessie Stanley
- Ⓓ Both Ford and Einstein

10. Which of the authors above would most strongly disagree with Ford's interpretation of success?

- Ⓐ Albert Einstein
- Ⓑ Steve Jobs
- Ⓒ Bessie Stanley
- Ⓓ None of the above.

The Assassination of President Lincoln
April 14, 1865

Shortly after 10 p.m. on April 14, 1865, actor John Wilkes Booth entered the presidential box at Ford's Theatre in Washington D.C., and fatally shot President Abraham Lincoln. As Lincoln slumped forward in his seat, Booth leapt onto the stage and escaped through the back door. A doctor in the audience rushed over to examine the paralyzed president. Lincoln was then carried across the street to Petersen's Boarding House, where he died early the next morning.

Lincoln was the first president assassinated in U.S. history. Why did Booth do it? He thought it would aid the South, which had just surrendered to Federal forces. It had nearly the opposite effect, ending Lincoln's plans for a rather generous peace. Booth did not act alone. This "wanted" poster appeared everywhere, offering a reward for the arrest of Booth and his accomplices. The conspirators were all captured, and Booth was shot while trying to escape from Union soldiers.

The whole country grieved the death of President Lincoln. As the nine-car funeral train carried President Lincoln home for burial in Springfield, Illinois, people showed up at train stations all along the way to pay their respects.

"The Assassination of President Lincoln." The Assassination of President Lincoln. N.p., n.d. Web. 15 July 2013. <http://www.americaslibrary.gov/jb/civil/jb_civil_lincoln_1.html>.

The Martyr
BY Herman Melville

Indicative of the passion of the people
on the 15th of April, 1865

Good Friday was the day
  Of the prodigy and crime,
When they killed him in his pity,
  When they killed him in his prime
Of clemency and calm—
  When with yearning he was filled
  To redeem the evil-willed,
And, though conqueror, be kind;
  But they killed him in his kindness,
  In their madness and their blindness,
And they killed him from behind.

        There is sobbing of the strong,
          And a pall upon the land;
        But the People in their weeping
                    Bare the iron hand:
        Beware the People weeping
          When they bare the iron hand.

He lieth in his blood—
  The father in his face;
They have killed him, the Forgiver—
  The Avenger takes his place,
The Avenger wisely stern,
  Who in righteousness shall do
  What heavens call him to,
And the parricides remand;
  For they killed him in his kindness,
  In their madness and their blindness.
And his blood is on their hand.

        There is sobbing of the strong,
          And a pall upon the land;
        But the People in their weeping
            Bare the iron hand:
        Beware the People weeping
          When they bare the iron hand.

Source: "Words for the Hour": A New Anthology of American Civil War Poetry, edited by Faith Barrett and Cristanne Miller (University of Massachusetts Press, 2005).

11. Part A
Which phrase below describes Booth and his accomplices?

Ⓐ in his kindness
Ⓑ in their madness and their blindness
Ⓒ the Forgiver
Ⓓ the Avenger

Part B
What was Melville's purpose in writing the poem above?

Ⓐ To express the emotions around Lincoln's death
Ⓑ To show how well Melville knew about the incident
Ⓒ To express the love of Lincoln
Ⓓ To explain how Lincoln died

12. Part A
What would the first passage be used for?

Ⓐ writing a song
Ⓑ inspiration for art
Ⓒ comic video
Ⓓ informational speech

12. Part B
Based on the passage, who helped Booth?

Ⓐ Mrs. Todd and the maid
Ⓑ Lee and Grant
Ⓒ Surratt and Harold
Ⓓ the CIA and Booth

End of Reading: Informational Text

Answer Key and
Detailed Explanations

Chapter 3
Reading: Informational Text

Lesson 1: Key Ideas and Details

Question No.	Answer	Detailed Explanations
1	B	Answer choice two is correct. Choice one describes how Verdi felt about the organ and man in town, and choices three and four talk about the spinet being fixed. Only choice two references how much he enjoyed practicing – so much so that he wore it out.
2	D	The answer choice four is correct. The other choices talk about what skunks eat, but choice four specifically discusses how much they eat.
3	C	The answer choice three is correct. Choices one and two are not true because the author doesn't need to provide the info in choice one and does provide the info negated in choice two. Choice four is true for the passage, but does not connect with skunks being omnivores.
4	A	Answer choice one is correct. The other choices explain what the skin does, but none come closer than choice one to explaining WHY it is being developed.
5	C	Answer choice three is correct. It explains that dogs can smell low blood sugar, so the reader can infer that's what helps diabetic patients. The other choices talk about the training research, and diabetics in general.
6	A	Answer choice one is correct. The researcher wants to reproduce the sensitivity in a way that will help patients. Dogs already have the sensitivity, so choices two and three are not correct, and choice four, while plausible, doesn't seem very useful.
7	C	Option C is the correct answer choice as a large number of people can be benefitted if a method of reproducing the sensitivity is found.
8	A	Answer choice one is correct. Rule three discusses what happens if you are tardy. Other choices relate to being prepared and knowing what to do when class starts or if you miss class.
9	A	Answer choice one is correct. The other choices talk about the effects and aftermath of his decision.
10	B	Answer choice two is correct. Booth was an actor, so that likely helped him gain access to the theatre. The other choices do not help answer the question.

Question No.	Answer	Detailed Explanations
11	D	Answer choice four is correct. The other three passages tell (with choice two telling about Booth, not Lincoln), but answer choice four gives a specific example of how people responded to Lincoln's death.

Lesson 2: Get Right to the Point

Question No.	Answer	Detailed Explanations
1	B	All answer choices seem to be correct, but the best answer is the second choice. The article does discuss fall weather and trees, but it does not <u>focus</u> on weather. Also, the point is not the life cycle of TREES, but the process of the leaves turning in the fall and dropping from the trees.
2	A	The first answer choice is the best one because the passage explains why leaves change colors, why there are different colors and why and how they fall off of trees. The second answer choice is not the best. The passage explains the different colors, but it explains more than just that, so it is not the best answer. The third answer choice is not correct because the excerpt mentions certain regions of the country, but that is not what the remainder of the passage is about. The fourth answer is not the best answer because chlorophyll is discussed, but that is a small portion of the passage.
3	C	Answer choice three is the best answer. The first choice is only about winter sports. The second answer is closer to what the article is about, however the third answer is BEST. The last answer is not appropriate. Popular Sports is too broad. The article was about a specific sporting event that is extremely old, so the third answer choice is the most accurate.
4	C	The last answer choice is the best choice. The passage discusses how various parts of the pyramids were possibly constructed. No one is sure exactly how they were built; they only have theories.
5	B	Answer choice number one is not the best answer because the passage did not discuss the people used to build the pyramids, only the techniques of the actual construction. Answer choice number two is the best answer because the passage discusses several beliefs or theories as to how the pyramids were constructed. Answer choice number three is not the best answer because carving the boulders or stones is only part of how the pyramids were built. This answer choice is incomplete. Answer choice number four is not the best choice because the discussion of architecture is at the beginning of the passage and is referring to how structures are built in modern times.

Question No.	Answer	Detailed Explanations
6	A	Answer choice one is the best answer. All choices are basically correct, but the first one is the best for the passage. He was from Italy, he did play the spinet every day and probably wore it out sooner than most. But, the point of the passage is to tell the reader that the young boy loved his music and was committed to playing every day.
7	A	Answer choice one is the best answer. Lincoln was concerned that the country might stay divided even after the war ended. He was attempting to get people to understand that if the country did not come back together as one nation, all the men who died in the Civil War would have died for nothing. He believes to honor the dead, the country should stay as one.
8	A	Answer choice one is the best answer. The other answer choices are related to the passage, except for three, but they are not the BEST answers. The best choice indicates that Woo is very good at action scenes and loves to do them. Answer choice three is not at all reasonable for this passage.
9	B	Answer choice two is the correct answer. Answer choice one is a true statement, but it is not the complete answer for the question. Answer choice three is interesting, and the author sort of hints at this concept in the beginning of the passage, but it is not the point of the passage. The people of Katonah were upset, but they chose to move before someone forced them to move. So, they are not really angry, but more proactive.
10	B	Answer choice two is the best answer. The article is about strikes and unions but that is not the overall focus of the story. And the article does not really elaborate on the "why" of the strike, only the end and what happened to the men.
11	C	Answer choice three is the best answer. The article explains how to get started and details the easy steps and low cost.

Question No.	Answer	Detailed Explanations
12 Part A	B	Answer choice number one is not the correct choice because the passage did not mention any of his friends. Also, the book his writings are in was not necessarily published when he wrote them. Publishing was not an option at the time Archimedes lived. Answer choice number two is the best choice because all of the book titles suggest that they were about new inventions or using tools they already had in new ways to improve the lives of the people of Archimedes' time. Answer choice number three uses an absolute (all) which suggest that no one was interested in anything other than inventions, and this would not be true. In addition, Archimedes books were not written in the way people do today. Answer choice number four is true, but it is not the BEST answer because it does not take the entire passage's information into account.
12 Part B		While any person might find Archimedes interesting and be able to appreciate how his writing influence math and science today, the BEST answer for this is Engineer. Engineers design things such as roads, cars, chemical uses. They need to know a great deal about math.
13	C	Answer choice three is the best answer. The plants are endangered and the laws are in place to help ensure the unique plant's future.

Lesson 3: Relationship Between People and Events

Question No.	Answer	Detailed Explanations
1	A	Answer choice number one is the best answer choice. If the reader substitutes "because" for "due," it is easier to see a relationship. Because indicates a connection of two or more items.
2	A	Order words indicate the order events occurred. First, second, third, lastly, finally are words that aid the reader in knowing the order events occurred.
3	B	Answer choice number two. These words are transition words that are used when writing a piece that is cause and effect.
4	D	The correct answer choice is the fourth answer. The word "as" indicates to the reader that two or more things are occurring at the same time. The sentence says that "As the president slumped, Booth..."
5	A	The first paragraph states the events in order. After Booth entered the theater, he shoots Lincoln. So, the SECOND thing that occurred was for Booth to shoot Lincoln.
6	C	Answer choice three is the best answer. The third paragraph tells the reader that the country grieved or mourned the death of Lincoln. This paragraph also says that because of this the people came to train stations to watch his body go by on the train.
7	D	The bolded sentence explains why Booth shot Lincoln and what the effect of that shooting had on the peace effort. Booth thought that if he killed Lincoln, it would help the south (cause and effect). The cause is still the same, but in reality the true effect was that it created more stress among the participants of the war.
8		The second paragraph discusses why Booth did what he did and the order (sequence) of events that led to Booth's demise.

Lesson 4: Getting Technical

Question No.	Answer	Detailed Explanations
1	A	Answer choice one is the best selection. The passage says that the nano hairs are made of polymers and plastic. These are not natural or organic.
2	C	Answer choice three is the best answer. "Artificial skin can be used to cover prosthetic leg" hints that all parts are not real/natural.
3	C	Answer choice three is the best answer. The article describes what has to be recorded and tracked, and it mentions using sensors to do this.
4	C	Answer choice number three is the best selection. The passage mentions under childhood feet which implies that these are items a child might run across while walking outside. NONE of the other three choices apply to this passage.
5	B	Answer choice two is the best answer. Impure means not perfect or clean. The passage mentions water being impure and then later discusses how water was unfit to drink. Therefore not safe to drink is the best choice.
6	B	Answer choice two is the best. The passage is about workers who did not work in a holdout for more money. When a worker strikes, he/she is trying to get more money by causing the trouble for the employers in hopes they'd give the workers more money.
7	C	The answer choice three is the best answer. The first line tells the reader what skunks eat, and it mentions eating fruits, veggies and other animals.
8	C	Answer choice number three is the best answer. The phrase "unable to find live animals to eat," indicates that scavenger means to eat dead animals.
9	C	Answer choice three is the best answer. The phrase "press the portions outward" explain that "relief" means to not be flat, but to be above the picture.
10	B	Answer choice two is the best answer. This passage is about counting the votes to elect President McKinley. The process is described and includes the Senate and the House of Representatives. These are parts of the U. S. Government.

Question No.	Answer	Detailed Explanations
11 Part A	C	Answer choice three is the best answer. The question asks what the teacher means by rude gestures by asking which choice is NOT rude. The other answer choices would be rude to others.
11 Part B	A	Answer choice number one is the best choice. The hunting is used to explain that the students should not hunt someone to treat poorly.
12 Part A	C	Answer choice three is the best answer choice. The line directly above the example tells the reader what to do and to be specific; use lots of supporting evidence.
12 Part B	B	Answer choice two is the best answer. The directions ask the student to make two lists. One of important characters in the novel Someone Was Watching and their own novel. The question asks what they were to do with the novel Someone Was Watching.

Lesson 5: How is it Built? Analyzing structure

Question No.	Answer	Detailed Explanations
1	A	Answer choice one is the best answer. Each paragraph covers a different aspect of the life of the Bushmen. Answer choice two is not at all reasonable. The passage does not narrow down to one aspect. Answer choice three is incorrect because the passage is not organized in the order something happened. Answer four is incorrect too because there is nothing to compare. This is an informative passage.
2	A	Answer choice one is the best answer to the question. The second answer is part of the passage, but does not address the question asked. The last two answer choices are in the passage, but they are not "sections" that would answer the question.
3	D	Answer choice four is the correct answer. The title of the book tells the reader the subject of the book. Each chapter title is a place on the farm where specific flowers would grow. Answers one and two are correct, but four is the most correct. Answer three does not make sense for this question.
4	D	Answer choice four is the correct answer. This section discusses the odor that skunks' spray causes. It also discusses how to alleviate the smell by giving suggestions on what to use to bathe the affected person/animal. None of the remaining three answers discuss removing the smell from a person or animal.
5	D	Answer choice four is the best answer. Answer choice one is correct, but not a complete answer. Answer choice two is also correct, but not as good answer as choice number four. Answer choice three is not correct for this passage. Therefore, answer choice four is the best answer because it is the most complete.
6	A	Answer choice one is the correct answer. The article tells of a tightrope walker. It chronicles a period of time in the walker's life. It is done so in the order that the events happened, thus the answer is chronological.
7	B	Answer choice two is the correct answer. There are no true headings for the advertisement (choice one), and choice three does not make sense. How can the person making the advertisement know what everybody else's interests are? The last answer choice is true, but not the best answer for the question.

Question No.	Answer	Detailed Explanations
8	A	Answer choice one is the correct answer. The title is at the top of the passage, but sections are labeled with headings to help the reader know what the main topic of the paragraph(s) will be. Graphics are not used, topics are, but the headings are the main way the reader knows the topics. Subheadings are not used.
9	D	Answer choice four is the correct answer. Humans would dump garbage, and so this is the heading that makes the most sense.
10	A	Answer choice one is the correct answer. The topic of the article is at the beginning. Each section is about a different tip or concern. This is a sub-topical organization.
11	C	Answer choice three is the correct answer. The format is set up to persuade someone by giving them information on a product/service. So, this is an advertisement.
12	B	Answer choice two is correct. The tours are presented with some of the same categories. One tour has more, but both have identical aspects.

Lesson 6: What's the Author's Angle?

Question No.	Answer	Detailed Explanations
1	A	Answer choice number one is the best one. The other three answers are not positive or encouraging. The first choice is positive of Verdi.
2	B	Answer choice number two is the best answer. The author describes the Czar's personality and discusses what others thought of him. The author mentions the Czar's gentleness and desire to not be so firm as his father, yet most of the people did not understand this, so he was not well thought of. The author feels the Czar was trying to do well and was misunderstood.
3	A	Answer choice number one is the best choice. The article describes how the old books will be discounted and that the facilities are "greatly increased." This tells the reader that the author is pleased with his new store.
4	C	Answer choice three is the best choice. The passage mentions the charts and graphs and then states it is not a pretty picture book. Therefore the author is not to agree with the statement that it is a pretty book.
5	C	Answer choice number three is the best answer. Although the author thinks that the invention is limiting due to having to know how to do the process, he does think that the invention is very good!
6	B	Answer choice number two is the best choice. The author chronicles what the striking workers did and how they felt. Then the author mentions that they worked really hard but were not successful. The author indicates he's sad for the workers' lack of success.
7	C	Answer choice three is the best answer. The residents knew they were going to have their town destroyed, so they made the decision to move themselves and maintain their town.
8	B	Answer choice number two is the best. The author explains his opinion of collecting cards. The tone is pleasant and explains how/why one would want to collect cards.
9	C	Answer choice three is the correct answer. The author states in the first part of the passage that children are curious and want to know things. This indicates that he believes the books listed will be interesting and useful to children.

Question No.	Answer	Detailed Explanations
10	B	Answer choice two is the correct answer. A testimonial is a technique of advertising where someone who has used the product shares their experiences (positive). This is intended to encourage others to use/buy the product as well.
11 Part A	C	Answer choice three is correct. By giving an example or anecdotal story, the reader feels a more personal connection. This connection helps the reader relate to the story, thus making it more meaningful.
11 Part B	D	Answer choice four is correct. The time and cost of training a dog is intense. The author wants the reader to know that the dogs are valuable for the owner, but also to understand that training is time consuming and expensive.
11 Part C	A	Answer choice number one is the best answer. By stating that a diabetic person could go into a coma the author tells the reader that diabetes is a serious disease and the research being done is important and valuable.
12	B	Answer choice two is the correct choice. The reader should be aware of any opinions or beliefs the author might have. This is important because the author's own beliefs often cause the information to be shared in a way to support the author. This does not mean the author is wrong, or should not be given credit, but the reader needs to keep this in mind while reading.
13	C	Answer choice three is the correct answer. The remaining three choices are supposed to have opinions. A news report should only include the facts: who, what, when, where. The author should not interject his opinion.

Lesson 7: Comparing Media

Question No.	Answer	Detailed Explanations
1	A	Answer choice one is correct. A time-lapse video of the leaves changing color may be included in a documentary to help someone understand how the leaves change color. Paintings are just representations, not the real thing, animals hibernating are an example given in the text but not helpful, and subtitles wouldn't do much more than the text itself.
2	C	Answer choice three is correct. A diagram of the process would be most helpful. The other three could be used to make it more entertaining or to add minor details.
3	B	Answer choice two is correct. While a diagram would be helpful and the picture and photograph would be interesting, letting students see and compare the leaves would be best.
4	C	Answer choice three is the best answer. Choices one and four are too recent to be useful and answer choice two is not possible because video didn't exist during the original Olympics.
5	B	Answer choice two is the best answer. Having students play the games will make the passage more interactive and help them understand the different sports it talks about.
6	A	Answer choice one is the best answer. The piece talks about the Olympics, so they should air it near the Olympics competition so that it makes more sense.
7	B	Answer choice two is correct. The passage talks about Egyptian pyramids and how they were built, so it would best be paired with images of the building process. Answer choice three is plausible, but not directly related to building.
8	A	Answer choice one is correct. The opening paragraph references some of today's breath-taking structures in the world today, so it'd make sense to open the documentary with pictures of skyscrapers. Choices two and three would come later in the documentary, while choice four is too ordinary to be included.
9	C	Answer choice three is correct. Plays are usually fiction, so it would most likely focus on a specific worker or group of workers and tell their story. Choice one is likely but the pyramids wouldn't be the main focus. Choice four could be part, but not the entire thing and choice two does not fit the play genre.

Question No.	Answer	Detailed Explanations
10	B	Answer choice two is the correct answer. Since plays normally tell stories, this passage could easily inspire a play about Verdi's childhood. A news story is not likely because this passage is from the past, a song would be awkward, and the narrative format doesn't really fit a slideshow.
11 part A	D	Answer choice four is the correct answer. The spaceflights in both time frames carried humans, and often more than one.
11 Part B	A	Answer choice one is correct. The main difference between the two missions is time in space (Gagarun's time was 7.2 times longer) and the fact that Shepard flew his own spacecraft. Both splashed down and only Shepard flew his own spacecraft.
11 part C	C	Answer choice three is the best answer. The other answer choices were true in either the '60's and '80's. Or both.
12	B	Answer choice two is the correct answer. Since plays normally tell stories, this passage could easily inspire a play about Verdi's childhood. A news story is not likely because this passage is from the past, a song would be awkward, and the narrative format doesn't really fit a slideshow.

Lesson 8: What's the Author's Point?

Question No.	Answer	Detailed Explanations
1	C	Answer choice three is correct. A scientist should present the information without any slant or bias to a specific belief or cause. A journalist might want to tell a story with more exciting aspects to get viewers, a student might not know enough facts and information to be completely accurate, and an activist might have a cause they want focus on, so they might not be as fair at the information as a scientist should be.
2	C	Answer choice three is correct. One could interview the author, but what if he/she did not research properly? Reading an encyclopedia is a good start, but the historian who specializes in Egypt would be the best source for verifying the information. Going to Egypt might be fun, but that would not necessarily tell the reader if the information in the article is factual.
3	C	Answer choice three is the best answer. It is verifiable. "All accounts" could be interviewed to see if that is really what people believe. The remaining answers involve opinions. Saying someone is too weak, or pretty, or smart is an opinion. What one person believes is too weak is not necessarily what another believes. And no one but Nicholas knows if he is overcome. So, the only reasonable answer is three.
4	A	Answer choice one is the correct answer. Nicholas could verify what happened, but he is involved in the incident; he might not have seen everything. There is no paper at that time to consult, and if there was, this story would not be in the paper. The author of the article believes it to be so, but that does not mean it actually happened. The best answer is to ask someone who saw what happened. Preferably one who only witnessed the event, not one who was involved.
5	A	Answer choice one is NOT a fact. It is an opinion that this store is better than any other in the city. That cannot be proven. The other choices are in fact something that could be verified.

Question No.	Answer	Detailed Explanations
6	D	Answer choice four is the correct answer. A child would need to follow directions in various places. The backyard is not varied enough. Just buying the book will not help prove the bolded portion of the information. Interviewing the author is pointless. Obviously he/she believes it will work, or they would not have included the information in the book.
7	C	Answer choice three is the correct answer. The word funny is not provable. What is funny to one person is not necessarily funny to another. The remaining three answer choices are facts that can easily be proven by details and information easily obtained.
8	B	The article tells the reader where he/she can find more background information on the strike (No.'s 7 & 10); answer choice two is the correct answer. The other answer choices do not make sense. To find information on a specific event, just "other magazines" is not detailed enough to find the necessary information. Newspapers might be a good source, but since the author tells the reader where the information is, looking through old newspapers is not necessary. And an encyclopedia would not have that information recorded yet. The news is too new.
9	B	Answer choice two is correct. The passage is factual information. Opinions of anyone are not included.
10	C	Answer choice three is the correct answer. He does not include readers' viewpoints and the other two answers are correct, but the third answer is the most correct.
11 Part A	B	Answer choice two is the correct answer. The remaining answer choices are opinion statements. For example "quite high movie price" is not the same for everyone. What one person might consider too high could be ten dollars. Others might not think twenty-five dollars is okay. The other statements are similarly written: the letter writer's opinion.
11 Part B	C	Answer choice three is the correct answer. The movie theater was substandard, but there were other issues too. Answer choice two is not correct because the author was not happy at all with the theater. Answer choice four is partially correct. He does want to be reimbursed for the popcorn, but he wants to be reimbursed for everything.

Question No.	Answer	Detailed Explanations
12 Part A	A	Enjoy, good and exciting are opinion words. So those answer choices are not factual or correct. The proper answer choice is the first one. The answer can be verified by the advertisement.
12 Part B	A	Answer choice one is the best answer. The other answer choices are related to the acitivites, because the people would have some experience with the tours. However, the tour operator would know more than the other three people.
13	D	Answer choice four is correct. If a person did not know how to ride a bicycle, he/she would not consider a bike tour. And a tour would be for tourists, so they would not have their own bikes. And a tour of Brooklyn is more likely for someone who has NOT been to Brooklyn before. Otherwise they would not need a tour.

Lesson 9: Equal? Alike? Different? Comparing Authors

Question No.	Answer	Detailed Explanations
1	C	Answer choice number three is the correct selection. If someone had been able to intervene, it would have helped the victim in the first passage. The other three answers are good answers in general, but the third answer best fits the situation of the boy in passage A.
2	A	Answer choice one is the correct answer. The first passage tells an incident, the second passage is informational. They are both about bullying, but from a different genre.
3	A	Answer choice one is correct. The first passage tells about a young man who was a victim of bullying. The second passage is informational and contains information, that mostly adults would know. So, the first answer choice is the correct one.
4	C	Answer choice three is correct. Both passages explain bullying.
5	B	Answer choice two is correct. All three of the other answers are forms of bullying, but not the experience of the victim in the first passage.
6	B	Answer choice two is the best answer. Einstein was someone who was not always thinking and behaving "normal." His ideas were very unusual for his time, so the free thinking of Stanley is more aligned with the scientist.
7	C	Answer choice three is the correct answer. Ford was a creative person, but his ideas were more business minded. So, his ideas were more "customary" or normal.
8	D	Both Einstein and Stanley wanted a better world.
9	B	Answer choice number two is the correct answer. Ford was responsible for the assembly line, something that most people could do, and it helped to change the way industry ran in America. But, his ideas and attitudes were more for the regular person, whereas the others were very broad and difficult for many people to grasp.
10	C	Answer choice three is correct. Stanley gives more of an air of societal success, which in itself is more likely to be criticized.

Question No.	Answer	Detailed Explanations
11 Part A	B	Answer choice two is the best answer. In the passage we learn that Booth did not know that the South had surrendered, and in the poem being mad (crazy with anger) and blind (without knowledge) describes Booth and his helpers.
11 Part B	A	Answer choice one is the best option. Poetry is written for entertainment or to evoke emotions. This poem expresses how upset the American people were at Lincoln's death.
12 Part A	D	Answer choice four is the best answer. The first passage has more details that can be verified, so it would be the best to use for an informational speech.
12 Part B	C	Answer choice three is the best answer. The image in the article shows pictures and names Booth's accomplices.

Chapter 4 - Language

The objective of the Language standards is to ensure that the student is able to accurately use grade appropriate general academic and domain specific words and phrases related to Grade 7.

To help students to master the necessary skills, we encourage the student to go through the resources available online on EdSearch to gain an in depth understanding of these concepts. The EdSearch page for each lesson can be accessed with the help of the url or the QR code provided.

Chapter 4

Lesson 1: Phrases and Clauses are Coming to Town

You can scan the QR code given below or use the url to access additional EdSearch resources including videos and mobile apps related to *Phrases and Clauses are Coming to Town.*

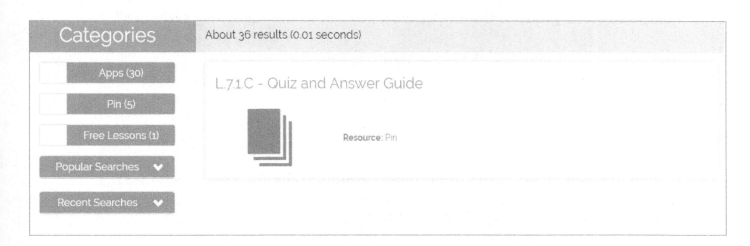

Categories	About 36 results (0.01 seconds)
Apps (30)	L.7.1.C - Quiz and Answer Guide
Pin (5)	
Free Lessons (1)	Resource: Pin
Popular Searches ⌄	
Recent Searches ⌄	

ed)Search   ***Phrases and Clauses are Coming to Town***

URL	QR Code
http://www.lumoslearning.com/a/l71	

1. What type of word group is the following?

Walking down the street

(A) Phrase
(B) Dependent Clause
(C) Independent Clause
(D) Dependent Phrase

2. What type of word group is the underlined portion of the following sentence?

After leaving school, <u>I realized I left my science textbook in my locker.</u>

(A) Phrase
(B) Dependent Clause
(C) Independent Clause
(D) Complete Phrase

3. What type of word group is the underlined portion of the following sentence?

<u>Next Saturday</u>, my family is going to the beach.

(A) Phrase
(B) Dependent Clause
(C) Independent Clause
(D) Complete Clause

4. What type of word group is the underlined portion of the following sentence?

I need a new cell phone because my old phone <u>fell in the toilet</u>.

(A) phrase
(B) dependent clause
(C) independent clause
(D) prepositional clause

5. What type of word group is the underlined portion of the following sentence?

I need a new cell phone <u>because my old phone fell in the toilet</u>.

(A) Phrase
(B) Dependent Clause
(C) Independent Clause
(D) Complete Clause

6. What type of word group is the underlined portion of the following sentence?

The actor <u>who starred in the movie version of one of my favorite books</u> did a horrible job playing the main character.

Ⓐ phrase
Ⓑ dependent clause
Ⓒ independent clause
Ⓓ interrupter phrase

7. What type of word group is the underlined portion of the following sentence?

<u>I decided to hope for the best</u>, but to expect the worst.

Ⓐ phrase
Ⓑ dependent clause
Ⓒ independent clause
Ⓓ dependent phrase

8. What type of word group is the underlined portion of the following sentence?

Fireworks are <u>amazing and beautiful</u> to me.

9. What type of word group is the underlined portion of the following sentence?

Good things tend to happen to you <u>when you least expect them</u>.

10. What type of word group is the underlined portion of the following sentence?

<u>Carley and Lori both bought their prom dresses from the same boutique</u> and their shoes from the same shoe store.

Chapter 4

Lesson 2: Good Sentences are Built on Agreement

You can scan the QR code given below or use the url to access additional EdSearch resources including videos and mobile apps related to *Good Sentences are Built on Agreement.*

 **Good Sentences are Built on Agreement**

URL	QR Code
http://www.lumoslearning.com/a/l71	

1. Which of the following verb forms correctly fills in the blank in the following sentence?

Almost everybody _____ glad we do not have school next Monday.

Ⓐ is
Ⓑ are
Ⓒ were
Ⓓ am

2. Which of the following sentences has correct subject-verb agreement?

Ⓐ Each of my sisters have their rooms.
Ⓑ Marco's car needs a new transmission and a new clutch.
Ⓒ My cat don't fit through the kitty door because its stomach is so fat.
Ⓓ Drinking water help you lose weight.

3. Which of the following verb forms correctly fills in the blank in the following sentence?

Even though Randy _____ tomatoes, he loves spaghetti sauce.

Ⓐ hate
Ⓑ hates
Ⓒ hated
Ⓓ like

4. Which of the following sentences has correct subject-verb agreement?

Ⓐ Every one of us have a purpose in life.
Ⓑ Angela and her best friend goes out for pizza every Friday night.
Ⓒ I hope my favorite football team play well this weekend.
Ⓓ Why do my neighbors always get louder at night?

5. Which of the following verb forms correctly fills in the blank in the following sentence?

Neither of my parents _____ going on vacation.

Ⓐ enjoy
Ⓑ enjoys
Ⓒ enjoying
Ⓓ are enjoying

6. Which of the following versions of the sentence has correct subject-verb agreement?

Ⓐ A positive attitude and motivation make school easier.
Ⓑ A positive attitude and motivation makes school easier.
Ⓒ A positive attitude and motivation is making school easier.
Ⓓ A positive attitude and motivation maked school easier.

7. Which sentence has correct subject-verb agreement?

Ⓐ Both my cat and my dogs enjoy eating "people" food.
Ⓑ Both my cat and my dogs enjoys eating "people" food.
Ⓒ Both my cat and my dogs enjoying eating "people" food.
Ⓓ Both my cat and my dogs eats "people" food.

8. Which of the following verb forms correctly fills in the blank in the following sentence?

Lindsay, my favorite of all my cousins, _____ coming to visit me in October.

Ⓐ am
Ⓑ is
Ⓒ are
Ⓓ will

9. Which of the following verb forms correctly fills in the blank in the following sentence?

Some people _____ watching golf tournaments. Others find the tournaments very boring.

Ⓐ enjoy
Ⓑ enjoys
Ⓒ enjoying
Ⓓ enjoyed

10. Which version of this sentence has correct subject-verb agreement?

Ⓐ An ant which climbs on a picnic table risk being squashed.
Ⓑ An ant which climb on a picnic table risk being squashed.
Ⓒ An ant which climbs on a picnic table risks being squashed.
Ⓓ An ant which climbing on a picnic table risking being squashed.

11. Which version of this sentence has correct subject-verb agreement? Circle the correct answer choice.

     Ⓐ Usually Sam or Alec are the referee for our intramural soccer game.
     Ⓑ Usually Sam or Alec were the referee for our intramural soccer game.
     Ⓒ Usually Sam or Alec is the referee for our intramural soccer game.
     Ⓓ Usually Sam or Alec was the referee for our intramual soccer game.

12. Which version of this sentence has correct subject-verb agreement? Circle the correct answer choice.

     Ⓐ At the end of the rainbow was a leprechaun and a pot of gold.
     Ⓑ At the end of the rainbow were a leprechaun and a pot of gold.
     Ⓒ At the end of the rainbow is a leprechaun and a pot of gold.

Name: _____ Date: _____

Chapter 4

Lesson 3: Managing Modifiers

You can scan the QR code given below or use the url to access additional EdSearch resources including videos and mobile apps related to *Managing Modifiers*.

ed Search	*Managing Modifiers*
URL	**QR Code**
http://www.lumoslearning.com/a/l71	

1. Which of the following adverbs fits best in the blank in this sentence?

My uncle's computer which was made in 1987 connects _____ to the Internet.

Ⓐ angrily
Ⓑ slowly
Ⓒ quickly
Ⓓ fast

2. What piece of punctuation should always appear between two coordinate adjectives?

Ⓐ A semi-colon
Ⓑ A comma
Ⓒ A period
Ⓓ A colon

3. What part of speech is the underlined word in the following sentence?

After a long, drawn out argument, the girl and her mother hugged for a long time and decided the girl's curfew was <u>hardly</u> worth fighting about.

Ⓐ Adverb
Ⓑ Adjective
Ⓒ Noun
Ⓓ Verb

4. Select the sentence with the adjective underlined.

Ⓐ Marta <u>hardly</u> knew where to find her orange sweater.
Ⓑ The large, angry dog <u>rushed</u> towards the mailman.
Ⓒ Everyone knows that <u>kind</u> words get a person better results than insults do.
Ⓓ I wanted to go to the movies this weekend, but I can't <u>afford</u> to because I don't get paid until next Thursday.

5. Select the version of the sentence with the adjective underlined.

Ⓐ <u>Because</u> my alarm clock didn't go off this morning and there was traffic due to an accident on the highway, I was very late for my appointment with Dr. Huang.
Ⓑ Because my alarm clock didn't <u>go off</u> this morning and there was traffic due to an accident on the highway, I was very late for my appointment with Dr. Huang.
Ⓒ Because my alarm clock didn't go off this morning and there was <u>traffic</u> due to an accident on the highway, I was very late for my appointment with Dr. Huang.
Ⓓ Because my alarm clock didn't go off this morning and there was <u>heavy</u> traffic due to an accident on the highway, I was very late for my appointment with Dr. Huang.

6. Select the version of the sentence with the adverb underlined.

Ⓐ When Megan's <u>best</u> friend told her she no longer wanted to be friends, Megan angrily slammed down the phone smashing it to pieces.

Ⓑ When Megan's best friend told her she no longer <u>wanted</u> to be friends, Megan angrily slammed down the phone smashing it to pieces.

Ⓒ When Megan's best friend told her she no longer wanted to be friends, Megan <u>angrily</u> slammed down the phone smashing it to pieces.

Ⓓ When Megan's best friend told her she no longer wanted to be friends, Megan angrily slammed down the phone <u>smashing</u> it to pieces.

7. Which of the following adjectives best completes this sentence?

The huge, _____ fire destroyed seven out of the twelve businesses in the downtown area.

Ⓐ large
Ⓑ violent
Ⓒ contained
Ⓓ temporary

8. Select the sentence with the adverb underlined.

Ⓐ Teenagers <u>rarely</u> think their parents know very much.
Ⓑ Our <u>ugly</u>, overgrown garden looks more like a weed patch than a vegetable garden.
Ⓒ Alesandro caught a ten-foot long <u>wide-mouthed</u> bass from the lake.
Ⓓ I can't figure out why it takes me longer to shower than it does to do my <u>homework</u>.

9. Which of the following sentences shows coordinate adjectives correctly punctuated and is written precisely.?

Ⓐ The bride's flowing, long, wedding, dress drew everyone's attention.
Ⓑ The rich, dark chocolate cake, my grandmother makes is my favorite dessert.
Ⓒ Rarely, can you find a short, interesting book to read when you have to write a book report.
Ⓓ Last nights dinner was a healthy.

10. What part of speech is the underlined word in the following sentence?

After a <u>long, drawn</u> out argument, the girl and her mother hugged for a long time and decided the girl's curfew was hardly worth fighting about.

Ⓐ Adjective
Ⓑ Adverb
Ⓒ Coordinate Adjective
Ⓓ Pronoun

11. What part of speech is the underlined word?

Bill <u>thought</u> it was strange that his older brother offered to give him money for pizza. Write your answer in the box given below.

12. What part of speech is the underlined word?

The <u>plain-looking</u> woman looked forward to her makeover. Write your answer in the box given below.

13. What part of speech is the underlined word?

Sandra was worried she did not do <u>well</u> on her algebra test.

Chapter 4

Lesson 4: Using Coordinate Adjectives

You can scan the QR code given below or use the url to access additional EdSearch resources including videos and mobile apps related to *Using Coordinate Adjectives*.

 **Search**

Using Coordinate Adjectives

URL	QR Code
http://www.lumoslearning.com/a/l72	

1. Where should a comma be placed in the following sentence?

The fascinating intelligent old man told us all about his experiences during the war.

Ⓐ fascinating, intelligent
Ⓑ intelligent, old
Ⓒ experiences, during
Ⓓ the, fascinating

2. Which choice best combines the following sentences with coordinate adjectives?

Slippery roads are common during the winter.
Slippery roads are also dangerous roads.

Ⓐ Slippery and dangerous roads are common during the winter.
Ⓑ Slippery, dangerous roads are common during the winter.
Ⓒ Slippery, and also dangerous, roads are common during the winter.
Ⓓ Slippery roads are common during the winter and are dangerous.

3. Which sentence contains coordinate adjectives?

Ⓐ The loud African parrot squawked at me.
Ⓑ Angry, frustrated customers stormed the store.
Ⓒ The sleepy little baby rubbed his eyes.
Ⓓ Adorable baby jaguars ran around at the zoo.

4. Which sentence uses coordinate adjectives correctly?

Ⓐ He was wearing running, black and striped shoes.
Ⓑ He was wearing black striped running shoes.
Ⓒ He was wearing black, striped running shoes.
Ⓓ He was wearing black, running striped shoes.

5. Which sentence uses coordinate adjectives incorrectly?

Ⓐ She was wearing an angora, red sweater.
Ⓑ She was wearing a comfy, fluffy angora sweater.
Ⓒ She was wearing a yellow, fluffy angora sweater.
Ⓓ She was wearing a soft, fluffy angora sweater.

6. Which sentence uses coordinate adjectives correctly?

Ⓐ He was wearing purple, rubber boots.
Ⓑ He travelled along a curvy, slippery highway.
Ⓒ He visited his aging, maternal grandmother.
Ⓓ He needs a cold, diet soda.

7. Which sentence uses coordinate adjectives correctly?

Ⓐ Mr. Crank was an angry, bitter old man.
Ⓑ Mr. Crank was an angry old man.
Ⓒ Mr. Crank was a bitter old man.
Ⓓ Mr. Crank was an old, bitter angry man.

8. How could the following sentence be changed to use coordinate adjectives correctly?

Alisha wanted to go to a tropical, warm, sunny island for Christmas.

Ⓐ Remove tropical from the sentence.
Ⓑ Move tropical after sunny and separate them with a comma.
Ⓒ Move tropical after sunny and do not add a comma.
Ⓓ Move warm before tropical.

9. How could the following sentence be changed to use coordinate adjectives correctly? Circle the correct answer choice.

Mom wanted a cashmere, red sweater for her birthday.

Ⓐ Switch cashmere and red and remove the comma.
Ⓑ Remove the comma between cashmere and red.
Ⓒ Switch cashmere and red, remove the comma, and add another adjective with a comma before red.
Ⓓ Add another adjective before cashmere, separating it from the others with a comma.

10. Which choice correctly combines the two sentences using coordinate adjectives? Circle the correct answer choice.

My dog lived a long life.
My dog lived a happy life.

Ⓐ My dog lived a long, happy life.
Ⓑ My dog lived a long happy life.
Ⓒ My dog lived a long life and it was happy.
Ⓓ My dog lived a long life and a happy life.

Chapter 4

Lesson 5: Spellcheck!

You can scan the QR code given below or use the url to access additional EdSearch resources including videos and mobile apps related to *Spellcheck!*

 **Spellcheck!**

URL	QR Code
http://www.lumoslearning.com/a/l72	

1. Which word in the following sentence is misspelled?

We all go threw difficult times in our lives when we feel sad and lonely.

Ⓐ threw
Ⓑ difficult
Ⓒ lives
Ⓓ lonely

2. Which of the following word is misspelled?

Ⓐ Fierce
Ⓑ Sleigh
Ⓒ Experement
Ⓓ Weird

3. Which word is misspelled in the following sentence?

My favorite meal at the restaraunt is pasta with mushrooms and broccoli.

Ⓐ favorite
Ⓑ restaraunt
Ⓒ mushrooms
Ⓓ broccoli

4. Which word is misspelled in the following sentence?

I was recognised as the top spelunker at least week's cave exploration

Ⓐ recognised
Ⓑ spelunker
Ⓒ exploration
Ⓓ tournament

5. Which of the following words contains a spelling mistake?

Ⓐ Appendix
Ⓑ Rupture
Ⓒ Paniked
Ⓓ Arguing

6. Which of the following words is misspelled?

Ⓐ Accessory
Ⓑ Harass
Ⓒ Neccessary
Ⓓ Possession

7. Which word completes the following sentence?

Make sure you have _____ umbrella with you because it is supposed to rain today.

Ⓐ you're
Ⓑ your

8. Which word completes the following sentence?

Every young girl grows up and becomes a _____.

Ⓐ woman
Ⓑ women

9. What is the correct spelling of the word that completes this sentence?

It is better to give than to _____.

Ⓐ receive
Ⓑ recieve
Ⓒ recive
Ⓓ reacieve

10. Which word completes the following sentence?

We arrived at the play _____ late to be seated. We had to stand in the back of the theater to watch the play.

Ⓐ to
Ⓑ too
Ⓒ two

11. Which word in these sentences is spelled incorrectly?

My little sister has an incredible imagenation. She thinks there is a monster living in her closet and an elf under her bed. Write your answer in the box below.

12. Which word in this sentence is spelled incorrectly?

Because Kay's mother is concerned about her daughter's happyness, she always does everything she can to help Kay avoid being unhappy. Write your answer in the box below.

13. Which word in this sentence is spelled incorrectly?

After I made chicken for dinner, my husband told me he prefered beef with his meals. Write your answer in the box below.

Chapter 4

Lesson 6: Precise and Concise Language

You can scan the QR code given below or use the url to access additional EdSearch resources including videos and mobile apps related to *Precise and Concise Language.*

 **Precise and Concise Language**

URL	QR Code
http://www.lumoslearning.com/a/l73	

1. Which choice best rewrites the following sentence with precise, concise language?

I am having a good day.

Ⓐ I am having a great day.
Ⓑ I am having a really good day.
Ⓒ I am having an extremely productive day.
Ⓓ I am having a really, really good day.

2. Which choice uses the most precise and concise language?

Ⓐ Hunting animals, like those who are endangered, is very wrong and not okay to do.
Ⓑ Hunting animals, like those who are endangered, is very wrong.
Ⓒ Hunting endangered animals is very wrong.
Ⓓ Hunting endangered animals is illegal.

In the first line of her book report, Maria writes:
The novel I read is about a pig whose name is Wilbur and he lives on a farm.

3. Which is NOT something Maria can do to make her sentence more precise?

Ⓐ Include the title of the book instead of "the novel I read."
Ⓑ Change "whose name is" to "named"
Ⓒ Say "who lives on a farm" instead of "and he lives on a farm."
Ⓓ Add more details about Wilbur.

In the first line of her book report, Maria writes:
The novel I read is about a pig whose name is Wilbur and he lives on a farm.

4. Which choice represents the MOST precise opening line Maria could write?

Ⓐ *Charlotte's* Web is about a pig named Wilbur who lives on a farm.
Ⓑ The novel I read is about a pig named Wilbur and he lives on a farm.
Ⓒ The novel I read is about a pig whose name is Wilbur who lives on a farm.
Ⓓ *Charlotte's* Web is about a pig named Wilbur and he lives on a farm.

Alfonso is writing a restaurant review. He writes the following:
The baked goods were delicious.

5. How can Alfonso be more precise with his review?

Ⓐ Change "baked goods" to a specific baked good he tried.
Ⓑ Change "delicious" to "good".
Ⓒ Change "baked goods" to "bakery items"
Ⓓ Change "The" to the name of the restaurant.

Alfonso is writing a restaurant review. He writes the following:
The baked goods were delicious.

6. Which sentence below does NOT make Alfonso's sentence more precise?

Ⓐ   The baked goods were incredibly yummy and delicious.
Ⓑ   The donuts were soft and warm.
Ⓒ   The chocolate chip cookies were ooey and gooey.
Ⓓ   The cakes and cookies were the best I've ever had.

After seeing a play, Yuri writes the following sentence:
The actresses wore dresses.

7. Which is NOT something Yuri can do to make the sentence more precise?

Ⓐ   Describe a particular actress's dress
Ⓑ   Add more details about the dresses
Ⓒ   Include what the actors wore too
Ⓓ   Describe the color of the dresses

After seeing a play, Yuri writes the following sentence:
The actresses wore dresses.

8. Which sentence makes Yuri's sentence more precise while still being concise?

Ⓐ   The actresses wore frilly dresses from the Victorian era.
Ⓑ   The actresses wore red, frilly, beautiful dresses.
Ⓒ   The lead actress, Mona Kent, and the others wore a frilly Victorian dress.
Ⓓ   All of the actresses wore frilly Victorian dresses.

While spending a week at camp, George writes the following letter home to his parents:
I love camp. I love it because we play sports. I also love it because we go canoeing. And I love it because we get to sing songs by the campfire.

9. How can George make the sentence "I love it because we play sports" more precise

While spending a week at camp, George writes the following letter home to his parents:
I love camp. I love it because we play sports. I also love it because we go canoeing. And I love it because we get to sing songs by the campfire.

10. Which choice makes George's letter most precise and concise? Circle the correct answer choice.

Ⓐ I love camp. I love it because we play sports, go canoeing, and sing songs by the campfire.
Ⓑ I love camp. I love it because we play basketball and football, go canoeing, and sing songs by the campfire.
Ⓒ I love camp because we play basketball and football, go canoeing, and sing songs by the campfire.
Ⓓ I love camp because we play sports, go canoeing, and sing songs by the campfire.

Chapter 4

Lesson 7: Figuring it Out with Context Clues

You can scan the QR code given below or use the url to access additional EdSearch resources including videos and mobile apps related to *Figuring it Out with Context Clues.*

 **Figuring it Out with Context Clues**

URL	QR Code
http://www.lumoslearning.com/a/l74	

Still, there was something that was bothering Sam. The tryouts for the tennis team were on the same day as his mom's birthday, and he knew his family was planning a huge surprise party for her. He didn't want to hurt his mom's feelings by missing the party, but he also didn't want to miss his one shot at being a champion tennis player just because the tryouts were on his mom's birthday. He was in a <u>quandary</u>; he didn't know what to do.

1. What is the meaning of the word "quandary" in the above passage?

    Ⓐ a state of elation
    Ⓑ a state of certainty
    Ⓒ a state of perplexity
    Ⓓ a simple state of mind

Hold him, everybody! In goes the <u>hypodermic</u>—Bruno squeals — 10 c.c. of the antidote enters his system without a drop being wasted. Ten minutes later: condition unchanged! Another 10 c.c. Injected! Ten minutes later: breathing less torturous— Bruno can move his arms and legs a little although he cannot stand yet. Thirty minutes later: Bruno gets up and has a great feed! He looks at us disdainfully, as much as to say, 'What's barium carbonate to a big black bear like me?' Bruno was still eating. I was really happy to see him recover.

2. What is the meaning of the word "hypodermic"?

    Ⓐ aortic
    Ⓑ skin
    Ⓒ orally administered drugs
    Ⓓ injection

Of all the life forms on earth, those living in the rivers, lakes, and oceans seem to be most interesting to people. We are extremely curious about these <u>aquatic</u> creatures. Countless movies, television shows, books and magazines focus on animals living in the water.

3. What is the meaning of the underlined word in this passage?

    Ⓐ fish
    Ⓑ blue-colored
    Ⓒ exciting
    Ⓓ living in water

What will you do with me if my father, the king, does not pay the $5 million ransom for my return?" asked the lovely princess as the kidnapper pushed her into his carriage.

"Well, my dear," the kidnapper replied with a <u>sinister</u> smile, "your father has two choices. He can either give me the money or he can say goodbye to his daughter…forever!"

4. What is the meaning of sinister as it is used in this passage?

- Ⓐ helpful
- Ⓑ evil
- Ⓒ crazy
- Ⓓ angry

The committee worked for weeks to write a set of rules for the new rock climbing club at our middle school. The students, parents, and teachers in the group wanted to make sure that the rules would be easy to follow and easy to read. To help the club members better understand the rules, they wrote a <u>preamble</u> explaining how they came up with these rules to put at the front of the set of rules.

5. What is the meaning of the underlined word in this passage?

- Ⓐ introduction
- Ⓑ cover
- Ⓒ rule
- Ⓓ page

From "Bruno the Bear"
From <u>A Bond of Love</u>

The bear became very attached to our two dogs and all the children living in and around our farm. He was left quite free in his younger days and spent his time playing, running into the kitchen, and going to sleep in our beds.

One day an accident befell him. I put down poison (barium carbonate) to kill the rats and mice that had got into my library. Bruno entered the library as he often did and ate some of the poison. **Paralysis** set into the extent that he could not stand on his feet. But he dragged himself on his stumps to my wife, who called me. I guessed what had happened. Off I rushed him in the car to the vet's residence. A case of poisoning! Tame Bear—barium carbonate—what to do? Out came his medical books, and a feverish reference to index began: "What poison did you say, sir?" he asked, "Barium carbonate," I said.

"Ah yes—B—Ba—Barium Salts—Ah! Barium carbonate! Symptoms— paralysis—treatment—injections of . … Just a minute, sir. I'll bring my syringe and the medicine." Said the doc.

I dashed back to the car. Bruno was still floundering about on his stumps, but clearly, he was weakening rapidly; there was some vomiting, he was breathing heavily, with heaving flanks and gaping mouth. I was really scared and did not know what to do. I was feeling very guilty and was running in and out of the vet's house doing everything the doc asked me.

"Hold him, everybody!" In goes the hypodermic—Bruno squeals — 10 c.c. of the antidote enters his system without a drop being wasted. Ten minutes later: condition unchanged! Another 10 c.c. Injected! Ten minutes later: breathing less torturous— Bruno can move his arms and legs a little although he cannot stand yet. Thirty minutes later: Bruno gets up and has a great feed! He looks at us disdainfully, as much as to say, 'What's barium carbonate to a big black bear like me?' Bruno was still eating. I was really happy to see him recover.

6. Based on its use in this selection, what can you infer the meaning of the bold word is?

Ⓐ Inability to eat
Ⓑ Inability to move
Ⓒ Poisoning
Ⓓ Confusion

As Sade was about to bungee jump off the bridge, she had a <u>fleeting</u> thought of death. Luckily, the thought was gone as quickly as it came.

7. What is the meaning of the underlined word?

Ⓐ frightening
Ⓑ passing rapidly
Ⓒ remaining for a long period of time
Ⓓ clear

The baseball players and the owner of the team could not come to a contract agreement. The two parties had been arguing for months. Finally, an <u>arbitrator</u> was brought in to help come up with an agreement that both parties could agree on.

8. What is the meaning of the underlined word?

Ⓐ Person who bets on the odds of winning
Ⓑ Person who argues for one side of a disagreement
Ⓒ Person who settles disagreements
Ⓓ Person who decides a disagreement

Even though the snake only <u>grazed</u> the leg of my pants, I was still extremely frightened and upset.

9. What is the meaning of the underlined word?

Ⓐ Ate a small amount
Ⓑ Circled around
Ⓒ Lightly touched
Ⓓ Looked at

Although the other children were <u>regaled</u> by the musician, Terry found him dull.

10. What is the meaning of regaled?

Ⓐ Entertained
Ⓑ Bored
Ⓒ Afraid
Ⓓ Interested

Without warning, a police officer materialized at the scene for the crime. The thieves were surprised by his sudden appearance.

11. What does materialize mean? Circle the correct answer choice.

Ⓐ Disappeared
Ⓑ Surprised
Ⓒ Created
Ⓓ Appeared suddenly

Hitler's plan to dominate Europe went awry when America joined the war.

12. What does awry mean? Circle the correct answer choice.

Ⓐ Wrong
Ⓑ Not according to plan
Ⓒ Well
Ⓓ According to plan

In medical school students must dissect cadavers to learn about human anatomy.

13. What is a cadaver? Circle the correct answer choice.

Ⓐ A computer model
Ⓑ A frog
Ⓒ A human body
Ⓓ A criminal

Chapter 4

Lesson 8: Re+view - Roots and Affixes

You can scan the QR code given below or use the url to access additional EdSearch resources including videos and mobile apps related to *Re+view - Roots and Affixes.*

 **ed Search**

Re+view - Roots and Affixes

URL	QR Code
http://www.lumoslearning.com/a/l74	

1. Determine the meaning of the word autonomous based on the following affixes.

Auto-=self
Nom=order
-ous=having the quality of

Ⓐ ordering something for yourself
Ⓑ being different than other people
Ⓒ having the qualities of self and order
Ⓓ being able to do something by yourself

2. The affix *path* means "to feel". What is the meaning of *empathetic* in the following sentence?

Because Mrs. Anderson is an empathetic person, she tries to help everyone in her church who is suffering.

Ⓐ nice
Ⓑ caring
Ⓒ helpful
Ⓓ cruel

Aqua-=water
Phobos=fear

3. If Juan is aquaphobic, what would be true about him?

Ⓐ He would love to go to the swimming pool.
Ⓑ He would wash the dishes after dinner each night.
Ⓒ He would avoid taking baths and showers.
Ⓓ He would want a fish as a pet.

4. A person who is antisocial would NOT enjoy...

Ⓐ going to a big party.
Ⓑ spending time alone in his or her room.
Ⓒ playing video games.
Ⓓ hiking by him or herself.

5. Determine the meaning of the word digress based on the following affixes.

di-= to the opposite
gress=to go

Ⓐ the opposite of going
Ⓑ move away from the main topic
Ⓒ go on vacation
Ⓓ opposed to something

The word postmortem is made up of two affixes:
post- + mortem
mortem means "life"

6. Based on your understanding of prefixes, when can you infer that something that is postmortem occurs?

Ⓐ Before someone is born
Ⓑ During someone's life
Ⓒ After someone is dead
Ⓓ When someone is living

The suffix -an means "from".

7. What can you assume is true about the person in the following sentence?

Lars was proud to be a Norwegian.

Ⓐ Lars is from nowhere in particular.
Ⓑ Lars is from Norwalk, Connecticut.
Ⓒ Lars is from Norway.
Ⓓ Lars is from Norfolk, Virginia.

8. Based on the prefix, *octogenarian* most likely means?

Ⓐ A kind of sea creature
Ⓑ A person who is in his or her eighties
Ⓒ A kind of book
Ⓓ The next generation

9. Based on the suffix, brimful most likely means?

- (A) Capable
- (B) Full of
- (C) Smaller
- (D) Few

10. Based on the prefix, unacceptable means?

- (A) Sick
- (B) Bad
- (C) Good
- (D) Angry

11. Match the prefix with it's meaning.

Related to water   Related to the universe   Related to sleep

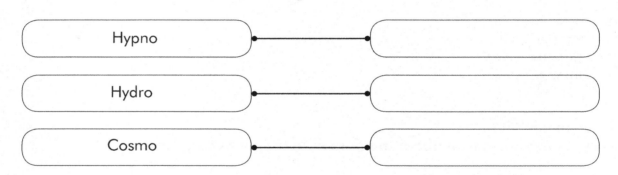

Hypno

Hydro

Cosmo

12. Match the word to its correct prefix.

From   Play   Electric

Re

Hydro

Trans

13. A letter or group of letters added at the end of a word which makes a new word is called a _____.

Chapter 4

Lesson 9: Consulting Sources

You can scan the QR code given below or use the url to access additional EdSearch resources including videos and mobile apps related to *Consulting Sources*.

 **Consulting Sources**

URL	QR Code
http://www.lumoslearning.com/a/l74	

While reading his science textbook, Jorge comes across the following sentence:
Animals are part of different ecosystems around the world.

1. If he wanted to find the meaning of "ecosystems," where would be the best place to look so he can find the definition quickly?

Ⓐ In a dictionary
Ⓑ In the glossary
Ⓒ In a thesaurus
Ⓓ In another chapter

While reading his science textbook, Jorge comes across the following sentence:
Animals are part of different ecosystems around the world.

2. If Jorge wanted to find words similar to the word "ecosystems" where would be the best place to look?

Ⓐ In a dictionary
Ⓑ In the glossary
Ⓒ In a thesaurus
Ⓓ In another chapter

While reading his science textbook, Jorge comes across the following sentence:
Animals are part of different ecosystems around the world.

3. Jorge decides to look up the word "ecosystem" in a dictionary. Where will he find the word?

Ⓐ Before ecology
Ⓑ After edifice
Ⓒ Between ecology and edifice
Ⓓ Between ebb and ecology

While reading his science textbook, Jorge comes across the following sentence: Animals are part of different ecosystems around the world.

When Jorge finds the word "ecosystem" in the dictionary he sees the following:

Ecosystem n. (ek-o-sys-tem)
1. a community of interacting organisms
2. a general term to describe a complex system

4. What do the letters in parentheses represent?

- Ⓐ The word's part of speech
- Ⓑ How to pronounce the word
- Ⓒ The main meaning of the word
- Ⓓ The secondary meaning of the word

While reading his science textbook, Jorge comes across the following sentence: Animals are part of different ecosystems around the world.

When Jorge finds the word "ecosystem" in the dictionary he sees the following:

Ecosystem n. (ek-o-sys-tem)
1. a community of interacting organisms
2. a general term to describe a complex system

5. Based on the dictionary entry, what part of speech is the word "ecosystem"?

- Ⓐ Adjective
- Ⓑ Noun
- Ⓒ Pronoun
- Ⓓ Verb

While reading his science textbook, Jorge comes across the following sentence:
Animals are part of different ecosystems around the world.

When Jorge finds the word "ecosystem" in the dictionary he sees the following:

Ecosystem n. (ek-o-sys-tem)
1. a community of interacting organisms
2. a general term to describe a complex system

6. Which definition best fits the word "ecosystem" in the sentence Jorge read?

    Ⓐ   A community of interacting organisms
    Ⓑ   A general term used to describe a complex system

Lynn is looking for a synonym to use in her essay, so she opens the thesaurus. She looks up the following entry.

delay v. 1. *Storms delayed the construction process.* curb, detain, hamper, hinder, hold.
2. *He delayed his admission until he got back from Europe.* postpone, hold, put off, shelve.
3. *Don't delay, the sale is almost over.* hedge, hang back, hesitate, pause, stall.

7. Why does the thesaurus include the sentences in italics?

    Ⓐ   To help the reader get ideas about what to write
    Ⓑ   To help the reader distinguish between the meanings of the word by providing examples
    Ⓒ   To help the reader find the perfect word
    Ⓓ   To help the reader see the different parts of speech of the word

Lynn is looking for a synonym to use in her essay, so she opens the thesaurus. She looks up the following entry.

delay v. 1. Storms delayed the construction process. curb, detain, hamper, hinder, hold. 2. He delayed his admission until he got back from Europe. postpone, hold, put off, shelve. 3. Don't delay, the sale is almost over. hedge, hang back, hesitate, pause, stall.

8. Lynn is writing a news article for the school paper. She wants a synonym for "delay" that says the lack of the principal's signature is delaying the arrival of the new vending machines. Which is the best synonym for her to use?

    Ⓐ   Hesitate
    Ⓑ   Put off
    Ⓒ   Hinder
    Ⓓ   Shelve

Lynn is looking for a synonym to use in her essay, so she opens the thesaurus. She looks up the following entry.

delay v. 1. Storms delayed the construction process. curb, detain, hamper, hinder, hold. 2. He delayed his admission until he got back from Europe. postpone, hold, put off, shelve. 3. Don't delay, the sale is almost over. hedge, hang back, hesitate, pause, stall.

9. Lynn wants to write a piece that encourages students to express the concerns to the principal without causing her to delay. Which would be the BEST synonym to use in her piece? Circle the correct answer choice.

   Ⓐ Hesitate
   Ⓑ Put off
   Ⓒ Hinder
   Ⓓ Shelve

Lynn is looking for a synonym to use in her essay, so she opens the thesaurus. She looks up the following entry.

delay v. 1. Storms delayed the construction process. curb, detain, hamper, hinder, hold. 2. He delayed his admission until he got back from Europe. postpone, hold, put off, shelve. 3. Don't delay, the sale is almost over. hedge, hang back, hesitate, pause, stall.

10. Lynn writes the following sentence: "The delay caused the vendors to take back their deal." She wants to find a synonym for "delay," but this particular thesaurus entry won't help. Which choice best explains why? Circle the correct answer choice.

   Ⓐ The thesaurus entry focuses on delay as a verb, not a noun.
   Ⓑ The thesaurus entry only contains three forms of the verb delay.
   Ⓒ The thesaurus entry covers the word "delay."
   Ⓓ The thesaurus entry is not the best place to find a word, the dictionary is.

Chapter 4

Lesson 10: How to Look it Up - Which Fits? Multiple Meaning Words

You can scan the QR code given below or use the url to access additional EdSearch resources including videos and mobile apps related to *How to Look it Up Which Fits? Multiple Meaning Words*.

How to Look it Up - Which Fits? Multiple Meaning Words

URL	QR Code
http://www.lumoslearning.com/a/l74	

Amelia worked very hard on her Social Studies project, but there were many mistakes in the essay part of the project. Her teacher didn't want to discount the effort Amelia put into the project, so she raised her grade from a C to a B.

1. Which definition of the word discount best fits its use in the following paragraph?

Ⓐ take an amount of money off of a bill or a price
Ⓑ paying interest on a loan before the payment is due
Ⓒ not count
Ⓓ leave out or not pay attention to

Even though the seventh grade class had never taken an overnight field trip before, the principal decided to approve Mr. Juarez's request to take his students to the beach for two days to study whales.

2. Which meaning of the word approve is used in the following sentence?

Ⓐ talk about in a positive way
Ⓑ officially agree to
Ⓒ agree to informally
Ⓓ show

Because the assistant manager was the manager's subordinate, he had to work on Christmas Day while the manager had the day off to spend with her family.

3. Which definition of the word subordinate best fits its use in the following sentence?

Ⓐ someone in a lower position
Ⓑ not as important
Ⓒ someone who depends on someone else
Ⓓ not as good

This morning I was awoken at 5:00AM by a **racket**! My next door neighbor was mowing his lawn with his noisy, old lawn mower. This was not a great way to start the day!

4. What is the definition of the bold word in this sentence?

Ⓐ piece of sports equipment used to play tennis
Ⓑ dishonest business deal
Ⓒ loud noise
Ⓓ illegal activity

Baseball Card Collecting

Looking for a new hobby? Do you like baseball? If you answered "yes" to these two questions, then baseball card collecting might be a fun pastime for you to begin! Ever since candy and gum manufacturers started putting cards with pictures of popular baseball players into the packages in the 1800's to encourage young people to buy their sweets, kids have been collecting baseball cards. Now, more than 200 years later, baseball card collecting has become a popular hobby for children and adults alike.

5. Based on this paragraph, what can you infer "sweets" are?

Ⓐ Gum
Ⓑ Candy
Ⓒ Baseball cards
Ⓓ pastries

The workers from the power company told us to beware of downed powerlines after the storm because many of the wires were **live**.

6. Which definition of live is used in this sentence?

Ⓐ to have life
Ⓑ at the time the event is occurring
Ⓒ emitting electrical power
Ⓓ to dwell in

I was so happy when I discovered the local news channel was broadcasting the award show **live** instead of on a ten minute delay.

7. Which definition of live is used in this sentence?

Ⓐ to have life
Ⓑ at the time the event is occurring
Ⓒ emitting electrical power
Ⓓ to dwell in

I felt lightheaded from the chemicals I used to **strip** the paint from the patio furniture.

8. Which definition of strip is used in this sentence?

Ⓐ to remove
Ⓑ long, narrow piece of cloth
Ⓒ to remove clothes
Ⓓ to clear out

The chess club decided to **bar** Igor from joining because he talked too much during chess matches.

9. Which definition of bar is used in this sentence?

Ⓐ A square of material
Ⓑ A place where people eat and drink
Ⓒ To prevent
Ⓓ To equip

10. Which is NOT a meaning that the word track can have?

Ⓐ Circular running surface often used for races
Ⓑ Monitor
Ⓒ Footprint left by an animal
Ⓓ Watch carefully

When their mother caught them taking cookies from the pantry, the children bolted out the back door.

11. What does bolt mean in the sentence above? Circle the correct answer choice.

Ⓐ A missile designed to be shot from a crossbow
Ⓑ A rod used to fasten a door
Ⓒ To move suddenly
Ⓓ To quickly run away

Mother shined the silver platter until it was brilliant.

12. What does brilliant mean in the sentence above? Circle the correct answer choice.

Ⓐ Glittering
Ⓑ Distinctive
Ⓒ Very smart
Ⓓ A gem

After many years of studying yoga, Kelly was able to master dozens of poses.

13. What does master mean in the sentence above? Circle the correct answer choice.

Ⓐ An artist with great skill
Ⓑ One who has authority over another
Ⓒ To become very skilled in a performance
Ⓓ To overcome a fear

Chapter 4

Lesson 11: Give it a Shot - Figures of Speech

You can scan the QR code given below or use the url to access additional EdSearch resources including videos and mobile apps related to *Give it a Shot - Figures of Speech.*

 **ed Search**

Give it a Shot - Figures of Speech

URL	QR Code
http://www.lumoslearning.com/a/l75	

As soon as Hector ate the fifteenth hotdog, he knew he had made a mistake entering the hot dog eating contest. His stomach felt <u>like a ton of bricks</u> with all that meat and bread in it!

1. What is the meaning of the underlined figure of speech?

Ⓐ light and empty
Ⓑ queasy and nauseous
Ⓒ heavy and full
Ⓓ hard and solid

Kim had spent the last three days writing the speech she was going to give the students during the assembly. She wanted more than anything to be elected as the president of the student council. When she looked down at the paper in her hand, she realized she was holding her math homework, not a copy of the speech. Kim looked up to see hundreds of pairs of eyes looking at her. Not wanting to give up on her dream of being elected and not wanting to appear unprepared, <u>Kim gave her speech off the cuff</u>.

2. What is the meaning of the underlined figure of speech?

Ⓐ quickly
Ⓑ quietly
Ⓒ embarrassedly
Ⓓ freely

Kim had spent the last three days writing the speech she was going to give the students during the assembly. She wanted more than anything to be elected as the president of the student council. When she looked down at the paper in her hand, she realized she was holding her math homework, not a copy of the speech. Kim looked up to see hundreds of pairs of eyes looking at her. Not wanting to give up on her dream of being elected and not wanting to appear unprepared, Kim gave her speech off the cuff.

3. What does the author mean by "hundreds of pairs of eyes"?

Ⓐ Many people were watching Kim carefully.
Ⓑ Many people were laughing at Kim.
Ⓒ Many people were watching Kim angrily.
Ⓓ Many people were smiling at Kim.

The unit on quadratic equations that we are studying in Math right now is so confusing. <u>I may die</u> trying to learn this information!

4. What is the author trying to convey to the reader through the underlined phrase?

    Ⓐ How exhausting quadratic equations are
    Ⓑ How physically ill Math class makes her
    Ⓒ How much effort she is having to put into learning quadratic equations
    Ⓓ How math is deadly

Brittany had never met anyone quite like Brian. When the two spent time together, she felt <u>as if no one else in the world existed</u> other than she and Brian.

5. What is the meaning of the underlined phrase?

    Ⓐ Their love took them to another world separate from others.
    Ⓑ Nothing else mattered when the two were together.
    Ⓒ Everyone tends to leave a couple in love alone.
    Ⓓ He was the only man she'd met.

Nikki came home after her curfew three nights in a row. Her father didn't want this to become a problem, so he decided to <u>nip it in the bud</u> by grounding her for a week.

6. What is the meaning of the underlined figure of speech?

    Ⓐ punish
    Ⓑ stop immediately
    Ⓒ encourage
    Ⓓ stop gradually

After Cece's mother watched her spend the first week of summer vacation sitting on the couch watching television, she signed her daughter up to volunteer at the local retirement home.
When Cece complained, her mother told her, "Idle hands are the devil's handiwork."

7. What does Cece's mother mean by this statement?

Ⓐ Laziness causes nothing but trouble.
Ⓑ Watching too much television is sinful.
Ⓒ Cece's hands are looking like the Devil's.
Ⓓ Wasting time is not a good idea.

Sammy's English teacher last year was extremely strict and gave her students hours of homework each night. So far, his new English teacher, Mr. Tucker, seemed very nice and had only given one short homework assignment. Sammy thought this year's English class was going to be <u>a walk in the park</u>.

8. What is the meaning of the underlined figure of speech?

Ⓐ difficult
Ⓑ easy
Ⓒ confusing
Ⓓ fun

After working in the yard mowing and planting shrubs for eight hours in the hot sun, Doreen decided to <u>call it a day</u>.

9. What is the meaning of the underlined figure of speech?

Ⓐ go to bed
Ⓑ stop working
Ⓒ talk to a friend on the phone
Ⓓ watch the sun set

My older brother never does the jobs my mother asks him to do around the house. I always end up having to do his chores. He's always <u>passing the buck</u> to me.

10. What is the meaning of the underlined figure of speech?

Ⓐ paying for jobs
Ⓑ ignoring
Ⓒ forcing to do work
Ⓓ putting the responsibility on

My dad takes care of the house and my mother <u>brings home the bacon.</u>

11. What does the underlined figure of speech mean? Circle the correct answer choice.

    Ⓐ Raises pigs
    Ⓑ Goes to the grocery store
    Ⓒ Earns an income to support the family
    Ⓓ Is looking for a job

During the audit it became apparent that many problems with the business had been <u>swept under the rug</u>. Now that they were known, changes would be made.

12. What does the underlined figure of speech mean?

    Ⓐ Hidden but not resolved
    Ⓑ Taken care of quietly
    Ⓒ Illegally managed
    Ⓓ Repeated

Robert vowed to <u>turn over a new leaf</u> and earn high grades in all of his classes for a change.

13. What does the underlined figure of speech mean?

    Ⓐ To commit to improving oneself
    Ⓑ To pretend to be a new person
    Ⓒ To look for ways to be different
    Ⓓ To hide one's shortcomings.

Name: _____   Date: _____

Chapter 4

Lesson 12: We're Related - Word Relationships

You can scan the QR code given below or use the url to access additional EdSearch resources including videos and mobile apps related to *We're Related - Word Relationships*.

 **Search**

We're Related - Word Relationships

URL	QR Code
http://www.lumoslearning.com/a/l75	

1. What is the relationship between the words serial and cereal?

Ⓐ They are synonyms.
Ⓑ They are antonyms.
Ⓒ They are homonyms.
Ⓓ They are opposites.

2. What is the relationship between the words annoying and unpleasant?

Ⓐ They are synonyms.
Ⓑ They are antonyms.
Ⓒ They are homonyms.
Ⓓ They are homographs.

3. Which of the following words is an antonym of the underlined word in the sentence?

Augustus enjoys <u>helping</u> others, so he volunteers at the local food bank.

Ⓐ aiding
Ⓑ entertaining
Ⓒ confusing
Ⓓ harming

4. Which of the following words is a synonym of the underlined word in the sentence?

Now that I have enough money, I can <u>purchase</u> the videogame I have been wanting for months.

Ⓐ sell
Ⓑ look for
Ⓒ buy
Ⓓ win

5. Which of the following words is an antonym of the underlined word in the sentence?

My cousin and I used to enjoy spending weekends together at her house, but after she started hanging out with people I don't like, I have nothing but <u>animosity</u> for her.

Ⓐ love
Ⓑ dislike
Ⓒ anger
Ⓓ sadness

6. What is an antonym of the underlined word?

Books in the library are <u>classified</u> according to subject.

Ⓐ organized
Ⓑ catalogued
Ⓒ ordered
Ⓓ disorganized

7. What is a synonym for the word in bold?

Lewis was **patient** as he waited for his appointment.

Ⓐ Tolerant
Ⓑ Complaining
Ⓒ Impatient
Ⓓ Fed up

8. What is a synonym for the word in bold?

"Ouch! That **smarts**!" exclaimed Julia when she stepped on a tack.

Ⓐ Stings
Ⓑ Is intelligent
Ⓒ Is confusing
Ⓓ Sounds loud

9. The words in bold above are

It took an **hour** for **our** parade to pass.

Ⓐ Homonyms
Ⓑ Synonyms
Ⓒ Antonyms
Ⓓ Homophones

10. What is an antonym for the word in bold?

I couldn't cut anything with that **dull** knife.

Ⓐ Sharp
Ⓑ Boring
Ⓒ Interesting
Ⓓ Comfortable

The **courageous** explorer wasn't afraid of anything.

11. Cowardly is a _____ for the word in bold above.

Ⓐ Homonym
Ⓑ Synonym
Ⓒ Antonym

By signing the document we **waived** our right to ask for more money at a later date. We were committed to the amount on the contract.

12. Abandon is a ____ for the word in bold above.

Ⓐ Homonym
Ⓑ Synonym
Ⓒ Antonym

Chapter 4

Lesson 13: Would You Rather Own a Boat or a Yacht? Denotation and Connotation

You can scan the QR code given below or use the url to access additional EdSearch resources including videos and mobile apps related to *Would You Rather Own a Boat or a Yacht? Denotation and Connotation*.

Would You Rather Own a Boat or a Yacht? Denotation and Connotation

URL	QR Code
http://www.lumoslearning.com/a/l75	

Omar is always making jokes and trying to get others to laugh. Even when a situation is serious, he tries to make light of it by joking. When Omar told his friends that his grandmother was very sick and might die, everyone thought he was just joking around. Omar was trying to share something very sad, but his friends thought he was being <u>facetious</u>.

1. The denotation of facetious is "amusing or funny". Based on the context of its use in this paragraph, what is the connotation of the word?

Ⓐ positive
Ⓑ negative

Selma is often late to work, and when she does arrive there, she is lazy and rude to the customers. Selma's boss, Nick, met with her to talk with her about her job performance. Nick said Selma has many good qualities, but he needs to <u>boot</u> her from her job immediately.
The word *boot* means "to end someone's employment."

2. Based on this paragraph, the connotation of this word is...

Ⓐ negative
Ⓑ positive
Ⓒ neutral

The manager of the sandwich shop takes home the leftover rolls and bread each night to feed his children and his wife. He does this because his family is <u>needy</u>.

3. If the underlined word was changed to greedy, how would the connotation of the sentence change?

Ⓐ The reader would think of the manager as someone who wants, but does not need the leftovers.
Ⓑ The reader would think of the manager as someone who needs, but does not want the leftovers.
Ⓒ The reader's view of the manager will not change because the connotation of both words is the same.

Noah's mother grounded him for a week because his room was so <u>filthy</u>.

4. If the underlined word was changed to untidy, how would the connotation of the sentence change?

Ⓐ The reader would think that Noah's room was disorganized, but not extremely dirty.
Ⓑ The reader would think that Noah's room was extremely dirty instead of being just disorganized.
Ⓒ The reader's view of Noah's room would not change because the connotation of both words is the same.

Billy lives for football season. He is a <u>devoted</u> fan of the Chicago Bears.
Billy lives for football season. He is an <u>obsessed</u> fan of the Chicago Bears.
Devoted and *obsessed* are considered synonyms. However, each has a different connotation.

5. How does the connotation of the sentence change when *devoted* is changed to *obsessed*?

Ⓐ Devoted has a more positive connotation than obsessed does
Ⓑ Devoted has a more negative connotation than obsessed does
Ⓒ There is no change in connotation when the words are exchanged.

When the Water-Shed Commission said that it must move or be destroyed, the <u>residents</u> of Katonah gathered together, and decided that rather than be wiped off the face of the map, it would pick up its houses and move itself.

6. How would the connotation of this sentence change if the underlined word was changed to *taxpayers*?

Ⓐ Residents focuses on the people being pushy. Taxpayers focuses on the people doing what they are supposed to do.
Ⓑ Taxpayers focuses on the people living in houses with their families. Residents focuses on the money they pay to the government.
Ⓒ Residents focuses on the people living in houses with their families. Taxpayers focuses on the money they pay to the government.
Ⓓ Residents focuses on the people pulling together. Taxpayers makes the people sound divided.

The idea is to make it impossible for England to <u>interfere</u> if we wish to make a treaty with another country.

7. How does the connotation of this sentence change if the underlined word is changed to *help*?

    Ⓐ Interfere has a positive connotation, but help has a negative connotation.
    Ⓑ Help has a positive connotation, but interfere has a negative connotation.
    Ⓒ The connotation will not change because both words have the same meaning.

Carley has <u>a large</u> amount of homework to do this weekend.

8. What word should replace the underlined words to emphasize the size of the amount of work Carley has?

    Ⓐ a big
    Ⓑ a tiny
    Ⓒ an enormous
    Ⓓ a moderate

Lori had a <u>bad</u> fear of snakes and spiders.

9. What word could replace the underlined word to show that Lori's fear is very strong?

    Ⓐ dreadful
    Ⓑ small
    Ⓒ strong
    Ⓓ trivial

Julius is a <u>very good</u> student. He has had all A's on his report cards since kindergarten.

10. What word could replace the underlined words to emphasize Julius' skills?

    Ⓐ mediocre
    Ⓑ unexceptional
    Ⓒ special
    Ⓓ exceptional

The woman's behavior during the performance was childish.

11. Childish has a _____ connotation.

Ⓐ Positive
Ⓑ Negative
Ⓒ Neutra

Mother spent the afternoon talking to our nosy neighbor, Mrs. Jones.

12. What word would change the connotation of this sentence to neutral. Circle the correct answer choice.

Ⓐ Interested
Ⓑ Talkative
Ⓒ Chatty
Ⓓ Annoying

Chapter 4

Lesson 14: Learning and Using Academic Vocabulary

You can scan the QR code given below or use the url to access additional EdSearch resources including videos and mobile apps related to *Learning and Using Academic Vocabulary*.

 **Learning and Using Academic Vocabulary**

URL	QR Code
http://www.lumoslearning.com/a/l76	

"Bruno the Bear"
Excerpt from <u>The Bond of Love</u>

For the next three hours, she would not leave that cage. She gave him tea, lemonade, cakes, ice cream, and whatnot. Then 'closing time' came and we had to leave. My wife cried bitterly; Bruno cried bitterly; even the hardened curator and the keepers felt depressed. As for me, I had reconciled myself to what I knew was going to happen next.

"Oh please, sir," she asked the curator, "may I have my Bruno back"? Hesitantly, he answered, "Madam, he belongs to the zoo and is Government property now. I cannot give away Government property. But if my boss, the superintendent, agrees, certainly, you may have him back."

There followed the return journey home and a visit to the superintendent's office. A tearful pleading: "Bruno and I are both fretting for each other. Will you please give him back to me?" He was a kind-hearted man and consented. Not only that, but he wrote to the curator, telling him to lend us a cage for transporting the bear back home.

Back we went to the zoo again, armed with the superintendent's letter. Bruno was driven into a small cage and hoisted on top of the car; the cage was tied securely, and a slow and careful return journey back home was accomplished.

Once home, a squad of workers were engaged for special work around our yard. An island was made for Bruno. It was twenty feet long and fifteen feet wide and was surrounded by a dry moat, six feet wide and seven feet deep. A wooden box that once housed fowls was brought and put on the island for Bruno to sleep in at night. Straw was placed inside to keep him warm, and his 'baby,' the gnarled stump, along with his 'gun,' the piece of bamboo, both of which had been sentimentally preserved since he had been sent away to the zoo, were put back for him to play with. In a few days, the workers hoisted the cage on to the island, and Bruno was released. He was delighted; standing on his hind legs, he pointed his 'gun' and cradled his 'baby.' My wife spent hours sitting on a chair there while he sat on her lap. He was fifteen months old and pretty heavy too!

1. Which word from the passage describes "a keeper or custodian of a collection"?

Ⓐ superintendent
Ⓑ squad
Ⓒ curator
Ⓓ worker

2. **Which word from the passage describes "a high-ranking official" or "someone who manages an organization"?**

   Ⓐ superintendent
   Ⓑ squad
   Ⓒ curator
   Ⓓ worker

3. **Which word from the passage describes "a group of people assembled to complete a task"?**

   Ⓐ property
   Ⓑ squad
   Ⓒ curator
   Ⓓ workers

Fall leaves
USDA Forest Service

We almost always think of trees as being green, but there is one time of year when their leaves turn a myriad orange, red, yellow, and brown: the beautiful and chilly days of fall. Those living in the Eastern or Northern United States come to anticipate the change in color starting in September or October every single year. But what causes the leaves to change color, and why?

Just like many animals that hibernate for the winter, trees experience a unique change during the winter months. During summer, for instance, plants use the process of photosynthesis to transform carbon dioxide found in the air into organic compounds like sugars using energy from the sun. During the winter, however, there is less light to go around, and their ability to create food from the photosynthesis process is limited.

What does that have to do with a leaf's color? The substance that allows trees to turn carbon dioxide into food (chlorophyll) is also the cause of the leaf's green sheen. As the photosynthesis process wanes in the colder months due to the lack of sun, so does its greenish hue, allowing other elements present in the leaf to show through. Believe it or not, the yellows and oranges that appear in fall have actually been there all year in the form of nutrients like carotene (also found in carrots). The intense green color of the chlorophyll had simply overshadowed them. But what about the reds and browns? And what causes the leaves to fall away after they change color? The bright reds and purples in each leaf come from a strong antioxidant that many trees create on their own because of their protective qualities. The antioxidant helps protect the trees from the sun, lower their freezing levels, and protect them from frost. As winter comes, so does the need for the antioxidant (similar to the way a dog gets more fur during winter to stay warmer).

4. Based on the passage, what gives carrots their orange color?

Ⓐ chlorophyll
Ⓑ photosynthesis
Ⓒ antioxidant
Ⓓ carotene

5. Based on the passage, what substance helps give leaves their green color?

Ⓐ chlorophyll
Ⓑ photosynthesis
Ⓒ antioxidant
Ⓓ carotene

6. Based on the passage, what is photosynthesis?

Ⓐ A process that helps get energy from sunlight and produce food
Ⓑ A substance that helps turn carbon dioxide into food
Ⓒ A protective chemical that helps protect trees from the sun
Ⓓ A chemical that gives leaves their orange and yellow colors

7. Based on the passage, what is an antioxidant?

Ⓐ A process that helps get energy from sunlight and produce food
Ⓑ A substance that helps turn carbon dioxide into food
Ⓒ A protective chemical that helps protect trees from the sun
Ⓓ A chemical that gives leaves their orange and yellow colors

Bushmen

With so much technology around us each day, it is hard to imagine that anyone in the world would live without television, let alone a cell phone or radio. Still, there are a few cultures that maintain an extremely primitive lifestyle, nearly untouched by the modern world. One of those is commonly known as the Bushmen of Kalahari.

The Bushmen, also known as the "Basarwa" or "San" are found throughout southern Africa in regions of the Kalahari Desert. Nomadic hunters and gatherers by nature, they roam the region living in small kinship groups and, relatively isolated from the rest of society, have developed an extremely unique culture not otherwise seen or understood by modern man.

Unlike English, which is built on a complex system of sounds and letters, the Bushmen speak an extremely unique language made exclusively of clicking sounds. The sounds are created with a sucking action from the tongue, and even the click language itself can vary widely from tribe to tribe, making it extremely difficult to communicate with non-Bush people.

In addition to language, the Bushmen have a very different way of living. Similar to Eskimos, groups of Bushmen will live in "kinship" societies. Led by their elders, they travel together, with women in the group gathering food while men hunt for it. Children, on the other hand, have no duties other than playing. In fact, leisure is an extremely important part of the Bushmen society. Dance, music and humor are essential, with a focus on family rather than technology or development. Because of this, some people associate the Bush culture with a backward kind of living or low status

Because of the increased speed of advancement and urban development, the Bushmen culture is in danger. Some have already been forced to switch from hunting to farming due to modernization programs in their countries. Others have been forced to move to certain areas of their countries so that modernization can continue to occur there. With so much development, it's clear that though the Bushmen culture is very rich, it is also in danger of extinction. It is unclear how long the Bush culture will continue.

https://en.wikipedia.org/wiki/Bushmen

8. Based on the passage, what is the best meaning of primitive?

    Ⓐ New and modern
    Ⓑ Not sophisticated or developed
    Ⓒ Cultural traits or traditions
    Ⓓ Languages unlike English

9. The passage describes kinship societies. If the word "kin" means "family or relations," then kinship societies are most likely... Circle the correct answer choice.

    Ⓐ Groups of individuals who came together from different tribes
    Ⓑ Groups of individuals from the same family
    Ⓒ Groups of individuals who are married
    Ⓓ Groups of individuals who follow one leader

10. Based on the passage, what is the meaning of the word modernization? Circle the correct answer choice.

    Ⓐ Keeping traditional practices and traditions
    Ⓑ Bringing computers and other cutting-edge technology
    Ⓒ Incorporating new practices and ideas
    Ⓓ Speaking a new language, such as English

End of Language

Answer Key and
Detailed Explanations

Chapter 4: Language

Lesson 1: Phrases and Clauses are Coming to Town

Question No.	Answer	Detailed Explanations
1	A	Answer choice one is correct. There is no subject but there is a verb, so this is a phrase. A phrase is a meaningful group of words which may appear to contain either a subject OR a verb--but NOT both. A phrase can NOT stand alone as a sentence. A clause is a meaningful group of words which contains a subject and a verb. There are two types of clauses: 1) independent and 2) dependent.
2	C	Answer choice three is correct. An independent clause contains all of the parts of a complete sentence: a subject, verb and a complete thought.
3	A	Answer choice one is correct. A phrase contains only a subject or a verb. This phrase has only a subject (Saturday). A phrase is a meaningful group of words which may appear to contain either a subject OR a verb--but NOT both. A phrase can NOT stand alone as a sentence. A clause is a meaningful group of words which contains a subject and a verb. There are two types of clauses: 1) independent and 2) dependent.
4	A	Answer choice one is correct. The part of the sentence contains a verb. A phrase is a meaningful group of words which may appear to contain either a subject OR a verb--but NOT both. A phrase can NOT stand alone as a sentence. A clause is a meaningful group of words which contains a subject and a verb. There are two types of clauses: 1) independent and 2) dependent.
5	B	Answer choice two is correct. A dependent clause contains a subject and a verb, but cannot be a sentence by itself because it begins with a dependent word such as "because". A phrase is a meaningful group of words which may appear to contain either a subject OR a verb--but NOT both. A phrase can NOT stand alone as a sentence. A clause is a meaningful group of words which contains a subject and a verb. There are two types of clauses: 1) independent and 2) dependent.

Question No.	Answer	Detailed Explanations
6	A	Answer choice one is correct. A phrase is a meaningful group of words which may appear to contain either a subject OR a verb--but NOT both. A phrase can NOT stand alone as a sentence. A clause is a meaningful group of words which contains a subject and a verb. There are two types of clauses: 1) independent and 2) dependent.
7	C	Answer choice three is correct. This clause contains a subject, verb and it completes a thought. A phrase is a meaningful group of words which may appear to contain either a subject OR a verb--but NOT both. A phrase can NOT stand alone as a sentence. A clause is a meaningful group of words which contains a subject and a verb. There are two types of clauses: 1) independent and 2) dependent.
8	Phrase	A phrase is a meaningful group of words which may appear to contain either a subject OR a verb--but NOT both. A phrase can NOT stand alone as a sentence. A clause is a meaningful group of words which contains a subject and a verb. There are two types of clauses: 1) independent and 2) dependent. The underlined portion is a phrase.
9	Clause	A phrase is a meaningful group of words which may appear to contain either a subject OR a verb--but NOT both. A phrase can NOT stand alone as a sentence. A clause is a meaningful group of words which contains a subject and a verb. There are two types of clauses: 1) independent and 2) dependent. The underlined portion is a clause.
10	independ en - dent clause	A clause is a meaningful group of words which contains a subject and a verb. There are two types of clauses: 1) independent and 2) dependent. An independent clause is a clause that can stand alone as a sentence. A dependent clause (or subordinate clause) is one that cannot stand alone as a complete sentence (i.e., it does not express a complete thought). The underlined portion is an independent clause.

Lesson 2: Good Sentences are Built on Agreement

Question No.	Answer	Detailed Explanations
1	A	Answer choice one is correct. Everybody is a singular subject, so it requires a verb that ends in is.
2	B	Answer choice two is correct. Subjects and verbs must match in number (number of items in the subject) and person (1st, 2nd or 3rd). In this sentence the subject, "car", is singular and third person. The verb "needs" is also singular, third person.
3	B	Randy is a singular subject. Therefore, the verb related to this subject must end in is.
4	D	Answer choice four is correct. The verb do is singular because the subject my is also singular.
5	B	Answer choice two is correct. Neither is the subject of this sentence. Neither is a singular subject. Therefore, the verb related to it must end in -s.
6	A	Answer choice one is correct. The subject is plural, so the verb must be plural as well (no -s)
7	A	Answer choice one is correct. The subject of this sentence is plural, so the verb must also be plural.
8	B	Answer choice two is correct. If the reader ignores the phrase set off by commas, it is easier to see that LINDSAY is a single person. Thus the singular be verb is should be used.
9	A	Answer choice one is correct. People is a plural form of person. The verb must be plural (no -s). Answer choice four cannot be used, although it "sounds right" because the next sentence's tense does not agree with this verb tense.
10	C	Answer choice three is correct. One ant needs the singular verb forms (ending in -s).
11	C	Answer choice three is correct. Sam OR Alec requires that the verb tense be singular. If the reader took either name out and read it with just one name, it would be the verb tense of is. Therefore, with the OR between the names, the verb tense remains singular.
12	B	Answer choice two is correct. This sentence can be confusing. If the reader switched the order to "A rainbow and a leprechaun were at the end of the rainbow," it would be easier to discern which verb tense. A compound predicate requires a plural form of the verb was.

Lesson 3: Managing Modifiers

Question No.	Answer	Detailed Explanations
1	B	Answer choice two is the correct answer. An adverb ends in -ly. The fact that the computer is older tells the reader that it is probably not very fast or effective. So, it cannot be quickly. Fast is not appropriate due to the meaning and form of the word. Angrily does not apply to the computer's connection. It might apply to the computer operator, but not the actual machine.
2	B	Answer choice two is the correct answer. When two adjectives appear next to one another, they should be separated by a comma. It is similar to the listing rule of comma usage.
3	A	Answer choice one is correct. Adverbs modify (affect) verbs.
4	C	Answer choice three is the best answer. Kind (adjective) describes the type of words (noun).
5	D	Answer choice four is the correct answer. The word heavy describes the traffic which is a noun. Adjectives modify (explain) nouns.
6	C	Answer choice three is the correct answer. Adverbs modify (explain/affect) verbs. Adverbs usually end in -ly. Because angrily (adverb) explains how Megan slammed (verb) the phone, it is the correct answer.
7	B	Answer choice two is the best answer. The fire is temporary, it was or will be contained (eventually), and large is a synonym of huge, so these answers are not correct. Violent describes how serious and intense the fire was.
8	A	Answer choice one is the correct answer. Often adverbs appear after the verb, but they do not have to. Rarely (adverb) describes how teenagers think (verb).
9	C	Answer choice three is correct. The other choices have more than comma issues or do not apply. Short and interesting are adjectives to describe a book. They need to be separated by a comma. Dark chocolate is confusing because dark does describe the chocolate, but it is also a type of chocolate. Flowing and long are awkward. Usually it would be written long, flowing. Also, others aren't precise.
10	C	Answer choice three is correct. Two adjectives together (long and drawn out) describe the noun argument.

Question No.	Answer	Detailed Explanations
11	Verb	Thought is an action. It cannot be seen, but it is still a willful act.
12	Adjective	Plain-looking describes how the woman appeared.
13	Adverb	Usually adverbs end in -ly, but in this case, the word well (adverb) is describing HOW they performed (did) on the test.

Lesson 4: Using Coordinate Adjectives

Question No.	Answer	Detailed Explanations
1	A	Answer choice one is correct. Commas go between coordinate adjectives. Since you can place an "and" between fascinating and intelligent, they are coordinating adjectives.
2	B	Answer choice two is correct. Commas go between coordinate adjectives. Since you can place an "and" between slippery and dangerous, they are coordinate adjectives.
3	B	Answer choice two is correct. Commas go between coordinate adjectives. Since you can place an "and" between angry and frustrated, they are coordinate adjectives.
4	C	Answer choice three is correct. Commas go between coordinate adjectives and coordinate adjectives are interchangeable. Running is not interchangeable, but black and striped are and should be separated with a comma.
5	A	Answer choice one is correct. Commas go between coordinate adjectives and coordinate adjectives are interchangeable. Angora is not interchangeable as it's a specific type of sweater.
6	B	Answer choice two is correct. Commas go between interchangeable coordinate adjectives. Only the adjectives in choice two are interchangeable.
7	A	Answer choice one is correct. Commas go between coordinate adjectives and coordinate adjectives are interchangeable. Only angry and bitter are interchangeable in this sentence.
8	C	Answer choice three is correct. Coordinate adjectives are separated by a comma and are interchangeable. In this sentence, tropical is not interchangeable so it needs to go before island.
9	C	Answer choice three is correct. Coordinate adjectives are separated by a comma and are interchangeable. In this sentence, red and cashmere aren't coordinate adjectives, so you need to add another adjective. Cashmere is also not interchangeable so it needs to be placed right before sweater.
10	A	Answer choice one is correct. Coordinate adjectives are separated by a comma.

Lesson 5: Spellcheck!

Question No.	Answer	Detailed Explanations
1	A	"Threw" is a homonym of "through" (the correct spelling for this case). "Threw" is the word that means the past tense of "to throw".
2	C	The correct spelling of this word is "experiment."
3	B	The correct spelling of this word is "restaurant."
4	A	The correct spelling of this word is "recognized." The British spelling of the word is "recognised."
5	C	The correct spelling of the word is "panicked."
6	C	The correct spelling of the word is "necessary."
7	B	The correct answer is two. You're is the contraction for you are, so your is correct.
8	A	Answer choice one is the correct tense, singular.
9	A	Answer choice one is correct. i before e except after c, and in cases where it says long a or long e.
10	B	Answer choice two is correct. Too, indicates an extent of something. Too much money, time etc. Also in addition.
11	imagination	The wrongly spelled word is imagenation. It should be spelled as Imagination.
12	happiness	The wrongly spelled word is happyness. It should be spelled as happiness.
13	preferred	The wrongly spelled word is prefered. It should be spelled as preferred.

Lesson 6: Precise and Concise Language

Question No.	Answer	Detailed Explanations
1	C	Answer choice three is correct. All of the other choices are general. Choice three is more specific and precise.
2	D	Answer choice four is correct. Answer choices one and two are longer and more redundant. Answer choice three is better, but can still be cleaned up.
3	D	Answer choice four is correct. To be more precise, Maria would want to change or remove information, not add information.
4	A	Answer choice one is correct. The first choice is specific and condenses the line without losing information.
5	A	Answer choice one is correct. The first choice will give Alfonso the opportunity to give specific details.
6	A	Answer choice one is correct. The first choice is still vague, even though it adds "yummy" the other choices make the words "baked goods" and the adjectives more specific.
7	C	Answer choice three is correct. Including what the actors wore would not be more precise.
8	D	Answer choice four is correct. It references that all of the actresses were involved, but condenses the description of the dresses, keeping it precise but concise.
9		The sentence could be made more specific as follows - I love it because we go canoeing and we get to sing songs by the campfire. Being precise means being specific. Canoeing and singing songs by the campfire are specific activities.
10	C	Answer choice three is correct. Even though choice four is shorter, choice three is concise and specific (precise).

Lesson 7: Figuring it Out with Context Clues

Question No.	Answer	Detailed Explanations
1	C	Answer choice three is correct. When someone finds themselves in a quandary, it is usually because they have to make a choice. This causes them to have to weigh the pros and cons of the decisions. The boy in this story has to make a decision, and it is causing him stress. He is in a quandary.
2	D	Bruno receives medicine through a shot injection. The answer choice is D. Also it is used as a noun in the story.
3	D	Answer choice four is the correct answer. The sentences discuss animals living in rivers and lakes. Also the second sentence mentions animals living in water.
4	B	Answer choice two is correct. Smiling in the mood of this part of a story is odd, so the reader can determine it is not a happy smile. This coupled with the fact that the daughter is being kidnapped tells the reader that the smile is a mean or negative intent.
5	A	Answer choice one is the correct answer. Based on the passage, it states "to help the club better understand the rules" is a hint that something before the rules must be read.
6	B	Answer choice two is correct. The sentence continues to explain that Bruno could not stand or move. This tells the reader that paralysis must mean inability to move.
7	B	Answer choice two is correct. When something is fleeting, it is very quick. The following sentence says: "luckily it was gone as quickly as it came." This helps the reader understand the meaning of fleeting.
8	C	Answer choice three is correct. The sentence(s) mention a disagreement. Then, "an arbitrator was brought in to help" is stated. This tells the reader that an arbitrator can help with a dispute, and that they must be a person who helps settle arguments.
9	C	Answer choice three is correct. "Only grazed my pants...I was still upset" tells the reader that only grazed means barely.
10	A	Answer choice one is correct. The words "even though" coupled with "found dull" tell the reader that something different than dull is intended. They should understand the opposite of dull could be entertained.

Question No.	Answer	Detailed Explanations
11	D	Answer choice four is correct. The words "without warning" and "suddenly appeard" tell the reader that materialized means to suddenly appear from nowhere.
12	B	Answer choice two is correct. To "go awry when..." tells the reader that until the "then," the planned events were different. So, awry must meant to go off the planned path.
13	C	Answer choice three is correct. Medical studnets must learn about the body's anatomy, and they cannot do that on a live human, or it would kill the people being dissected. So,cadaver must mean dead human.

Lesson 8: Re+view - Roots and Affixes

Question No.	Answer	Detailed Explanations
1	C	Answer choice three is correct. Autonomous means to be in control of self.
2	B	Answer choice two is correct.
3	C	If he is phobic of aqua, he is afraid of water. Being afraid of water would make it difficult to get in to water. The other answer choices are about someone who LIKES water.
4	A	Answer choice one is correct. Anti is opposite and social means to be in society. So opposite or against society would mean a person who is antisocial would not enjoy a big social event.
5	B	Answer choice two is the correct answer. To digress means to get away from, or to stray from focus.
6	C	Answer choice three is correct. A postmortem is something studied or done after death.
7	C	Answer choice three is correct. The suffix added to many country names indicates a person from that country.
8	B	Answer choice two. Octo (like octagon in a stop sign) means 8. And octogenarian is a person in their 80's.
9	B	Answer choice two is correct. Full to the brim; brimful.
10	B	Answer choice two is the correct answer. Acceptable is okay. The prefix -un means not.
11		Hypno refers to sleep Hydro is related to water and Cosmo is related to the universe
12		The correct words are: Replay, Hydroelectric, and Transform.
13		It is the definition of Suffix

Lesson 9: Consulting Sources

Question No.	Answer	Detailed Explanations
1	B	Answer choice two is correct. To find the answer quickly, Jorge should look up the meaning in the glossary of the textbook.
2	C	Answer choice three is correct. Using a glossary or dictionary will get him the definition, but a thesaurus will provide similar words.
3	C	Answer choice three is correct. Words in dictionaries are in alphabetical order so he will find it between ecology and edifice.
4	B	Answer choice two is correct. The words in parentheses will help Jorge know how to pronounce the word "ecosystem."
5	B	Answer choice two is correct. The n. shows that the word "ecosystem" is a noun.
6	A	Answer choice one is correct. The dictionary gives two definitions, but the one closest to what Jorge read is "a community of interacting organisms."
7	B	Answer choice two is correct. The sentences in italics help the reader distinguish between the different meanings of the word by providing examples of usage.
8	C	Answer choice three is correct. The synonym she needs is most related to the first definition of delay, so hinder is a good choice.
9	A	Answer choice one is correct. The synonym she needs is most related to the third definition of delay, so hesitate is a good choice.
10	A	Answer choice one is correct. The thesaurus entry covers delay as a verb, not as a noun. Students should look closely at the part of speech before choosing a synonym.

Lesson 10: "How to Look it Up Which Fits? Multiple Meaning Words"

Question No.	Answer	Detailed Explanations
1	D	Answer choice four is correct. In this case the teacher did not want the student to think she did not recognize the effort.
2	B	Answer choice two is correct. Approve means to give approval, or say okay.
3	A	Answer choice one is correct. Sub means below, and a manager would have the power to schedule who he wanted when he wanted them. Subordinate means underling or person below another on a hierarchy.
4	C	Answer choice three is correct. A racket that awakes someone is a noise. This is slang for noisy activity.
5	B	Answer choice two is correct. It is typical to refer to candy and dessert type foods as "sweets." The reader knows the word sweets in this passage means candy because the passage states that candy companies put the cards in the packages to encourage the kids to buy the candy.
6	C	Answer choice three is correct. Sometimes after a storm electrical lines are down. If the power company warns someone from wire, one that is "live," then the consumer should assume it is dangerous. And dangerous to a power company means electricity.
7	B	Answer choice two is correct. If they were going to broadcast "without a delay," then the reader understands that "live" means as it is happening.
8	A	Answer choice one is correct. Strip, when used as a verb, means to take off. So, to strip paint means to remove it.
9	C	Answer choice three is correct. The sentence discusses how someone had misbehaved, and then had a consequence. So, to the reader, bar should mean prohibit, or keep from.
10	D	Answer choice four is the correct answer. Monitor is similar to answer four, but track does not mean to watch "carefully."

Question No.	Answer	Detailed Explanations
11	D	Answer choice four is correct. To bolt in this sentence is to move away from someone or place in a hurry.
12	A	Answer choice one is correct. In this sentence, Brilliant means glittering. To polish something to a brilliant shine is to make it glitter and bright.
13	C	Answer choice three is correct. Master in this case is a verb, meaning that the person has a great deal of skill.

Lesson 11: Give it a Shot - Figures of Speech

Question No.	Answer	Detailed Explanations
1	C	Answer choice three is correct. Bricks are heavy and 2000 pounds would be extremely heavy.
2	D	Answer choice four is the correct answer. Off the cuff usually means with no notes or talking points. The person just "does it."
3	A	Answer choice one is the correct answer. There probably were hundreds of pairs of eyes, since there were likely several hundred people in the auditorium, but this is an expression that illustrates to the reader how nervous Kim was.
4	C	Answer choice three is the best answer. This is a hyperbole, an exaggeration, to make a point of how difficult the work is.
5	B	Answer choice two is correct. This statement is intended to illustrate to the reader how focused on her boyfriend she is.
6	B	Answer choice two is the correct answer. This is an idiom. It does not mean what the actual words say, but it is understood that this means to stop something before it really gets started.
7	A	Answer choice one is correct. This is an idiom that was used many years ago. It means that if a person doesn't stay busy, she could find herself somewhere she does not belong.
8	B	Answer choice two is correct. A walk in the park would be an easy and enjoyable stroll. So, this saying indicates something will be easy to accomplish.
9	B	Answer choice two is correct. This is a common idiom that means to decide the work day is complete.
10	D	Answer choice four is correct. This means to not do work, or make decisions. It is meant to indicate someone is avoiding what they are to do.
11	C	Answer choice three is the answer. Brings home bacon or good means to provide for a family.
12	A	Answer choice one is correct. If something is under the rug, it appears to be okay, but really it is just hidden. Nothing is resolved or "cleaned up."
13	A	Answer choice one is correct. This idiom means to make a change for the better.

Lesson 12: We're Related - Word Relationships

Question No.	Answer	Detailed Explanations
1	C	Homonyms are words that sound the same when they are pronounced, but that are spelled differently and usually have different meanings.
2	A	Synonyms are words that have similar meanings. They can usually replace each other in a sentence and the sentence will hold the same meaning.
3	D	Antonyms are words that mean the opposite of one another.
4	C	Synonyms are words that have the same meaning as each other.
5	A	Antonyms are words that have opposite meanings.
6	D	Disorganized is an antonym of classified.
7	A	Answer choice one is correct. Patient and tolerant are similar in meaning.
8	A	Answer choice one is a synonym of "smarts" as it is used.
9	A	Answer choice one is correct. They sound the same, but have different spellings and meanings.
10	A	Answer choice one is correct. In the case of the knife, the opposite would mean sharp, as in easy to cut.
11	C	Answer choice three is correct. The opposite of courageous is cowardly.
12	B	Answer choice two is correct. In business "waived rights/claims" means to give up or leave.

Lesson 13: Would You Rather Own a Boat or a Yacht?
Denotation and Connotation

Question No.	Answer	Detailed Explanations
1	B	Facetious is not generally used in a positive way.
2	A	Boot has negative connotations. It is not used in positive situations.
3	A	**Needy** has positive connotation because it focuses on needing something, but not being able to provide it for yourself. **Greedy** has negative connotations because it means someone is taking more than he or she needs simply because he or she wants it.
4	A	The word **untidy,** is not an extremely positive word, but it doesn't imply something is extremely dirty. The word **filthy** means that something is not only messy, but also dirty.
5	A	Answer choice one is the correct answer. Devoted generally means loving, and obsessed conjures images of someone who is excessively preoccupied or focused.
6	C	Answer choice three is correct. This word switch changes the focus of the sentence and its feelings slightly. Taxpayer is not a warm word.
7	B	Answer choice two is the best answer. Help is something people ask for and want. Interfering is something that is considered intrusive and unwanted. So, the second answer is the best way to make the sentence positive.
8	C	Answer choice three is correct. Large is a fairly neutral word, but enormous has a lot more emotion with it. Depending on the sentence it could be both positive and negative, so it is a neutral word.
9	A	Answer choice one is much stronger a word than "bad." This word gives a broader meaning to just how much Lori fears snakes.
10	D	Answer choice four is best. Exceptional sets him above just average or pretty good. It means his work is way beyond the norm.
11	B	Answer choice two is correct. An adult behaving in a childish manner is not desired, so it has a negative connotation.
12	A	Answer choice one is the best answer. If the neighbor's questions are welcomed, she is interested (positive). If the questions are not welcome, then the neighbor is nosy (a negative feeling).

Lesson 14: Learning and Using Academic Vocabulary

Question No.	Answer	Detailed Explanations
1	C	Answer choice three is correct. A curator is a keeper or custodian of a collection, such as the collection of animals at the zoo.
2	A	Answer choice one is correct. A superintendent is a high-ranking official or someone who manages the zoo.
3	B	Answer choice two is correct. The passage says "a squad of workers," so the answer is squad, not workers.
4	D	Answer choice four is correct. The passage says carotene is present in yellow and orange leaves, so it can be inferred it also gives carrots their orange color.
5	A	Answer choice one is correct. The passage says chlorophyll helps gives leaves their green color.
6	A	Answer choice one is correct. The passage describes photosynthesis as a process.
7	C	Answer choice three is correct. The passage describes an antioxidant as a protective substance/coating.
8	B	Answer choice two is correct. Primitive describes something not sophisticated or developed. For example, early man is often considered primitive.
9	B	Answer choice two is correct. A kinship society is most likely formed with groups of individuals from the same families.
10	C	Answer choice three is correct. Modernization does not just involve technology (choice two), but bringing in new ideas and practices.

OST FAQs

What will OST Assessment Look Like?

In many ways, the OST assessments will be unlike anything many students have ever seen. The tests will be conducted online, requiring students complete tasks to assess a deeper understanding of the Ohio Learning standards. The students will take the Summative Assessment at the end of the year. The time for the ELA Summative assessment for each grade is given below:

Estimated Time on Task in Minutes		
Grade	Part 1	Part 2
3	90	90
4	90	90
5	90	90
6	105	105
7	105	105
8	105	105

How is this Lumos tedBook aligned to OST Guidelines?

The practice tests provided in the Lumos Program were created to reflect the depth and rigor of the OST assessments based on the information published by the test administrator. However, the content and format of the OST assessment that is officially administered to the students could be different compared to these practice tests. You can get more information about this test by visiting The ohio department of education website.

What item types are included in the Online OST Test?

Because the assessment is online, the test will consist of a combination of new types of questions:

1. Drag and Drop
2. Evidence based selected response (EBSR)
3. Extended Constructed Response
4. Hot Text Selective Highlight
5. Drop Down
6. Multiple Choice – Single Correct Response, radial buttons
7. Table Fill-in
8. Multiple Choice – Multiple Response, check boxes
9. Matching Table
10. Numeric Response
11. Grid

For more information on 2021-22 Assessment year, Visit
http://www.lumoslearning.com/a/ost-2021-faqs
OR Scan the **QR Code**

How Can the Lumos Study Program Prepare Students for OST Tests?

At Lumos Learning, we believe that year-long learning and adequate practice before the actual test are the keys to success on OST test. We have designed the Lumos study program to help students get plenty of realistic practice before the test and to promote year-long collaborative learning.

This is a Lumos tedBook™. It connects you to Online OST Assessments and additional resources. You can access these resources using a number of devices including personal computers, Android/iOS phones and tablets. The Lumos StepUp Online Assessment is designed to promote year-long learning. It is a simple program students can securely access using a computer or device with internet access. Students will get instant feedback and can review their answers anytime. Each student's answers and progress can be reviewed by parents and educators to reinforce the learning experience.

Why Practice with Repeated Reading Passages?

Throughout the Lumos Learning Practice workbooks, students and educators will notice many passages repeat. This is done intentionally. The goal of these workbooks is to help students practice skills necessary to be successful in class and on standardized tests. One of the most critical components to that success is the ability to read and comprehend passages. To that end, reading fluency must be strengthened. According to Hasbrouck and Tindal (2006), "Helping our students become fluent readers is absolutely critical for proficient and motivated reading" (p. 642). And, Nichols et al. indicate, (2009), "fluency is a gateway to comprehension that enables students to move from being word decoders to passage comprehenders" (p. 11).

Lumos Learning recognizes there is no one-size-fits-all approach to build fluency in readers; however, the repeated reading of passages, where students read the same passages at least two or more times, is one of the most widely recognized strategies to improve fluency (Nichols et al., 2009). Repeated reading allows students the opportunity to read passages with familiar words several times until the passage becomes familiar and they no longer have to decode word by word. As students reread, the decoding barrier falls away allowing for an increase in reading comprehension.

The goal of the Lumos Learning workbooks is to increase student achievement and preparation for any standardized test. Using some passages multiple times in a book offers struggling readers an opportunity to do just that.

References
Hasbrouck, J., and Tindal, G. (2006). Oral reading fluency norms: A valuable assessment tool for reading teachers. Reading Teacher, 59(7), 636644. doi:10.1598/RT.59.7.3.
Nichols, W., Rupley, W., and Rasinski, T. (2009). Fluency in learning to read for meaning: going beyond repeated readings. Literacy Research & Instruction, 48(1). doi:10.1080/19388070802161906.

Discover Engaging and Relevant Learning Resources

Lumos EdSearch is a safe search engine specifically designed for teachers and students. Using EdSearch, you can easily find thousands of standards-aligned learning resources such as questions, videos, lessons, worksheets and apps. Teachers can use EdSearch to create custom resource kits to perfectly match their lesson objective and assign them to one or more students in their classroom.

To access the EdSearch tool, use the search box after you log into Lumos StepUp or use the link provided below.

http://www.lumoslearning.com/a/edsearchb	

The Lumos Standards Coherence map provides information about previous level, next level and related standards. It helps educators and students visually explore learning standards. It's an effective tool to help students progress through the learning objectives. Teachers can use this tool to develop their own pacing charts and lesson plans. Educators can also use the coherence map to get deep insights into why a student is struggling in a specific learning objective.

Teachers can access the Coherence maps after logging into the StepUp Teacher Portal or use the link provided below.

http://www.lumoslearning.com/a/coherence-map	

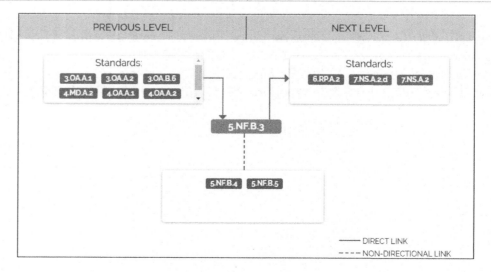

What if I buy more than one Lumos Study Program?

Step 1

Visit the URL and login to your account.
http://www.lumoslearning.com

Step 2

Click on 'My tedBooks' under the "Account" tab.
Place the Book Access Code and submit.

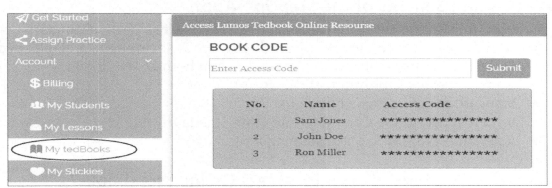

Step 3

To add the new book for a registered student, choose the
○ Existing Student button and select the student and submit.

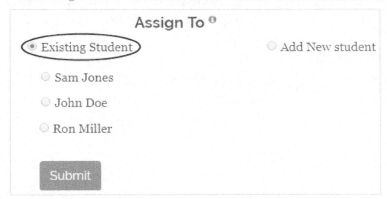

To add the new book for a new student, choose the ○ Add New student
button and complete the student registration.

Assign To ⓘ

○ Existing Student   ⦿ Add New student

Register Your TedBook

Student Name:*	Enter First Name	Enter Last Name
Student Login*		
Password*		

Submit

Lumos StepUp® Mobile App
FAQ For Students

What is the Lumos StepUp® App?

It is a FREE application you can download onto your Android Smartphones, tablets, iPhones, and iPads.

What are the Benefits of the StepUp® App?

This mobile application gives convenient access to Practice Tests, Common Core State Standards, Online Workbooks, and learning resources through your Smartphone and tablet computers.

- Eleven Technology enhanced question types in both MATH and ELA
- Sample questions for Arithmetic drills
- Standard specific sample questions
- Instant access to the Common Core State Standards
- Jokes and cartoons to make learning fun!

Do I Need the StepUp® App to Access Online Workbooks?

No, you can access Lumos StepUp® Online Workbooks through a personal computer. The StepUp® app simply enhances your learning experience and allows you to conveniently access StepUp® Online Workbooks and additional resources through your smartphone or tablet.

How can I Download the App?

Visit **lumoslearning.com/a/stepup-app** using your Smartphone or tablet and follow the instructions to download the app.

QR Code
for Smartphone
Or Tablet Users

Lumos StepUp® Mobile App FAQ
For Parents and Teachers

What is the Lumos StepUp® App?

It is a free app that teachers can use to easily access real-time student activity information as well as assign learning resources to students. Parents can also use it to easily access school-related information such as homework assigned by teachers and PTA meetings. It can be downloaded onto smartphones and tablets from popular App Stores.

What are the Benefits of the Lumos StepUp® App?

It provides convenient access to

- Standards aligned learning resources for your students
- An easy to use Dashboard
- Student progress reports
- Active and inactive students in your classroom
- Professional development information
- Educational Blogs

How can I Download the App?

Visit **lumoslearning.com/a/stepup-app** using your Smartphone or tablet and follow the instructions to download the app.

**QR Code
for Smartphone
Or Tablet Users**

Progress Chart

Standard	Lesson	Page No.	Practice		Mastered	Re-practice /Reteach
CCSS			Date	Score		
RL.7.1	Prove It! (With Evidence from the Text)	11				
RL.7.1	Use Those Clues - Make an Inference	22				
RL.7.2	And the Point of This is...?	36				
RL.7.2	What is it All About?	53				
RL.7.3	One Thing Leads to Another	67				
RL.7.3	When and Where?	87				
RL.7.3	Who or What?	106				
RL.7.4	A Matter of Attitude	120				
RL.7.5	How it's Made and What it Means	131				
RL.7.6	What a Character!	144				
RL.7.7	Finding Patterns - Comparing and Contrasting	156				
RL.7.9	Based on a True Story - History and Fiction	172				
RI.7.1	Key Ideas and Details	209				
RI.7.2	Get Right to the Point	217				
RI.7.3	Relationship Between People and Events	234				
RI.7.4	Getting Technical	239				
RI.7.5	How is it Built? Analyzing structure	249				
RI.7.6	What's the Author's Angle?	266				
RI.7.7	Comparing Media	277				
RI.7.8	What's the Author's Point?	286				
RI.7.9	Equal? Alike? Different? Comparing Authors	300				

Standard	Lesson	Page No.	Practice		Mastered	Re-practice /Reteach
CCSS			Date	Score		
L.7.1.A	Phrases and Clauses are Coming to Town	331				
L.7.1.B	Good Sentences are Built on Agreement	334				
L.7.1.C	Managing Modifiers	338				
L.7.2.A	Using Coordinate Adjectives	342				
L.7.2.B	Spellcheck!	345				
L.7.3.A	Precise and Concise Language	349				
L.7.4.A	Figuring it Out with Context Clues	353				
L.7.4.B	Re+view - Roots and Affixes	359				
L.7.4.C	Consulting Sources	363				
L.7.4.C L.7.4.D	How to Look it Up Which Fits? Multiple Meaning Words	368				
L.7.5.A	Give it a Shot - Figures of Speech	372				
L.7.5.B	We're Related - Word Relationships	377				
L.7.5.C	Would You Rather Own a Boat or a Yacht? Denotation and Connotation	381				
L.7.6	Learning and Using Academic Vocabulary	386				

Lumos Learning
Developed by Expert Teachers

Grade **7**

OHIO Math

OST Practice

Updated for 2021-22

ONLINE

2 OST Practice Tests

11 Question Types

COVERS 30+ SKILLS

Available

- At Leading book stores
- Online www.LumosLearning.com